Peoples of the
Old Testament
World

1995

PUBLICATION AWARD

BIBLICAL
ARCHAEOLOGY
SOCIETY

Peoples of the Old Testament World

Edited by
Alfred J. Hoerth
Gerald L. Mattingly
&
Edwin M. Yamauchi

Foreword by Alan R. Millard

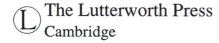

The Lutterworth Press
Cambridge

Baker Books
A Division of Baker Book House Co
Grand Rapids, Michigan 49516

© 1994 by Alfred J. Hoerth, Gerald L. Mattingly, and Edwin M. Yamauchi

North American edition

Published by Baker Books
a division of Baker Book House Company
P.O. Box 6287, Grand Rapids, Michigan 49516-6287
United States of America

Second printing, April 1996

Library of Congress Cataloging-in-Publication Data

Peoples of the Old Testament world / edited by Alfred J. Hoerth, Gerald L. Mattingly and
Edwin M. Yamauchi ; foreword by Alan R. Millard.
    p.   cm.
    Includes bibliographical references and indexes.
    ISBN 0-8010-4383-2
    1. Middle East—History—To 622. 2. Ethnology—Middle East. 3. Bible. O.T.—
History of Biblical events. I. Hoerth, Alfred J. II. Mattingly, Gerald L. III. Yamauchi,
Edwin M.
    DS62.23.P46   1994
    221.9′5—dc20   93-40419

United Kingdom edition

Published by The Lutterworth Press
P.O. Box 60, Cambridge, England CB1 2NT
United Kingdom

First edition 1996

ISBN 0 7188 2953 0

A catalogue record is available from the British Library.

Printed in the United States of America

Contents

Illustrations

Foreword

Alan R. Millard

Rankin Professor in Hebrew and Ancient Semitic Languages
University of Liverpool

"The Lord has chosen you out of all the people on the face of the earth to be his people," said God through Moses (Deut. 7:6). Ancient Israel lived in a world of many nations and it had to interact with them. The Bible tells a certain amount about some, very little about others. Some appear briefly, then disappear; others recur through several books and clearly had a major impact on Israel's history. Knowing about these peoples should broaden understanding of the biblical text, helping to answer questions such as, "Who were the Hittites?" or "Why were the Assyrians so feared?" It is easy to look in a Bible dictionary to find a short account of the people that the Bible names; the purpose of this book is to give more information about the major ones than such entries usually allow, with references for detailed study. Readers will soon see that the Bible is a major source for knowledge about some peoples (e.g., Philistines, Edomites, and Canaanites), while for others (e.g., Egyptians and Assyrians) their own inscriptions reveal so much about them that the Bible is marginal to their history.

The Bible often views Israel's contemporary states with a hostile eye, for political and especially religious reasons. Accordingly, historians read those texts critically to counter that bias. In some cases that has lead to a negative attitude that refuses to give credit to biblical statements unless other evidence supports them. The course of research on the ancient Near East over the past century and a half has shown repeatedly how well the Hebrew Scriptures reflect the realities their authors know. The insecurity of states like Israel and Judah becomes very clear, with neighbors frequently hostile and great powers approaching from the horizon. To be captured in a raid, like Naaman's maid

(2 Kings 5), or to be exiled wholesale was a risk that many ran throughout history, not a new experience when Samaria or Jerusalem fell. The prophecies of Amos, Isaiah, Jeremiah, and others gain in power and urgency as the current affairs of those days are understood, and this only becomes possible as the stories of the other nations are uncovered.

Besides the thousands of written documents recovered from the biblical world, there is a vast array of archeological evidence. Buried buildings, pots and pans, iron knives, golden bowls, children's graves—all combine to bring the past to life, to remind us that we are reading about actual human beings like ourselves. The kings had their great palaces and temples, displaying their wealth and power, but supporting them were merchants and artisans, farmers and slaves. Archeologists can never restore a picture of the past completely, as often their major find is the refuse of antiquity, and even then the smells have vanished. Therefore, there are many gaps in our knowledge. In addition, it has to be remembered that material remains usually yield less exact information than inscriptions, so the written records have a special value, notably when other written texts are being interpreted.

The essays in this volume weave together the results of recent study and discovery, long-known facts, and the biblical text to create pictures of the peoples of the Old Testament world. The authors have made them as complete and accurate as possible, aiming to give a better understanding of the distinctive feature of ancient Israel—God's revelation of himself through its history.

Preface

Alfred J. Hoerth

Director of Archaeology
Wheaton College

This book is an outgrowth of Wheaton College's long-standing interest in Near Eastern archeology, a subject that was introduced into Wheaton's curriculum by Joseph P. Free in 1936. A full major was offered by 1940, and the first majors were graduated in 1942. Professor Free also instituted an annual archeology conference that brought leading scholars to the campus. In the early years of this conference, such luminaries as G. Ernest Wright, Cyrus H. Gordon, and William F. Albright were featured speakers.

In the 1960s, Robert E. Cooley (now president of Gordon-Conwell Theological Seminary) became director of the Archaeology and Near Eastern Studies Program at Wheaton College. He helped shape the present focus of the department—to lead students toward an understanding of the historical, cultural, and intellectual backgrounds of ancient Near Eastern civilizations, especially that of the Bible. Under Dr. Cooley's leadership, Wheaton's annual archeology conferences continued, and speakers who could share their specialized knowledge with students, scholars, and laypeople were brought to the campus. This conference is still convened annually, attracting three hundred to four hundred people.

In 1989, the conference title was "Peoples of the Old Testament World," a theme suggested by Gerald L. Mattingly of Johnson Bible College (Knoxville, Tennessee). Significant new archeological and historical data have accumulated since Donald J. Wiseman edited the important volume, *Peoples of Old Testament Times* (Oxford: Clarendon, 1973), and the conviction grew among the planners that the 1989 Wheaton conference could be the catalyst for an up-to-date survey of ancient Near Eastern peoples. To that end the eight conference speakers met at the close of the conference, and Mattingly and Edwin M. Yamauchi (professor of history at Miami University in Oxford, Ohio) consented to put their expertise and drive into this venture. Thanks to them, additional scholars contributed to the project so that other—though not all—relevant "peoples" would be covered. We hope that this collection of studies will be of benefit to all scholars and students of the Bible who seek to learn more about the historical-cultural context of the Old Testament narratives.

Like any endeavor of this kind, *Peoples of the Old Testament World* required input from many people. In addition to the contributors, the editors wish to thank the dedicated staff at Baker Book House, who offered enthusiastic support for this project. In particular, we appreciate the expertise and encouragement of Allan Fisher, Jim Weaver, Maria E. denBoer, and David Aiken. It was a pleasure to work with them.

Abbreviations

ABD	*The Anchor Bible Dictionary*
ANEP	*The Ancient Near East in Pictures Relating to the Old Testament*
ANET	*Ancient Near Eastern Texts Relating to the Old Testament*
CAH	*Cambridge Ancient History*
ISBE	*International Standard Bible Encyclopedia*
LXX	Septuagint
MT	Masoretic Text
NIV	New International Version
NRSV	New Revised Standard Version
NT	New Testament
OT	Old Testament
TDOT	*Theological Dictionary of the Old Testament*

Gen.	1–2 Kings	Song	Obad.
Exod.	1–2 Chron.	Isa.	Jon.
Lev.	Ezra	Jer.	Mic.
Num.	Neh.	Lam.	Nah.
Deut.	Esth.	Ezek.	Hab.
Josh.	Job	Dan.	Zeph.
Judg.	Ps.	Hos.	Hag.
Ruth	Prov.	Joel	Zech.
1–2 Sam.	Eccles.	Amos	Mal.

Note: Unless otherwise indicated all dates are B.C.

Contributors

Bill T. Arnold holds a Ph.D. from Hebrew Union College and is Professor of Old Testament and Semitic Languages at Ashland Theological Seminary.

Walter R. Bodine holds a Ph.D. from Harvard University and lives in Dallas.

William C. Gwaltney Jr. holds a Ph.D. from Hebrew Union College and is Stephens Professor of Bible at Milligan College.

James K. Hoffmeier holds a Ph.D. from the University of Toronto and is Professor of Archaeology and Old Testament at Wheaton College.

Harry A. Hoffner Jr. holds a Ph.D. from Brandeis University and is Professor of Hittitology at the Oriental Institute at the University of Chicago.

Kenneth G. Hoglund holds a Ph.D. from Duke University and is Assistant Professor of Religion at Wake Forest University.

David M. Howard Jr. holds a Ph.D. from the University of Michigan and is Associate Professor of Old Testament and Semitic Languages at Trinity Evangelical Divinity School.

Gerald L. Mattingly holds a Ph.D. from Southern Baptist Theological Seminary and is Professor of Biblical Studies at Johnson Bible College.

Wayne T. Pitard holds a Ph.D. from Harvard University and is Associate Professor of Hebrew Bible at the University of Illinois.

Keith N. Schoville holds a Ph.D. from and is Professor of Hebrew and Semitic Studies at the University of Wisconsin.

William A. Ward holds a Ph.D. from Brandeis University and is Professor of Egyptology and Director of the Program in Ancient Studies at Brown University.

Edwin M. Yamauchi holds a Ph.D. from Brandeis University and is Professor of History at Miami University.

Randall W. Younker is a Ph.D. candidate at the University of Arizona and is Director of the Institute of Archaeology at Andrews University.

Archeological Periods of Syria-Palestine

Only approximate, these dates are constantly being refined in light of new archeological evidence. For this reason there may be differences between the dates used by the essayists in this volume and those below.

Paleolithic	before 14,000		
Epipaleolithic	14,000–8000		
Neolithic	8000–4200		
Chalcolithic	4200–3300		
Early Bronze	3300–2000	I	3300–3000
		II	3000–2800
		III	2800–2400
		IV	2400–2000
Middle Bronze	2000–1550	I (formerly IIA)	2000–1800
		II (formerly IIB)	1800–1650
		III (formerly IIC)	1650–1550
Late Bronze	1550–1200	I	1550–1400
		II	1400–1200
Iron	1200–539	I	1200–930
		IIA	930–721
		IIB	721–605
		IIC	605–539
Persian	539–332		
Hellenistic	332–63	Early	332–198
		Late	198–63
Roman	63 B.C.–A.D. 324	Early	63 B.C.–A.D. 135
		Late	135–324

Source: Adapted with permission from Philip J. King, *American Archaeology in the Mideast: A History of the American Schools of Oriental Research* (Philadelphia: ASOR, 1983), page 282.

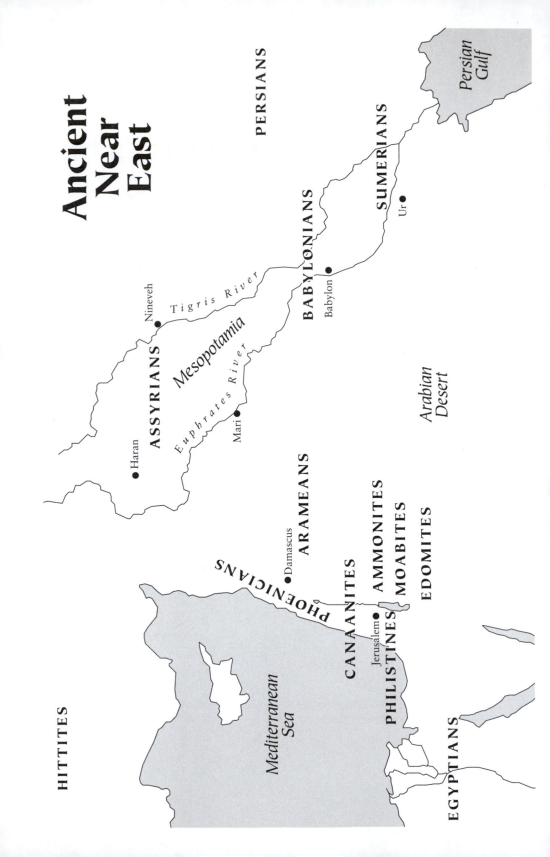

Ancient Near East

HITTITES

PERSIANS

BABYLONIANS

SUMERIANS

Ur

ASSYRIANS

Nineveh

Tigris River

Mesopotamia

Euphrates River

Haran

Mari

Babylon

Persian Gulf

Arabian Desert

ARAMEANS

Damascus

PHOENICIANS

CANAANITES

AMMONITES

MOABITES

EDOMITES

Jerusalem

PHILISTINES

Mediterranean Sea

EGYPTIANS

Part 1

Mesopotamia

Sumerians

Walter R. Bodine

Listen to me, you who pursue righteousness
and who seek the LORD:
Look to the rock from which you were cut
and to the quarry from which you were hewn.
—Isaiah 51:1

Study of the Sumerians

The Sumerians are the only one of the thirteen groups to which a chapter of this volume is devoted who are not mentioned in the Bible.[1] Yet

---

Author's note: This essay has benefited from the critical comments of John Huehnergard, Thorkild Jacobsen, Stephen Lieberman, Piotr Steinkeller, and Edwin Yamauchi.

1. Perhaps for this reason the Sumerians were not given separate treatment in *Peoples of Old Testament Times*, ed. Donald J. Wiseman (Oxford: Clarendon, 1973). Yet my statement must be qualified. Hebrew *šinʿār*, which occurs eight times in the Hebrew Bible (Gen. 10:10; 11:2; 14:1, 9; Josh. 7:21; Isa. 11:11; Dan. 1:2; Zech. 5:11), appears to represent the Sumerian term for "Sumer-Akkad" and thus refers to the area that includes the homeland of the Sumerians. While the proposal to identify Hebrew *šēm* (the ancestor of Israel via Abraham [Gen. 10:21; 11:10–26]) etymologically with Sumer ("Shumer" in cuneiform) is doubtful (Arno Poebel, "The Name of Elam in Sumerian, Akkadian, and Hebrew," *American Journal of Semitic Languages and Literatures* 48 [1931–32]: 25–26; followed by Samuel N. Kramer, *The Sumerians: Their History, Culture, and Character* [Chicago: University of Chicago Press, 1963], 297–99, who errantly cites Poebel's article as appearing in vol. 58 [1941] of *AJSL*), Sumerian influence in Israel's backgrounds is a foregone conclusion because of the pervasive influence of Sumerian culture on all of the ancient Near East, as will be stressed below. More pointedly, the biblical text traces Abraham's origins to the city of Ur (Gen. 11:28, 31; 15:7), a prominent urban center of the Sumerians. It has been argued that the Ur in question (i.e., "Ur of the Chaldeans") is not the Sumerian city, but a northern Ur, perhaps in the vicinity of Haran on the upper Euphrates, e.g., Cyrus H. Gordon, "Abraham and the Merchants of Ura," *Journal of Near Eastern Studies* 17 (1958): 28–31; idem, "Abraham of Ur," in *Hebrew and Semitic Studies Presented to Godfrey Rolles Driver*, ed. D. Winton Thomas and William D. McHardy (Oxford: Clarendon, 1963), 81–83. For a response to the earlier article by Gordon, see Harry W. F. Saggs, "Ur of the Chaldees: A Problem of Identification," *Iraq* 22 (1960): 200–209.

their influence on ancient Israel, as well as the rest of the ancient Near East, is as fundamental as that of most of the other peoples discussed here.

That the Sumerians have not been as well known is due to several factors. One is the lack of attention given them in the Bible. While virtually every field of ancient Near Eastern studies has by now established its autonomy as a discipline worthy of inquiry in its own right, and this is preeminently true of Assyriology (a term still used for the study of the Sumerian and Semitic peoples of ancient Mesopotamia), it remains true that one of the primary attractions to graduate study in ancient Near Eastern civilizations is the Hebrew Bible. Another factor in the relative obscurity of the Sumerians is the linguistic unrelatedness of their language to any other known language of the ancient world (or of any period). Comparative linguistic work in Semitic, in the broader field of Afroasiatic, and even in Indo-European in the case of Hittite and Old Persian, draws one into the study of the other languages of the ancient Near East, but not of Sumerian, except as it illuminates Akkadian.[2] Perhaps most significant is the high degree of uncertainty that yet surrounds the study of the Sumerian language itself. The earliest texts are still largely unintelligible, as are some features of the language throughout its history. Added to all of this, the very existence of the Sumerians as a people was only established toward the end of the nineteenth century.

Great strides have been taken toward the recovery of Sumerian civilization. Through roughly the first half of our century, excavations were carried out at most of the major occupation sites of the Sumerians, and a wealth of clay tablets inscribed in Sumerian were recovered. These texts are still in the process of being copied and published, and pioneering studies continue to clarify the Sumerian language. Especially in the latter part of the century, Assyriologists have produced definitive editions of Sumerian texts.[3]

---

2. "Akkadian" is a cover term that includes the Semitic languages or, perhaps better, dialects of ancient Mesopotamia: Old Akkadian, Assyrian, Babylonian, and various peripheral dialects from outlying areas.

3. Of all the civilizations of the ancient Near East, Mesopotamia is the best documented. It has been conservatively estimated that a quarter million clay tablets recovered through excavation are inscribed in Sumerian. Most of these tablets are fragmentary, and they are separated in different museums and private collections around the world. The great majority are business documents recording economic, legal, and other administrative matters. Fortunately, multiple copies of literary works were commonly made, so that lost portions of given compositions can often be filled out by duplicates. Kramer estimates that tablets containing literary compositions amount to about 5,000, making up close to 300 compositions with some 30,000 lines; Samuel N. Kramer, *From the Poetry of Sumer: Creation, Glorification, Adoration*, Una's Lectures 2 (Berkeley: University of California Press, 1979), 11–12. His estimate is probably low, depending on what one means by literature and how compositions are identified. Only a fraction of the Sumerian tablets that lie buried in the Middle East have been dug up, as is evidenced by the com-

In the course of this century's investigations, it has become clear that the other civilizations that developed in the ancient Near East were deeply influenced by that of the Sumerians, the earliest to achieve its apex of cultural development. Some of the many influences that emanated from early Sumer include writing,[4] the city-state, the accumulation of capital, the wheel, the potter's wheel, monumental architecture (including various architectural features such as the arch, dome, and vault), the sexagesimal number system,[5] written legal documents, schools, and the cylinder seal.[6]

The extent of Sumerian influence on the rest of the ancient Near East was highlighted in the mid-1970s by the discovery at Ebla, an ancient Syrian site, of a large archive of clay tablets written in Sumerian and in Semitic (Eblaite, now believed to be either an early dialect of Akkadian or another form of East Semitic alongside Akkadian) and dating from the mid-third millennium. Until the discovery of the Ebla archive, it was assumed that third-millennium Syria was culturally insignificant. The tablets reveal a city-state that rivaled the major centers of Mesopotamia and was deeply influenced by Sumerian culture. The Sumerian language suddenly became indispensable for the study of the early history of Syria-Palestine, and the early diffusion of Sumerian culture was made even more evident.

Protoliterate Period

Most of the features of civilization mentioned above emerged in Mesopotamia before the beginning of written records. In fact, many aspects of Sumerian civilization appear to have reached their height around the time that writing first appeared and shortly thereafter, during what is often called

---

positions that are known thus far only in part or from literary catalogs that list numerous compositions not yet recovered; Kramer, *From the Poetry of Sumer*, 12–13.

4. Writing also arose early in Egypt, and direct links with Mesopotamia cannot be established with certainty. A plausible explanation of how writing developed in Mesopotamia is that of Denise Schmandt-Besserat, "An Archaic Recording System and the Origin of Writing," *Syro-Mesopotamian Studies* 1/2 (1977): 31–70. Her proposal, however, is disputed by, e.g., Roy Harris, *The Origin of Writing* (LaSalle, Ill.: Open Court, 1986), 73; and Stephen J. Lieberman, "Of Clay Pebbles, Hollow Clay Balls, and Writing: A Sumerian View," *American Journal of Archaeology* 84 (1980): 339.

5. The Sumerians employed a primarily sexagesimal system, i.e., one having the number sixty as its basic unit. Such a system is reflected today in our measurement of time, circles, and angles.

6. A number of features of civilization that emerged first in Sumer are discussed in the popular book by Samuel N. Kramer, *History Begins at Sumer: Thirty-nine Firsts in Man's Recorded History*, 3d ed. (Philadelphia: University of Pennsylvania Press, 1981).

the Protoliterate period (ca. 3400–2900).[7] The earliest written tablets come from the sites of ancient Uruk and Jemdet Nasr (with a scattering from other places, especially in the Diyala region) and date from as early as 3100. The language of these texts appears to be Sumerian, suggesting that the Sumerians invented writing. Some scholars argue for a non-Sumerian substratum in the Sumerian language, which would point to another and possibly an earlier ethnic group that was incorporated into the Sumerian population, but cannot be otherwise identified. This posited substratum is usually referred to as Proto-Euphratean or Ubaidian, but the linguistic evidence used to support its existence is still in question.

The home of the Sumerians was in Mesopotamia, the land between the Tigris and Euphrates rivers above the Persian Gulf. Their population was concentrated in the lower part of the alluvial plain that constitutes southern Mesopotamia and is generally referred to as Babylonia. Prominent among their cities were Eridu, Ur, Larsa, Uruk (biblical Erech), Bad-tibira, Lagash, Nina, Girsu, Umma, Shuruppak, Isin, and Nippur. Although walled settlements were known from earlier, Neolithic times in Mesopotamia, it appears that the cities of Sumer were unwalled in the fourth millennium, suggesting a relatively peaceful period.

In search of the earliest detectable form of government in Mesopotamia, Assyriologists have found evidence of an assembly of free adult citizens that convened on an ad hoc basis to make decisions for the good of the community. The assembly was bicameral, consisting of a council of elders and an assembly of all able-bodied men. The gathering of the assembly could be occasioned, for example, by offensive behavior of individuals that called for punitive action, large-scale projects such as canal digging that necessitated communal organization, or the threat of aggression by another city-state and the consequent need of leadership in armed resistance. In order to deal with such emergencies the assembly would choose a leader to carry out its decisions.[8]

---

7. For Mesopotamian chronology before the Dynasty of Akkad, I follow Edith Porada, "The Relative Chronology of Mesopotamia, part 1: Seals and Trade (6000–1600 B.C.)," in *Chronologies in Old World Archaeology*, ed. Robert W. Ehrich (Chicago: University of Chicago Press, 1965), 133–200; for Akkad and thereafter, John A. Brinkman, "Mesopotamian Chronology of the Historical Period," in A. Leo Oppenheim, *Ancient Mesopotamia: Portrait of a Dead Civilization*, rev. ed. completed by Erica Reiner (Chicago: University of Chicago Press, 1977), 335–48.

8. This reconstruction derives from the research of Thorkild Jacobsen, especially two essays in *Toward the Image of Tammuz and Other Essays on Mesopotamian History and Culture*, ed. William L. Moran, Harvard Semitic Series 21 (Cambridge: Harvard University Press, 1970): "Primitive Democracy in Ancient Mesopotamia" (pp. 157–70; reprinted from *Journal of Near Eastern Studies* 2 [1943]: 159–72) and "Early Political Development in Mesopotamia" (pp. 132–56; reprinted from *Zeitschrift für Assyriologie* 52 [1957]: 91–140). Additional references to these essays are cited according to the pagination of *Toward the Image of Tammuz*.

Several Sumerian words are employed for offices of leadership at this early period. While at first the office of *en* may have included political power, it soon came to be primarily associated with the cult; and the term came to mean "high priest" or "high priestess," that is, the spiritual head of the temple, whose residence was within the temple precincts. The *lugal* ("big man") was from the outset more of a political office, though not exclusively so. The *lugal* resided in his own dwelling, separate from the temple, known as the *é-gal* ("big house"), which became the palace, as the *lugal* became the equivalent of the Mesopotamian king. Perhaps from his role as war leader, his position grew in importance until he was the most powerful person in his city-state; and his office became hereditary. A third term, *ensí*, is not entirely clear, but may refer to a more limited position, perhaps that of an administrator of a city under the wider authority of a *lugal* when a larger sphere of authority was operative. Some believe that another term, *nin*, referred at first to the female counterpart of both the *en* and the *lugal*; but, like *en*, it may have originally been used of either sex, since it appears in the names of male gods (e.g., Ningirsu, Ninurta).

If one were to think in terms of the modern distinction between secular and sacred, then the early Sumerian homeland should be viewed as a sacred milieu. The center of the city was the temple, the home of the chief deity of the city, often with smaller temples dedicated to the spouse or children of the city deity. The ruler and the people alike viewed themselves as servants of this deity. Temple property and, indeed, the entire city were seen as the property of the deity; a highly organized bureaucracy administered the temple cult, land, industry, and commerce. In older scholarship a picture was drawn of a temple economy in which in very early times the temple owned all the land.[9] This was an exaggeration, since evidence of private ownership of land appears in Early Dynastic texts.[10] It may be that the larger part of the land was owned by the temples in the early periods in southern Babylonia, where the Sumerians were dominant, while private property was more extensive in northern Babylonia, which was dominated by Semites.[11]

---

9. For a clear statement see Adam Falkenstein, "The Sumerian Temple City," intro. and trans. by Maria deJ. Ellis, *Monographs of the Ancient Near East* 1/1 (1974): 1–21. The theory was first developed by Anton Deimel in a 1920s series of articles in *Orientalia*. A critique that includes a survey of much of the literature may be found in Benjamin Foster, "A New Look at the Sumerian Temple State," *Journal of the Economic and Social History of the Orient* 24 (1981): 225–41.

10. A large part of this research is published in Russian. An English summary of some of it may be found in Igor M. Diakonoff, "Structure of Society and State in Early Dynastic Sumer," *Monographs of the Ancient Near East* 1/3 (1974): 1–16.

11. This is the proposal of Dietz O. Edzard, "The Early Dynastic Period," in *The Near East: The Early Civilizations*, ed. Jean Bottéro, Elena Cassin, and Jean Vercoutter (New York: Delacorte, 1967), 74–77.

In the south, with the Sumerian system of city-states, the leading deity of the capital of a city-state held authority over the entire region, while the deities of lesser cities and towns within it were honored locally in their own areas.[12] The religious capital of Sumer was the city of Nippur, the home of Enlil. According to Sumerian texts, the assembly of the gods met at Nippur to receive the nomination of a king by his city deity and to confer upon him the kingship. It may be that an assembly of free citizens of all Sumer met in Nippur to make decisions, perhaps from the late Protoliterate period through the first phase of the Early Dynastic period that followed.[13] Indications of this are found in the observations that Nippur remained aloof when warfare raged among other cities of Sumer, that no ruling dynasty claimed it as their capital, and yet that control of Nippur gave a ruler claim to control over all of Sumer and Akkad.

The Sumerians worshiped a number of important deities. An (or Anu), whose home was at Uruk, was regarded as the highest god of the pantheon, though by the time of the known texts he had receded to a rather inactive role. His name is also the word for "sky." Royal authority was his, and the institution of kingship was first granted by him. The actual ruler of the Sumerian pantheon was Enlil ("lord wind"), who lived in his temple, Ekur, in Nippur. Enlil was viewed both as the powerful provider for his people and the fearful executor of the judgmental decrees of the divine council. Also prestigious among the deities was Enki, the god of wisdom and cunning. He was also the god of the watery deep, the Abzu, and had his home at Eridu. The goddess Ninhursag (also known as Ninmah or Nintur) was more prominent than Enki at first, though her prominence later waned. Sometimes considered the spouse of Enlil, she was viewed as a divine mother by early Sumerian kings, who spoke of themselves as being nourished by her milk. Nanna, the moon god, resided at Ur; and Utu, the sun god, at Larsa (and at Sippar in the north). Enlil's son, Ninurta, god of victorious warfare and plant and animal fertility, had his temple, Eshumesha, at Nippur and was virtually identified with Ningirsu, whose temple, Eninnu, was at Girsu.[14] Nanshe was the goddess of fish and birds and the interpreter of dreams. The goddess Inanna had her temple, Eanna, at Uruk. This multifaceted goddess represented the productivity of the storehouse, thunderstorms, war, and the morn-

---

12. Piotr Steinkeller, "Mesopotamia, History of (Third Millennium)," in *The Anchor Bible Dictionary*, ed. David N. Freedman et al., 6 vols. (New York: Doubleday, 1992), 4:725. I am grateful to Prof. Steinkeller for providing me with a prepublication copy of this essay.

13. Jacobsen, "Early Political Development," 139–41.

14. Jerrold S. Cooper, *The Return of Ninurta to Nippur*, Analecta Orientalia 52 (Rome: Pontifical Biblical Institute Press, 1978), 10–11.

ing and evening stars. Identified early with Akkadian Ishtar, she finally became the most important goddess in all of western Asia.

Of the published Sumerian literary compositions, there are about twenty that feature gods and goddesses and have been classified in modern terms as myths. These compositions are vital for the modern effort to reconstruct the understanding of reality of the ancient Sumerians, for the stories a people tell are a primary avenue to the core concepts of their culture.[15] Yet this avenue, in the case of the Sumerians, is not well lighted for several reasons: the uncertainties that persist about the translation of the texts, the settings in which the stories were delivered, and their sociological function. Above and beyond these difficulties, some of which are gradually being ameliorated, stands the awesome gap that separates our modern Western worldview from that of the ancient Mesopotamians.

For these reasons, caution is needed lest we draw interpretive conclusions too quickly from the Sumerian texts. For example, the myth usually entitled "Enlil and Ninlil" tells of the young goddess Ninlil bathing in a canal of Nippur, against her mother's counsel. Enlil, upon seeing her, propositions her and carries out his intention, overriding her mild demur. Through the union Ninlil is impregnated with the moon god Nanna. Subsequently Enlil is banished from Nippur by the assembly of gods because of his deed. En route to the netherworld, Ninlil follows him and allows him (under the guise of three other individuals) to impregnate her three more times with three netherworld deities. The tale concludes with a declaration of praise to Enlil. How is this myth to be understood? From the section recounting Enlil's banishment, one scholar finds evidence of Sumer's high moral standards;[16] but this stands in tension with the conclusion to the myth where Enlil is extolled as the sovereign one who promotes fertility. In a deeper reading of the text, another scholar perceives a "strange undertone of inevitability."[17] Yet such levels of meaning are still largely elusive. Still another scholar writes more recently of this myth: "It does not yet seem possible to understand the composition's more profound mythological meanings."[18]

One of the myths in which the god Enki is central, "Enki and the World

15. Livia Polanyi, "What Stories Can Tell Us about Their Teller's World," *Poetics Today* 2 (1981): 98–99.

16. Kramer, *From the Poetry of Sumer*, 40.

17. Thorkild Jacobsen, "*Sumerian Mythology*: A Review Article," in *Toward the Image of Tammuz and Other Essays on Mesopotamian History and Culture*, ed. William L. Moran, Harvard Semitic Series 21 (Cambridge: Harvard University Press, 1970), 127 (reprinted from *Journal of Near Eastern Studies* 5 [1946]: 128–52).

18. Jerrold S. Cooper, "Review of *Enlil und Ninlil: Ein sumerischer Mythos aus Nippur* by Hermann Behrens," *Journal of Cuneiform Studies* 32 (1980): 180.

Order," opens with praise and self-praise to Enki. Then the god pronounces blessing on Sumer, the city of Ur, and the lands of Meluhha and Dilmun. Elam and Marhashi are dealt with severely, but a gift is given to the Martu. Essential aspects of human life and the natural environment are then set in place. At this point the goddess Inanna comes before Enki to complain that she has been slighted in the distribution of divine prerogatives, in comparison with her sister deities. Enki replies by calling Inanna's attention back to the prerogatives that she has already received. Unfortunately the ending of the text is too fragmentary to allow for a meaningful translation, so that Inanna's response is uncertain.

In one of the myths of Inanna, "Inanna and Enki," the theme of the goddess's desire for increased prerogatives is also central. Such prerogatives are viewed as the possession of divinely ordained decrees covering over one hundred aspects of civilization and human life. The Sumerian term for these is *me*.[19] In order to obtain the *me*, Inanna journeys by boat to the Abzu, the watery dwelling of Enki, who has the decrees in his care. She is received and dined by Enki and, during the banquet, while he is drunk, he gives her all of the divine *me*. She promptly loads them on her boat and sets out for her home, Uruk. Upon regaining his sobriety, Enki realizes what he has done and dispatches his messenger and a group of sea monsters to overtake Inanna and recover the *me*. While they do overtake her at several stops, each time she is successful, with the help of the god Ninshubur, in retaining her prized cargo, which she finally brings safely to Uruk amid celebration.

In "Enki and the World Order," the aspiration of Inanna for a wider dominion seems to be focal to the story. In "Inanna and Enki," the goddess obtains all of the *me* and transports them to Uruk, likely reflecting the elevation of Uruk or Inanna or both at some historical point. In another composition, a hymn known as "The Exaltation of Inanna," the goddess is extolled as the possessor of all of the *me*. She is the "Lady of all the me's . . . the guardian of all the great me's!"[20] In still another hymn, "the holy crown of An has been placed upon (her) head . . . the holy scepter of An has been placed in her hand."[21] In these several myths and hymns there seem to be glimpses into the

---

19. There have been many studies of the meaning of Sumerian *me*. A recent discussion is Gertrud Farber-Flügge, *Der Mythos "Inanna und Enki" unter besonderer Berücksichtigung der Liste der me*, Studia Pohl 10 (Rome: Pontifical Biblical Institute Press, 1973), with references to previous literature on p. 116 n. 121, to which should be added William W. Hallo and Johannes J. A. van Dijk, *The Exaltation of Inanna*, Yale Near Eastern Researches 3 (New Haven: Yale University Press, 1968), 49–50 (Hallo's view).

20. Hallo and van Dijk, *Exaltation of Inanna*, 15 (lines 1, 6).

21. Åke W. Sjöberg, "A Hymn to Inanna and Her Self-Praise," *Journal of Cuneiform Studies* 40 (1988): 169 (1:6, 8).

rise of Inanna in the Mesopotamian pantheon, a process that can be traced in later texts about her Semitic counterpart, Ishtar.[22]

Early Dynastic Period

The first period for which written records can be employed to any extent is known as Early Dynastic. By this time the basic shape of Sumerian culture had been determined, and there are indications that its high point had already been reached and decline had set in. The continuity of the civilization of the Early Dynastic age with the earlier period is shown by the persistence of styles in pottery and cylinder-seal manufacturing and the ongoing function of the scribal schools. New departures in government are indicated by the establishment of the institution of kingship and the erection of palaces later in Early Dynastic times (at Kish, Mari, and possibly Eridu). Increased warfare among city-states is attested by the appearance of city walls. While the Sumerians were dominant during this period, at least in the southern area, there is evidence that suggests a strong Semitic influence in northern Babylonia (in the vicinity of Kish and Shuruppak [modern Fara]).[23] As far back as evidence allows one to trace the presence of Semites alongside Sumerians in Mesopotamia, it seems that the military conflicts that occurred between them were not motivated primarily by ethnic differences, but by other factors.[24]

The Early Dynastic period is usually divided into three parts: Early Dynastic I (2900–2750), Early Dynastic II (2750–2600), and Early Dynastic III (subdivided into IIIA [2600–2500] and IIIB [2500–2335]). Textual evidence for centers of political influence during the early phases of the Early Dynastic age comes primarily from the Sumerian King List, which contains a listing of political centers and rulers with incredibly long reigns, followed by a reference to the flood, and then a resumption of political centers and their successive kings, written in a different style, with lengths of reigns that decrease until they are realistic by our standards. In addition to the inflated reigns of earlier kings, the king list pictures a unified Sumer and Akkad with one ruler following another, a picture that is not historical. Even more significant for the use of this text for historical reconstruction is the question

22. Hallo and van Dijk, *Exaltation of Inanna*, 48–49, 60–61.
23. Robert D. Biggs, "Semitic Names in the Fara Period," *Orientalia* 36 (1967): 55–66.
24. Thorkild Jacobsen, "The Assumed Conflict between the Sumerians and Semites in Early Mesopotamian History," in *Toward the Image of Tammuz and Other Essays on Mesopotamian History and Culture*, ed. William L. Moran, Harvard Semitic Series 21 (Cambridge: Harvard University Press, 1970), 187–92 (reprinted from *Journal of the American Oriental Society* 59 [1939]: 485–95).

of its literary genre and especially its purpose.[25] It is a literary text and not a historical one—but, then, neither is any Sumerian text, at least in any sense in which we would use the term. Yet none of these qualifications amounts to saying that the individuals named in the text were not historical persons who did, in fact, occupy a position of authority in their given cities. The opposite can be demonstrated in some cases, apart from the king list. Nevertheless, the Early Dynastic centers of authority and individual rulers known primarily from the Sumerian King List must be viewed with the understanding that the boundary between literary fiction and historical reality is ambiguous.

The first seat of Mesopotamian kingship after the flood was at Kish according to the king list, which may be reflected in the usage of the title "King of Kish" by later Mesopotamian monarchs. Etana, an early king of Kish (many feel the earliest, though he does not occupy the first position in the king list), is described as "the one who consolidated all lands,"[26] seemingly an allusion to a unifying of the country under his rule. He is also spoken of as "the one who to heaven ascended,"[27] a reference to the myth, known from Akkadian sources, of Etana's flight to heaven with the aid of an eagle to obtain a plant that would remedy his childlessness. The ending of the myth is lost.[28] A later successor of Etana in the king list, Enmebaraggesi, is named in two inscriptions that confirm the historicity of his reign.

The city succeeding Kish as the center of power was Uruk, to the south. The second ruler in the First Dynasty of Uruk, Enmerkar, is said in the king list to have built Uruk. Since the capital of his father, the founder of the dynasty, is said to have been located in Eanna, the temple of Inanna, this could suggest a site with a holy place that was later expanded into an urban center, though other interpretations are possible. Enmerkar is the first of four successive kings who are celebrated in later heroic literature. In several tales he is found in conflict with the ruler of Aratta (a power far to the east), emerging victorious and establishing a trade relationship whereby he provides for the needs of his people. Lugalbanda, Enmerkar's successor, is a brave and swift messenger who assists Enmerkar in confrontations with Aratta and also negotiates his own adventures.

25. Piotr Michalowski, "History as Charter: Some Observations on the Sumerian King List," *Journal of the American Oriental Society* 103 (1983): 237–48.

26. Thorkild Jacobsen, *The Sumerian King List*, Assyriological Studies 11 (Chicago: University of Chicago Press, 1939), 81 (2:18).

27. Ibid. (2:16–17).

28. Translations of texts referred to in the essay, when such are not cited, can be located through the list of suggested readings appended to this essay, in many cases most conveniently in the volumes by Jacobsen (*Harps*), Kramer (*Sumerians*), and Pritchard (*ANET*).

The next king of Uruk, Dumuzi (Babylonian Tammuz), is elevated to the level of deity as he becomes the husband of the goddess Inanna, their love, courtship, and marriage being extolled in the literature. Their fortunes turn, however, when Inanna is put to death upon her visit to the underworld. Allowed to return and find a substitute, she finally comes upon her husband Dumuzi, who is not lamenting for her. Enraged, she designates him; and, after twice eluding his captors, he is taken off in her place. Alternately, in another myth, Dumuzi is killed by outsiders upon whom Inanna takes revenge. The Dumuzi/Tammuz cult was practiced widely and long throughout the ancient Near East. It is referred to in the Bible in Ezekiel 8:14.

The best known of the kings of the First Dynasty of Uruk was Gilgamesh (originally Bilgamesh in Sumerian), whose exploits were rehearsed in several literary compositions. In "Gilgamesh and Agga," Gilgamesh and his servant Enkidu, together with the army of Uruk, face a siege against their city by the forces of Kish, led by Agga (or Akka), their king. Uruk triumphs as Agga is captured in the midst of his army by a successful sortie led by Enkidu.[29] Gilgamesh, apparently in response to an earlier kindness of Agga, then releases Agga to return to his own city. "Gilgamesh and Huwawa" tells of Gilgamesh (together with Enkidu, seven spirits appointed by Utu, and fifty chosen men) setting out to the Cedar Forest to establish his enduring fame. Upon arriving after a dangerous journey, Gilgamesh immediately cuts down a cedar, which wakes the monster Huwawa, guardian of the forest. The latter dons his radiance and goes forth to momentarily overwhelm Gilgamesh. Being restored, Gilgamesh tricks Huwawa into giving up his protective auras by a ruse (which varies among the versions of the story). Gilgamesh then pities the creature and would spare him, but Enkidu is opposed and slays Huwawa, an action that incurs Enlil's disapproval.

Other Sumerian stories of Gilgamesh include the following. The poorly preserved "Gilgamesh and the Bull of Heaven" tells how the Bull of Heaven is sent by Inanna against Uruk after she obtains permission to do so from An by threatening to appeal to the other gods if he refuses. "The Death of Gilgamesh" relates Enlil's address to Gilgamesh to the effect that he is not destined for immortality (though he has been granted dominion and heroism); it then tells of Gilgamesh's death, lists Gilgamesh's family and servants, and recounts how Gilgamesh made offerings to the gods for them. "Gilgamesh, Enkidu, and the Netherworld" tells of Inanna bringing a *huluppu* tree to her city and planting it. After it was taken over by three creatures whom she could

---

29. Jacob Klein, "The Capture of Agga by Gilgameš (GA 81 and 99)," *Journal of the American Oriental Society* 103 (1983): 201–4, amplifying the interpretation of Jacobsen, "Early Political Development," 381–82 n. 55.

not deal with, Gilgamesh delivered the tree back to her and then had two implements (*pukku* and *mekkû*) made for himself from it. With these he in some way (how is not clear) oppressed the people of Uruk. When the implements fell into the netherworld, Gilgamesh was unable to retrieve them; so Enkidu volunteered to do so. Because he failed to heed Gilgamesh's warnings, he was held fast. Gilgamesh obtained help from Enki and (through Enki) from Utu, so that Enkidu's spirit was permitted to return and converse with Gilgamesh. Enkidu described the netherworld as he had experienced it.

Stories of Gilgamesh are best known from an Akkadian version of twelve tablets with copies dating to the seventh century.[30] The final half of the last Sumerian story mentioned above was the direct source of the twelfth tablet of this Akkadian version, which is a literal translation of the Sumerian that fits only awkwardly with the eleven tablets that precede it in the Akkadian. Those eleven tablets constitute an integrated composition of considerable literary artistry, which has been shown to derive from a creative development of earlier sources tracing back, in part, to some of the Sumerian tales outlined above.[31]

Probably the best known section of the Akkadian epic, because of its similarity to the biblical account in Genesis 6–9, is the flood story in the eleventh tablet. The flood story can be traced back to Sumerian through a fragmentary tablet only one-third of which has been preserved.[32] In this Sumerian text, Gilgamesh is not mentioned, suggesting that the flood story was later combined with the Gilgamesh traditions. The text tells of the creation of humans and animals, the institution of kingship in five antediluvian cities under the care of the tutelary deities, the decision of the divine council to send the flood, communication about the flood to the man Ziusudra, the coming of the flood, Ziusudra's survival in a boat, his offering of sacrifice, and his endowment with eternal life and settlement in the land of Dilmun.[33]

In the king list Uruk was succeeded by Ur, whose kings, unlike those of Uruk and Etana of Kish, are not known from later literary works. The first

---

30. A recent, accessible translation of the first eleven tablets of this version is Maureen G. Kovacs, *The Epic of Gilgamesh* (Stanford: Stanford University Press, 1989).

31. Samuel N. Kramer, "The Epic of Gilgameš and Its Sumerian Sources: A Study in Literary Evolution," *Journal of the American Oriental Society* 64 (1944): 7–23, 83; Jeffrey H. Tigay, *The Evolution of the Gilgamesh Epic* (Philadelphia: University of Pennsylvania Press, 1982).

32. Samuel N. Kramer, "The Sumerian Deluge Myth: Reviewed and Revised," *Anatolian Studies* 33 (1983): 115–21, interacting extensively with Miguel Civil, "The Sumerian Flood Story," in Wilfred G. Lambert and Alan R. Millard, *Atra-ḫasīs: The Babylonian Story of the Flood* (Oxford: Clarendon, 1969), 138–45, 167–72; and Thorkild Jacobsen, "The Eridu Genesis," *Journal of Biblical Literature* 100 (1981): 513–29.

33. Usually identified with the island of Bahrain in the Persian Gulf, though this is disputed for the period before the late third millennium; Theresa Howard-Carter, "The Tangible Evidence for the Earliest Dilmun," *Journal of Cuneiform Studies* 33 (1981): 210–23.

"Peace" panel of the sounding box of a harp (the "Standard of Ur"), 2500 B.C. (height: 8";
length: 19")   *Courtesy of the British Museum*

two, Mesannepada and Annepada, however, have been attested on a marble
temple inscription. The names of two other rulers, Akalamdug and
Meskalamdug (not known from the Sumerian King List, perhaps because
they ruled before Ur gained wide hegemony), have been found in Ur's royal
burial ground.

The burial ground, excavated by Sir Leonard Woolley, was a remarkable
discovery. The finds include a golden replica of a man's hairstyle from King
Meskalamdug's grave; the golden head of a bull with eyes, beard, and horn
tips made of lapis lazuli attached to the sounding box of a lyre; two male
goats standing upright, each with its front legs in a small tree; mosaic inlays
of war and celebration scenes in an artifact that has come to be called the
"Standard of Ur"; the elaborate headdress of Queen Puabi (earlier read as
Shubad); and other magnificent objects.[34] Also stirring, in a gruesome way, is
Woolley's discovery of the burial of a retinue of royal servants with the royal
family upon the death of their king. Upward of eighty persons were found
buried in one chamber. It is uncertain whether this was an authentic Sumerian
custom, for it was apparently rare and cannot be attested after this time.

---

34. Color prints of some of the most noteworthy of these may be found in Peter R. S. Moorey,
*Ur "of the Chaldees": A Revised and Updated Edition of Sir Leonard Woolley's Excavations at
Ur* (Ithaca: Cornell University Press, 1982), 51–103.

In Early Dynastic III the institution of kingship with dynastic succession was firmly established. Pressure from the Elamites to the east, already reflected in stories of earlier rulers, mounted. Significant for the historian is the increase in contemporary documents that can be relatively well understood and whose contents can be expected to yield more historical information, especially royal inscriptions. The bulk of these documents comes from the city-state of Lagash. In the shifting balance of power, there was a union of Uruk and Ur, which later included Umma, and perhaps an alliance between Kish and Akshak to the north, with Lagash apparently standing alone.[35] The inscriptions repeatedly draw attention to conflict between Lagash and Umma over the territory between them, known as the *guedinna* ("the edge of the plain"), land that was productive for agriculture. The sources indicate that this dispute was arbitrated earlier by Mesalim (often spelled Mesilim), a ruler who bore the title "King of Kish." Rulers of Lagash and Umma entered into the ongoing dispute throughout the remainder of the Early Dynastic age and beyond.

Ur-Nanshe, the founder of the First Dynasty of Lagash, left numerous short inscriptions on stone recounting his temple building and other activities. Eannatum (also spelled Eanatum), his grandson, briefly assumed the title "King of Kish" early in his reign. His best known monument is the "Stele of Vultures," named for the birds of prey that are depicted feasting on his conquered enemies. One side of the sculpture portrays the king and the phalanx of his army, and the other has the king's god, Ningirsu, holding the king's enemies in a net. Eannatum fought the armies of Kish, Akshak, and Mari within his own state of Lagash; thus, his warfare was defensive.

UruKAgina[36] followed the last of Ur-Nanshe's dynasty to the rulership of Lagash. The fortunes of Lagash had been in decline since the reign of Eannatum, and it is likely that many social abuses had come in the wake of waning military power. UruKAgina moved to counter these abuses and is remembered for his reforms (preserved in two copies). He reversed abuses of royal authority, encroachments on temple lands and personnel, oppression of workers, excessive collection of revenue, mistreatment of the poor and defenseless, and undesirable family practices. All of these reforms he claims he carried out on behalf of Ningirsu, whose prerogatives he was restoring.

The final defeat of Lagash and its ruler, UruKAgina, in the Early Dynastic period came at the hands of Lugalzagesi, *ensí* of Umma. Lugalzagesi achieved

---

35. This follows Jerrold S. Cooper, "Reconstructing History from Ancient Inscriptions: The Lagash-Umma Border Conflict," *Sources from the Ancient Near East* 2/1 (1983): 8–9.

36. The earlier reading of this ruler's name, Urukagina, has been revised to Uruinimgina; but the revision is in dispute. The transcription employed here acknowledges this difference of opinion.

further success, to the extent that he proclaimed himself "King of Uruk"[37] and "King of Sumer," identified himself with the chief deities of all of Sumer, and claimed recognition by peoples from the Persian Gulf to the Mediterranean. He expressed imperial aspirations that at least became reality in the following period, though likely not during his reign.

Kingdom of Akkad

During the next period Semites were politically dominant in Mesopotamia. Their presence is discernible from the earliest documentable times, with greater concentration in the north. Early rulers of Kish were Semitic. Yet in the present period, not only were the rulers Semitic, they installed a network of Semitic authorities under them (though also allowing native rulers to remain); their language was used in official inscriptions alongside Sumerian; and their capital city, Akkad (often spelled Agade, in distinction from the region of Akkad), came to dominate all of Mesopotamia.

The founder of the Dynasty of Akkad was Sargon, also known as Sargon the Great (2334–2279). According to later tradition, he was born in secret and cast adrift on the Euphrates in a reed basket from which he was taken up and reared as a gardener until he was favored by the goddess Ishtar and given a place in the court of King Ur-Zababa of Kish. From this position, he established himself as ruler at a new capital, Akkad, the location of which has not been determined, though it may have been in the vicinity of Babylon. The sequence of his conquests is not clear. Certainly his victory over Lugalzagesi was pivotal. Records entered in Enlil's temple at Nippur and faithfully copied there picture campaigns from the Persian Gulf to the Mediterranean and beyond this to the east and north.

While vigorously pursuing military dominance, Sargon showed respect for Sumerian cultural and religious traditions. For example, he installed his own daughter Enheduanna in the office of high priestess of the moon god Nanna at Ur. (This practice was subsequently followed by Babylonian rulers to the time of Nabonidus [555–539].) Possessed of extraordinary literary ability, Enheduanna left two collections of hymns that she authored, extolling in one case the goddess Inanna and in the other the temples of Sumer and Akkad. It may be that certain literary features of these hymns reflect a deliberate movement of Sargon carried forth by his daughter to equate Sumerian Inanna and Semitic Ishtar.[38] This syncretism of Sumerian and Semitic traditions was to become characteristic of ancient Mesopotamian civilization to the extent that

37. Lugalzagesi may have ruled Uruk by virtue of its close ties with Umma, rather than by conquest; Cooper, "Reconstructing History," 34.
38. Hallo and van Dijk, *Exaltation of Inanna*, 11.

in later times, when the Sumerians had ceased to exist as a distinct people and their language had passed from living usage, the two streams are virtually impossible to separate, so that Assyriologists are accustomed to speaking of the symbiosis of the two.

Sargon's successors had to deal with repeated revolts, which are attested already in the later years of his own reign. The third ruler to follow Sargon, Naram-Sin (2254–2218), was compared to his forebear in greatness. In addition to the titles of Sargon ("King of Akkad," "King of Kish," "King of the Land" [i.e., Sumer]), Naram-Sin styled himself "King of the Four Quarters" (i.e., universal ruler); and then, most significantly, he placed before his name the cuneiform sign for divinity. This practice was continued by a few later rulers in Mesopotamia, but a concept of divine kingship never developed in any full sense of the term, as it did, for example, in Egypt. Nor is its significance well understood. While Naram-Sin campaigned in all directions and could boast of many triumphs, his dominion was an uneasy one. Extensive traditions grew up around his reign, as with Sargon, that treated his success with ambivalence. His successor, Shar-kali-sharri, saw the kingdom of Akkad disintegrating.

After several decades during which general anarchy seems to have prevailed, the final destruction came in the reign of Naram-Sin according to a Sumerian composition known as the "Curse of Akkad." This text describes the earlier favor of Enlil and the prosperity of Akkad, and then sacrilege on the part of Naram-Sin in invading Nippur and desecrating Enlil's sanctuary, the Ekur. In his rage Enlil is said to have brought in the foreign Gutians as his instrument of judgment. (In actual fact, in addition to the Gutian invasion, internal disruption and the opposition of the Elamites, Hurrians, and Lullubi were also involved in the fall of Akkad.) The devastation the Gutians effected is portrayed in the "Curse of Akkad." In order to calm Enlil, eight of the leading deities pronounced a curse on Akkad, which was immediately carried out. In the worldview of the ancient Mesopotamian, the events of history were understood to be a playing out on the human level of the decisions made on the divine plane. Noteworthy in this composition is the attribution of the fall of Akkad to the act of Naram-Sin. The direct linking of human action with divine action as cause and consequence is not without parallel in Mesopotamian literature, especially later in the first millennium; but such a connection is not typical earlier, for example, in the Sumerian King List, in city laments (to be discussed below), or in Ur III royal correspondence.[39] There, divine action, as when gods or goddesses pronounce destruction, appears to be unre-

39. Jerrold S. Cooper, *The Curse of Agade* (Baltimore: Johns Hopkins University Press, 1983), 29–30.

lated to human responsibility and arbitrary, perhaps inevitable.[40]

The Gutians continued to make periodic raids into Mesopotamia from the Zagros Mountains for about half a century and exerted their power primarily in northern Babylonia. Continuity with the Sumerian past was maintained in the south, for example, in the Lagash region, where a succession of governors (*ensí*) retained autonomy.[41] The best known of these is Gudea, who engaged in many building activities at home and far-reaching foreign trade. Gudea's inscriptions include two large clay cylinders that have preserved the most extensive Sumerian literary composition recovered to date, containing close to fourteen hundred lines. The text commemorates Gudea's rebuilding of the Eninnu temple of Ningirsu at Girsu, which was at that time the capital of the city-state of La-

Statue of Gudea, ca. 2150 B.C. (height: 17.25″)
*Courtesy of the Metropolitan Museum of Art,
Harris Brisbane Dick Fund, 1959*

40. Cf. n. 17 above for Jacobsen's observation of the notion of inevitability in a mythological text.

41. It is generally believed that these rulers, the Second Dynasty of Lagash, were defeated and their dynasty brought to an end by the new Third Dynasty of Ur, which will be discussed shortly. There is evidence, however, that suggests that two of these governors, Gudea and Nammahni (also spelled Nammahani and Namhani), were contemporaries of the first king of the new Ur Dynasty, Ur-Nammu, indicating that Lagash lost its independence only during Ur-Nammu's reign; Piotr Steinkeller, "The Date of Gudea and His Dynasty," *Journal of Cuneiform Studies* 40 (1988): 47–53.

gash.[42] Having been commissioned by Ningirsu in two dreams to build his temple, Gudea goes about his task carefully: he unites his people, obtains necessary materials and workers, completes the temple, and introduces the god and his consort to their new home.

The expulsion of the Gutians was accomplished by Utuhegal of Uruk. Their defeat opened the way for the resumption of Sumerian rule. It was not Utuhegal or his city-state of Uruk that was to exercise this rule, however. After seven years Utuhegal was overcome by one of his subordinates, Ur-Nammu (sometimes spelled Ur-Namma) of Ur.

Ur III Dynasty

The dominance of the city-state of Ur under the dynasty (2112–2004) founded by Ur-Nammu was a period of Sumerian renaissance. Ur's dominion encompassed southern and central Mesopotamia as far north as Sippar, extended further northward along the Tigris to a point slightly beyond Ashur and eastward into Elam (apparently at one point well beyond the capital of Susa), and included vassal states even further removed whose degree of dependence varied from one reign to another.[43] The kingdom was administered from Ur and, secondarily, from Uruk and Nippur. A highly organized bureaucracy made for a tight and effective administration that produced prosperity and security throughout a good two-thirds of the century-long reign of the dynasty. Building programs were extensive, and arts, literature, and education flourished.

The kingship of Ur-Nammu was acknowledged by the priesthood of Enlil at Nippur, and he took the new title of "King of Sumer and Akkad," indicating his rule over southern and central Mesopotamia as far as the Lower Diyala region. His coronation was celebrated in a literary genre, the royal hymn, which extolled the choice of the king by the gods.

Ur-Nammu has been credited with a collection of laws, but the author may have been his son Shulgi.[44] Several collections such as this have been

---

42. Earlier scholarship identified Tello as Lagash (which is modern al-Hiba); rather, Girsu is to be identified with the site of Tello; see Vaughn E. Crawford, "Lagash," *Iraq* 36 (1974): 29–35.

43. Piotr Steinkeller, "The Administrative and Economic Organization of the Ur III State: The Core and the Periphery," in *The Organization of Power: Aspects of Bureaucracy in the Ancient Near East*, ed. McGuire Gibson and Robert D. Biggs, 2d ed., Studies in Ancient Oriental Civilization 46 (Chicago: Oriental Institute, 1991), 30–41.

44. Johannes J. A. van Dijk, *apud* Fatma Yildiz, "A Tablet of Codex Ur-Nammu from Sippar," *Orientalia* 50 (1981): 93–94 n. 20a; Samuel N. Kramer, "The Ur-Nammu Law Code: Who Was Its Author?" *Orientalia* 52 (1983): 453–56; Steinkeller, "Administrative and Economic Organization," 21 n. 10.

recovered from Mesopotamia. They are usually called "codes," though they do not appear to have been documents that were referred to in the courts while actual cases were being decided. They were more likely what we would call scientific treatises on the law, which originated in the schools.[45] This is the earliest of these collections, of which the most famous is that of Hammurapi (often spelled Hammurabi) of Babylon. The "Ur-Nammu" laws, preserved only in small part, deal with situations similar to those of later times, but differ in that they impose financial penalties for bodily harm against other people, in contrast to death or mutilation comparable to the crime (the "eye for an eye" principle of talion) known from later Semitic collections.

Ur-Nammu's reign was filled with building activities. Royal residences, wharves, irrigation works, and temples that had fallen into disrepair under the Gutian domination were renewed. It was the prerogative of the king to rebuild the temples of the land, and this would customarily be done on the site of the previous temple complex, producing a layered structure as destruction levels were built upon. By the reign of Ur-Nammu, if not before (earlier evidence is lacking), renovation levels were deliberately constructed in this manner; and the ziggurat was born, a layered tower with a shrine presumed to have been on the top level. The ziggurat of the temple complex of Nanna at Ur is the best preserved, but Ur-Nammu also constructed ziggurats at Nippur, Uruk, Eridu, and other cities.

The reign of Ur-Nammu's son Shulgi was an illustrious one. That there were military campaigns is shown by year-date formulas,[46] and it appears that these were largely successful. Trade routes were reopened, and trade and industry prospered; so did literature and the scribal schools. Although most copies of Sumerian literature come from the later Old Babylonian period, it is clear that much of it was created at this time. The schools of Nippur and Ur are accredited to Shulgi, and the king claimed to have been trained as a scribe, a rare boast even for a Mesopotamian king. Shulgi resumed the title "King of the Four Quarters" alongside his father's "King of Sumer and

---

45. Fritz R. Kraus, "Ein zentrales Problem des altmesopotamischen Rechtes: Was ist der Codex Hammu-rabi?" *Genava* 8 (1960): 283–96; Jean Bottéro, "Le 'Code' de Hammurabi," *Annali della Scuola normale superiore de Pisa* 12 (1982): 409–44 (now available in English as "The 'Code' of Hammurabi," in *Mesopotamia: Writing, Reasoning, and the Gods*, trans. Zainab Bahrani and Marc Van De Mieroop [Chicago: University of Chicago Press, 1992], 156–84); Raymond Westbrook, "Cuneiform Law Codes and the Origins of Legislation," *Zeitschrift für Assyriologie* 79 (1989): 200–222.

46. In Sumer from the Akkad period through the Old Babylonian period, years, instead of being numbered as in our modern designations, derived their names from noteworthy events that took place in the preceding years, a practice that Sumerologists refer to as "year-date formula" or "year-name."

Akkad" and had himself treated as divine, like Naram-Sin. Shrines were established for him, and more royal hymns were written in his honor than for any other Mesopotamian monarch.

Two of Shulgi's sons, Amar-Sin and Shu-Sin, succeeded him to the throne; and both were deified. Little is known of Amar-Sin's reign; he died of a "shoebite," presumably a foot disease. A people who had been mentioned in earlier periods appear during the reign of Shu-Sin as a serious threat. They are the Semites from west of the Euphrates, known generally as the Amorites (*Martu* in Sumerian, *Amurrum* in Akkadian). Shu-Sin's inscriptions tell of his building an extensive wall somewhere between Ur and Mari, "which keeps away the Tidnum" (one of the Amorite tribes). His efforts were less than effective, so much so that his successor, Ibbi-Sin, was forced to build walls and fortifications around even the districts of Ur and Nippur. Gradually one after another of Ur's provinces withdrew their loyalty, and the kingdom was lost. It was an army from the east, from Elam and Shimashki,[47] that sacked Ur and led Ibbi-Sin away as a captive.

Isin-Larsa Period

The fall of the Ur III kingdom was not yet the end of Sumerian dominance, at least in the south; but it was the beginning of the end. With the fall of Ur, northern and central Mesopotamia were fragmented into competing kingdoms. In the south, where Sumerian culture was most deeply entrenched, a unity of sorts was maintained for about the next century by the city of Isin. Its first king, Ishbi-Erra (often spelled Ishbi-Irra) from Mari, had been a subordinate of Ibbi-Sin until he proclaimed himself ruler of Isin. Gaining control of Nippur, Uruk, Eridu, and, later in his reign, Ur itself, Ishbi-Erra took over the administrative system of Ur. He and his successors employed the Sumerian language in their official correspondence, though they themselves were Semites. Some of the Sumerian literature composed during this period has been recovered in excavations at Nippur, though there was undoubtedly much more than has been retrieved.

There are several compositions that can be classified as "city laments" that come from this period. One of these, the "Lamentation over the Destruction of Sumer and Ur," most clearly appears to have been written to legitimize the

---

47. The allies of the Elamites in the overthrow of Ur are generally referred to in the literature as the "Su people" (which has been understood in several different ways). For their identification as the people of Shimashki (a state that arose in southwestern Iran about the time of the Ur III Dynasty), see Piotr Steinkeller, "On the Identity of the Toponym LÚ.SU(.A)," *Journal of the American Oriental Society* 108 (1988): 197–202.

Isin Dynasty by establishing its continuity with the Ur III kings.[48] Another that also has the city of Ur as its subject and likely had the same general purpose is the "Lamentation over the Destruction of Ur." It depicts devastation overtaking the cities of Sumer, including Ur itself; the goddess Ningal (consort of Nanna) poignantly lamenting her inability to turn An, Enlil, and the divine council from their decree of destruction; the judgment falling like a mighty storm; Ur lying in ruins in the aftermath; Ningal bewailing her loss; and an appeal to Ningal and Nanna to return to their city and let it be rebuilt. Two other city laments can be precisely dated during the First Isin Dynasty, for they both contain a reference to a later ruler of that dynasty, Ishme-Dagan. These are the "Uruk Lament" and the "Nippur Lament."[49] The "Eridu Lament" may also date to the same reign, though this is not demonstrable.[50] Each of the city laments concludes with a prayer for the return of the city deity or deities and, thus, for restored favor on the city. Since they all probably date to the First Isin Dynasty, it would seem that they all had the same underlying purpose. As the restoration of the cities of Sumer was called for and the deities of these cities invoked, the rulers of the city of Isin who were promoting this restoration would be affirmed as the legitimate successors to kingship over Sumer.

Under Ishme-Dagan, the fourth ruler in the Dynasty of Ishbi-Erra, there appear again the efforts of the king to abolish social grievances, as with Uru-KAgina of Lagash in earlier times. That this should be necessary may speak of growing unrest in the kingdom of Isin; this is supported by references in texts from the reign of Ishme-Dagan to the raids of the Amorites and to a defeat of that king at the gates of Kish.

Lipit-Ishtar (sometimes spelled Lipit-Eshtar), son of Ishme-Dagan and last member of the Dynasty of Ishbi-Erra, left a collection of laws set between a prologue and an epilogue, a pattern seen in the later and better known laws of Hammurapi. Lipit-Ishtar is presented in the prologue as "the wise shepherd" (a common figure for Mesopotamian kings) who is commissioned "to establish justice in the land" (a phrase that may refer to debt an-

---

48. Piotr Michalowski, *The Lamentation over the Destruction of Sumer and Ur*, Mesopotamian Civilizations 1 (Winona Lake, Ind.: Eisenbrauns, 1989), 6–8; idem, "History as Charter," 242.

49. M. W. Green, "The Uruk Lament," *Journal of the American Oriental Society* 104 (1984): 275–76 (12:9, 14); an edition of the "Nippur Lament" is being prepared by H. L. J. Vanstiphout. I know of the mention of Ishme-Dagan in the latter through Michalowski, *Lamentation over the Destruction of Sumer and Ur*, 6.

50. M. W. Green, "The Eridu Lament," *Journal of Cuneiform Studies* 30 (1978): 127–67. Other, more fragmentary compositions may also belong to this category; but these are the main extant city laments.

nulment). As with the earlier laws of Ur-Nammu, financial penalties are imposed for damages.

The measure of centralization in the Sumerian south that Isin had been able to maintain ended when Gungunum, an Amorite ruler of Larsa, took control of Ur and then Uruk. Later, Nippur, which had passed back and forth between Isin and Larsa, came under the control of Larsa; and finally Isin itself fell to Rim-Sin, the third of a series of Elamite rulers and the last king of Larsa. Rim-Sin attached great importance to the event, dating documents from the last thirty years of his reign by it. It did not prove to be so significant, however. The end of Isin's dominance, actually signaled by the transfer of Ur to Larsa under Gungunum, inaugurated a period of fragmentation among competing cities that would end only with the ascendancy of Babylon under Hammurapi (1792–1750).

Sumer's Legacy

Although the Sumerians no longer existed as a distinct political entity after the conquest of Mesopotamia by Hammurapi of Babylon, their influence lived on. The vast bulk of literature composed in Sumerian that has been excavated so far derives from the Old Babylonian period. The Sumerian language, although it died out as a living language at least by this time, if not earlier, continued in use as a religious and literary language for more than a millennium. The civilization of the Semites who succeeded the Sumerians as the rulers of Mesopotamia was indelibly marked by that which was Sumerian. As it is put in an analysis of the Semitic side of ancient Mesopotamia: "The Sumerians left their imprint in varying degrees on all things Mesopotamian."[51]

In the introduction to this essay, I listed some of the specific items in world civilization that probably derive from Sumerian origins. Yet such a listing can in no way adequately portray the debt of later civilizations to the Sumerians, for "to reckon only with those Mesopotamian relics that have survived up to now is like counting the pieces of furniture inherited from remote ancestors, forgetting that the ancestors have shaped the lives of our forefathers and, indirectly, our own life."[52]

The Western world owes a debt to the Sumerians that has not yet been calculated. The classical civilizations of Greece and Rome, out of which Western civilization sprang most directly, were engaged in cultural interaction with the ancient Near East from their beginnings; and all of the ancient Near East was

---

51. A. Leo Oppenheim, *Ancient Mesopotamia: Portrait of a Dead Civilization*, rev. ed. completed by Erica Reiner (Chicago: University of Chicago Press, 1977), 4.

52. Georges Roux, *Ancient Iraq*, 3d ed. (Baltimore: Penguin, 1992), 425.

influenced, in varying degrees, by the Sumerians.[53] Although the Sumerians were conquered by the Semites, in a deeper sense, "the conquered conquered the conquerors," for the Babylonians "took over Sumerian culture and civilization lock, stock, and barrel," "exercised no little influence on their less cultured neighbors," and "as much as the Sumerians themselves, helped to plant the Sumerian cultural seed everywhere in the ancient Near East."[54]

One line for the influence of the Sumerians on the West is through the Bible, which was produced in the ancient Near East and which has had such a formative role in the development of Western civilization. In a time, at least in the United States, when emphasis is being placed on multiculturalism, that is, on the varied sources of an increasingly pluralistic society, it is urgent, for the sake of an informed historical perspective, that the origins of Western civilization be traced backward beyond Greece and Rome, where the search usually ends, to the ancient Near East and, in this process, that the Sumerians be given their due.[55]

Recommended Reading

For the student who wants to read more about the Sumerians, I recommend the following, limited to sources in English. The liveliest and most current research most often appears in technical journals, and the following books (especially Hallo, Oppenheim, Postgate, and Roux) cite relevant journals up to the time of their writing. I have arranged the titles in a preferred order of reading for the ambitious student who will undertake them all, and I have annotated them for the student who must be selective.

Hallo, William W., and William K. Simpson. *The Ancient Near East: A History.* New York: Harcourt Brace Jovanovich, 1971. One of the two best books to begin with. Hallo's part through page 97 treats the Sumerians.
Roux, Georges. *Ancient Iraq.* 3d edition. Baltimore: Penguin, 1992. One of the two best books to begin with. Chapters 5–11 are especially relevant for the Sumerians.
Bottéro, Jean, Elena Cassin, and Jean Vercoutter (eds.). *The Near East: The Early Civilizations.* Translated by R. F. Tannenbaum. New York: Dela-

---

53. Because of this influence, even though the Sumerians are not mentioned explicitly in the Hebrew Bible, the reference from Isa. 51:1, cited at the beginning of this essay, can be read as a call to ponder the legacy of ancient Sumer.

54. Kramer, *Sumerians*, 288–89.

55. If this is done well, I believe that it will result in an appreciation of aspects of the Bible that have been lost to our Western perspective and a discovery of continuities that we share with peoples of the East.

corte, 1967. The chapters on Mesopotamia by Falkenstein, Edzard, and Bottéro are a sensitively written history.

Kramer, Samuel N. *The Sumerians: Their History, Culture, and Character.* Chicago: University of Chicago Press, 1963. A classic study.

Jacobsen, Thorkild. *The Treasures of Darkness: A History of Mesopotamian Religion.* New Haven: Yale University Press, 1976. An empathetic synthesis of Mesopotamian religion.

Jacobsen, Thorkild. *The Harps That Once . . . : Sumerian Poetry in Translation.* New Haven: Yale University Press, 1987. A nuanced rendering of a large selection of Sumerian literary texts.

Pritchard, James B. (ed.). *Ancient Near Eastern Texts Relating to the Old Testament.* 3d edition. Princeton: Princeton University Press, 1969. Though the Sumerian selections are limited, they include a wide sampling of the kinds of texts available.

Saggs, Harry W. F. *The Greatness That Was Babylon: A Survey of the Ancient Civilization of the Tigris-Euphrates Valley.* 2d edition. London: Sidgwick & Jackson, 1988. Helpful topical organization.

Jones, Tom B. (ed.). *The Sumerian Problem.* Major Issues in History. New York: Wiley, 1969. Offers a feel for the struggle that accompanied the resurrection of the Sumerians to historical study.

Lloyd, Seton. *Foundations in the Dust: The Story of Mesopotamian Exploration.* Revised edition. New York: Thames & Hudson, 1980. An interesting account of archeological work in Mesopotamia.

Nissen, Hans J. *The Early History of the Ancient Near East, 9000–2000 B.C.* Translated by Elizabeth Lutzeier and Kenneth J. Northcott. Chicago: University of Chicago Press, 1988. A history based primarily on archeological data.

Kramer, Samuel N. *In the World of Sumer: An Autobiography.* Detroit: Wayne State University Press, 1986. The life story of one of the leading Sumerologists.

Oppenheim, A. Leo. *Ancient Mesopotamia: Portrait of a Dead Civilization.* Revised edition completed by Erica Reiner. Chicago: University of Chicago Press, 1977. Although dealing only with the Semites, it is recommended for study of the Sumerians because of the author's grasp of Mesopotamian cultural history.

Postgate, J. Nicholas. *Early Mesopotamia: Society and Economy at the Dawn of History.* London: Routledge, 1992. Although it appeared after this essay had been submitted and, thus, could not be cited, this work is mandatory for all who study the Sumerians. I have placed it last so that the reader who works through the entire corpus will have the benefit of that wider exposure when undertaking it, though it could be read earlier and should not be omitted from any partial selection.

Babylonians

Bill T. Arnold

*Zedekiah rebelled against the king of Babylon. So in the ninth
year of Zedekiah's reign, . . . Nebuchadnezzar king of Babylon
marched against Jerusalem with his whole army.*
—2 Kings 24:20–25:1

The Babylonians were a notable people during the Old Testament
period for two reasons. First, from a purely historical perspective, they were
God's instrument of destruction against Jerusalem late in the story of his people. Second and perhaps more importantly, they transmitted and in some
cases even originated most of the cultural and religious foundations for the
Old Testament world. They and their predecessors the Sumerians established
the philosophical and social infrastructure for Israel's neighbors. So, in addition to the historical contacts between the Babylonians and Israelites, it is important to understand the Babylonian contributions to Old Testament
culture and society.

Name and Origin

The earliest form of the name "Babylon" appears to have been *Babil*,
the origin and meaning of which are lost to antiquity. The word may have
been of Sumerian origin, since the city's existence may be traced to just before
the Akkadian Empire (2334–2193).[1] The first Akkadian form of the name,

---

1. Potsherds have been reported from the surface of the site from the latter part of the Early
Dynastic period; see McGuire Gibson, *The City and Area of Kish* (Miami: Field Research,
1972), 37 n. 49; and André Parrot, *Babylon and the Old Testament*, trans. B. E. Hooke (New
York: Philosophical Library, 1958), 69. For the most part excavations have extended only to the
Neo-Babylonian levels. It has not been possible to do much with deeper and earlier stratums,
due to the problem of ground water. The dates in this paper follow John A. Brinkman, "Mesopotamian Chronology of the Historical Period," in A. Leo Oppenheim, *Ancient Mesopotamia:*

Bāb-ilim ("gate of God"), was probably a secondary development derived through popular etymology.[2] The later plural form, *Bāb-ilāni*, became *Babulōn* in Greek, resulting in the modern name "Babylon."

Ancient Mesopotamian literature preserves conflicting traditions concerning the naming of Babylon. The chronographic and omen literature attribute the name of the city to Sargon of Akkad (2334–2279), who allegedly dug up a mound of dust from Babylon and set it up near his own city of Akkad in a symbolic act stressing his role as conqueror. It was at this time that he named the place "Babylon."[3] Elsewhere, the name of Babylon is attributed to the gods. In the opening paragraphs of the Code of Hammurapi, the great gods Anu and Enlil named the city when they established Marduk the god of Babylon as preeminent over humankind. In the Babylonian Creation Epic (*"Enuma Elish"*), Marduk announces that he has built and named the city as residence for his divine fathers.[4]

The Bible contains its own tradition concerning the name of Babylon in the opprobrious interpretation given for the name in Genesis 11:9. Whereas

---

Portrait of a Dead Civilization, rev. ed. completed by Erica Reiner (Chicago: University of Chicago Press, 1977), 335–48. Chronological precision is still impossible for most of Babylonian history before the first millennium. I have followed what has become a consensus among most Assyriologists for the controversial Old Babylonian period: that is, the use of the so-called middle chronology (Brinkman, "Mesopotamian Chronology," 346 n. 4).

2. It used to be accepted *prima facie* that the Akkadian was a direct translation of an older and more original Sumerian name *Ka-dingirra*, also meaning "gate of God." But Ignace J. Gelb demonstrates that Akkadian *Bāb-ilim* was in fact older than Sumerian *Ka-dingirra* and that it was probably a secondary development of *Babil* due to popular etymology; see "The Name of Babylon," *Journal of the Institute of Asian Studies* 1 (1955): 1–4. It is also suggested that the name is a Semitic pronunciation of a proto-Euphratean *Papil/Papal*; see William White Jr., "Babylon, City of," in *The New International Dictionary of Biblical Archaeology*, ed. Edward M. Blaiklock and Roland K. Harrison (Grand Rapids: Zondervan, 1983), 85.

3. This tradition is found in the Weidner Chronicle 50–51 and the Chronicle of Early Kings A:18–19; see A. Kirk Grayson, *Assyrian and Babylonian Chronicles* (Locust Valley, N.Y.: Augustin, 1975), 149, 153–54. However a copy of the Weidner Chronicle recently found at Sippar reverses Sargon's action, claiming he built a city opposite Babylon that he named Akkad; see Farouk N. H. Al-Rawi, "Tablets from the Sippar Library I: The 'Weidner Chronicle': A Supposititious Royal Letter concerning a Vision," *Iraq* 52 (1990): 10, line 18. On this tradition in the omen literature, see A. Kirk Grayson, "Divination and the Babylonian Chronicles," in *La Divination en Mésopotamie Ancienne et dans les Régions Voisines: XIVᵉ Rencontre Assyriologique Internationale (Strasbourg, 2–6 Juillet 1965)* (Paris: Presses Universitaires de France, 1966), 73 n. 4.

4. Code of Hammurapi 1:17 (*ANET* 164). The *"Enuma Elish"* quotes Marduk as saying: "I will name it Bāb-ili, (which means) the residences of the great gods" (5:129; *ANET* 502). "Homes of the great gods" is an etymological "translation" of Akkadian *bāb-ili*; see Benno Landsberger and J. V. Kinnier Wilson, "The Fifth Tablet of Enuma Eliš," *Journal of Near Eastern Studies* 20 (1961): 178.

Akkadian speakers used popular etymology to devise an exalted meaning ("gate of God"), Genesis uses a Hebrew wordplay to refute the lofty claim. Instead, the city represented humanity's unified rebellion against God and was therefore marked by confusion (Hebrew *bālal* means "to confuse"), turning the gate of heaven into confusion of speech and the dispersion of humanity.

Geographical Parameters

The boundaries of Babylonia varied greatly according to the political vicissitudes of the turbulent Tigris-Euphrates valleys. South of modern Baghdad, these rivers form an alluvial plain that was the geographical heartland of Babylonia. Most of the significant cities were located on the Euphrates or one of its canals. This heartland was vulnerable to many hostile forces throughout Babylonia's political history, due to a severe lack of natural geographical barriers. The Euphrates corridor in the northwest occasioned numerous invasions of seminomadic populations during the millennium and a half under consideration here. The marshes in the south offered no resistance to invaders from the plains of Persia or from the Persian Gulf itself. Invaders could also descend upon the urban centers of central Babylonia from the Zagros Hills to the east and northeast.

The city of Babylon did not enjoy the prestigious history of many older cities in Sumer. But in the second millennium, it gradually became the political center of the country. Under Hammurapi's brief hegemony, the dimensions of an empire with Babylon as its center extended for the first time beyond southern Mesopotamia into the northwestern bend of the Euphrates River. These political boundaries reached nearly the same dimensions under some of the Kassite rulers of the Middle Babylonian period. The vast empire of Nebuchadnezzar II exceeded the traditional borders of Babylonia, though he shared the northern regions of western Asia with the Medes. But these expansive empires were normally short lived, and the Babylonians seldom controlled territory beyond southern Mesopotamia for prolonged periods of time.

Political History

The city of Babylon is known to have existed in the third millennium. The earliest reference to the city dates to the first Semitic empire (that of Sargon of Akkad, about 2350). A year-date formula[5] of Shar-kali-sharri, Sargon's great-grandson and last king of the dynasty, commemorates the

---

5. In early Babylonia, each year derived its name from a noteworthy event that took place in the preceding year, a practice Assyriologists refer to as "year-date formula" or "year-name."

construction of two new temples in Babylon.[6] Later chronicles preserve the tradition that Sargon himself dug a pit there and gave the city its name.[7] Babylon was a relatively unimportant provincial capital with a local governor during the Neo-Sumerian period (Ur III).

At the turn of the millennium, ethnic migrations began that would change the destinies of Babylonia. Both the Akkadian and Sumerian empires near the end of the millennium noted the appearance of new nomadic groups that became increasingly more hostile. The Sumerians called these groups *Martu* ("the West"), which became *Amurru* for Akkadian speakers (and "Amorites" to us). This was the second of four great Semitic migrations to take place over two millenniums, each bringing dramatic ethnic and political changes.[8] Over the next two centuries, the Amorites settled into Mesopotamia, founding new cities and populating others in the south and several along the northern river valleys. Among these new Amorite political centers the most important were Isin, Larsa, Eshnunna, and Kish in the south, Mari and Ashur further north, and Qatna

Steward Ebih-Ilu from Mari, early 3d millennium B.C. (height: 20.7″)
Courtesy of the Louvre Museum

6. Johannes Renger, "The City of Babylon during the Old Babylonian Period," *Sumer* 35 (1979): 208; and Thorkild Jacobsen, "Babylon (OT)," in *Interpreter's Dictionary of the Bible*, ed. George A. Buttrick et al. (Nashville: Abingdon, 1962), 1:334.

7. Grayson, *Assyrian and Babylonian Chronicles*, 149 (Weidner Chronicle 51), 153–54 (Chronicle of Early Kings A:18–19).

8. Successively the Akkadians, Amorites, Arameans, and Arabs; see Dietz O. Edzard, "The Early Dynastic Period" and "The Old Babylonian Period," in *The Near East: The Early Civilizations*, ed. Jean Bottéro, Elena Cassin, and Jean Vercoutter; trans. R. F. Tannenbaum (New York: Delacorte/London: Weidenfeld & Nicolson, 1967), 58–59, 180–86; Ignace J. Gelb, "The Early History of the West Semitic Peoples," *Journal of Cuneiform Studies* 15 (1961): 27.

and Aleppo in the northwest. But at Babylon, an Amorite named Sumu-abum established a dynasty in 1894 that would eventually carry the city to new heights of political and cultural significance.

Old Babylonians

History shows that whenever a high civilization is conquered by seminomadic groups, the newly settled population assimilates and adopts the older culture as its own (so the Akkadian Semites assumed Sumerian culture and the Hyksos became Egyptian). By around 1800 the assimilation of the older Mesopotamian culture was underway among the Amorites. The dynasties of the various city-states became "Babylonian" in nature, adopting Akkadian language and culture. They were recognizable as Amorites only by their West Semitic names.[9]

This "Babylonian" culture flourished in numerous cities throughout Mesopotamia. By the time of Hammurapi (1792–1750), sixth in the Amorite Dynasty at Babylon, the region of the Tigris-Euphrates valleys was marked by a balance of power among the increasingly powerful Amorite city-states. Previous scholarship tended to portray the "age of Hammurapi" as a Babylonia-centered phenomenon. But the growing number of contemporary documents from this period (especially the archives from Mari) have transformed this notion into a

Female worshiper from Mari, early 3d millennium B.C. (height: 7.6″)

Courtesy of the Louvre Museum

9. Terminology for the historical periods of Babylonia differs considerably. I refer in the most general way to the Old Babylonian (2000–1595), Middle Babylonian (1595–1000), and Neo-Babylonian (1000–539) periods. What I call the early Neo-Babylonian period falls between the end of the Kassite Dynasty and the beginning of the Chaldean Dynasty, or roughly 1155–625.

Head of Hammurapi from Susa, 1792–
1750 B.C. (height: 5.9″)
Courtesy of the Louvre Museum

picture of a cosmopolitan Near East with a multi-centered base of political power shared by several cities. In fact, a now famous letter from Mari contains an appraisal of international affairs by a royal official: "There is no king who, of himself, is the strongest. Ten or fifteen kings follow Hammurapi of Babylon, the same number follow Rim-Sin of Larsa, the same number follow Ibal-pi-El of Eshnunna, the same number follow Amut-pi-il of Qatanum [Qatna], twenty kings follow Yarim-Lim of Yamhad [Aleppo]."[10]

This balance of power allowed Hammurapi to devote his energies in the first years of his reign to defensive and religious building activities and internal administration. Of his first twenty-nine years, only three of his year-date formulas record military campaigns.[11] In point of fact, his neighbor to the north, Shamshi-Adad I of Ashur, commanded the favorable position early in Hammurapi's reign, even occupying Mari and controlling the Middle Euphrates Valley. It was only through an adroit use of shifting coalitions that Hammurapi was able to avoid being overrun by Shamshi-Adad or by the dangerous armies of Eshnunna to his north and Larsa to his south. The politics of the age demanded such tenuous

10. This political assessment was made by Itûr-Asdu, an official of King Zimri-Lim of Mari; see Georges Dossin, "Les Archives Épistolaires du Palais de Mari," *Syria* 19 (1938): 117–18. No single state could boast superiority in natural resources and labor, so the more ambitious rulers strengthened their hand with coalitions and diplomacy; see J. M. Munn-Rankin, "Diplomacy in Western Asia in the Early Second Millennium B.C.," *Iraq* 18 (1956): 108–10.

11. In his seventh, tenth, and eleventh years Hammurapi took several cities, the most important of which were Uruk and Isin. In his second year-date formula, he is said to have "established justice (*mîšarum*) in the country," an apparent reference to legal reforms that may have culminated in his famous law code. See *ANET* 269–70.

alliances, so that a "king's success was a function of the king's skill in maneu-vering the counters of this dangerous game."[12] The stellar rise of Babylon is a tribute to Hammurapi as a man of personal genius and exceptional gifts. He was a leader who left an indelible mark on his successors.

Once Shamshi-Adad died (ca. 1782) Assyrian strength waned, and Mari was able to regain independence under Zimri-Lim. Over the next decade or so, Hammurapi fortified strategic cities in northern Babylonia, while accepting an uneasy coalition with Rim-Sin of Larsa (an Elamite Dynasty, though still perhaps Amorite). This relationship of convenience for mutual defense was necessary only because of the geographical proximity of Babylon and Larsa. While Hammurapi maintained the truce, Rim-Sin subdued Isin, Uruk, and other potentially hostile cities to Babylon's south. Then, when Hammurapi felt secure in his position, he embarked on aggressive military campaigns aimed at consolidating his personal hold on southern Mesopotamia (carefully pre-served in his year-date formulas). In his thirtieth year (1764), he successfully defeated an Elamite coalition comprised of troops from Assyria, Eshnunna, and elsewhere. After this victory, Hammurapi for the first time began to use the brazen titulary from the great third-millennium empires in his year-date formulas: "The leader, beloved of Marduk, after having defeated the army that Elam . . . had raised in masses, through the mighty power of the great gods, reestablished the foundations of the Empire of Sumer and Akkad."[13]

The next year (1763), Hammurapi turned on his neighbor at Larsa, Rim-Sin. With the fall of Larsa, all the southern rival cities fell to Hammurapi. For the first time since the Neo-Sumerian Empire at Ur, all of southern Mesopo-tamia was united under a single throne. Meanwhile, Hammurapi enjoyed a warm relationship with Zimri-Lim of Mari (letters between the two reveal mutual trust and cooperation). They allowed ambassadors to report on mili-tary and political situations observed in the respective cities, even to the de-gree of requesting and exchanging contingents of troops.[14] But now that Hammurapi controlled the south, this friendly cooperation was destined to end, and in 1761 Hammurapi turned on his old friend Zimri-Lim. Two years later, he destroyed the walls of Mari, and in his thirty-seventh through thirty-

---

12. Edzard, "Old Babylonian Period," 204. Hammurapi seems to have cleverly fragmented his opposition during this time with diplomatic activity, all while he was carefully building his own power base; see Hartmut Schmökel, *Hammurabi von Babylon* (Darmstadt: Wissenschaft-liche Buchgesellschaft, 1975); Horst Klengel, *Hammurapi von Babylon und seine Zeit* (Berlin: Deutscher Verlag der Wissenschaften, 1976); and Franz M. T. de Liagre Böhl, "King Ḥammu-rabi of Babylon in the Setting of His Time," in *Opera Minora* (Groningen-Djakarta: Wolters, 1953), 344.

13. Year 30 (*ANET* 270).

14. Cyril J. Gadd, "Hammurabi and the End of His Dynasty," in *CAH* 2/1:180–81.

ninth years he subdued Eshnunna and other lesser threats in Assyria to the north. For the last portion of his reign, the whole of Mesopotamia proper was his. Only the western kingdoms of Aleppo and Qatna were beyond his reach.

The prologue to Hammurapi's famous law code proudly lists the prominent cities of Mesopotamia that were subject to him, including the older influential cities of the south, the Assyrian centers in the north, and those along the Middle Euphrates.[15] His titulary used expressions from the powerful Old Akkadian Empire in a new way, and Hammurapi clearly viewed himself a successor to the first great empires of the third millennium.

Though Hammurapi's empire may have rivaled the Ur III kingdom in geographical parameters, the same can not be said of its duration. Merely a decade after his death, his son Samsu-iluna recorded the first encounter with a new element in Near Eastern history: the Kassites.[16] Though Hammurapi's successors were able to maintain a meager dynasty for a century and a half, they ruled an empire nothing like that shaped by Hammurapi. Yet his unification of Mesopotamia left a mark on the collective psyche of the country and created a new role for the previously insignificant city of Babylon. Because of the grandeur and strength of his brief empire, all of southern Mesopotamia would henceforth be known as "Babylonia." No city would rival Babylon for the next two millenniums, until the Greeks built Seleucia.[17]

Middle Babylonians

During the century and a half in which Hammurapi's five successors ruled Babylonia (1750–1595), the once great empire was reduced considerably. The north was soon lost to the Kassite newcomers, and the south to a dynasty that later tradition would call the "First Sealand Dynasty." But the final blow to the Amorite Dynasty at Babylon came from the Hittites, the Indo-Europeans from Anatolia. Murshili I (1620–1595) swept down the Euphrates from northwestern Syria, taking Aleppo and Mari along the way and forging into Babylonia with little resistance. But shortly after the sack of Babylon (1595), Murshili hastened home, only to die in a palace conspiracy, and the Hittites withdrew, leaving a political vacuum in Babylonia.[18]

Events after the fall of Babylon are obscured by the dearth of documentary evidence, leading many scholars to refer to this period as a "dark age." Even the length of this age is nebulous, making chronological precision impossible for second-millennium Mesopotamian history. Apparently the first beneficia-

---

15. *ANET* 164–65.
16. Year-date formula of Samsu-iluna's ninth year (*ANET* 271).
17. Joan Oates, *Babylon*, rev. ed. (New York: Thames & Hudson, 1986), 67.
18. Harry W. F. Saggs, *The Greatness That Was Babylon*, 2d ed. (London: Sidgwick & Jackson, 1988), 77.

ries of the Hittite raid on Babylon were the rulers of a dynasty from the so-called Sealand in the southern marshes of Babylonia. This dynastic line traced itself back to the time of Hammurapi's son Samsu-iluna and apparently engaged him in warfare.[19] Little is known of this dynasty besides the royal names of its rulers, and these names imply aspirations to lead a revival of Sumerian culture in the south. After the Hittite withdrawal, the sixth dynast from the Sealand took northern Babylonia, holding the city itself briefly.[20] After six more rulers, the Sealand Dynasty fell to the Kassites, who now were strong enough to hold all of Babylonia.

The picture that emerges from this shadowy Middle Babylonian period is far different from the political situation in Babylonia in the first half of the second millennium. Instead of Amorite city-states of various sizes that slowly but decisively supplanted the older Sumero-Akkadian culture, Babylonia is now dominated by a different ethnic element in Mesopotamia, the Kassites. They established a new empire at Babylon, reducing the role of the indigenous Semitic population there, just as the Indo-Aryan Hurrians had done in upper Mesopotamia in the Mitanni Empire. In fact, during the last three-and-a-half centuries of the second millennium, Babylonia proper was something of a melting pot in which numerous ethnolinguistic groups were present in significant numbers.[21]

The Kassites appeared as foreign invaders in western Babylonia prior to the fall of Babylon to the Hittites.[22] The original Kassite homeland in the

19. According to a number of Samsu-iluna's year-date formulas (*ANET* 271; Gadd, "Hammurabi," 220–22).

20. Although the Sealand Dynasty's hold on Babylon was ephemeral, it was able to hold off the Kassites in the north for a century or more. This accomplishment alone was enough to insure a legacy, which is documented in the important historical text known as the "Babylonian King List A" (*ANET* 272). This text outlines the history of Babylonia from the First Dynasty of Babylon (Hammurapi's) to about 600 by simply listing successive claimants to the throne of Babylon, which served as a figurative capital for the respective dynasties; see William W. Hallo and William K. Simpson, *The Ancient Near East: A History* (New York: Harcourt Brace Jovanovich, 1971), 106–7.

21. John A. Brinkman identifies, among others, Assyrians, Elamites, Hurrians, Lullubi, and the Aḫlamū (who were precursors of the Arameans); see "Hurrians in Babylonia in the Late Second Millennium B.C.: An Unexploited Minority Resource for Socio-Economic and Philological Analysis," in *Studies on the Civilization and Culture of Nuzi and the Hurrians: In Honor of Ernest R. Lacheman,* ed. Martha A. Morrison and David I. Owen (Winona Lake, Ind.: Eisenbrauns, 1981), 28.

22. For a convenient survey of our knowledge of the Kassites, see John A. Brinkman, "Kassiten," in *Reallexikon der Assyriologie,* ed. Erich Ebeling and Bruno Meissner (Berlin: de Gruyter, 1980), 5:464–73. See also Edwin M. Yamauchi, "Kassites," in *The New International Dictionary of Biblical Archaeology,* ed. Edward M. Blaiklock and Roland K. Harrison (Grand Rapids: Zondervan, 1983), 276–78; and John A. Brinkman, *Materials and Studies for Kassite History* (Chicago: University of Chicago Press, 1976).

Zagros Mountains is unknown. But soon after the Hittites withdrew, Kassites were firmly established in northern Babylonia. By around 1475, they had taken Babylon itself from the Sealand Dynasty and unified all of Babylonia (which they called Kar-Duniash) into a single Kassite Dynasty. With occasional interludes, they ruled over a unified empire (with Babylon as its religious capital) until about 1155—the longest dynasty in Babylonian history.[23]

After enigmatic beginnings, the Kassite Dynasty used a Babylonian base to establish a major power of the ancient Near East for over three hundred years. Though never dominant militarily, the Kassites were generally successful at defending their borders by concluding treaties with Assyria and Egypt and by using nonmilitary means of diplomacy with other potential enemies. Through these diplomatic efforts they brought political stability to southern Mesopotamia unlike anything known in the Old Babylonian period. Occasional military threats were posed by Assyria to the north and Elam to the east, and Kassite forces were engaged in border skirmishes with these enemies. Assyria under Tukulti-Ninurta I (1243–1207) actually conquered Babylonia, sacked the city, and used Assyrian governors to rule Babylon for seven years.[24] Ultimately, though, it was an Elamite invasion that led to the fall of the Kassite Dynasty in 1155.[25]

The Kassites adopted the traditional Sumero-Akkadian culture to such an extent that little is known of their own language, literature, and religion.[26] The degree to which the Kassites were assimilated into Mesopotamian culture is evident in the new capital city built by Kurigalzu I (early fourteenth century) on the outskirts of modern Baghdad. Known as Dur-Kurigalzu ("fortress of Kurigalzu") it contained temples dedicated to prominent Sumerian deities and is dominated by a traditional stepped tower (ziggurat) like those of older Sumerian cities. In fact, the Kassite rulers appear to have erected and repaired shrines only for the traditional Mesopotamian deities instead of honoring their own pantheon of approximately two dozen gods.[27]

---

23. Babylonian King List A names thirty-six kings who ruled for 576 years, 9 months (*ANET* 272).

24. Grayson, *Assyrian and Babylonian Chronicles*, 175–76 (Chronicle P 4:3–7). See J. M. Munn-Rankin, "Assyrian Military Power 1300–1200 B.C.," in *CAH* 2/2:284–94.

25. Several Elamite records relate details of the campaign; see René Labat, "Elam and Western Persia, c. 1200–1000 B.C.," in *CAH* 2/2:485–86.

26. Brinkman, "Kassiten," 471–73.

27. Ibid., 472; "Mesopotamia," in *Encyclopaedia Judaica* (Jerusalem: Keter, 1971), 16:1499; and Georges Roux, *Ancient Iraq*, 3d ed. (Baltimore: Penguin, 1992), 249.

Babylonian culture enjoyed a new level of international prestige during the Kassites' long dynasty. In fact, the wide influence of Mesopotamian culture in the ancient Near East may be largely due to the length and stability of this dynasty that had so thoroughly assimilated the culture. During this period, Babylonian scribal scholarship flourished and Mesopotamian literature spread throughout the Fertile Crescent. Babylonian medicine and art were widely influential.[28] Furthermore, the Babylonian dialect of Akkadian became the *lingua franca*, employed by rulers throughout western Asia during this international age, as illustrated by the famous letters of el-Amarna in Egypt.[29]

Early Neo-Babylonians

Around the beginning of the Iron Age (about 1200), cataclysmic changes began to occur in the ancient Near East that altered the political map of the region. Major powers on the eastern rim of the Mediterranean Sea collapsed (notably Egypt and the Hittites) and others declined in a chain reaction across western Asia.[30] Within a century the political order that had existed for over three hundred years dissolved and in the vacuum a new ethnic entity emerged in the form of the Aramean city-states of Syria.[31] Babylonia proper was not directly or immediately affected by the collapse of powerful nations to the west, but the ever-increasing prominence of the Arameans contributed to the temporary decline of Assyria after the fall of Tukulti-Ninurta I.[32] By the beginning of the first millennium, Arameans controlled not only southern Syria, but the western territories of Babylonia.

28. Brinkman, "Kassiten," 468–69.

29. Letters between Akhenaten and the successors of Kurigalzu show that the royal families were linked by marriage and that the rulers addressed each other as "brother," implying equal status; see Oates, *Babylon*, 90.

30. Though details are unavailable, many scholars assume these developments started with the fall of Troy (about 1250) and the subsequent fall of the Mycenaean cities on the mainland of Greece. Survivors supposedly fled by sea along the coasts, disrupting the established powers and creating a dominolike effect that upset the long established powers. These newcomers are best attested in the Egyptian sources and are known collectively as "Sea Peoples"; see Richard D. Barnett, "The Sea Peoples," in *CAH* 2/2:359–78; and Kenneth A. Kitchen, "Sea Peoples," in *The New International Dictionary of Biblical Archaeology*, ed. Edward M. Blaiklock and Roland K. Harrison (Grand Rapids: Zondervan, 1983), 404–5.

31. See the chapter in this volume on Arameans and Wayne T. Pitard, *Ancient Damascus: A Historical Study of the Syrian City-State from Earliest Times until Its Fall to the Assyrians in 732 B.C.E.* (Winona Lake, Ind.: Eisenbrauns, 1987), 81–89. The age of international communication was officially over, and the Babylonian dialect ceased to be used as the *lingua franca*.

32. Harry W. F. Saggs, *The Might That Was Assyria* (London: Sidgwick & Jackson, 1984), 56, 61–62.

The three centuries after the fall of the Kassites are marked by a succession of several dynasties featuring native Babylonian rulers.[33] In fact, this seems to be unique in the history of Babylonia, being the only period when native Babylonians controlled the country instead of foreign dynasties.[34] By contrast, the Amorites built the Old Babylonian Empire, the Kassites were dominant during the Middle Babylonian period, and the Chaldeans in the Neo-Babylonian.

The first successor to the Kassites is known as the "Second Dynasty of Isin," because the initial kings of the dynasty traced family origins back to Isin, the site of a powerful dynasty earlier in the second millennium.[35] This dynasty ruled Babylonia from 1157 to 1026 and the names and approximate dates for eleven dynasts may be reconstructed from native sources.[36]

During the early years of this dynasty, the Elamites to the east continued to plague northern Babylonia. But the fortunes of Babylonia changed with the fourth dynast, Nebuchadnezzar I (1125–1104).[37] This ruler left an indelible mark on successive generations by avenging the Elamite sack of Babylon. The Elamites had taken the Marduk statue captive as a symbol of victory when they defeated the Kassites and continued to hold it in their capital city, Susa. Nebuchadnezzar launched a surprise attack during the heat of mid-summer, reaching Susa and recovering the Marduk statue. The Elamites had been a constant threat to Babylonia, but they were of little consequence for the next three centuries. Nebuchadnezzar's victory restored the national morale of Babylonia and the statue was returned to its shrine in Babylon, accompanied by popular rejoicing. As an important religious consequence of this event, Marduk achieved a new level of supremacy in the Babylonian pantheon. This once relatively insignificant deity had

33. Native Babylonian in that they were not *recently* migrated to Mesopotamia. They were an amalgamation of various ethnic components that were by now indistinguishable; see John A. Brinkman, *A Political History of Post-Kassite Babylonia, 1158–722 B.C.*, Analecta Orientalia 43 (Rome: Pontifical Biblical Institute Press, 1968), 260–85.

34. John A. Brinkman suggests that this era (i.e., 1158–812) be called "Babylonia for the Babylonians"; see "Foreign Relations of Babylonia from 1600 to 625 B.C.: The Documentary Evidence," *American Journal of Archaeology* 76 (1972): 278.

35. Or perhaps Isin was the first capital of the new ruling house; see John A. Brinkman, "Isin," in *Reallexikon der Assyriologie*, ed. Erich Ebeling and Bruno Meissner (Berlin: de Gruyter, 1980), 5:184.

36. Babylonian King List A (*ANET* 272) is incomplete, but may be supplemented with royal economic and chronographic texts; see Brinkman, "Isin," 184.

37. The first of three or four Mesopotamian kings to bear this distinguished name. Care must be used to avoid confusing this king with the powerful Nebuchadnezzar II (604–562) of the Neo-Babylonian Empire and one or perhaps two usurpers during the Persian period; see David B. Weisberg, *Texts from the Time of Nebuchadnezzar*, Yale Oriental Series, Babylonian Texts 17 (New Haven: Yale University Press, 1980), xix–xxiv.

assumed an increasingly visible role since the Old Babylonian period. Neb-uchadnezzar's dramatic recovery of the Marduk statue now elevated him to the position of supreme deity, which has been interpreted as an early step in the direction of monotheism, though perhaps henotheism would be more accurate.[38]

The remainder of the Second Dynasty of Isin is less well attested. After several years of border skirmishes with Assyria, these two countries directed their attention to a common threat: the Arameans who were invading Baby-lonia and Assyria from the west during a time of general famine.[39] The final dynasts left few original sources and little is known about the last phase of the dynasty or about the circumstances surrounding the fall of the Second Dynasty of Isin. It seems likely that the devastating Aramean invasions in the northwest weakened and eventually toppled the ruling dynasty. These en-croachments from the northwest must have been a factor in determining that the next regime would be associated with the Sealand in the south.[40]

Over the next half century (1026–979), Babylonia was ruled by a succes-sion of three brief and undistinguished dynasties: the Second Sealand Dy-nasty (1026–1005) ruled from the south; the Bazi Dynasty (1004–985) was comprised of three Kassite tribal rulers; and the so-called Elamite Dynasty (984–979) managed only a single dynast.[41] For the next century and a half, Babylonian political history is marked by two features: continued Aramean infiltration and the important relationship with Assyria to the north. The Arameans disrupted internal stability, making a powerful political base im-possible. The relationship with Assyria would dominate Babylonian history for the next several centuries.

The instability is apparent from the paucity of documentary evidence from the years 979–811. Dynastic affiliations of the succeeding rulers of

38. Wilfred G. Lambert, "The Reign of Nebuchadnezzar I: A Turning Point in the History of Ancient Mesopotamian Religion," in *The Seed of Wisdom: Essays in Honour of T. J. Meek*, ed. W. S. McCullough (Toronto: University of Toronto Press, 1964), 3–13. Marduk had a priv-ileged position in the Old Babylonian pantheon, though he appears subordinate to Anu and Enlil in the prologue to the Code of Hammurapi (*ANET* 164). On boundary stones and dedicatory inscriptions of the Kassite period, he continued to occupy a subordinate position. But one text from the time of Nebuchadnezzar I calls Marduk *šar ilāni* ("king of the gods") and from this time forward his kingship over the gods is commonly attested. Though the great literary piece known by the Akkadian title "*Enuma Elish*" is commonly called "the Babylonian creation myth," the central theme is not creation but the "assertion and justification of the supremacy of Marduk and of his city Babylon"; see Harry W. F. Saggs, *The Encounter with the Divine in Me-sopotamia and Israel* (London: Athlone, 1978), 58.

39. Brinkman, "Isin," 186.

40. Ibid., 186–87.

41. Babylonian King List A records several names for rulers of these dynasties in fragmen-tary fashion (*ANET* 272).

Nabu-apla-iddina (left), son of Adnaya, and King Nabu-apla-iddina (right), 870 B.C. (height: 6.9″; width: 4.2″; thickness: 1.4″)

Courtesy of the British Museum

Babylon are impossible to outline for this period.[42] For most of the tenth century, Babylonia was marked by an east–west orientation. Aramean tribal groups kept the west in a constant state of disruption and controlled the important trade route along the Euphrates, while the sparse available evidence suggests Babylonia's orientation lay toward the east. Beginning around 911, the political focus changed and new political factors ushered in a predominantly north–south axis. To the north, Babylonia encountered Assyrian military strength again—this time due to the resurgence of Assyrian might under Ashur-dan II (934–912) and Adad-nirari II (911–891). In the south, a new tribal group that would eventually become an important political player in Babylonian history first began to make its presence

42. Babylonian King List A is too fragmentary to detail the sequence of kings for Babylonia at this time (*ANET* 272). Brinkman prefers to speak in general of "uncertain dynasties" for this period; see *Post-Kassite Babylonia*, 166–213.

known: the Chaldeans.[43] At the end of this period, Shamshi-Adad V of Assyria invaded Babylonia for four successive years (814–811). After capturing and deporting two Babylonian kings to Assyria in 813 and 812, the country was reduced to a point of anarchy. One Babylonian chronicle reports that "there was no king in the land," a state of affairs that seems to have lasted at least twelve years.[44] For the next two centuries, Chaldeans in southern Babylonia would compete with Assyria for control of northern Babylonia.

Neo-Babylonians

The Chaldeans of southern Babylonia first appear in the cuneiform sources of the ninth century. They were more sedentary than the Arameans, who continued to plague western Babylonia as loosely organized seminomads. The Chaldeans were organized in tribal groups called "houses" and were settled in the swamps and lakes of the lower courses of the Tigris and Euphrates rivers.[45] They seem to have adapted quickly to Babylonian culture, controlling the trade routes of the Persian Gulf area and thereby accumulating considerable wealth with which they paid handsome tribute to the Assyrians. But this was only a temporary ploy, since all the while they were growing in number and strength. Chaldeans became contenders for the Babylonian throne by the middle of the eighth century. Indeed, much of the political history of Babylonia in the early first millennium can be described as a transition from Kassite to Chaldean hegemony.[46]

Conflict between Assyria and Babylonia during the ninth century had weakened northern Babylonia considerably. But with the death of Adad-

---

43. For a recent survey of these political developments in Babylonia for 1000–811, see John A. Brinkman, "Babylonia c. 1000–748," in *CAH* 3/1:295–309.

44. Grayson, *Assyrian and Babylonian Chronicles*, 182 (Chronicle 24 rev. 8). The exact number of years is broken in the text, but Brinkman argues it is probably at least twelve; see *Post-Kassite Babylonia*, 213 n. 1327.

45. The largest and most influential Chaldean tribes were Bit-Dakkuri south of Borsippa, Bit-Amukani further south along the Euphrates, and Bit-Yakin to the east along the Tigris. The smaller Aramean tribes were loosely organized around the fringes of the settled areas; see Manfried Dietrich, *Die Aramäer Südbabyloniens in der Sargonidenzeit (700–648)*, Alter Orient und Altes Testament 7 (Neukirchen-Vluyn: Neukirchener Verlag/Kevelaer: Butzon & Bercker, 1970), 1–6; but see the remarks in John A. Brinkman, "Notes on Arameans and Chaldeans in Southern Babylonia in the Early Seventh Century B.C.," *Orientalia* 46 (1977): 304–25. The Chaldeans and Arameans were both West Semitic and many scholars have assumed they were identical. But the native Assyrian and Babylonian sources consistently distinguished between them. They are also distinguished by differences in tribal organization, the dates of their respective appearances in history, and contrasting levels of Babylonization; see Brinkman, *Post-Kassite Babylonia*, 266–67 (especially n. 1716), 273–75.

46. Brinkman, "Babylonia c. 1000–748," 288.

nirari III (783), the Assyrian Empire was temporarily halted by a weak central government, economic problems, and a new threat to its north, Urartu.[47] The Chaldeans were now ready to fill the political vacuum created by a declining Assyria and a ravaged northern Babylonia. A certain Eriba-Marduk from the Bit-Yakin tribe of the Chaldeans came to the Babylonian throne. Later tradition honors him with the title "reestablisher of the foundation(s) of the land," which presumably means he restored the stability of Babylonia.[48]

The next noteworthy ruler of Babylon marked the beginning of a new era for later historians. From the time of Nabonassar (747–734), ancient scholars began to keep systematically precise records of historical events.[49] Nabonassar was evidently not Chaldean and he apparently attempted to exclude Chaldeans from power. His inability to control either the Chaldeans or Arameans left Babylonia hemmed in on every hand and he was able to maintain order only with the help of a new neighbor to the north. Tiglath-pileser III rose to the throne of Assyria as the result of a revolution (745) and quickly established his reputation as an empire builder. He sustained Nabonassar's reign, but soon after the latter's death, Babylonia was weakened by minor revolts.

Mukin-zeri, a Chaldean from southern Babylonia, took advantage of the instability in Babylon and assumed the throne in 731.[50] Tiglath-pileser had been preoccupied in Syria, but moved to depose Mukin-zeri, which he finally accomplished three years later. In an attempt to consolidate his hold on the south, Tiglath-pileser himself assumed the throne of Babylon. He thus became the first Assyrian ruler in more than four centuries to unite Assyria and

47. Saggs, *Might That Was Assyria*, 82–84; and Edwin M. Yamauchi, *Foes from the Northern Frontier: Invading Hordes from the Russian Steppes* (Grand Rapids: Baker, 1982), 31–35.

48. Eriba-Marduk was the first powerful Chaldean monarch of Babylonia. Evidence is insufficient to determine his dates precisely, but he reigned for at least nine years and his rule terminated shortly before 760. He drove out the Arameans who had inhabited portions of Babylon and Borsippa, repaired the throne of Marduk at Esagil, as well as other building activities; see Brinkman, *Post-Kassite Babylonia*, 221–24.

49. The "Neo-Babylonian Chronicle Series," a valuable new historiographic source for this period, records outstanding events of each year beginning with the reign of Nabonassar; see Grayson, *Assyrian and Babylonian Chronicles*, 10–24, 69–111. See Brinkman, *Post-Kassite Babylonia*, 226–34, for details of this king's reign. Greek astronomers recognized the "Nabonassar era" as a turning point in the history of science, and the term "Chaldean" came to mean "astronomer" in Hellenistic times; see Francesca Rochberg-Halton, "New Evidence for the History of Astrology," *Journal of Near Eastern Studies* 43 (1984): 115.

50. Also known as Nabu-mukin-zeri, he was from the Bit-Amukani tribe of the Chaldeans, but little else is known of him; see Brinkman, *Post-Kassite Babylonia*, 235–40, for details of his reign.

Babylonia in a dual monarchy, setting a precedent for Assyrian rulers for the next century.[51]

Tiglath-pileser's son, Shalmaneser V (726–722), inherited the dual monarchy and successfully ruled Babylon for five years. But soon after his death, another Chaldean, Merodach-baladan II, seized the Babylonian throne and consolidated his hold by uniting the previously fragmented Chaldean tribes.[52] This consummate politician and military strategist was able to rule Babylonia—free from Assyrian interference—for a full decade (721–710).[53] But ultimately, Sargon II (721–705) and the might of the Neo-Assyrian Empire proved too much for him. In 710, Sargon ousted Merodach-baladan and assumed the throne of Babylonia in a dual monarchy for five years. But Merodach-baladan's brief reign illustrates the recurring movement in Babylonia to retain national autonomy free of Assyrian rule. The unity and spirit of independence that he established in the Chaldean tribes of southern Babylonia culminated in the rise of the Chaldean Dynasty of the Neo-Babylonian Empire, which eventually would participate in the destruction of Assyria.

For the century after Merodach-baladan, the powerful monarchs of the Neo-Assyrian Empire expended considerable energy and resources trying to maintain control of Babylonia. Sargon's son and successor, Sennacherib (704–681), tried several modes of governing Babylonia.[54] First he himself assumed the throne of the dual monarchy as his predecessors had done. But successive revolts one month apart led Sennacherib to try a new strategy, installing a pro-Assyrian native Babylonian. After this too failed, Sennacherib finally installed his son, the crown prince, on the throne of Babylon. But the

---

51. Saggs, *Might That Was Assyria*, 89–92. Tukulti-Ninurta I (1244–1207) of Assyria had claimed the title "King of Babylon(ia)." But in point of fact, he was not recognized as king in the native Babylonian tradition; see John A. Brinkman, "Elamite Military Aid to Merodach-baladan," *Journal of Near Eastern Studies* 24 (1965): 161 n. 1.

52. Merodach-baladan II, a wealthy prince of the Bit-Yakin tribe, was also able to secure a military alliance with Elam to the east in his anti-Assyrian efforts. The Old Testament bears testimony to his capable diplomatic efforts at forging an international coalition against Assyria (2 Kings 20:12–19; Isa. 39). For details on Merodach-baladan, see John A. Brinkman, "Merodach-baladan II," in *Studies Presented to A. Leo Oppenheim*, ed. Robert D. Biggs and John A. Brinkman (Chicago: Oriental Institute, 1964), 6–53; and R. J. van der Spek, "The Struggle of King Sargon II of Assyria against the Chaldaean Merodach-baladan (710–707 B.C.)," *Jaarbericht . . . ex Oriente Lux* 25 (1978): 56–66.

53. The evidence suggests Chaldean rule was not univocally accepted throughout Babylonia. But Merodach-baladan managed to placate, or at least dominate, the small pro-Assyrian faction in the urban centers of northern Babylonia, while staying one step ahead of the Assyrians by avoiding direct contact with their overwhelming military forces; see Brinkman, "Merodach-baladan II," 38–40.

54. For these details, see John A. Brinkman, "Sennacherib's Babylonian Problem: An Interpretation," *Journal of Cuneiform Studies* 25 (1973): 90–94. See also Saggs, *Might That Was Assyria*, 99–103.

young prince was captured and taken to Elam where he was presumably murdered. After a decade and a half of trouble in the south and the loss of his son, Sennacherib ruthlessly devastated Babylon. For the next eight years until his death, the city languished with no official king, though there is evidence that southern Babylonia suffered less economically than did the north.[55]

Esarhaddon (680–669) abandoned his father's austere anti-Babylonian attitude and resumed control of Babylonia under the dual monarchy of previous Assyrian monarchs. During his reign, enforced Assyrian rule provided stability in Babylonia, and the country appears to have experienced gradual economic growth and moderate prosperity.[56] Upon his death, the empire was divided according to his instructions between his sons: Ashurbanipal (668–627) in Assyria and Shamash-shum-ukin (667–648) in Babylonia. This arrangement was intended to perpetuate the peace and stability that Esarhaddon had provided, but this was not to be. The sibling kingdoms fell into a bloody civil war and after four years (652–648) the Assyrians were able to regain control of the south.[57] Assyria emerged from the conflict seriously weaker: it had cost Ashurbanipal an inordinate amount of resources and energy to defeat Babylonia, and the vulnerability of the Assyrian Empire had become apparent. In addition, Babylonia experienced a quick economic recovery from the war. The Assyrian threat to Babylonian nationalism actually served as a catalyst to unify resistance movements among the various tribal and ethnically diverse elements of Babylonia. After the quick postwar economic and cultural recovery, Babylonia was on the threshold of political achievements comparable to Hammurapi's great empire over a millennium before.[58]

With the death of Ashurbanipal, Nabopolassar (625–605) seized the throne of Babylon and established a new dynasty variously known as the

---

55. John A. Brinkman, *Prelude to Empire: Babylonian Society and Politics, 747–626 B.C.*, Babylonian Fund Occasional Publications 7 (Philadelphia: University Museum, 1984), 69–70.

56. Ibid., 70–84.

57. It seems likely that Manasseh of Judah joined Elam, Arabia, and various other anti-Assyrian forces in western Asia in a Babylonian coalition in support of Shamash-shum-ukin (which is suggested by 2 Chron. 33:11–13); see Bustenay Oded, "Judah and the Exile," in *Israelite and Judaean History*, ed. John H. Hayes and J. Maxwell Miller (Philadelphia: Westminster, 1977), 454–56.

58. Brinkman (*Prelude to Empire*) emphasizes Assyria's role as a catalyst in unifying the disjointed groups in Babylonia, which explains the rapid rise and remarkable strength of the Neo-Babylonian Empire in light of the chaotic weakness of Babylonia in the early first millennium. The rise of Assyria also made strange bedfellows in Syria-Palestine, such as Ahab's peace with Ben-Hadad II (1 Kings 20:31–34) and Pekah's with Rezin (2 Kings 16:5–7). Further parallels may be found in the Persian threat that unified Greek clans and set the stage for the golden age of Greece.

Neo-Babylonian or Chaldean Empire.[59] Early in his reign, the Assyrian military machine was still a threat to Babylonian independence. Nabopolassar managed to hold power with only brief interludes until 614, when a new power in ancient Near Eastern politics laid siege to Ashur, one of the four great capitals of Assyria. The Medes were successors to Elamite power in Iran, and under Cyaxares (625–585) they took the city and began massacring the inhabitants.[60] Nabopolassar arrived on the scene after the city had actually fallen, and by the ruins of Ashur he established an alliance with his new powerful neighbor, Cyaxares.[61] This treaty delegated northern Mesopotamia to the Medes and left Nabopolassar free in central Mesopotamia and Syria. He was a major participant in the fall of the other Assyrian capitals, including Nineveh, fulfilling the prophecies of Nahum and Zephaniah (Zeph. 2:13–15).

Assyria's last gasp was a futile alliance with Egypt who, in a sudden reversal of policy, realized that Babylonia was now its main threat. In 609, Josiah attempted to block the path of Pharaoh Neco II at Megiddo, who was headed north to assist the remnants of the Assyrian army near Carchemish on the northwest bend of the Euphrates. Though Josiah lost his life in the attempt (2 Kings 23:29; 2 Chron. 35:20–23), his involvement impaired the Egyptians and contributed to the Babylonian victory. Because of old age or ill health, Nabopolassar began leaving the command of the Babylonian army to the crown prince, Nebuchadnezzar II (604–562).[62] The young general led his forces in an impressive and decisive victory against the Egyptians at Carchemish in the spring of 605 (Jer. 46:2). All of Syria-Palestine lay before Nebuchadnezzar as he pursued the Egyptians south. But in mid-August, Nabopolassar died in Babylon, and Nebuchadnezzar raced across the desert and claimed the throne in less than a month.[63] During brief raids into Pales-

---

59. The use of "Chaldean" may be misleading. There is no unambiguous evidence that Nabopolassar and his successors were ethnically Chaldean. The term is used by biblical and classical authors to denote this dynasty. But in these sources "Chaldean" is usually synonymous for "Babylonian" and has no ethnic significance; see Brinkman, *Prelude to Empire*, 110–11 n. 551. The only source connecting Nabopolassar with the Sealand is late and of questionable reliability; see Donald J. Wiseman, *Nebuchadrezzar and Babylon*, Schweich Lectures 1983 (Oxford: Oxford University Press for the British Academy, 1985), 5–6.

60. For details on the Medes and their role in the fall of Assyria, see Edwin M. Yamauchi, *Persia and the Bible* (Grand Rapids: Baker, 1990), 31–56.

61. Grayson, *Assyrian and Babylonian Chronicles*, 93 (Fall of Nineveh Chronicle 28–30); and Donald J. Wiseman, *Chronicles of Chaldaean Kings (626–556 B.C.) in the British Museum* (London: British Museum, 1956), 14, 57–59. The new alliance was one of "good will and good relations [i.e., peace]"; see Donald J. Wiseman, "'Is It Peace?'—Covenant and Diplomacy," *Vetus Testamentum* 32 (1982): 311–26.

62. Wiseman, *Nebuchadrezzar and Babylon*, 13–15.

63. Grayson, *Assyrian and Babylonian Chronicles*, 99–100 (Chronicle 5:10–11).

tine over the next seventeen months, Nebuchadnezzar besieged Jerusalem and captured Daniel and his friends (Dan. 1:1; Jer. 46:2).[64]

Nebuchadnezzar quickly fell heir to most of the former territories of the Assyrian Empire. With the friendly Medes consolidating their power to the north and east, Nebuchadnezzar was free to concentrate on the Euphrates Valley and Syria-Palestine as far as Egypt. Thus he was able once again to establish Babylonia as the leading power in the ancient Near East and his reign may be compared to Hammurapi's in strength and size. But there were pockets of resistance, especially in Palestine. After a battle with the Egyptians in 601 in which both sides suffered great losses, Jehoiakim of Judah suddenly switched allegiance away from Babylonia, assuming Egypt was now the stronger of the two world powers.[65] Nebuchadnezzar personally led the Babylonian forces to Judah. Jehoiakim died before the siege of Jerusalem, leaving his son Jehoiachin on the throne. The city fell on 16 March 597.[66] Nebuchadnezzar captured Jehoiachin, deported him and other members of the royal family to Babylon, and replaced him with an uncle, Zedekiah (2 Kings 24:17).

After Nebuchadnezzar easily suppressed an insurrection attempt in Babylon (595), Zedekiah again led Judah to align with Egypt.[67] Nebuchadnezzar's response was fierce and quick. He laid siege to Jerusalem on 15 January 588 (2 Kings 25:1; Jer. 39:1; Ezek. 24:1–2), and it fell on 19 July 586.[68] Nebuchadnezzar's general, Nebuzaradan, so thoroughly razed the city that the trauma left a lasting legacy in the Jewish psyche (as evidenced in the Book of Lamentations). Archeological evidence suggests that the population of Judah

64. The Babylonian sources are quiet on these events (see Wiseman, *Nebuchadrezzar and Babylon*, 24). The apparent contradiction between Dan. 1:1 and Jer. 46:2 is because Daniel was using the Babylonian year-date system that does not count the accession year, while Jeremiah used a system that includes the accession year; see Edwin R. Thiele, *The Mysterious Numbers of the Hebrew Kings*, 3d ed. (Grand Rapids: Zondervan, 1983), 183.

65. To the dismay of Jeremiah (27:5–11). See Wiseman, *Nebuchadrezzar and Babylon*, 29–30.

66. The exact date is recorded in the Babylonian Chronicle, which reflects the strategic importance Jerusalem held at this time; see Grayson, *Assyrian and Babylonian Chronicles*, 102 (Chronicle 5 rev. 12–13).

67. Wiseman, *Nebuchadrezzar and Babylon*, 34–36.

68. Unfortunately the Babylonian Chronicle texts do not exist past Nebuchadnezzar's tenth year (595), and the date of the fall of the city is thus in question. Some evidence suggests the fall occurred in the summer of 587; for arguments see John N. Oswalt, "Chronology of the OT," in *ISBE* 1:685. Letters from the nearby city of Lachish bear eloquent testimony to conditions during the siege. One of these letters states, "We keep on the lookout for the fire signals of Lachish . . . because we do not see Azekah" (Lachish ostracon 4; *ANET* 322). Azekah, which was between Jerusalem and Lachish and was presumably supposed to relay messages by smoke signal, had apparently already fallen to the Babylonians; for a defense of this view of the letter against recent reinterpretations, see Anson F. Rainey, "Watching Out for the Signal Fires of Lachish," *Palestine Exploration Quarterly* 119 (1987): 149–51.

fell from a quarter of a million in the eighth century to half that after the fall of Jerusalem.[69] Judah apparently attempted independence once more in 582, but this was easily squelched by Nebuzaradan (Jer. 52:30).

The scope of Nebuchadnezzar's imperial aspirations may be seen in his thirteen-year siege and apparent victory at Tyre (Josephus, *Against Apion* 1:21 §156; and Ezek. 26:7–14) and an invasion of Egypt in 570.[70] His empire surpassed Hammurapi's in geographical dimensions, yet in his inscriptional remains Nebuchadnezzar prided himself more in domestic rebuilding activities. Indeed, his military campaigns were motivated to a large degree by the desire to take booty to finance his ambitious rebuilding of Babylon and twelve other cities in Babylonia.

Nebuchadnezzar's famous pride (Dan. 4:30 [MT 4:27]) was not without justification. He was clearly responsible for transforming Babylon into the greatest city of the ancient world; its modern ruins spread over two thousand acres to form the largest ancient site in Mesopotamia.[71] Its magnificent walls were entered by eight gates, each named after a god. The famed Ishtar Gate played an important religious role in the life of the city and is fortunately the best preserved. The surface of the entrance was covered with blue enameled bricks, which served as background for alternating red-and-white dragons (symbolic of Marduk) and bulls (symbolic of Adad). The gate was approached by means of an impressive processional street, sixty-five feet wide in places and paved with white limestone and red breccia. Bordering the street were walls that were found still standing as high as forty feet. They were decorated with lions six feet in length (symbolic of Ishtar) with red or yellow manes on a blue ceramic background. It was along this street that the king would accompany the statue of Marduk in grand procession each spring during the New Year festival. It was believed that he and the inhabitants of Babylonia participated in the renewal of nature and the naming of destiny for the coming year.[72] One can only image the awe inspired by this ceremony in such a dazzling setting.

The Babylonian renaissance under Nabopolassar and Nebuchadnezzar brought with it a religious revival, which is reflected in the architecture of the

---

69. Edwin M. Yamauchi, "Nebuchadnezzar," in *The New International Dictionary of Biblical Archaeology*, ed. Edward M. Blaiklock and Roland K. Harrison (Grand Rapids: Zondervan, 1983), 333.

70. Historical evidence from the latter part of Nebuchadnezzar's reign is sparse and the evidence of his Egyptian invasion is open to other interpretations; see Wiseman, *Nebuchadrezzar and Babylon*, 39–40.

71. Edwin M. Yamauchi, "Babylon," in *Major Cities of the Biblical World*, ed. Roland K. Harrison (Nashville: Nelson, 1985), 32, 36–41. Herodotus (1:178) asserts, "In addition to its enormous size it surpasses in splendor any city of the known world."

72. *ANET* 331–34.

period. Perhaps the most famous structure is the seven-staged brick temple-tower named *Etemenanki* ("house of the foundation of heaven and earth"). The typical Mesopotamian pyramid (or *zigguratu*, "temple-tower") was an artificial mound for a temple. Sennacherib had destroyed this "tower of Babel," but it was repaired by both Nabopolassar and Nebuchadnezzar and must have been an imposing structure, with estimates of its height reaching three hundred feet.

There were a number of royal palaces, but Nebuchadnezzar built a magnificent new palace late in his reign. The ruins of this structure contained a museum in which he housed a large collection of "antiquities," revealing his interest in archeology and history. Classical authors credit the building of the so-called Hanging Gardens of Babylon to Nebuchadnezzar.[73] These ancient sources describe elaborate roof gardens for his Median wife who missed her luxuriant homeland. These beautiful buildings and structures, including as many as fifty temples, made Babylon one of the wonders of the ancient world.

Nebuchadnezzar died in 562 after a forty-three-year rule.[74] His reign is one of the most amply documented periods of Babylonian history, yielding royal inscriptions, chronicles, private and administrative texts, legal materials, and letters. History has honored his dynasty as the apex of Babylonia's wealth and political power—but it would all be lost in less than a quarter of a century.

Nebuchadnezzar was followed in rapid succession by three ineffective dynasts: his son Evil-Merodach (561–560), his son-in-law Neriglissar (559–556), and the latter's son Labashi-Marduk (556). Evil-Merodach immediately released Jehoiachin who had been imprisoned by Nebuchadnezzar for thirty-six years and gave him royal recognition, including a regular allowance for the rest of his life (2 Kings 25:27–30; Jer. 52:31–34). This historical event has been wonderfully confirmed by Babylonian ration tablets, which mention King Yaukin of Judah.[75] Neriglissar (probably the Nergal-sharezer of Jer. 39:3, 13) apparently assassinated Evil-Merodach and took the throne himself. A chronicle from Neriglissar's third year (557) records a successful mil-

73. Among others, Berossus describes the extravagant gardens (quoted by Josephus, *Antiquities* 10:11:1 §226).

74. Many have denied the account of Nebuchadnezzar's dementia in Dan. 4, assuming that the story is a reflection of Nabonidus's exile in Taima. This theory lacks any evidence, and there is no reason to question the account in Dan. 4; see Yamauchi, "Nebuchadnezzar," 334.

75. Yaukin is the Akkadian form of Jehoiachin; see Edwin M. Yamauchi, *The Stones and the Scriptures* (Grand Rapids: Baker, 1981), 85; and Ronald H. Sack, *Amêl-Marduk, 562–560* B.C.: *A Study Based on Cuneiform, Old Testament, Greek, Latin, and Rabbinical Sources*, Alter Orient und Altes Testament, Sonderreihe 4 (Neukirchen-Vluyn: Neukirchener Verlag/Kevelaer: Butzon & Bercker, 1972).

Stele of Nabonidus before the symbols of the deities Sin, Shamash, and Ishtar, 6th century B.C. (height: 22.8″; width: 18.1″; thickness: 9.8″)
Courtesy of the British Museum

itary campaign in Cilicia against a king who had raided a Babylonian protectorate in Syria.[76] Of Labashi-Marduk, little is known.

It is customary to include Nabonidus (555–539) in this dynasty, though technically he was a usurper and a leading figure in the murder of Nebuchadnezzar's grandson Labashi-Marduk. Nabonidus was not from the royal family and could claim no support for the throne.[77] His mother was Adad-guppi, a prominent centenarian from Haran, the important religious center in northern Mesopotamia. Her biography, preserved on a tomb inscription, relates her remarkable devotion to Sin, the moon god of Haran.[78] This may explain Nabonidus's rabid devotion to Sin, while paying lip service to other deities of Babylonia.

Nabonidus participated in the conspiracy against Labashi-Marduk, though he never intended kingship for himself. It is probable that the conspirators were led by Belshazzar, Nabonidus's son. As the safest way to secure the throne for himself in the future, Belshazzar championed his father as the new

76. Grayson, *Assyrian and Babylonian Chronicles*, 20–21, 103–4.
77. Paul-Alain Beaulieu, *The Reign of Nabonidus, King of Babylon 556–539 B.C.*, Yale Near Eastern Researches 10 (New Haven: Yale University Press, 1989), 67–68.
78. *ANET* 560–62. Adad-guppi has often been called a high priestess of Sin, but this goes beyond the available evidence; see Beaulieu, *Reign of Nabonidus*, 68.

ruler.[79] Nabonidus appears at times to be a man haunted by his conscience and uncertain of his own legitimacy to the throne. His staunch devotion to Sin proved particularly unpopular to the Babylonian citizenry. His antiquarian interests surpassed those of his predecessors, and they were probably motivated by a political design to show continuity with the great Sargonic empire of the late third millennium.[80]

For reasons that are still unclear, Nabonidus installed Belshazzar as regent in Babylon three years after he became king, and he then led an army through Syria, Lebanon, and finally into northwestern Arabia. He stayed ten years at the Arabian oasis of Taima (biblical Tema), five hundred miles from Babylonia, failing to return to the capital for the annual New Year festival honoring Marduk.[81] Whatever his personal motivation, his subjects in Babylon considered Nabonidus's prolonged absence a self-imposed exile.[82] When Cyrus II captured Babylon without a fight in October 539, its people welcomed him as a liberator.[83] The Persian capture of Babylon ended the last native Semitic empire in ancient Mesopotamia. For the first time in Babylonian history, foreigners controlled the country without assimilating its culture, and the region became a province in a large empire whose center was outside the borders of Mesopotamia. For the next millennium, Indo-Europeans would dominate Babylonia.

Culture and Religion

Babylonia enjoyed a prestigious role in world history because it was the prominent instrument by which the Sumero-Akkadian culture was transmitted to the rest of western Asia. In particular, the immediate cultural surroundings of the Old Testament Israelites were profoundly influenced by Babylonian culture. The Assyrians in northern Mesopotamia were enamored

79. Belshazzar may have been the real power behind the throne throughout Nabonidus's reign; see ibid., 90–98.

80. Ibid., 138–43.

81. For a recent survey of the conjectures regarding Nabonidus's actions, see ibid., 178–85. It seems likely that Belshazzar and his supporters convinced Nabonidus to go into voluntary exile in Arabia, hoping to avoid confrontation between Nabonidus's religious convictions and the powerful clergy of Marduk at Babylon. His banishment to Taima is thus explained as the result of political differences between Nabonidus and his powerful son (pp. 184–85).

82. This explains why Belshazzar is the king of Dan. 5 instead of Nabonidus and why Daniel is offered the "third" position in the kingdom; see Edwin M. Yamauchi, "Nabonidus," in *ISBE* 3:469.

83. The fall of the city is recorded by Herodotus (1:191) and Xenophon (*Cyropedia* 7:26–37). For more on the fall of Babylon and the account of Dan. 5, see Yamauchi, *Persia and the Bible*, 85–87.

with the cultural mystique of their southern neighbors, and other Old Testament peoples were at least familiar with Babylonian culture and religion. The widespread use of the native Mesopotamian writing system of cuneiform bears eloquent testimony to the influence of the Babylonians.

Language

Writing was invented in southern Mesopotamia when the Sumerians discovered they could use wedgelike shapes on various materials to represent words.[84] The wedge-shaped writing (known as cuneiform, from Latin *cuneus* ["wedge"] and *forma* ["form"]) was commonly incised into wet clay, which was the most readily available medium. Often the scribe would then bake the clay tablets in the sun or in an oven, resulting in tablets that were extremely durable. For more permanent records, the cuneiform would be chiseled into stone. During the third millennium, the writing system evolved from pictographic logograms or word signs (in which one sign represented one word) to syllabic representation (in which a single sign stood for one syllable). In this way, cuneiform signs were capable of spelling out a word and could therefore easily be used to write any language.

Semitic speakers coming into Mesopotamia quickly adapted the cuneiform system to their own languages. In the second millennium, the Semitic languages divided into dialects that mirrored the historical realities: Assyrian in the north and Babylonian in the south. But the useful cuneiform system spread far beyond the Semitic-speaking world. Elamites and Persians in ancient Iran, Hittites in Asia Minor, and Ugaritic speakers in Syria all used cuneiform in one variation or another for their own respective languages. The most eloquent illustration of the influence of Babylonian culture is that Babylonian became the *lingua franca* during the Kassite period. Even the Egyptian royal court was accustomed to cuneiform writing.

Literature

The cuneiform system of writing lent itself easily to various occasions, as the need arose. For economic and legal transactions, clay tablets were deposited in archival collections that were expected to last for a few generations only. For more permanent records, texts were inscribed on monuments of stone,

---

84. Stanislav Segert, "Writing," in *ISBE* 4:1148–49. It is still uncertain if the Sumerians themselves actually invented writing, or whether they were merely the first to exploit the new invention. Sumerian is certainly the earliest of seven primitive systems of writing, which leads many to assume the other systems developed under Sumerian influence. On the problem of "monogenesis" versus "polygenesis," see Ignace J. Gelb, *A Study of Writing*, 2d ed. (Chicago: University of Chicago Press, 1963), 212–20.

such as Hammurapi's famous law code.[85] But the Babylonian *belles lettres*, or literary texts, were preserved by repeated copying in scribal schools, particularly in the Old Babylonian period.[86]

The Babylonians were clearly infatuated with the Sumerian culture that preceded them in the third millennium. The Sumerians had been true cultural innovators, not only in the invention of writing but in establishing new literary forms. The Amorites of the Old Babylonian period preserved what was by then a declining culture, and many of the Babylonian masterpieces are adaptations of the older Sumerian versions. Most of this literature may be categorized as epics (which deal with the memorable deeds of humans) or myths (devoted to the exploits of gods). Of the numerous important literary works from Babylonia, only a few examples can be introduced here.

One of the greatest expressions of the Babylonian worldview is the creation story, better known by the Akkadian title, "*Enuma Elish.*"[87] The seven tablets were probably composed during the Kassite period, though the date is much disputed, and none of our copies antedate the first millennium. The story tells of a cosmic conflict between the leading deities, in which the monstrous Ti'amat, mother goddess personifying the primeval ocean, was killed by the young and daring Marduk. Using her carcass, Marduk created the present universe; using the blood of her co-conspirator, he and his father created humankind to do the hard labor of the universe, leaving the deities free from work. Out of gratitude to Marduk for rescuing them from Ti'amat, the gods built for him the city of Babylon. The piece ends with the gods assembling for a feast at Esagil, Marduk's new temple. They acknowledge him as supreme deity of the universe and enumerate his fifty honorific names. During later Babylonian history, this composition was recited on the fourth day of the New Year festival at Babylon and played a significant role in the religious and social life of the community.[88]

The greatest literary piece to come from Babylonian soil is the "Gilgamesh Epic," a touching account of how an ancient king of Uruk rebelled against

85. The text is preserved on a diorite stele, now housed in the Louvre (*ANET* 163–80; *ANEP*, figs. 244, 246).

86. Babylonian literature is best preserved in the Old Babylonian scribal school at Nippur and the Middle Assyrian and royal Neo-Assyrian libraries at Ashur and Nineveh.

87. The first words of this composition are *enuma elish* ("when on high") (*ANET* 60–72, 501–3).

88. "*Enuma Elish*" is not the only creation myth from Babylonia, but it is the longest. The "Epic of Atrahasis" presents in historical sequence both the creation of humanity and its near extinction in the flood, and therefore provokes natural comparisons with Genesis; see Wilfred G. Lambert and Alan R. Millard, *Atra-ḫasīs: The Babylonian Story of the Flood* (Oxford: Clarendon, 1969).

death when he lost his friend Enkidu.[89] On the eleventh of the twelve tablets, Gilgamesh, who was probably a historical figure from around 2600, meets Utnapishtim, who has been called the "Babylonian Noah." Utnapishtim relates how he achieved immortality when he was forewarned of a divine plan to flood the world. He survived the flood in a large reed boat accompanied by his family and pairs of all animals. But this event was unrepeatable and gives Gilgamesh little hope for immortality. He himself fails three tests by which he could have received immortality. But in defeat he resigns himself to the inevitability of death and takes comfort in his achievements.

Another important literary type from Babylonia is the so-called wisdom literature.[90] The Sumerians had developed many wisdom types, such as proverbs, maxims, precepts, disputes, etc. To these, the Babylonians added two lengthy poems dealing with topics familiar to readers of the Old Testament. "The Poem of the Righteous Sufferer" (or *Ludlul Bēl Nēmeqi* ["I will praise the Lord of Wisdom"]) was probably a product of the Kassite period, dealing with the problem of suffering. The righteous narrator was abandoned by the gods, opposed by the king, victimized by the courtiers, afflicted with diseases, and finally rejected as a social outcast. After obtaining no relief from the clergy in charge of exorcism, the sufferer discovers the source of his trouble. It was not the king or the courtiers who were responsible, but almighty Marduk himself. In a series of dreams, the pious hero learns that Marduk's wrath has been appeased and his fortunes immediately begin changing. This "Babylonian Job" hardly compares with the spiritual insight and grandeur of the biblical Book of Job, yet the similarities are obvious.

The second wisdom poem worthy of note is "The Babylonian Theodicy," which takes the form of a discussion between a sufferer and his friend. The poem of twenty-seven stanzas of eleven lines each is an elaborately composed acrostic (i.e., the eleven lines of each stanza begin with the same syllable).[91] The sufferer outlines the evils of social injustice, while the friend attempts to reconcile this with the established views on the divinely ordered justice of the

89. See the chapter in this volume on the Sumerians and *ANET* 72–99, 503–7. The text is a composite narrative from early in the second millennium, which was based on four or more Sumerian stories; see Thorkild Jacobsen, *The Treasures of Darkness: A History of Mesopotamian Religion* (New Haven: Yale University Press, 1976), 208–15; and Jeffrey H. Tigay, *The Evolution of the Gilgamesh Epic* (Philadelphia: University of Pennsylvania Press, 1982).

90. This body of literature corresponds in subject matter to Old Testament wisdom literature and naturally evokes comparisons between the two. But Babylonian wisdom literature is nearly devoid of the emphasis on pious living so prevalent in the wisdom books of the Old Testament (Prov. 1:7). On the discussion in the next two paragraphs, see Wilfred G. Lambert, *Babylonian Wisdom Literature* (Oxford: Clarendon, 1960).

91. The initial acrostic reads "I, Saggil-kīnam-ubbib, the incantation priest, am adorant of the god and the king"; see Lambert, *Babylonian Wisdom Literature*, 63.

universe. The two finally agree on the conviction that humans are unjust, and this is because the gods made them so.

One body of nonliterary texts that bears striking parallels to the biblical texts is the legal corpus.[92] Hammurapi promulgated an official code of laws that by then already stood in an ancient legal tradition. Ur-Nammu had published a collection of laws in the Ur III period, and in the Isin-Larsa period Lipit-Ishtar left a collection in the same outline used by Hammurapi: prologue, corpus of laws, and epilogue.[93] It is still uncertain what impact these law codes had on the actual legal practices of the society.

Art

Babylonian art, as is true of its culture in general, is an interesting amalgamation of Sumerian and Semitic tastes and styles. The Babylonians used most of the same art forms and media of expression used throughout Mesopotamian history: cylinder seals, sculpture, metal work, etc. But each major period of Babylonian history brought its distinctive innovations.

The Old Babylonian period witnessed the introduction of wall painting and minor changes in the traditional styles of cylinder seals. There is also evidence that artisans mass-produced clay plaques and figurines early in the period, but otherwise they seem to have continued the older Mesopotamian styles.[94] An innovation of the Kassite period is the "boundary stone" (Akkadian *kudurru* is a new term in this period). These sculptured stones one or two feet in height, with divine symbols in relief representing the deities who protect the monument, marked grants of land and field boundaries.[95] The innovations of the Neo-Babylonian period were mostly architectural in nature. Nabopolassar and his successors adapted the Assyrian type of mural relief to the use of enameled brick (as in the spectacular Ishtar Gate described above).

92. The fundamental study is Godfrey R. Driver and John C. Miles, *The Babylonian Laws*, 2 vols. (New York: Oxford University Press, 1952–55). On the identical and near-identical parallels, see Samuel Greengus, "Law in the OT," in *Interpreter's Dictionary of the Bible: Supplementary Volume*, ed. Keith R. Crim (Nashville: Abingdon, 1976), 533–34; and Raymond Westbrook, "Biblical and Cuneiform Law Codes," *Revue Biblique* 92 (1985): 247–64.

93. See the chapter in this volume on the Sumerians for these earlier law codes; for Hammurapi's law code, see *ANET* 163–80. Another collection from just before Hammurapi was produced by the kingdom of Eshnunna; see Albrecht Goetze, *The Laws of Eshnunna*, Annual of the American Schools of Oriental Research 31 (New Haven: American Schools of Oriental Research, 1956); Reuven Yaron, *The Laws of Eshnunna* (Jerusalem: Magnes, 1969); and *ANET* 161–63.

94. Gadd, "Hammurabi," 217–18.

95. As an architectural innovation, the Kassites introduced baked bricks into exterior decoration, along with the use of deities in human form; see Oates, *Babylon*, 99–100.

Science

The Babylonians made significant advances in many fields of scientific endeavor, particularly mathematics and astronomy. Hundreds of multiplication and division tables as well as many problem texts from the Old Babylonian scribal school at Nippur evidence a surprising aptitude in mathematics during this period. The high level of algebraic achievement by the early Babylonians has led some to compare this period with the early Renaissance.[96] In addition to the decimal system familiar to Western culture (which uses powers of 10), Babylonian scholars also used a sexagesimal system (employing powers of 60) originally devised by the Sumerians and coming down to us in the form of the 60-minute hour and the 360-degree circle.

Babylonian astronomical observations date at least to the end of the Old Babylonian period.[97] Though these early observations were probably recorded for divination and religious motives, astronomy eventually distinguished itself from astrology as a separate science. By the Neo-Babylonian period, scholars display an impressive ability to combine accurate astronomical observation with advanced mathematical calculation, resulting in a sophisticated lunar-solar calendar that was thoroughly predictable and free from mere observation.[98] This innovation directly inspired the calendar of orthodox Judaism.

Religion

Several Old Testament authors were familiar with the character of Babylonian religion. But ancient Mesopotamian culture lay obscured beneath the sands of time for millenniums before it was retrieved in the past century and a half. Is it possible to speak with confidence from a modern Western perspective about religious beliefs and practices in ancient Babylonia?

There is no consensus among scholars in answering this question. One eminent authority traces the history of Mesopotamian religion through four thousand years of development in which the gods were viewed first as providers for the necessities of life, then as protectors against enemies, next as parents with whom personal relationships were possible, and finally (in the

---

96. For an introduction to the topic, see Saggs, *Greatness That Was Babylon*, 399–407.

97. The so-called Venus Tablets from the time of Ammiṣaduqa (1646–1626) record the rising and setting of the planet Venus.

98. In order to reconcile the solar year with their lunar-based year, which was eleven days shorter, they devised a nineteen-year cycle of intercalary months. The precision and accuracy of this system makes it possible for modern scholars to date exactly many historical events as far back as 626; see Richard A. Parker and Waldo H. Dubberstein, *Babylonian Chronology, 626 B.C.–A.D. 75*, Brown University Studies 19 (Providence: Brown University Press, 1956).

first millennium) as cruel warriors.[99] Many view this reconstruction as interesting, but much too speculative. The opposite extreme argues that a Mesopotamian religion "cannot and should not be written" because of a lack of available evidence and, more seriously, because of the tremendous conceptual and cultural barriers that separate us from such an ancient polytheistic religion.[100] The elusive middle ground is possible to find, provided one remembers the limitations caused by the conceptual gulf between moderns and ancient Babylonia.[101]

The Babylonian pantheon, numbering into the thousands, was an interesting blend of Sumerian and Semitic deities that were basically related to natural phenomena.[102] Most of the great gods of Babylonia were given Semitic names, but were identical in character and function to their Sumerian counterparts: Anu (Sumerian An), the god of the heavens; Enlil (who kept his Sumerian name), the king of the lands; Ea (Sumerian Enki), the god of wisdom and magic whose dominion was the sweet water ocean under the earth. These three were grandfather, father, and son respectively and make up a cosmic triad of the greatest gods. Three other important deities are celestial in nature and also of the same family: Sin (Sumerian Nanna), the moon god, was also father of Shamash (Sumerian Utu), the sun god, and Ishtar (Sumerian Inanna), goddess of the planet Venus. Under Semitic influence, the last deity, as goddess of both love and war, assimilated the personality and functions of other goddesses.

In addition, there were Semitic innovations in the Babylonian pantheon. Adad, the weather god, was of secondary importance in Sumerian religion, but rose to prominence under the Amorite Dynasty of Hammurapi. Conversely, some important Sumerian deities are of lesser significance in the Babylonian pantheon (e.g., Tammuz [Sumerian Dumuzi]). But the most important development was the rise of Marduk to supremacy in the pantheon

---

99. Jacobsen, *Treasures of Darkness*. Among his other important publications on this topic, see "Mesopotamia," in *The Intellectual Adventure of Ancient Man*, by Henri Frankfort et al. (Chicago: University of Chicago Press, 1946), repr. as *Before Philosophy* (Baltimore: Penguin, 1949).

100. A. Leo Oppenheim, *Ancient Mesopotamia: Portrait of a Dead Civilization*, rev. ed. completed by Erica Reiner (Chicago: University of Chicago Press, 1977), 171–83, a position taken as a reaction to the early writings of Jacobsen.

101. In his attempt to demonstrate that the cultural continuum between modern humans and Mesopotamian religion is not as absolute as Oppenheim supposed, Saggs overemphasizes the continuum between Old Testament Israel and Babylonia; see *Encounter with the Divine*, 1–29.

102. Helmer Ringgren, *Religions of the Ancient Near East*, trans. John Sturdy (Philadelphia: Westminster, 1973), 52–68; J. J. M. Roberts, *The Earliest Semitic Pantheon: A Study of the Semitic Deities Attested in Mesopotamia before Ur III* (Baltimore: Johns Hopkins University Press, 1972), 152–54; and Jeremy Black and Anthony Green, *Gods, Demons and Symbols of Ancient Mesopotamia* (Austin: University of Texas Press, 1992).

as the city of Babylon rose politically in the second millennium (see the discussion of Nebuchadnezzar I above and n. 38).

These deities were sexual beings who married, raised families, and were subject to injury or even death. Humankind was created to relieve the gods from the burden of physical labor and to perform ritual service to the gods. Among such service was the provision of the deity's food, drink, and libation for his or her regular meals. The gods themselves prescribed the rituals in which they received portions of the sacrificial animals, the rest going to the king and temple officials. The king was perceived as the official representative of the deity and it was his responsibility to insure the fertility of the land through the careful observance of the New Year rituals. In the temples themselves, an elaborate priestly bureaucracy was responsible for maintaining the temple and its deity.[103]

The temple itself could spread over many acres and consist of several buildings. But the dominant feature of the temple complex was the ziggurat, a stepped tower of three to seven stages. The precise role and function of these towers is still an open question. They may have been connected to the idea that gods originally lived in mountains and the ziggurat served as a substitute.

Near the foot of this tower stood the temple itself, containing the cella or long narrow chamber in which the god was housed. The divine statue was usually carved from wood, adorned with precious stones or metals, and stood on a raised platform or in a niche. The deity was actually thought to be present in its statue, which is borne out by a ritual performed soon after its manufacture. The idol's mouth and eyes were symbolically opened and the lifeless matter became "a receptacle of the divine presence."[104] Solomon's temple shared several features with these patterns, but one striking contrast was the lack of any visible deity in Israel's Holy of Holies.

The Babylonians saw the universe as a single closed system, in which events in one realm mirrored those of another. So events in the human domain reflected events in the divine realm, and successive observable events in nature may be connected by a cause-and-effect relationship. There developed in Babylonia a "pseudoscience" for observing unusual natural phenomena and the events that followed them. It was assumed that this sequence could be repeated in the future. Thus through divination, the will of the gods could be determined and the future could be predicted. Many such omen techniques

103. Saggs, *Greatness That Was Babylon*, 295–307.

104. Oppenheim, *Ancient Mesopotamia*, 186; Saggs, *Greatness That Was Babylon*, 309. See also Isa. 44:12–20 and Hab. 2:18–20.

were practiced, such as the observation of animals' entrails, oil in water, smoke from incense, the behavior of birds, celestial phenomena, etc.

At the turn of this century, when large quantities of new information from ancient Babylonia began to fuel intense interest, scholars were intrigued with parallels in biblical literature. Among some, this led to a "pan-Babylonian-ism," which assumed all ideas originated in Babylonia and moved westward.[105] Although this approach has long since been abandoned, some scholars continue to overemphasize the conceptual and cultural continuum between Mesopotamia and Israel.[106] A more balanced approach begins by recognizing that Israel and her neighbors shared a common culture, from which each one differed to varying degrees. So the biblical flood story shows distinct similarities in form and even content with the "Gilgamesh Epic." But the event is given a very different interpretation in the Old Testament.[107]

The Babylonians adapted and propagated the Sumero-Akkadian culture of the third millennium. Because of their unprecedented political significance during the Old and Neo-Babylonian periods, this cultural heritage contributed significantly to the common Semitic worldview during the ancient Near East. Old Testament Israel was squarely in the mainstream of that cultural pool. Yet it remains to be explored fully to what extent Israel differed from that heritage—indeed to what extent Israel may have reacted against it.

Recommended Reading

Edzard, Dietz O. "The Old Babylonian Period." Pp. 177–231 in *The Near East: The Early Civilizations*. Edited by Jean Bottéro, Elena Cassin, and Jean Vercoutter. Translated by R. F. Tannenbaum. London: Weidenfeld & Nicolson, 1967.

Hallo, William W., and William K. Simpson. *The Ancient Near East: A History*. New York: Harcourt Brace Jovanovich, 1971.

105. This climaxed in the work of Friedrich Delitzsch, *Babel und Bibel* (Leipzig: Hinrichs, 1902). For convenient summary, see Herbert B. Huffmon, "*Babel und Bibel*: The Encounter between Babylon and the Bible," *Michigan Quarterly Review* 22 (1983): 309–20.

106. For example, Bertil Albrektson, *History and the Gods: An Essay on the Idea of Historical Events as Divine Manifestations in the Ancient Near East and in Israel* (Lund: Gleerup, 1967); and Saggs, *Encounter with the Divine*.

107. The similarities between Israel and Babylonia have been well documented: the religiously dominated culture *vis à vis* modern materialism, the principle of association that governed intellectual processes, and the basic conservatism of both civilizations. But similarities such as these only serve to make the disparities more informative and hence justify a careful comparative method. See K. van der Toorn, *Sin and Sanction in Israel and Mesopotamia: A Comparative Study*, Studia Semitica Neerlandica 22 (Assen: Van Gorcum, 1985), 1–9.

Oates, Joan. *Babylon.* Revised edition. New York: Thames & Hudson, 1986.

Parrot, André. *Babylon and the Old Testament.* Translated by B. E. Hooke. New York: Philosophical Library, 1958.

Ringgren, Helmer. *Religions of the Ancient Near East.* Translated by John Sturdy. Philadelphia: Westminster, 1973.

Roux, Georges. *Ancient Iraq.* 3d edition. Baltimore: Penguin, 1992.

Saggs, Harry W. F. *The Greatness That Was Babylon: A Survey of the Ancient Civilization of the Tigris-Euphrates Valley.* 2d edition. London: Sidgwick & Jackson, 1988.

Walton, John H. *Ancient Israelite Literature in Its Cultural Context.* Grand Rapids: Zondervan, 1989.

Wiseman, Donald J. *Nebuchadrezzar and Babylon.* Schweich Lectures 1983. Oxford: Oxford University Press for the British Academy, 1985.

Assyrians

William C. Gwaltney Jr.

The Israelites persisted in all the sins of Jeroboam and did not turn away from them until the LORD removed them from his presence, as he had warned through all his servants the prophets. So the people of Israel were taken from their homeland into exile in Assyria.
          —2 Kings 17:22–23

Since the discovery of the archeological remains of ancient Assyria, attention has focused on recovering its history, literature, religion, and material culture. Based on cuneiform documents and physical remains, scholars of the last 150 years have resurrected the Assyrian people and their civilization from the tells of northern Iraq.[1] The historical remains of the Assyrians are significant since the Hebrew Scriptures remember them as the ravagers of Galilee and the destroyers of the once proud Samaria.[2] Furthermore, the Bible associates the Israelites with the Assyro-Babylonian world (Shinar, Nimrod, and Calah in Gen. 10:8–12, for example). We may now use these findings to reconstruct the history of the Israelites,[3] to trace from a historical

---

1. For a summary of the early exploration and excavation, see Harry W. F. Saggs, *The Might That Was Assyria* (London: Sidgwick & Jackson, 1984), chap. 18; Georges Roux, *Ancient Iraq*, 3d ed. (Baltimore: Penguin, 1992), chap. 2; and Seton Lloyd, *Foundations in the Dust: The Story of Mesopotamian Exploration*, rev. ed. (London: Thames & Hudson, 1980). For a history of the decipherment of the cuneiform languages, see Svend A. Pallis, *The Antiquity of Iraq: A Handbook of Assyriology* (Copenhagen: Munksgaard, 1956), chaps. 2–3; Cyrus H. Gordon, *Forgotten Scripts* (New York: Basic Books, 1968), chaps. 3–4.

2. Galilee: 2 Kings 15:29; Josephus, *Antiquities* 10:11:1 §220; Samaria: 2 Kings 17:1–6; Josephus, *Antiquities* 9:14 §§277–79.

3. See J. Maxwell Miller and John H. Hayes, *A History of Ancient Israel and Judah* (Philadelphia: Westminster, 1986), for a recent application of ancient Near Eastern material to the chronology of the Hebrew Bible.

perspective the involvement of the Assyrians in the world of ancient Israel, and to weigh the Assyrian contribution to Western civilization.

Land

Ancient Assyria's geographical orientation greatly influenced its attitudes and actions.[4] First, Assyria straddled the upper Tigris and its major tributaries, the Greater (Upper) Zab and the Lesser (Lower) Zab, and was thus at their mercy in flood time. Second, it was nearly surrounded by mountains: the Zagros on the east, the Armenian on the north, the Hamrin Hills in the south, and a low-lying ridge in the west that separated the Assyrian heartland from the Jazira steppe. The Assyrians, however, at times faced invasion from hostile tribes that streamed through the mountain passes in the east and north. Third, the Assyrian heartland confronted migrating westerners from time to time. Fourth, Assyria culturally identified itself with southern Mesopotamia from early historic times as Sumerian culture spread northward following the Tigris and Euphrates valleys.

Although the Assyrian homeland was compact and somewhat isolated, it was not completely cut off from the western Fertile Crescent. One of the two major overland routes ran north from southern Mesopotamia to Ashur, then on to Nineveh. From there it turned westward into the Jazira and ran through Shubat-Enlil (recently identified as Tell Leilan), then to Guzana (Tell Halaf), and on to Haran in the Balikh area. The route then crossed the Euphrates at either Carchemish or Emar (Meskene) for points west. People and commodities had passed along this well-worn path since prehistoric times. Since the Assyrians were not especially blessed with the raw materials needed by their burgeoning technologies, they learned to trade in all directions for needed *matériel*. Thus they came into contact with the "outside world" and, at the same time, became fiercely protective of their beloved homeland.

In spite of the uncertainties of river flooding and enemy invasion, the rolling Assyrian homeland proved to be a hospitable environment for the hardy early settlers. Weather patterns in ancient Iraq have not changed appreciably since 5000, so modern climatic and agricultural patterns provide a clue to the

---

4. Descriptions of the Assyrian heartland can be found in nearly every book written about the Assyrians. See especially Jørgen Laessøe, *People of Ancient Assyria: Their Inscriptions and Correspondence*, trans. F. S. Leigh-Browne (London: Routledge & Kegan Paul, 1963), chap. 2; Martinus A. Beek, *Atlas of Mesopotamia* (New York: Nelson, 1962), 9–18; and Roux, *Ancient Iraq*, chap. 2. See also J. Nicholas Postgate, "Some Remarks on Conditions in the Assyrian Countryside," *Journal of the Economic and Social History of the Orient* 17 (1974): 225–43; and W. Nützel, "The Climate Changes of Mesopotamia and Bordering Areas," *Sumer* 32 (1976): 11–25.

climate of ancient Assyria. Following the winter and early spring rains, the land breaks out with lush growth that wilts in May, with the approach of the intensely hot summer. The winter and spring rains, averaging 12–25 inches, usually provide enough moisture to produce a good cereal harvest without irrigation. Wheat, barley, fruit trees, vines, and vegetables also grow in the area.

Assyria flourished as a land of agricultural villages, but several major cities emerged in early historic times. The territory west of the Tigris was ruled by Ashur, the first capital. Nineveh controlled the land east of the Tigris and north of the Upper Zab, while Erbil was the primary city between the two Zab rivers. South of the Lower Zab, Arrapha dominated. To archeologists, four Assyrian cities—Ashur, Nineveh, Calah, and Dur-Sharrukin—are most important.[5] Their physical remains are impressive with their technological skills, especially in architecture, heavy construction, defenses, and artistic creativity.

The first city of the land was Ashur (modern Qala'at Sherqat), named for their chief god, and also the name of the land and the people.[6] Situated on a bluff overlooking the river, Ashur lay on the west bank of the Tigris about sixty miles south of Mosul. Founded in the third millennium by desert immigrants and honored with rich temples and royal tombs, Ashur retained its position as the Assyrian religious center until the end of the Neo-Assyrian Empire.

Nineveh, the last capital of Assyria, was one of the oldest cities of Mesopotamia, but attained its zenith only under Sennacherib and his successors.[7] Located on the east bank of the Tigris across from modern Mosul and occupying about 1,800 acres, its site includes two major tells, Nebi Yunus and Kouyun-

---

5. See Gordon G. Garner, *Royal Cities of Assyria* (Melbourne: Australian Institute of Archaeology, 1981).

6. The site of ancient Ashur was excavated by Walter Andrae between 1903 and 1914, with results given in his various publications; see the revision of Andrae's *Das wiedererstandene Assur* (Munich: Beck, 1977) by Barthel Hrouda. For a cataloging of the documents found, see Olof Pedersén, *Archives and Libraries in the City of Assur: A Survey of the Material from the German Excavations*, 2 vols. (Uppsala: Almqvist & Wiksell, 1985–86).

7. The Kouyunjik mound of Nineveh was the first tell in Mesopotamia to be excavated and has been dug into on several occasions, beginning in 1842 with Paul Émile Botta. Austen Henry Layard also excavated Nineveh from 1849 to 1851; see Layard's *Nineveh and Its Remains* (New York: Appleton, 1858); Gordon Waterfield, *Layard of Nineveh* (New York: Praeger, 1963); and Reginald C. Thompson and R. W. Hutchinson, *A Century of Exploration at Nineveh* (London: Luzac, 1929). Americans, led by David Stronach, made limited excavations in 1987 and 1989; preliminary reports appear in *Mār Šipri* 1/2 (1988): 1–2; 2/2 (1989): 1–2; and 4/1 (1991): 1–3. For new texts from Nineveh, see Frederick M. Fales, "New Assyrian Letters from the Kuyunjik Collection," *Archiv für Orientforschung* 27 (1980): 136–53. On the involvement of the Israelite prophets Jonah and Nahum with Nineveh, see Donald J. Wiseman, "Jonah's Nineveh," *Tyndale Bulletin* 30 (1979): 29–51; and Paul J. N. Lawrence, "Assyrian Nobles and the Book of Jonah," *Tyndale Bulletin* 37 (1986): 121–32.

jik. In the latter mound, early diggers located the famous library of Ashurbanipal, which remains one of the literary treasures of the ancient world.

Calah (modern Nimrud), located on the east bank of the Tigris about twenty miles south of Nineveh, was founded in the thirteenth century during one of Assyria's expansionistic eras. In the early part of the ninth century Calah became Assyria's capital under the famous Ashurnasirpal II. Shalmaneser III's Black Obelisk was found in Calah's ruins, as were the Nimrud ivories.[8]

In 717 Sargon II (721–705) began building Dur-Sharrukin ("Fort Sargon" = modern Khorsabad) as his new capital on a virgin site about twelve miles northeast of Nineveh.[9] Built in ten years, it was laid out as a square one mile on each side. It was a marvel of beauty, complete with palace, temples, and artistic wonders; but Sargon was not to enjoy his capital for long. About a year after its inauguration, Sargon died in battle; his son Sennacherib favored Nineveh over Dur-Sharrukin.

People

Long before 9000 the Assyrian foothills provided a haven for wandering tribes. During the "Neolithic revolution" early villages like Umm Dabaghiyeh and Tell Sotto and towns like Jarmo grew up.[10] Better strains of cereal grains were developed and various animals were domesticated, which made increasing population possible. Pottery technology spread rapidly. Social organization advanced beyond the extended family.

The earliest farming culture in the Assyrian heartland is named for Hassuna, located about twenty miles south of Mosul.[11] Dating from about 6000, this culture developed new technologies and long-distance trading, which testify to a growing sophistication. In southern Assyria, where rainfall is mar-

8. For a summary of the work at Nimrud, see Max E. L. Mallowan, *Nimrud and Its Remains*, 3 vols. (London: Collins, 1966).

9. Khorsabad was excavated by the French in 1843–44 and by the Americans in 1930–35; see Gordon Loud et al., *Khorsabad*, 2 vols., Oriental Institute Publications 38, 40 (Chicago: University of Chicago Press, 1936–38); and Pauline Albenda, *The Palace of Sargon, King of Assyria: Monumental Wall Reliefs at Dur-Sharrukin, from Original Drawings Made at the Time of Their Discovery in 1843–1844 by Botta and Flandin* (Paris: Éditions Recherche sur les Civilisations, 1986).

10. On Tell Sotto, see Saggs, *Might That Was Assyria*, 6–12; on Jarmo, see Robert J. Braidwood and B. Howe, *Prehistoric Investigations in Iraqi Kurdistan*, Studies in Ancient Oriental Civilization 31 (Chicago: University of Chicago Press, 1960). For Umm Dabaghiyeh, see Michael Roaf, *Cultural Atlas of Mesopotamia and the Ancient Near East* (New York: Facts on File, 1990), 47.

11. Seton Lloyd and Fuad Safar, "Tell Hassuna," *Journal of Near Eastern Studies* 4 (1945): 255–84; Takey Dabbagh, "Hassuna Pottery," *Sumer* 21 (1965): 93–111.

ginal for grain cultivation, the Samarran culture flourished.[12] The relation of this culture to Hassuna is still debated.[13]

The next people to appear in the Assyrian plains are the Halafian, after Tell Halaf on the Habur River.[14] Their pottery and technology suggest the arrival of a new people in greater Mesopotamia. Continuing for a thousand years in places, this group spread over a wide area from Cilicia to Kurdistan to Lake Van. Their point of origin is still debated, but they seem to represent a reasonably well-defined culture.

Unlike the Halafian, the Ubaid culture spread northward through Iraq and eventually covered the area from the Persian Gulf to Syria.[15] In Assyria the two cultures overlapped until finally the Ubaid outlasted the Halafian. Population density increased during this era. Some think that the Ubaidians in southern Mesopotamia should be considered "Proto-Sumerians" since there appears to be an unbroken cultural transition from Eridu to Hajji Muhammad, and then to Ubaid, Uruk, and Jemdet Nasr.[16] This latter culture leads directly into the Protoliterate Sumerian era. At any rate, the displacement of Halafian by Ubaidian in Assyria closed down the northern trade at least until the late Ubaid era when traffic in timber and copper with Syria brought Assyria into wider economic interchange again.

The era from about 4500 to 2500 in Assyria remains somewhat clouded. In the south, these two millenniums, known as the Uruk and Early Dynastic ages, are well known from archeological evidence.[17] Former agricultural towns became larger walled cities. Urbanization with all its attendant skills was on the march. Food production grew and population increased, making more complex social organization necessary. Craft skills flourished as never before. Newly created writing served bureaucratic ends.

---

12. Jack Finegan, *Archaeological History of the Ancient Middle East* (Boulder, Colo.: Westview, 1979), 6.

13. On Tell es-Suwwan, a major site, see Saggs, *Might That Was Assyria*, 13.

14. Max von Oppenheim, *Tell Halaf*, 4 vols. (Berlin: de Gruyter, 1943–62). See also Edwin M. Yamauchi, "Tell Arpachiyah," in *The New International Dictionary of Biblical Archaeology*, ed. Edward M. Blaiklock and Roland K. Harrison (Grand Rapids: Zondervan, 1983), 438.

15. Harry R. Hall and C. Leonard Woolley, *Al-ꞌUbaid*, Ur Excavations 1 (London: Oxford University Press, 1927).

16. For a discussion of the Eridu and Hajji Muhammad cultures, see Finegan, *Archaeological History*, 8–10; and Ann L. Perkins, *The Comparative Archeology of Early Mesopotamia*, Studies in Ancient Oriental Civilization 25 (Chicago: University of Chicago Press, 1949), 73–90. On Ubaid and Jemdet Nasr, see Finegan, *Archaeological History*, 10–14; and Perkins, *Comparative Archaeology*, 106–7.

17. See especially the discussion by Hallo in William W. Hallo and William K. Simpson, *The Ancient Near East: A History* (New York: Harcourt Brace Jovanovich, 1971), 34–54. On the archeological remains of the Warka and Protoliterate periods, see Perkins, *Comparative Archaeology*, chap. 4.

This urban Sumerian civilization migrated northward and made an increasing impact on Assyria.[18] Town fortifications and public buildings grew in size, even though temples reveal only a small degree of growth at most sites. One is tempted to interpret this evidence as demonstrating an early defensive posture against aggressive outsiders. Warfare was becoming an integral part of the regional ethos. Two significant sites of this era, Tell Brak on the Habur and Tepe Gawra near Nineveh, reveal a great degree of cultural influence from the south.[19] Trade again developed in all directions.

Assyria had to confront a new military and cultural force from the south in Sargon the Great of Akkad whose expansionism brought his armies into their land in the middle of the twenty-fourth century and annexed Assyria to the Akkadian Empire.[20]

Who were these northern people who came under the cultural domination of the Sumerians and later under the military domination of the Akkadians? We cannot be sure of their origins: Iran, Armenia, the Syrian desert, and southern Mesopotamia have all been suggested as their place of origin. Evidence from Ebla suggests that during the Early Bronze Age, at least, we may expect Semitic linguistic affinities for the peoples in the northern Fertile Crescent who came under early Sumerian cultural influence.[21] From the Middle Bronze Age onward, however, there can be little doubt of a Semitic origin for the Assyrian people. Some Hurrian and Indo-European elements may have been present,[22] but Assyria was primarily Semitic.

Early History

The protohistorical era of Assyria ends with the beginning of what is called the Old Assyrian period and the coming of the Amorites.[23] These nomadic westerners poured into the eastern Fertile Crescent, bringing with

18. Saggs, *Might That Was Assyria*, 16–19.

19. Perkins, *Comparative Archaeology*, chap. 5.

20. Roux, *Ancient Iraq*, 151–55; Hallo and Simpson, *Ancient Near East*, 54–60.

21. Paolo Matthiae, "Tell Mardikh: The Archives of the Palace," *Archaeology* 30 (1977): 244–53; idem, *Ebla: An Empire Rediscovered*, trans. Christopher Holme (Garden City, N.Y.: Doubleday, 1981); Robert D. Biggs, "The Ebla Tablets: An Interim Perspective," *Biblical Archaeologist* 43 (1981): 76–86.

22. For this view, see Hildegard Lewy, "Assyria: c. 2600–1816 B.C.," in *CAH* 1/2:729–70.

23. For a synthesis of the view of an "Old Assyrian Empire" extending into central Anatolia, see Julius Lewy, "On Some Institutions of the Old Assyrian Empire," *Hebrew Union College Annual* 27 (1956): 1–79; and Hildegard Lewy, "Anatolia in the Old Assyrian Period," in *CAH* 1/2:707–28. For the prevailing view of the Assyrian presence in Anatolia as a trading enterprise, see Louis L. Orlin, *Assyrian Colonies in Cappadocia* (The Hague: Mouton, 1970); and Mogens T. Larsen, *The Old Assyrian City-State and Its Colonies* (Copenhagen: Akademisk Forlag, 1976).

them dynamic change. Wherever they settled they formed strong and aggressive city-states founded upon the older established civilization. Eventually the struggle for hegemony erupted into war. When Hammurapi of Babylon later fought his way to mastery over all Mesopotamia, one of the Amorite kingdoms he had to subdue was Assyria.[24]

One document that purports to inform us about the origins of the early Assyrian kingdom is the "Assyrian King List," which lists the kings of Assyria down to Sargon II (721–705).[25] The first seventeen kings are identified as "kings living in tents."[26] The next ten kings form a single ancestral line going back to the seventeenth king of the previous group. Then appears a group of six kings without patronymy. Thereafter the king list gives each king's name, his relation to the previous king, and the number of years he ruled. Many hold deep suspicions about the early part of the list, but by the time of Shamshi-Adad I (1813–1781) we are on solid historical ground. This usurper was a contemporary of Babylon's Hammurapi and is well attested in numerous texts.

Dated from about 1910 to 1840, the six kings immediately preceding Shamshi-Adad are known to us from other Old Assyrian (or Cappadocian) texts.[27] The founder of this line, Ilushuma, is the last ruler in the previous sec-

24. Hallo and Simpson, *Ancient Near East*, 72–73, 84–103; Giorgio Buccellati, *The Amorites of the Ur III Period* (Naples: Instituto Orientale di Napoli, 1966); Dietz O. Edzard, *Die "Zweite Zwischenzeit" Babyloniens* (Wiesbaden: Harrassowitz, 1957); Jean R. Kupper (ed.), *La Civilisation de Mari*, XVe Rencontre Assyriologique Internationale (Paris: Société d'Édition "Les Belles Lettres," 1967).

25. *ANET* 564–66. For bibliography on the Assyrian King List, see Finegan, *Archaeological History*, 379–80. See also Hallo and Simpson, *Ancient Near East*, 97; Saggs, *Might That Was Assyria*, 23–26; Hayim Tadmor, "Observations on Assyrian Historiography," in *Essays on the Ancient Near East in Memory of Jacob Joel Finkelstein*, ed. Maria deJ. Ellis (Hamden, Conn.: Archon for the Connecticut Academy of Arts and Sciences, 1977), 209–13.

26. See Fritz R. Kraus, *Könige die in Zelten Wohnten* (Amsterdam: Noord-Hollandsche Uitgevers, 1965).

27. Something like twenty thousand Old Assyrian tablets have been excavated in central Turkey, mainly from ancient Kanish (now known as Kültepe) near Kayseri. About five thousand of these have been published; see the bibliography in Karl Hecker, *Grammatik der Kültepe-Texte*, Analecta Orientalia 44 (Rome: Pontifical Biblical Institute Press, 1968), §§2–4. These documents inform us about the trading network established by the Assyrians, in which textiles and tin were shipped westward into Anatolia and traded for processed gold and silver to be sent back to Ashur and applied to further investments. This corpus is especially important for use in analyzing the economic terminology and procedures of the ancient world. The long-term success of this wide-ranging trading network demonstrates how aggressive and persistent the Assyrians were in pursuing their interests abroad through economic means. The archeological remains excavated in the merchant section of Kanish show that Assyrians had settled here side-by-side with native peoples. The documents, ranging from business texts to personal letters and from court records to marriage contracts, show the kind of symbiosis these people from several cultural and linguistic backgrounds had achieved for their mutual benefit.

tion of ten kings. Unfortunately we have only occasional historical references to the rulers before Ilushuma. Perhaps the leaders in the early part of the list were tribal chiefs. The rulers of Ilushuma's line went by the title *waklum* ("overseer").[28] They were followed by Shamshi-Adad's Amorite domination over the northland. Quickly, however, these infiltrating Semites settled down to a more urbanized lifestyle and extended their control over surrounding towns and tribes. They moved through the city-chief (*waklum*) stage of leadership as found in the Old Assyrian documents to that led by a king (*sharrum*). The original purpose for creating the Assyrian King List may have been to legitimize Shamshi-Adad's claim to kingship by tying his ancestry to that of an established family of Assyrian chieftains. The Assyrian King List describes Shamshi-Adad's rise to glory in these words:

> Shamshi-Adad, the son of Ilu-kabkabi, went away to Babylonia in the time of Naram-Sin; in the eponymy of Ibni-Adad, Shamshi-Adad came back from Babylonia; he seized Ekallatu; he stayed in Ekallatu for three years; in the eponymy of Atamar-Ishtar, Shamshi-Adad came up from Ekallatu and removed Erishu, son of Naram-Sin, from the throne, seized the throne, (and) ruled as king for 33 years.[29]

After solidifying his control in all Assyria, Shamshi-Adad turned against Mari, which he defeated and annexed.[30] He appointed his younger son (Yasmakh-Adad) to Mari's throne and his older son (Ishme-Dagan) as viceroy of Ekallatu, while he preferred to live in Shubat-Enlil (Tell Leilan).[31] Ashur remained Assyria's administrative and religious capital. Shamshi-Adad reopened Assyrian trade in central and eastern Anatolia and succeeded in maintaining this mighty kingdom, based on his military and administrative skills.

Following Shamshi-Adad's death, the Amorite Assyrian kingdom disintegrated as rapidly as it had been constructed. Within a short time the inef-

---

28. Larsen, *Old Assyrian City-State*, 129–47.

29. *ANET* 564.

30. The Mari texts have been published in the series "Archives Royales de Mari: Transcriptions et Traductions" (Paris: Imprimerie Nationale, 1946–). For a short synthesis of the Mari materials in English, see Hildegard Lewy, "Mari," in *Interpreter's Dictionary of the Bible*, ed. George A. Buttrick et al. (Nashville: Abingdon, 1962), 3:264–66; and Jack M. Sasson, "Mari," in *Interpreter's Dictionary of the Bible: Supplementary Volume*, ed. Keith R. Crim (Nashville: Abingdon, 1976), 567–71. For a wider bibliography, see Finegan, *Archaeological History*, 368–69. See also the periodical *MARI: Annales de Recherches Interdisciplinaires* (Paris: Éditions Recherche sur les Civilisations, 1982–).

31. Harvey Weiss, "Tell Leilan on the Habur Plains of Syria," *Biblical Archaeologist* 48 (1983): 6–34; idem, "Tell Leilan 1989: Leilan IIID–IIB Urbanization and State Formation," *Mār Šipri* 3/2 (1990): 1–3.

fective Yasmakh-Adad was overthrown by Zimri-Lim of the former dynasty of Mari, and the Middle Euphrates region of the Assyrian kingdom was lost. Ishme-Dagan made no effort to rescue his brother or retake Mari. The Amorite Assyrian kingdom of the Tigris remained independent under Ishme-Dagan until Hammurapi "overthrew the army of Subartu" late in his career.

Assyrian rule over northern Mesopotamia was now at an end. Ishme-Dagan was succeeded by Ashur-dugul, whom the Assyrian King List calls "the son of a nobody"—a signal of the political instability following Ishme-Dagan. The next kings in the king list are only names to us, reflected in the sparse historical records for the next three centuries in Assyria.

From about the middle of the fifteenth century the Mitanni began annexing Assyrian territory.[32] During this era Assyria was no longer treated as a political unit, but Arrapha, Erbil, Ashur, and Nineveh became separate units.

Middle Assyrian Revival

The fourteenth century witnessed the beginnings of a rebirth of Assyrian independence, which culminated in the Middle Assyrian Kingdom. Ashur-uballit I (1363–1328), who freed Assyria of Mitanni control, even called the Egyptian pharaoh "brother" as an equal.[33] Before the end of his reign he had intervened in Babylonian affairs and influenced the selection of its next king. This was only the start of Assyrian expansion, as the Assyrians continued to press their interests in the north and in Babylonia.

The century initiated by the reign of Adad-nirari I (1305–1274), Ashur-uballit's grandson, and concluded by that of Tukulti-Ninurta I (1243–1207) established a military and political scenario that was played out frequently during later centuries of Assyrian struggle.[34] Adad-nirari defeated the rem-

32. On the Mitanni kingdom and its involvement with Egypt, the Hittites, and the Assyrians, see Roux, *Ancient Iraq*, chap. 16; and Hallo and Simpson, *Ancient Near East*, 109–20, 264–65, 274.

33. See Amarna texts 15–16, Jörgen A. Knudtzon, *Die el-Amarna-Tafeln*, 2 vols., Vorderasiatische Bibliothek 2 (Leipzig: Hinrichs, 1908–15); Saggs, *Might That Was Assyria*, 42; and Pinchas Artzi, "The Rise of the Middle-Assyrian Kingdom according to el-Amarna Letters 15 and 16," in *Bar-Ilan Studies in History* (Ramat-Gan: Bar-Ilan University Press, 1978), 25–41. Twenty-five of these tablets appear in English translation in *ANET* 483–90. See also Peter Machinist, *Provincial Governance in Middle Assyria and Some New Texts from Yale*, Assur 3/2 (Malibu, Calif.: Undena, 1982); and Amir Harrak, "Historical Statements in Middle Assyrian Archival Sources," *Journal of the American Oriental Society* 109 (1989): 205–9. The entire Amarna corpus is now available in English translation: William L. Moran, *The Amarna Letters* (Baltimore: Johns Hopkins University Press, 1992).

34. See especially the treatment by Saggs, *Might That Was Assyria*, 46–55.

nants of the Mitanni kingdom at Hanigalbat, annexed it, and established Assyrian control over the northern area between the Tigris and the Euphrates. Later the boundary between Assyria and Babylonia was set at the Diyala River. Shalmaneser I (1273–1244), Adad-nirari's son and successor, encountered the emerging kingdom of Urartu based in the Lake Van region.[35] He forced the Urartians back into the northern mountains and broke a rebellion to resurrect Hanigalbat as an independent state, deporting the defeated rebels. Tukulti-Ninurta I, like his father and grandfather, expanded the borders in the west when he annexed Qutu and Ukumenu.[36] He then faced the question of how to pacify the Babylonians. The Babylonian problem forced the more powerful Assyrian monarch to walk a narrow line. Not to respond with enough force was to invite political intrigue or open revolt. To respond with too much force was to call down the curse of the Babylonian gods on the Assyrians. Finally, Babylonian goading forced Tukulti-Ninurta to let loose his armies on Babylon. The queen city, including its shrines dedicated to the ancient gods, was sacked. Assyrian propagandists defended the irreverence on the grounds that the gods of Babylon had rejected the city and commissioned Tukulti-Ninurta to punish it. To show Marduk's rejection the sacred image was carried to Ashur, where it was treated with due respect.[37] Tukulti-Ninurta was later executed by his son, who became the next king. This coup introduced a period of decline lasting until the reign of Ashur-resh-ishi I (1132–1115). Empire building was interrupted but not forgotten.

Beginning with Ashur-resh-ishi I and his son Tiglath-pileser I (1114–1076) the Middle Assyrian era attained its full flower. Once again Assyria's borders were established after northern frontier battles.[38] Tiglath-pileser ventured beyond Assyria's traditional northern boundaries into more distant regions all the way to the "Great Sea" (the Mediterranean).[39] He claims to have crossed the Euphrates twenty-eight times, mainly to stop another in-

---

35. On the kingdom of Urartu, see B. B. Piotrovsky, *The Ancient Civilization of Urartu*, trans. J. Hogarth (New York: Cowles, 1969); Richard D. Barnett, "Urartu," in *CAH* 3/1:314–71; Paul E. Zimansky, *Ecology and Empire: The Structure of the Urartian State*, Studies in Ancient Oriental Civilization 41 (Chicago: Oriental Institute, University of Chicago, 1985).

36. See Saggs, *Might That Was Assyria*, 51–52.

37. Ibid., 52.

38. Ibid., 59–60; Finegan, *Archaeological History*, 97; Roux, *Ancient Iraq*, 278–79; Richard D. Barnett, "Phrygia and the Peoples of Anatolia in the Iron Age," in *CAH* 2/2:417–42.

39. See Yutaka Ikeda, "Assyrian Kings and the Mediterranean Sea: The Twelfth to Ninth Centuries B.C.," *Abr-Nahrain* 23 (1984–85): 22–31. For new information on the reign of Tiglath-pileser I, see Veysel Donbaz and Amir Harrak, "The Middle Assyrian Eponymy of Kidin-Aššur," *Journal of Cuneiform Studies* 41 (1989): 217–25.

vading nomadic enemy, the Arameans, who had raided the western Assyrian frontier.[40]

Two sons of Tiglath-pileser followed him on the throne. During their reigns the Arameans reasserted themselves as a problem too difficult to be dealt with by Assyria alone.[41] Babylon and Assyria were driven together to cope with the new menace. Ashur-bel-kala (1073–1056), attempting to strengthen his defenses against the Arameans, married the Babylonian king's daughter to bring the Assyrian and Babylonian peoples together. The Aramean threat was temporarily thwarted in Mesopotamia, but the Assyrian king was no longer able to deal with the situation beyond the western border. During the interim between Ashur-bel-kala and Ashur-dan II (934–912) the Assyrian monarchy was totally occupied with maintaining itself against these pressures and with dynastic struggles. But a new day of empire building was awaiting the ninth-century kings.

Neo-Assyrian Emergence

Ashur-dan II and his four successors reestablished internal political stability, reasserted Assyrian expansion, and reopened international trade. Ashur-dan managed to recreate unified royal administration in the traditional Assyrian territory. His son Adad-nirari II (911–891) consolidated his father's kingdom and pushed beyond the Tur Abdin Range in the northwest and brought the Assyrians into confrontation with Aramean states in that region. The course was set for decades to come. Only border actions were needed to settle the Babylonian border.

Adad-nirari's son Tukulti-Ninurta II (890–884) regained territory in the northeast mountains. Some Arameans living within the new Assyrian boundaries became welcomed vassals. Wealth in the form of precious metal, aro-

40. On the Arameans, see Emil G. Kraeling, *Aram and Israel* (New York: Columbia University Press, 1918); Roger T. O'Callaghan, *Aram Naharaim: A Contribution to the History of Upper Mesopotamia in the Second Millennium* B.C., Analecta Orientalia 26 (Rome: Pontifical Biblical Institute Press, 1948); André Dupont-Sommer, *Les Araméens* (Paris: Maisonneuve, 1949); Abraham Malamat, "The Aramaeans," in *Peoples of Old Testament Times*, ed. Donald J. Wiseman (Oxford: Clarendon, 1973), 134–55; Benjamin Mazar, "The Aramean Empire and Its Relations with Israel," *Biblical Archaeologist* 25 (1962): 98–120, repr. in *The Biblical Archaeologist Reader*, vol. 2, ed. Edward F. Campbell Jr. and David N. Freedman (Missoula, Mont.: American Schools of Oriental Research/Scholars Press, 1975), 127–51; John A. Brinkman, *A Political History of Post-Kassite Babylonia, 1158–722 B.C.* (Rome: Pontifical Biblical Institute Press, 1968), 267–85.

41. For a possible explanation of these difficult times, see J. Neumann and Simo Parpola, "Climatic Change and the Eleventh-Tenth-Century Eclipse of Assyria and Babylonia," *Journal of Near Eastern Studies* 46 (1987): 161–82.

matics, camels, ivory, textiles, animals, iron, and grain poured into Assyrian depots on a regular basis. All this was preparatory to the grand scheme of Ashurnasirpal II (883–859), Tukulti-Ninurta II's son.

On becoming king, Ashurnasirpal faced revolts on the fringes of his kingdom.[42] He quickly responded and crushed the rebels in the Habur region, built more border forts in the northern Tigris area and in the west, and annexed territory southeast of the Diyala. Through all this he reasserted the political integrity of the homeland. Assyria's northern expansion caused Ashurnasirpal to build a new capital closer to the front. Calah (modern Nimrud) was built on the ruins of an abandoned town near the juncture of the Tigris and the Upper Zab. A stone stele from the 1951 dig in Calah's palace describes how the king built his new city and provided a dedicatory banquet for 69,574 guests for a ten-day celebration.[43] Eventually Ashurnasirpal crossed the Euphrates and ventured as far as the Mediterranean, during which campaign most kings offered their submission to this awesome lord. He took hostages to curtail rebellion and added new territory whose tribute would help meet the demands at home for glory and wealth.

Shalmaneser III (858–824) inherited from his father a kingdom stretching from the Mediterranean and the Taurus to the Zagros, from the Armenian Mountains to southern Kurdistan. Not content with simply maintaining these borders,

King Ashurnasirpal II, 883–859 B.C. (height: 3′ 6″)
Courtesy of the British Museum

42. On Ashurnasirpal, see A. Kirk Grayson, "Studies in Neo-Assyrian History: The Ninth Century B.C.," *Biblia et Orientalia* 33 (1976): 134–45; W. de Filippi, *The Royal Inscriptions of Aššur-Nāṣir-Apli II (883–859 B.C.),* Assur 1/7 (Malibu, Calif.: Undena, 1977); Julian E. Reade, "The Rassam Obelisk," *Iraq* 42 (1980): 18–22.

43. See A. Kirk Grayson, *Assyrian Royal Inscriptions* (Wiesbaden: Harrassowitz, 1976), 2:172–76; and *ANET* 558–60.

Shalmaneser launched numerous expeditions in the west aimed at conquering Damascus. He led his troops into Cilicia to corner that region's iron and to tap the lucrative western trade. In his sixth year (853), however, he confronted a formidable western military force near Qarqar on the Orontes River.[44] Twelve major "kings of Hatti" led by Damascus and Hamath formed a coalition to stop the Assyrians. Ahab of Samaria sent two thousand chariots and ten thousand infantry.[45] For the first time an Assyrian text mentions an Israelite king, Ahab of Israel.

From the time of Shalmaneser III the fortunes of Israel and Judah became linked to those of Assyria.[46] When Assyria was preoccupied with difficulties elsewhere, the two Israelite kingdoms could follow their own agendas; but when Assyria grew stronger, Israel and Judah had no choice but to come to terms with the "bee in the land of Assyria" (Isa. 7:18). Since Assyria was more powerful than the western kingdoms, Israel and Judah were usually required to submit and pay tribute. Occasionally they tried to go their own way—with disastrous results.[47]

The outcome of Shalmaneser's 853 campaign remains in doubt. He claimed to have defeated the enemy so that their corpses formed a bridge across the Orontes River. His records are silent about any followup campaigns for several years, however, which suggests that he actually had less military success at Qarqar than he claimed.[48] Shalmaneser made later forays into the west and received tribute from Jehu of Israel in 841.[49] Shalmaneser claims to have crossed the Euphrates for the twenty-first time in 838. He did not explain each crossing in his annals, but they appear to be raids against rebels.

44. For bibliography on Qarqar, see Edwin M. Yamauchi, "Qarqar," in *The New International Dictionary of Biblical Archaeology*, ed. Edward M. Blaiklock and Roland K. Harrison (Grand Rapids: Zondervan, 1983), 377.

45. *ANET* 279. On the chronology associated with the Battle of Qarqar, see John A. Brinkman, "A Further Note on the Date of the Battle of Qarqar and Neo-Assyrian Chronology," *Journal of Cuneiform Studies* 30 (1978): 173–75.

46. Primary Assyrian materials from the period of Shalmaneser III through the fall of Assyria are available in English in *ANET* 276–305.

47. See, e.g., the policies of Pekah (2 Kings 15:25–31) and Hoshea (2 Kings 15:30; 17:1–6).

48. For an evaluation of Shalmaneser III's career, see Hallo and Simpson, *Ancient Near East*, 125–29; and William W. Hallo, "From Qarqar to Carchemish: Assyria and Israel in the Light of New Discoveries," *Biblical Archaeologist* 23 (1960): 34–61, repr. in *The Biblical Archaeologist Reader*, vol. 2, ed. Edward F. Campbell Jr. and David N. Freedman (Missoula, Mont.: American Schools of Oriental Research/Scholars Press, 1975), 156–62.

49. See *ANET* 281 for the text of the famous Black Obelisk of Shalmaneser III, which records the tribute of Jehu(?) son of Omri. For an alternate interpretation of the "son of Omri," see P. Kyle McCarter Jr., "'Yaw, Son of 'Omri': A Philological Note on Israelite Chronology," *Bulletin of the American Schools of Oriental Research* 216 (1974): 5–7. For a later study of the Black Obelisk, see Alberto R. W. Green, "Sua and Jehu: The Boundaries of Shalmaneser's Conquest," *Palestine Exploration Quarterly* 111 (1979): 35–39, pls. iv–vi.

Although the battle at Qarqar between Shalmaneser III and the twelve-king coalition is not mentioned in the Bible, it nevertheless establishes a cornerstone date for devising a chronology for the two Israelite kingdoms. We may couple Ahab's activity in 853 with Jehu's tribute in 841 and use these dates to establish Israelite chronology in the middle 800s and clarify the dynastic transition during a troubled time in the northern Israelite kingdom.[50]

The latter years of Shalmaneser III were full of turmoil.[51] Two of his sons created a civil war that ended when Shamshi-Adad V (823–811) defeated his brother, seized the throne, and set about restoring order within Assyria and securing the borders. The Babylonian boundary was especially sensitive. Urartu in the north used the occasion to move southward. Tribute was withheld in the west. Israel had some breathing room from Assyrian aggression again.

Adad-nirari III (810–783), son of Shamshi-Adad V and his legendary wife Semiramis (Assyrian Sammuramat), was forced to campaign in southern Syria. Damascus and its allies had again organized a western coalition against the Assyrians. Thus Assyria under Adad-nirari confronted two stubborn foes in the north and the west: Urartu and the Damascus coalition. He advanced against Syria-Palestine, but a campaign against Urartu was beyond his resources. The Rimah Stele records Adad-nirari's claim to have received tribute from King Joash of Samaria.[52] This incursion in his fifth or sixth year (ca. 805) seems to lie behind the statement in 2 Kings 13:5 that Yahweh gave Israel a deliverer and they escaped from the hand of the Syrians.[53]

The reigns of Adad-nirari III's three successors were undistinguished. Shalmaneser IV (782–773) led several defensive actions against Urartu and Syria, but western activities were largely curtailed. Rebellion reemerged in Assyria. The governor of Calah eventually seized power, took the throne-name Tiglath-pileser III (744–727), and reopened the western front after putting things in order at home. During this hiatus in Assyrian control of the west (ca. 805–743), Israel and Judah were left to follow their own interests with-

50. See especially Hallo, "From Qarqar to Carchemish."

51. For a treatment of the era of Ashurnasirpal II, Shalmaneser III, and Shamshi-Adad V, see Grayson, "Studies in Neo-Assyrian History."

52. Miller and Hayes, *History of Ancient Israel and Judah*, 288 (photograph), 299 (translation); S. Page, "A Stele of Adad-nirari III and Nergal-eres from Tell al Rimah," *Iraq* 30 (1968): 139–53; Hayim Tadmor, "The Historical Inscriptions of Adad-nirari III," *Iraq* 35 (1973): 141–50.

53. William H. Shea, "Adad-nirari III and Jehoash of Israel," *Journal of Cuneiform Studies* 30 (1978): 101–13.

out superpower interference, but this was the last respite from eastern domination they were to enjoy.[54]

Reconstructing Tiglath-pileser III's career is difficult because his annals are not well preserved.[55] The general course of Assyrian affairs is clear, however. He began by consolidating his control over the Assyrian homeland and fixing the Babylonian border at the Diyala. Urartian presence in Syria had cut into Assyrian commerce, making an eventual clash inevitable. From 743 through 738 Tiglath-pileser directed his troops against the troublesome Urartians with great success and pushed them back into the mountains. The Syrian city-states were forced to submit, and tribute poured into Assyria once again. King Menahem of Israel paid a tribute of a thousand talents of silver for Tiglath-pileser's confirmation of his rule over Israel (2 Kings 15:19–20). From 737 to 735 Tiglath-pileser once again pursued the Urartians in the north. But in 734 he turned toward Babylon and the west—with painful results for both Babylon and Israel.

In Babylon, Mukin-zeri, chief of the Amukani tribe of the Chaldeans,[56] seized the throne in 734. Tiglath-pileser reacted first with diplomacy to undercut the usurper but after three years he moved his armies southward against Babylon. Mukin-zeri fled to the southern marshes with Assyrian troops in hot pursuit. In 729 Tiglath-pileser "took the hand of Marduk" in

54. On the relations between Assyria and Israel/Transjordan, see Benedikt Otzen, "Israel under the Assyrians: Reflections on Imperial Policy in Palestine," *Annual of the Swedish Theological Institute* 11 (1978): 96–110; Crystal M. Bennett, "Some Reflections on Neo-Assyrian Influence in Transjordan," in *Archaeology in the Levant: Essays for Kathleen Kenyon*, ed. Peter R. S. Moorey and Peter Parr (Warminster: Aris & Phillips, 1978), 164–71; Ronny Reich and Baruch Brandl, "Gezer under Assyrian Rule," *Palestine Exploration Quarterly* 117 (1985): 41–54; Paul R. Gilchrist, "Israel's Apostasy: Catalyst of Assyrian World Conquest," in *Israel's Apostasy and Restoration: Essays in Honor of Roland K. Harrison*, ed. Avraham Gileadi (Grand Rapids: Baker, 1988), 99–113 (esp. 105–11). For archeological evidence for Assyrian presence in Palestine, see J. B. Bloom, *Material Remains of the Neo-Assyrian Presence in Palestine and Transjordan* (Ph.D. diss., Bryn Mawr College, 1988).

55. For an evaluation of the career of Tiglath-pileser III, see Hallo, "From Qarqar to Carchemish," 169–74; Saggs, *Might That Was Assyria*, 85–92; Mordechai Cogan, "Tyre and Tiglath-pileser III," *Journal of Cuneiform Studies* 25 (1973): 96–99; Edwin M. Yamauchi, "Tiglath-pileser," in *The New International Dictionary of Biblical Archaeology*, ed. Edward M. Blaiklock and Roland K. Harrison (Grand Rapids: Zondervan, 1983), 451–53; Rykle Borger and Hayim Tadmor, "Zwei Beiträge zur alttestamentlichen Wissenschaft aufgrund der Inschriften Tiglathpilesers III.," *Zeitschrift für die Alttestamentliche Wissenschaft* 94 (1982): 244–51; Bustenay Oded, "Observations on Methods of Assyrian Rule in Transjordania after the Palestinian Campaign of Tiglath-pileser III," *Journal of Near Eastern Studies* 29 (1970): 177–86.

56. For the distinction between Chaldeans and Arameans, see John A. Brinkman, "Notes on Arameans and Chaldeans in Southern Babylonia in the Early Seventh Century B.C.," *Orientalia* 46 (1977): 304–25; idem, "Merodach-baladan II," in *Studies Presented to A. L. Oppenheim*, ed. Robert D. Biggs and John A. Brinkman (Chicago: Oriental Institute, 1964), 6–53; and idem, *Post-Kassite Babylonia*, 260–88.

the New Year's festival and became officially the king of Babylon under the name Pulu.[57]

In the west Tiglath-pileser encountered anti-Assyrian coalitions that had arisen after his departure in 738.[58] In 734 he subjugated Philistia as far as the "brook of Egypt," probably a reference to Wadi Besor.[59] Rebel kings were replaced in favor of pro-Assyrian puppets. Gaza became the border post at the western edge of the Assyrian Empire. In his campaigns of 733 and 732, Tiglath-pileser captured Damascus, removed Rezin, and incorporated the city into the Assyrian provincial system. Pro-Assyrian elements removed King Pekah in Samaria and installed the more pliable Hoshea.[60] A fragmentary annal expresses the situation in these words:

> Israel . . . all its inhabitants (and) their possessions I led to Assyria. They overthrew their king Pekah and I placed Hoshea as king over them. I received from them 10 talents of gold, 1,000(?) talents of silver as their tribute and brought them to Assyria.[61]

Second Kings 15:29 explains:

> In the days of Pekah king of Israel, Tiglath-pileser king of Assyria came and captured Ijon, Abel-beth-maacah, Janoah, Kedesh, Hazor, Gilead, and Galilee, all the land of Naphtali; and he carried the people captive to Assyria.

Galilee was made into an Assyrian province. The northern Israelite kingdom now consisted only of Samaria. Ammon, Moab, Edom, and Arabian tribes paid tribute,[62] while Judah was spared. King Ahaz (742–727) had refused to join the coalition of Rezin of Damascus and Pekah of Israel, and he now offered tribute to Tiglath-pileser for protection against Rezin's and Pekah's threats to remove him from Jerusalem's throne in favor of the mysterious "son of Tabeel" (Isa. 7:4–6).

Tiglath-pileser III was followed on Assyria's throne by his son Shalmaneser V (726–722). Second Kings 17:3–6 records this king's three-year

57. See "Pul king of Assyria" in 2 Kings 15:19 and 1 Chron. 5:26 (where he is called by both his Assyrian and Babylonian throne-names).

58. On Assyrian relations with Phoenicia, see Guy Bunnens, "Considerations Géographiques sur la Place Occupée par la Phénicie dans l'Expansion de l'Empire Assyrien," and Guy Kestemont, "Tyr et les Assyriens," both in *Studia Phoenicia*, ed. E. Gubel, Édouard Lipiński, and B. Servais-Soyez (Louvain: Peeters, 1983), 53–78, 169–93.

59. Nadav Naʾaman, "The Brook of Egypt and Assyrian Policy on the Border of Egypt," *Tel Aviv* 6 (1979): 68–90.

60. 2 Kings 15:29–30. See Borger and Tadmor, "Zwei Beiträge."

61. *ANET* 284. See 2 Kings 17:1–6 for the biblical account of Hoshea's career.

62. Oded, "Methods of Assyrian Rule in Transjordania."

siege and conquest of Samaria, which ended the northern Israelite king-dom.[63] Unfortunately Shalmaneser's reign is poorly documented, so we are not clearly informed of his activities in the west. Nor can we be certain of the circumstances of his death or why he was succeeded by someone other than his son. An uprising in Ashur caused by his attempt to impose forced labor there may have led to his downfall.[64] At any rate, the later copy of the Assyrian King List ends with the reign of Shalmaneser V without explaining the succession of Sargon II to the throne.

The career of Sargon II (721–705) is well documented.[65] He claimed to have captured Samaria in his first year and removed over 27,000 captives, after which he rebuilt the city better than it was before, imported a new population, and reorganized its government under an Assyrian governor.[66] He reinstated its tribute and moved on to deal with the rebellious king of Gaza. But Sargon had grave problems closer to home in Babylon. Merodach-bal-adan of the Yakin tribe of the Chaldeans allied himself with King Humbani-gash of Elam and then reasserted his kingship over Babylon.[67] Sargon turned

63. For a new interpretation of the involvement of Shalmaneser V and Sargon II in the collapse of Samaria, see John H. Hayes and Jeffrey K. Kuan, "The Final Years of Samaria (730–720 BC)," *Biblica* 72 (1991): 153–81.

64. See Saggs, *Might That Was Assyria*, 92.

65. For the reign of Sargon II of Assyria, see the following volumes in the series State Archives of Assyria (nos. 1, 4, 5, 8; Helsinki: Helsinki University Press): Simo Parpola, *The Correspondence of Sargon II*, part 1: *Letters from Assyria and the West* (1987); Ivan Starr, *Queries to the Sungod: Divination and Politics in Sargonid Assyria* (1990); G. B. Lanfranchi and Simo Parpola, *The Correspondence of Sargon II*, part 2: *Letters from the Northern and Northeastern Provinces* (1991); Hermann Hunger, *Astrological Reports to Assyrian Kings* (1992). See also Cyril J. Gadd, "Inscribed Prisms of Sargon II from Nimrud," *Iraq* 16 (1954): 173–201; Hayim Tadmor, "The Campaigns of Sargon II of Assur: A Chronological-Historical Study, *Journal of Cuneiform Studies* 12 (1958): 22–40, 77–100; Michael Ford, "The Contradictory Records of Sargon II of Assyria and the Meaning of *Palû*," *Journal of Cuneiform Studies* 22 (1968–69): 83–84; Daniel D. Luckenbill, *Ancient Records of Assyria and Babylonia* (Chicago: University of Chicago Press, 1927), vol. 2: §§1–230; Saggs, *Might That Was Assyria*, 92–98; A. Leo Oppenheim, "The City of Assur in 714 B.C.," *Journal of Near Eastern Studies* 19 (1960): 133–47; Nadav Naʾaman and Ran Zadok, "Sargon II's Deportations to Israel and Philistia (716–708 B.C.)," *Journal of Cuneiform Studies* 40 (1988): 36–46; Edwin M. Yamauchi, *The Stones and the Scriptures* (Grand Rapids: Baker, 1981), 75; Nadav Naʾaman, "The Historical Background to the Conquest of Samaria (720 BC)," *Biblica* 71 (1990): 206–25. See also Louis D. Levine, "Geographical Studies in the Neo-Assyrian Zagros," *Iran* 11 (1973): 1–27; 12 (1974): 99–124; idem, *Geographical Studies in the Neo-Assyrian Zagros* (Toronto: Royal Ontario Museum, 1974).

66. *ANET* 285.

67. Brinkman, "Merodach-baladan II"; Marvin A. Powell, "Merodach-baladan at Dur-Jakin: A Note on the Defense of Babylonian Cities," *Journal of Cuneiform Studies* 34 (1982): 59–61; R. J. van der Spek, "The Struggle of King Sargon II of Assyria against the Chaldean Merodach-baladan (710–707 BC)," *Jaarbericht . . . ex Oriente Lux* 25 (1978): 56–66. On the involvement of the Elamites in Mesopotamian affairs, see John A. Brinkman, "Elamite Military Aid to Merodach-baladan," *Journal of Near Eastern Studies* 24 (1965): 161–66; A. Kirk Gray-

his troops southward in 720, but was blocked at Der (Badrah) by the Elamite army, which he claimed to have defeated; however, he took no further action against Merodach-baladan for about ten years. Once again rebellion led by Hamath and Arpad was hatched in the west, in which Samaria joined. Sargon had no trouble ending this rebellion and reasserting his control over the west in 720. He returned for a show of strength in 717–716.[68] The north was another matter, however. Urartu remained a rival to Assyrian trade in the northern markets. In 714 Sargon made a major campaign against Urartu, defeated them, and brought back hoards of booty.[69] He also negotiated a pact of friendship with the legendary King Midas of Mushki (the Phrygians) for trade relations.

In 712 Sargon had to focus his attention on the west to deal with an anti-Assyrian rebellion in Ashdod. According to the Eponym Chronicle, Sargon stayed at home but sent his army, which quickly crushed the rebellion and annexed the territory (Isa. 20).[70] As an annalistic entry states, "I reorganized (the administration of) these cities [Ashdod, Gath, and Asdudimmu] and placed an officer of mine as governor over them and declared them Assyrian citizens and they bore my yoke."[71]

In 710 Sargon again focused his military actions on the Babylonians. After forcing Merodach-baladan back to the marshes, Sargon became Babylon's king (709). Trapped in his city, Dur-Yakin, Merodach-baladan paid a heavy tribute (707) and Sargon withdrew. Sargon then had to return to the northern mountains to meet a new foe, the Cimmerians (Gimirrai or Gomer in Gen. 10:2–3; 1 Chron. 1:5–6; Ezek. 38:6) who swept into Urartian territory and perhaps even into northern Assyria. Sargon died in battle and the Cimmerians moved on into Asia Minor and left the Assyrians to their empire.

Sargon's son Sennacherib (704–681) played the most prominent role in the Hebrew Bible of all Assyrian monarchs.[72] He was the first Assyrian king to

son, "Assyria's Foreign Policy in Relation to Elam in the Eighth and Seventh Centuries B.C.," *Sumer* 42 (1986): 146–48.

68. See Julian E. Reade, "Sargon's Campaigns of 720, 716, and 715 B.C.: Evidence from the Sculptures," *Journal of Near Eastern Studies* 35 (1976): 95–104.

69. See Paul E. Zimansky, "Urartian Geography and Sargon's Eighth Campaign," *Journal of Near Eastern Studies* 49 (1990): 1–21.

70. See Hallo, "From Qarqar to Carchemish," 158 n. 16, for bibliographical details relating to the Eponym Chronicle. See also Edwin R. Thiele, *The Mysterious Numbers of the Hebrew Kings*, 3d ed. (Grand Rapids: Zondervan, 1983), 67–78, 221–26.

71. *ANET* 286.

72. For a summary of Sennacherib's reign, see Daniel D. Luckenbill, *The Annals of Sennacherib*, Oriental Institute Publication 2 (Chicago: University of Chicago Press, 1924); Alexander Heidel, "The Octagonal Prism of Sennacherib in the Iraq Museum," *Sumer* 9 (1953): 117–88; Saggs, *Might That Was Assyria*, 98–105. See especially the judgment of Hallo about the later

attack Judah and lay siege to Jerusalem (2 Kings 18–20; 2 Chron. 29–32; and Isa. 36–39).[73] When the news of Sargon's death circulated, rebellion broke out in the west and in Babylonia. The intrigues of Egypt and Merodach-baladan no doubt contributed to the agitation. The western rebels included the kings of Sidon, Ashkelon, and Ekron, plus Hezekiah of Judah. In his third campaign (701) Sennacherib defeated the coastal rebels augmented by an Egyptian force under Taharqa.[74] After his resounding victory at Eltekeh, Sennacherib turned against Judah. He claimed to have besieged forty-six walled Judean cities plus innumerable unwalled villages and counted 200,150 people as booty.[75] Next he besieged Jerusalem and penned

---

Sargonids from Sennacherib onward that "the real spirit of the time is revealed, on the one hand, by such marvels of civil engineering as Sennacherib's aqueduct at Jerwan and, on the other, by the greatly increased attention to administrative matters reflected in the growing amount of royal correspondence"; Hallo and Simpson, *Ancient Near East*, 141.

73. Whether Sennacherib waged two campaigns against Judah or one has been debated for years, so that a vast literature exists concerning Sennacherib's career. For recent statements, see Christopher T. Begg, "Sennacherib's Second Palestinian Campaign: An Additional Indication," *Journal of Biblical Literature* 106 (1987): 685–86; and William H. Shea, "Sennacherib's Second Palestinian Campaign," *Journal of Biblical Literature* 104 (1985): 401–18. See also Brevard S. Childs, *Isaiah and the Assyrian Crisis*, Studies in Biblical Theology 2/3 (London: SCM/Naperville: Allenson, 1967); Alan R. Millard, "Sennacherib's Attack on Jerusalem," *Tyndale Bulletin* 36 (1985): 61–77; F. Gonçalves, *L'Expédition de Sennachérib en Palestine dans la Littérature Hébraïque Ancienne* (Louvain-la-neuve: Université Catholique de Louvain, 1986); and Paul E. Dion, "Sennacherib's Expedition to Palestine," *Église et Théologie* 20 (1989): 5–26. See most recently the article of Frank J. Yurco against the two-campaign view, "The Shabaka-Shebitku Coregency and the Supposed Second Campaign of Sennacherib against Judah: A Critical Assessment," *Journal of Biblical Literature* 110 (1991): 35–45.

74. For additional data on Sennacherib's third campaign, see Nadav Naʾaman, "Sennacherib's 'Letter to God' on His Campaign to Judah," *Bulletin of the American Schools of Oriental Research* 214 (1974): 25–39; idem, "Sennacherib's Campaign to Judah and the Date of the *lmlk* Stamps," *Vetus Testamentum* 29 (1979): 61–86. On the archeological evidence from biblical Lachish as it relates to Sennacherib's third campaign, see David Ussishkin, "The 'Lachish Reliefs' and the City of Lachish," *Israel Exploration Journal* 30 (1980): 174–95; idem, "Defensive Judean Counter-Ramp Found at Lachish in 1983 Season," *Biblical Archaeology Review* 10.2 (1984): 66–73; idem, "Restoring the Great Gate at Lachish," *Biblical Archaeology Review* 14.2 (1988): 42–47; William H. Shea, "Sennacherib's Description of Lachish and of Its Conquests," *Andrews University Seminary Studies* 26 (1988): 171–80; Hershel Shanks, "Destruction of Judean Fortress Portrayed in Dramatic 8th-Century BC Pictures," *Biblical Archaeology Review* 10.2 (1984): 48–65. See Miller and Hayes, *History of Ancient Israel and Judah*, 353–58, for a description of Hezekiah's preparations for war.

75. See Arthur Ungnad, "Die Zahl der von Sanherib deportierten Judaer," *Zeitschrift für die Alttestamentliche Wissenschaft* 18 (1942–43): 199–202, who makes a case for changing the number of those deported from 200,150 to 2,150 by claiming a scribal error. For support of the larger number, see Alan R. Millard, "Large Numbers in the Assyrian Royal Inscriptions," in *Ah, Assyria . . . : Studies in Assyrian History and Ancient Near Eastern Historiography Presented to Hayim Tadmor*, ed. Mordechai Cogan and Israel Ephʿal; Scripta Hierosolymitana 33 (Jerusalem: Magnes, 1991), 213–22; and Bustenay Oded, *Mass Deportation and Deportees in the Neo-Assyrian Empire* (Wiesbaden: Reichert, 1979).

up Hezekiah in Jerusalem "like a bird in a cage," to use Sennacherib's own words.[76] Hezekiah, now standing alone, decided to surrender and pay the tribute levied by Sennacherib as well as an annual payment. Whether Sennacherib followed up these victories with a foray into Egypt as Herodotus and Berossus recount remains undocumented from Assyrian records.[77] As one would expect, the Bible's statement that the major part of the Assyrian army was killed by the angel of death (2 Kings 19:35; 2 Chron. 32:21; Isa. 37:36) also remains undocumented in Assyrian records. Speculation of a plague based on the reports of Herodotus and Berossus is tenuous at best.

Sennacherib's problems were more serious in Babylon.[78] Merodach-baladan again proclaimed himself king of Babylon and united the local population against Assyrian hegemony. Sennacherib responded with force and in 703 defeated the Chaldeans, plundered the palace, took numerous prisoners, and appointed his factotum Bel-ibni as king of Babylon. Merodach-baladan retreated to the marshes only to reappear three years later stirring up sedition. In 700 Bel-ibni was replaced by Sennacherib's son Ashur-nadin-shumi, who maintained control for six years. Merodach-baladan offered no military resistance but took refuge with the Elamites, and there is no further record of him. Sennacherib was compelled to mount campaigns against the troublesome Elamites when Ashur-nadin-shumi was murdered in 694. Babylon paid the price for its rebellion and for killing Sennacherib's son when Sennacherib attacked and pillaged the city in 690–689. However, Sennacherib's harsh treatment of Babylon may have boomeranged by leading indirectly to his death in early 681.[79]

Sennacherib's end is told in 2 Kings 19:37, Isaiah 37:38, and Tobit 1:21. Two of his sons murdered him, but a younger son, Esarhaddon (Assyrian Aššur-aḫa-iddina), returned from the northern provinces with his troops and forced the conspirators to flee. He then seized the throne and consolidated his power. Esarhaddon's account of the events leading to his accession strangely fails to explain what happened to his father. Josephus (*Antiquities* 10:1:5 §§21–23) quotes Berossus to the effect that the two elder brothers were driven away by the citizens of Nineveh and fled into Armenia. Assyrian records do not tell the whole story, but one annal of Ashurbanipal recounts the following action after he had defeated some of his enemies:

76. *ANET* 288.

77. Herodotus 2:141; and Berossus in Josephus, *Antiquities* 10:1:4–5 §§20–23.

78. Louis D. Levine, "Sennacherib's Southern Front: 704–689 B.C.," *Journal of Cuneiform Studies* 34 (1982): 28–58; and John A. Brinkman, "Sennacherib's Babylonian Problem: An Interpretation," *Journal of Cuneiform Studies* 25 (1973): 89–95.

79. For additional evidence about the difficulties surrounding royal succession in the last days of Sennacherib, see Simo Parpola, "Neo-Assyrian Treaties from the Royal Archives of Nineveh," *Journal of Cuneiform Studies* 39 (1987): 161–89.

The others, I smashed alive with the very same statues of protective deities with which they had smashed my own grandfather Sennacherib—now (finally) as a (belated) burial sacrifice for his soul. I fed their corpses, cut into small pieces, to dogs, pigs, *zîbu*-birds, vultures, the birds of the sky, and (also) to the fish of the ocean.[80]

One Babylonian chronicle records that a son murdered Sennacherib in a failed coup.[81] Without doubt, the tradition in 2 Kings, Isaiah, and Tobit attributed Sennacherib's tragic end to the arrogant sacrilege of his attack on Jerusalem. Babylonian writers might have blamed Sennacherib's tragic end on his brutal sacrilege against their "holy city."

Esarhaddon's reign (680–669) began with civil war, which he quickly controlled.[82] Soon afterward, he obeyed an oracle to rebuild the devastated Babylon.[83] He thus struck the pose of a god-fearing peacemaker. The *Pax Assyriaca* remained intact during Esarhaddon's reign, as he managed to protect his northern flank against Scythian and Cimmerian (biblical Ashkenaz and Gomer) invasion and the ever-present Urartian danger. Elam was pacified as well, and the Medes, east of the Zagros, were not yet ready to menace the Assyrian homeland. But his control over the empire was stretched beyond effectiveness when Esarhaddon invaded Egypt in 675. After initial setbacks he finally (671) moved his army across the desert from Palestine into Egypt and defeated Pharaoh Taharqa at Memphis. In 669 he had to undertake another

---

80. *ANET* 288.

81. Basing his judgment on Harper letter 1091, Simo Parpola makes a case that the culprit was Arad-Ninlil, a son of Sennacherib; see "The Murderer of Sennacherib," in *Death in Mesopotamia: Papers Read at the XXVIᵉ Rencontre Assyriologique Internationale*, ed. Bendt Alster, Mesopotamia 8 (Copenhagen: Akademisk Forlag, 1980), 171–82. See also Emil G. Kraeling, "The Death of Sennacherib," *Journal of the American Oriental Society* 53 (1933): 335–46; Hallo, "From Qarqar to Carchemish," 185 n. 149. For the chronicle, see A. Kirk Grayson, *Assyrian and Babylonian Chronicles* (Locust Valley, N.Y.: Augustin, 1975), 81.

82. On Esarhaddon's career, see Anthony J. Spalinger, "Esarhaddon and Egypt: An Analysis of the First Invasion of Egypt," *Orientalia* 43 (1974): 295–326; Saggs, *Might That Was Assyria*, 104–8; Mordechai Cogan, "New Additions to the Corpus of Esarhaddon Historical Inscriptions," *Archiv für Orientforschung* 31 (1984): 72–75; Bustenay Oded, "Relations between the City-States of Phoenicia and Assyria in the Reigns of Esarhaddon and Ashurbanipal," in *Studies in the History of the Jewish People*, ed. Bustenay Oded (Haifa: University of Haifa Press, 1974), 31–42; Simo Parpola, *Letters from Assyrian Scholars to the Kings Esarhaddon and Assurbanipal*, 2 vols., Alter Orient und Altes Testament 5 (Neukirchen-Vluyn: Neukirchener Verlag/Kevelaer: Butzon & Bercker, 1970–83).

83. See John A. Brinkman, "Through a Glass Darkly: Esarhaddon's Retrospects on the Downfall of Babylon," *Journal of the American Oriental Society* 103 (1983): 35–42. On Esarhaddon's later plans to return Marduk's statue to Babylon, see Wilfred G. Lambert, "Esarhaddon's Attempt to Return Marduk to Babylon," in *Ad Bene et Fideliter Seminandum: Festgabe für Karlheinz Deller*, ed. Gerlinde Mauer and Ursula Magen, Alter Orient und Altes Testament 220 (Neukirchen-Vluyn: Neukirchener Verlag/Kevelaer: Butzon & Bercker, 1988), 157–74.

campaign against a rebellious Egypt. According to the Babylonian Chronicle, Esarhaddon died en route to Egypt.[84]

Esarhaddon appears but seldom and insignificantly in the Bible. He is mentioned as Sennacherib's successor in 2 Kings 19:37, Isaiah 37:38, and Tobit 1:21. He was remembered as the settler of foreigners in Palestine in Ezra 4:2 and 1 Esdras 5:69. Tobit (1:22) claims that Esarhaddon made Tobit's nephew Ahikar cupbearer and keeper of the signet, as also stated in the fifth-century Aramaic text from Elephantine, "The Words of Ahiqar."[85] King Manasseh of Judah is listed among the twenty-two kings of Hatti who had been summoned by Esarhaddon to bring timber and stone to Nineveh.[86] This occasion seems to lie behind the account in 2 Chronicles 33:10–13 of Manasseh's imprisonment, repentance, and prayer of contrition before the Lord (compare the "Prayer of Manasseh").

Assyria's Decline and Fall

In 672 Esarhaddon made extensive preparations for an orderly transition in government after his death. He designated one son, Ashurbanipal, king of Assyria and another son, Shamash-shum-ukin, king of Babylon. In a formal ceremony he forced Shamash-shum-ukin, the army, and Assyrian vassals to swear loyalty to Ashurbanipal.[87] On Esarhaddon's death, the plan was activated and worked until 652, when Shamash-shum-ukin led Babylon in revolt against his brother.[88] After a four-year war, Ashurbanipal won; but Assyria had been dealt a blow from which it did not recover. After 648 the order of *līmu* eponyms remains uncertain and historical records from Assyria give only disconnected views of the last years of Ashurbanipal and the Assyrian Empire. The government was in disarray.

The course of Ashurbanipal's kingdom before the Babylonian revolt is rel-

---

84. *ANET* 303.
85. *ANET* 428.
86. *ANET* 291.
87. For the oaths taken, see *ANET* 534–41. For other treaties associated with Esarhaddon and his successors, see A. Kirk Grayson, "Akkadian Treaties of the Seventh Century B.C.," *Journal of Cuneiform Studies* 39 (1987): 127–60; and Parpola, "Neo-Assyrian Treaties." For a bibliography of the inscriptions of the Assyrian era from Ashurbanipal onward, see Hallo, "From Qarqar to Carchemish," 186; Roux, *Ancient Iraq*, 329–36; Mordechai Cogan and Hayim Tadmor, "Gyges and Ashurbanipal: A Study in Literary Transmission," *Orientalia* 46 (1977): 65–85; and Anthony J. Spalinger, "Assurbanipal and Egypt: A Source Study," *Journal of the American Oriental Society* 94 (1974): 316–28.
88. For a summary of the intrigue between Ashurbanipal and Shamash-shum-ukin, see Richard C. Steiner and Charles F. Nims, "Ashurbanipal and Shamash-shum-ukin: A Tale of Two Brothers from the Aramaic Text in Demotic Script, part 1," *Revue Biblique* 92 (1985): 60–81.

Ashurbanipal and his queen dine, while entertained by musicians (the decapitated head of an Elamite rebel hangs on a tree at left), 668–627 B.C. (height: 5′ 6″)

Courtesy of the British Museum

atively clear, however. By 667 he had to deal with an uprising in Egypt led by Taharqa and Tanuatamun, which resulted in the sack of Thebes immortalized by Nahum 3:8–10.[89] In 664 Egypt came under the rule of Psammetichus I, who several years later began to draw Egypt away from Assyria so that by 650 Egypt finally expelled the Assyrians. Ashurbanipal was forced to relinquish Egypt to save southern Mesopotamia since Elam was in full revolt again. He quickly devastated and resubjugated Babylonia and Elam.

In 665 Tyre and Arvad led a rebellion in Hatti, which was put down by Ashurbanipal's troops. During the decade following these western revolts, he had to contend with problems involving the Lydians, Cimmerians, and Mannai, plus another uprising among the Elamites. Ashurbanipal had quieted the northwestern front rather well before the outbreak of the Babylonian revolt led by his brother.

After Shamash-shum-ukin's rebellion, Ashurbanipal spent two campaigns marching through Elam and looting the region, including its capital, Susa.[90] The brutal Assyrian treatment of the Elamite royal family and kingdom proved unwise, since the Assyrians lost Elam as a buffer in southwestern Iran, a buffer they badly needed against the Medes and Persians in the era following Ashurbanipal's death.

89. For an attempt to unravel the Egyptian campaigns of Ashurbanipal, see Spalinger, "Assurbanipal and Egypt."

90. On the sack of Susa, see Edwin M. Yamauchi, *Persia and the Bible* (Grand Rapids: Baker, 1990), 291–92.

Ashurbanipal's greatest legacy was his palace library, which is now housed in the British Museum as the Kouyunjik collection.[91] It remains one of the most notable collections of cuneiform documents ever excavated.

Ashurbanipal is mentioned only once in the Bible as "the great and noble Osnappar" (NRSV) who had settled foreigners, perhaps Elamites, in Samaria (Ezra 4:10).[92] He had to battle revolts in Egypt and Palestine on several occasions, which the biblical writers chose not to mention. He seems not to have attacked Jerusalem, which suggests that the house of David remained cooperative through the era. The last recorded Assyrian foray into Judah occurred in 643.[93] Apparently Judah was able to ignore its vassal status to Assyria beginning about 640 and somehow kept its sovereignty.

Ashurbanipal died in 627 and was followed by his son Ashur-etil-ilani, whose rule overlapped that of his father for several years.[94] Ashur-etil-ilani appears not to have lasted long after his father's death and was succeeded by his brother Sin-shar-ishkun who ruled until about 612. But Assyria's future was very much in doubt, since an aggressive Chaldean, Nabopolassar (625–605), had come to the throne of Babylon and created a coalition that was to bring the once invincible Assyrian kingdom to destruction.[95] They dismantled Assyria city by city beginning in 616 until finally Nineveh capitulated in 612 after a three-month siege.[96] Sin-shar-ishkun died in the city's ruins. The remnants of the Assyrian army fled to Haran, crowned Ashur-uballit II king, and prepared to make a final stand. The Assyrian army was crushed at Haran in 609. The Assyrian Empire ended in the west outside its own homeland.[97]

91. Mordechai Cogan and Hayim Tadmor, "Ashurbanipal Texts in the Collection of the Oriental Institute, University of Chicago," *Journal of Cuneiform Studies* 40 (1988): 84–96; Simo Parpola, "Assyrian Library Records," *Journal of Near Eastern Studies* 42 (1983): 1–29.

92. On the representation of the name Ashurbanipal and other Assyrian names in the Hebrew Bible, see Alan R. Millard, "Assyrian Royal Names in Biblical Hebrew," *Journal of Semitic Studies* 21 (1976): 1–14.

93. See Morton [= Mordechai] Cogan, *Imperialism and Religion: Assyria, Judah and Israel in the Eighth and Seventh Centuries B.C.E.* (Missoula, Mont.: Scholars Press, 1974), 70 and n. 31.

94. For a reconstruction of this era, see Saggs, *Might That Was Assyria*, 117–21; and Julian E. Reade, "The Accession of Sinsharishkun," *Journal of Cuneiform Studies* 23 (1970): 1–9.

95. Stefan Zawadzki, "The First Year of Nabopolassar's Rule according to the Babylonian Chronicle BM 25127: A Reinterpretation of the Text and Its Consequences," *Journal of Cuneiform Studies* 41 (1989): 57–64.

96. On the Median role in the fall of Nineveh, see C. Nylander, "Earless in Nineveh: Who Mutilated 'Sargon's' Head?" *American Journal of Archaeology* 84 (1980): 329–33.

97. On later memories of Assyria, see R. Drews, "Assyria in Classical Universal Histories," *Historia* 14 (1965): 129–42.

Religion and Culture

When analyzing three thousand years of Mesopotamian culture, it becomes difficult to distinguish between what is Sumerian, what is Babylonian, and what is Assyrian. Over the centuries extensive cultural interchange occurred. The Old Assyrian texts of the twentieth/nineteenth centuries show how much similarity existed between early Assyrian and southern Mesopotamian institutions. Yet, many elements of the distinctive Assyrian culture were already in use:

1. Years were designated by *līmu* eponyms.
2. Ashur, Adad, Sin, Shamash, and Ishtar were the chief deities of the Assyrian pantheon, although the Sumerian Anu, Enlil, Ea, and Nabu were honored as well.
3. The *akītu* (New Year's) festival was observed as early as the reign of Shamshi-Adad I.[98]
4. The title *rab-šākēh* ("chief cupbearer"), well known from its appearance in Neo-Assyrian times in the Bible (2 Kings 18–19; Isa. 36–37; Sir. 48:18), was in use.[99]
5. Assyrian merchants were exploring distant lands while engaged in an early form of capitalism for economic advantage; even the *waklum* had commercial interests in the international trade.

The archeological remains of the Old Assyrian trading colony in central Anatolia testify to the adaptability of Assyrian culture: the Assyrians lived side by side with "natives," intermarried with them, and adopted much of their frontier lifestyle.[100]

In the mind of the Assyrians the later imperial religion was closely bound to their corporate and private welfare. The decisive action of Ashur and the gods caused their success; so "serving" the gods was crucial for king and peasant. The religion of the empire may be reconstructed from the excavation reports of the temples of Ashur and other deities, plus various religious texts.[101]

---

98. See Govert van Driel, *The Cult of Aššur* (Assen: Van Gorcum, 1969), 163.

99. See text 40 in William C. Gwaltney Jr., *The Pennsylvania Old Assyrian Texts*, Hebrew Union College Annual Supplement 3 (Cincinnati: Hebrew Union College–Jewish Institute of Religion, 1983), 96–98.

100. See the excavation reports of the mercantile center of Kanish published by Tahsin Özgüç: *Türk Tarih Kurumu Tarafindan Yapilan Kültepe Kazisi Raporu, 1948*; *Türk Tarih Kurumu Tarafindan Yapilan Kültepe Kazisi Raporu, 1949* (with Nimet Özgüç); and *Kültepe-Kaniš* (Ankara: Türk Tarih Kurumu, 1950, 1953, 1959).

101. See especially Édouard Dhorme and René Dussaud, *Les Religions de Babylone et d'Assyrie* (Paris: Presses Universitaires de France, 1949); van Driel, *Cult of Aššur*; Helmer Ringgren,

The king himself was the leading actor in the cult of Ashur during the "high holy days" of their religious calendar in the last two months of the year and the first month of the new year—including a key role in the *akītu* festival. Unfortunately the preserved texts provide only partial descriptions of the rites and the king's role. One text suggests that a piece of the king's clothing could substitute for him in his absence.[102] Assyrian kings from Ashur-uballit I on were called "high priest" (Sumerian SANGA = Akkadian *šangû*). Ashur's temple personnel were headed by a "great high priest" (*šangû rabû*) and a "second priest" (*šangû šanû*).

Other cult personnel conducted dozens of ceremonies following a strict religious calendar. These rites included feeding the gods twice a day, bathing and dressing them, carrying them in processionals, performing music to accompany various ceremonies, reading omens, and conducting incantations to ward off evil. Some temple personnel had administrative duties involving construction and maintenance of buildings and allocation of physical and human resources. From earliest times temples became repositories of wealth as individuals and families made donations of precious metals, precious stones, and slaves.

Religion affected Assyrian provincial administration. The Neo-Assyrian government treated foreign territories in two ways: as vassal states and as annexed Assyrian provinces. They required loyalty oaths (*adû*) of all their subjects, in which Ashur and the "great gods" were invoked as guarantors. When subjects swore the oath, they were submitting to Ashur as lord (local gods might be invoked also). In annexed territories, the Assyrian pantheon became supreme. In vassal states, local gods continued to be worshiped but a representative of the vassal had to appear at the Assyrian court periodically to pay annual tribute and special "gifts." Thus they acknowledged Ashur as the most powerful of gods.

The Assyrians treated the gods of conquered people in different ways. They might destroy them for the metal and gems; they might lead them away in a solemn procession to Assyria, where they could dedicate them to Ashur or another of the major gods; or they might deposit them in a provincial capital on the Assyrian frontier. The statue of Marduk of Babylon was honored in ceremonies in which the Assyrian king himself participated. Esarhaddon treated with respect the gods his father had removed from Babylon by keep-

---

Religions of the Ancient Near East, trans. John Sturdy (Philadelphia: Westminster/London: SPCK, 1973); Cogan, *Imperialism and Religion*; Harry W. F. Saggs, *Everyday Life in Babylonia and Assyria* (New York: Dorset, 1965), chap. 9; and Thorkild Jacobsen, *The Treasures of Darkness: A History of Mesopotamian Religion* (New Haven: Yale University Press, 1976).

102. See van Driel, *Cult of Aššur*, 171.

ing them in temporary shrines while their Babylonian temples were under-going renovation. He also invoked the gods Bethel, Anath-Bethel, and Baal-zephon in a treaty with the vassal king of Tyre.[103] When Merodach-baladan fled Babylon before Sennacherib's attack, he took the statues of the gods with him to the Sealand. Sometimes the gods were allowed to remain behind in an allied vassal state. The Assyrians thought such deities had acknowledged Ashur's supremacy. Removal of the gods of a city did not close down the cult of those gods, however; new images could be created and dedicated to re-place those carried away.

The Assyrians, like their Babylonian neighbors, lived in a world inhabited and controlled by gods, demons, spirits, and ghosts of the dead. Some of these were benevolent while some were bent on destroying humans. We can only imagine the level of fear felt generally in Mesopotamia during the first millennium, but one mythological composition from about 1000 opens a small window on their collective soul: the "Erra Epic."[104] Erra, the god of slaughter, becomes enraged against the land, convinces Marduk to abandon the world into Erra's control, and then turns the world topsy-turvy through war. Erra is eventually pacified and a remnant of humanity is spared. One clay copy of this myth has a pierced handle so that it could be hung on the wall of a building. To recite the myth, or just to have a copy present, would counter the destructive forces found in the world. Omen divination, exor-cism, incantation, and astrology became an indispensable part of private and governmental life to discover and control the plans of these superhuman forces. No significant undertaking could be launched without the gods' ap-proval. Thus religion served the needs of the state as well as the needs of cit-izens.

Thorkild Jacobsen finds disturbing qualities in the *Zeitgeist* of the first mil-lennium, that is, a growing fear and brutality, a preoccupation with death, and a "blunting of sensibilities."[105] But he also finds a childlike trust and even tenderness in the prayers of the later rulers of the Assyrian Empire. This strange coupling of tenderness and savagery is disturbing to modern sensitiv-ities. Throughout Mesopotamian history, however, one senses a pervasive pessimism that the gods' decisions were arbitrary and amoral. Humans had no destiny beyond an afterlife in dust and gloom. The Assyrians learned from their gods that military power outweighed moral force. Even their laws were

---

103. Saggs, *Everyday Life in Babylonia and Assyria*, 193–94.
104. Felix Gössmann, *Das Era-Epos* (Würzburg: Augustinus, 1955); Luigi Cagni, *Das Erra-Epos*, Studia Pohl 5 (Rome: Pontifical Biblical Institute Press, 1970); idem, *The Poem of Erra*, Sources from the Ancient Near East 1/3 (Malibu, Calif.: Undena, 1977).
105. Jacobsen, *Treasures of Darkness*, 226–39.

Sennacherib at the siege of Lachish
in Judah in 701 B.C. (height of characters ranges from 7.1″ to 21.3″)
Courtesy of the British Museum

harsher. In spite of this crudity, an occasional voice bespeaking a nobler ethic
was heard, frequently in royal prayers to gods of judgment.

Assyrian art also served pragmatic ends.[106] Influenced by Babylonian and
"western" expression, their distinctive art forms began to emerge in the Middle Assyrian era. They excelled in various forms: architecture, metal crafting
(for tools, weapons, *objets d'art*, and jewelry), ceramic design, sculpture in
the round, seal cutting, furniture building with intricate inlay, and mural
painting. But the art form most associated with Assyria remains bas-relief
carving on slabs of stone that were placed on edge to panel palace corridors
and rooms. The ninth-century palace of Ashurnasirpal II at Nimrud has provided the earliest examples of this art form, which achieved its height in the
Nineveh palaces of Sennacherib and Ashurbanipal. The purpose for these realistic scenes of war and the hunt is unclear. Perhaps they were meant to in-

106. Seton Lloyd, *The Art of the Ancient Near East* (London: Thames & Hudson, 1961);
Cyril J. Gadd, *The Stones of Assyria* (London: Chatto & Windus, 1936); Richard D. Barnett and
Donald J. Wiseman, *Fifty Masterpieces of Ancient Near Eastern Art* (London: British Museum,
1969); Henri Frankfort, *The Art and Architecture of the Ancient Orient*, 4th ed. (Harmonds-
worth: Penguin, 1970); Julian E. Reade, *Assyrian Sculpture* (Cambridge: Harvard University
Press, 1983).

form the gods of their accomplishments, to glorify the king, or to strike fear in their enemies. Whatever their purpose, they provide the modern historian with information about royal Assyrian (and enemy) life, dress, and weaponry. Notable among the bas-relief war scenes is Sennacherib's siege of Lachish.[107] In secular scenes Assyrian artists gained a high degree of realism. In religious motifs they maintained an idealistic, formal expression. This artistic duality displays in the Assyrian mind a realism toward the world of physical reality and a formalism toward the transcendent world.

Recommended Reading

Beek, Martinus A. *Atlas of Mesopotamia*. London/New York: Nelson, 1962.

Cogan, Morton [= Mordechai]. *Imperialism and Religion: Assyria, Judah and Israel in the Eighth and Seventh Centuries* B.C.E. Missoula, Mont.: Scholars Press, 1974.

Contenau, Georges. *Everyday Life in Babylon and Assyria*. New York: Norton, 1966.

Driver, Godfrey R., and John C. Miles. *The Assyrian Laws*. Oxford: Clarendon, 1935.

Grayson, A. Kirk. *Assyrian and Babylonian Chronicles*. Locust Valley, N.Y.: Augustin, 1975.

———. *Assyrian Royal Inscriptions*. 2 vols. Wiesbaden: Harrassowitz, 1972–76.

———. "Mesopotamia, History of: History and Culture of Assyria." Vol. 4 / pp. 732–55 in *The Anchor Bible Dictionary*. Edited by David N. Freedman et al. New York: Doubleday, 1992.

Guild, N. *The Assyrian*. New York: Dell, 1987. [A historical novel that provides a view of Neo-Assyrian military and governmental intrigue as well as a sense of daily life.]

Hallo, William W. "From Qarqar to Carchemish: Assyria and Israel in the Light of New Discoveries." *Biblical Archaeologist* 23 (1960): 34–61. Reprinted in *The Biblical Archaeologist Reader*, vol. 2, pp. 152–88. Edited by Edward F. Campbell Jr. and David N. Freedman. Missoula, Mont.: American Schools of Oriental Research/Scholars Press, 1975.

Hallo, William W., and William K. Simpson. *The Ancient Near East: A History*. New York: Harcourt Brace Jovanovich, 1971.

Laessøe, Jørgen. *People of Ancient Assyria: Their Inscriptions and Correspondence*. Translated by F. S. Leigh-Browne. London: Routledge & Kegan Paul, 1963.

---

107. See n. 74.

Larsen, Mogens T. *The Old Assyrian City-state and Its Colonies*. Copenhagen: Akademisk Forlag, 1976.

Luckenbill, Daniel D. *Ancient Records of Assyria and Babylonia*. 2 vols. Chicago: University of Chicago Press, 1926–27.

———. *The Annals of Sennacherib*. Oriental Institute Publications 2. Chicago: University of Chicago Press, 1924.

Miller, J. Maxwell, and John H. Hayes. *A History of Ancient Israel and Judah*. Philadelphia: Westminster, 1986.

Oates, David. *Studies in the Ancient History of Northern Iraq*. London: Oxford University Press, 1968.

Oppenheim, A. Leo. *Ancient Mesopotamia: Portrait of a Dead Civilization*. Revised edition completed by Erica Reiner. Chicago: University of Chicago Press, 1977.

Ringgren, Helmer. *Religions of the Ancient Near East*. Translated by John Sturdy. Philadelphia: Westminster, 1973.

Roaf, Michael. *Cultural Atlas of Mesopotamia and the Ancient Near East*. New York: Facts on File, 1990.

Roux, Georges. *Ancient Iraq*. 3d edition. Baltimore: Penguin, 1992.

Saggs, Harry W. F. "The Assyrians." Pp. 156–78 in *Peoples of Old Testament Times*. Edited by Donald J. Wiseman. Oxford: Clarendon, 1973.

———. *Everyday Life in Babylon and Assyria*. New York: Dorset, 1987.

———. *The Might That Was Assyria*. London: Sidgwick & Jackson, 1984.

Thiele, Edwin R. *The Mysterious Numbers of the Hebrew Kings*. 3d edition. Grand Rapids: Zondervan, 1983 (esp. chap. 4).

Van Driel, Govert. *The Cult of Aššur*. Assen: Van Gorcum, 1969.

Yadin, Yigael. *The Art of Warfare in Biblical Lands in the Light of Archaeological Study*. 2 vols. New York: McGraw-Hill/London: Weidenfeld & Nicolson, 1963.

Yamauchi, Edwin M. *Foes from the Northern Frontier*. Grand Rapids: Baker, 1982.

Persians

Edwin M. Yamauchi

The LORD moved the heart of Cyrus king of Persia to make a proclamation throughout his realm . . . : "The LORD, the God of heaven, has given me all the kingdoms of the earth and he has appointed me to build a temple for him at Jerusalem in Judah."
—Ezra 1:1–2

Medes

The Medes and Persians were closely related Indo-European tribes who entered the Iranian plateau sometime after the middle of the second millennium according to the archeological evidence. They followed the route either east or west of the Caspian Sea and gradually infiltrated into the area of the northern Zagros Mountains in western Iran.

Important discoveries of early Iron Age settlements have been made at Marlik (south of the Caspian Sea) and Tepe Sialk (south of Tehran on the western edge of the vast interior desert). The widespread appearance of Iron Age III culture (800–550) in the Zagros has been associated with the rise of the Medes to power.

The capital of the Medes was Ecbatana (modern Hamadan) in the Zagros, located on the major route from Mesopotamia to the Iranian plateau. The northern frontier of the Medes was the territory of Mannea (biblical Minni; cf. Jer. 51:27), just south of Lake Urmia. Their southern border was the region of Ellipi in the southern Zagros. The eastern border is associated with a Mount Bikni, which may be Mount Elvend near Hamadan or Mount Demavand east of Tehran.

Only a few Median sites have been excavated. These sites, uncovered in the 1960s and 1970s, include Baba Jan Tepe excavated by Clare L. Goff, Godin Tepe excavated by T. Cuyler Young Jr., and Tepe Nush-i Jan excavated by David Stronach. The four structures found at the latter site include the oldest Iranian fire temple yet discovered. When the site was abandoned circa 600, it was carefully filled in with shale and mud. The excavator found some jewelry and other artifacts, which may possibly include booty taken from the Assyrians.[1]

The *Mādāia* ("Medes") are first mentioned in a text of the Assyrian king Shalmaneser III in 836. The name *Parsua* also occurs first in this monarch's reign in 844. The Medes are mentioned in the texts of every Assyrian king thereafter until the time of Ashurbanipal, sometimes being called "the mighty Medes," "the distant Medes," or "the Medes by the Salt Desert."[2]

The Assyrians were especially interested in obtaining horses from the Medes. A text of Tiglath-pileser III lists a total of at least 1,615 horses received as tribute from the Medes.[3] Tiglath-pileser III (744–727) invaded the Zagros region twice and Sargon II (721–705) six times. A stele of Sargon was found at Najafābād deep in Median territory.[4] There are eighteen references to Assyrian deportations from the area of Media.[5] What is of interest to students of the Bible is that Sargon replaced some of these deportees with newcomers from the land of Hatti, that is, Palestine (2 Kings 17:6).[6]

Sargon's texts, which list some fifty Median chieftains, indicate the highly decentralized situation of the Medes in the late eighth century, a situation indirectly corroborated by the Old Testament (Jer. 25:25; 51:11, 28 refer to Median "kings"). According to Herodotus (1:96–99) it was Deioces who united the Medes and established his capital at Ecbatana. Deioces has been dated according to the data given by Herodotus between 700 and 647.

Esarhaddon (680–669) in 672 imposed vassal treaties on Median princes, which pledged them to support his son Ashurbanipal.[7] Among the treaty tablets found at Nimrud by Max Mallowan are some of the largest cuneiform tablets discovered. The tablets were found smashed to smithereens in the throne room, no doubt by the Medes when they helped to sack Nimrud in 612.

1. Interim excavation reports by David Stronach and others may be found in the journal *Iran*: 7 (1969): 1–20; 11 (1973): 129–40; 13 (1975): 187–88; 16 (1978): 1–28.

2. Simo Parpola, *Neo-Assyrian Toponyms*, Alter Orient und Altes Testament 6 (Neukirchen-Vluyn: Neukirchener Verlag/Kevelaer: Butzon & Bercker, 1970), 130–31.

3. See Stuart C. Brown, "Media and Secondary State Formation in the Neo-Assyrian Zagros: An Anthropological Approach to an Assyrian Problem," *Journal of Cuneiform Studies* 38 (1986): 112 n. 14.

4. Louis D. Levine, "Prelude to Monarchy," in *Iranian Civilization and Culture*, ed. C. J. Adams (Montreal: McGill University Press, 1972), 42; idem, *Two Neo-Assyrian Stelae from Iran* (Toronto: Royal Ontario Museum, 1972).

5. Bustenay Oded, *Mass Deportations and Deportees in the Neo-Assyrian Empire* (Wiesbaden: Reichert, 1979), 26.

6. Daniel D. Luckenbill, *Ancient Records of Assyria and Babylonia* (Chicago: University of Chicago Press, 1927), 2:183; *ANET* 284–85.

7. Esarhaddon's brothers killed their father Sennacherib in 681 (2 Kings 19:37; Isa. 37:38).

The rise of a united Median state in the early seventh century is attested in Assyrian texts.[8] During the last years of Esarhaddon's reign, liver-omen texts refer to his concern about Kashtariti, a chief of the central Zagros who united the Medes, Manneans, and Cimmerians in an anti-Assyrian coalition. Kashtariti is identified by many scholars with the Median king whom Herodotus (1:102) named Phraortes, though this has been contested.

According to Herodotus, Phraortes died while fighting in a battle against the Assyrians. But there is no record of such a conflict in texts of Ashurbanipal (668–627) for the usual date proposed for Phraortes' death (653). A related question is the date of the twenty-eight-year domination of "Asia" by the Scythians, an invading nomadic tribe from the Russian steppes (Herodotus 1:103; 4:1).[9] Most scholars place the Scythian interregnum after Phraortes and before Cyaxares, that is, between 653 and 625.[10]

René Labat lowers the dates of Phraortes to 647–625 and subsumes the Scythian period (625–597) wholly within the reign of Cyaxares.[11] Alan R. Millard divides the Scythian interregnum into two phases: (1) twenty years dominating Asia (645–625), that is, eastern Turkey, and (2) eight years of dominance in Media during the first years of Cyaxares.[12] The Medes finally expelled the Scythians, who resettled in the Ukraine north of the Black Sea. It is possible that the threat of foes from the northern frontier mentioned by Jeremiah may refer to Scythian horsemen.[13]

Scholars agree upon the dates of Cyaxares (625–585), whose long forty-year reign saw the ascendancy of the Medes to their greatest heights (Herodotus 1:106). In alliance with the Chaldeans, he helped overthrow the Assyrians and extended the Median kingdom westward through Urartu to eastern Anatolia.[14] In 614 the Medes took the great city of Ashur. Two years later the Medes and Chaldeans launched a joint attack upon the Assyrian capital of

8. Igor M. Diakonoff, "Media," in *The Cambridge History of Iran*, vol. 2: *The Median and Achaemenian Periods*, ed. Ilya Gershevitch (Cambridge: Cambridge University Press, 1985), 110.

9. On the Scythians, see Tamara T. Rice, *The Scythians*, 3d ed. (New York: Praeger, 1961); Edwin M. Yamauchi, *Foes from the Northern Frontiers: Invading Hordes from the Russian Steppes* (Grand Rapids: Baker, 1982), chap. 4; idem, "The Scythians: Invading Hordes from the Russian Steppes," *Biblical Archaeologist* 46 (1983): 90–99; Renate Rolle, *The World of the Scythians* (Berkeley: University of California Press, 1989).

10. For the traditional chronology of Median kings derived from Herodotus see Diakonoff, "Media," 112–13.

11. René Labat, "Kaštariti, Phraorte et les Débuts de l'Histoire Mède," *Journal Asiatique* 249 (1961): 2–4.

12. Alan R. Millard, "The Scythian Problem," in *Glimpses of Ancient Egypt*, ed. J. Ruffle et al. (Warminster: Aris & Phillips, 1979), 119–22.

13. Yamauchi, *Foes from the Northern Frontiers*, chap. 5.

14. Ibid., chap. 2.

Nineveh. A remnant of the Assyrians fled to Haran, where they were over-
come in 609. During the last five years of his reign Cyaxares fought with
Alyattes of Lydia (Herodotus 1:73–74), a conflict ended by the mediation of
Labynetus (Herodotus 1:74), whom some identify with Nabonidus.

The last king of an independent Median kingdom was Astyages (585–
550). His daughter Mandana married a Persian, Cambyses I, and gave birth
to the famous Cyrus the Great. Cyrus led the Persians in a successful revolt
against his grandfather Astyages and the Medes in 550.[15] Thereafter the
Medes were to play a subordinate though an important role under the Persians in the Achemenid period (550 to 330).

Persians

Cyrus II (559–530)

The kings of the Persian Empire were known as Achemenians after an eponymous ancestor, Achemenes (ca. 700). Achaemenes' grandson was Cyrus I
(640–600?), who had a son serve as a hostage at Ashurbanipal's court in
Nineveh. His successor was Cambyses I (600–559), the father of Cyrus II, the
founder of the Persian Empire. From the reign of Cyrus II until their conquest
by Alexander (ca. 330), the Persians developed one of the largest of all ancient empires, at its greatest extent stretching from the Hellespont in the
northwest and the Nile in the southwest to the Indus in the east.

Cyrus II (the Great) began his thirty-year reign over the Persians circa 559.
In 550 Cyrus decisively defeated Astyages' army probably in the plain of
Pasargadae, where he later built his capital. The Nabonidus Chronicle confirms Herodotus's account (1:127) that Cyrus was aided in his victory by the
defection of some of the Medes.

Cyrus next turned his forces against the Lydians in western Anatolia. After
an indecisive battle, the Lydian king Croesus retired to his capital at Sardis
under the mistaken belief that Cyrus would not pursue as winter was approaching. Cyrus's conquest of Lydia in 546 soon paved the way for the take-
over of the Ionian Greek settlements on the west coast of Asia Minor.

The Persians then attacked their erstwhile allies the Babylonians, whose
last king was Nabonidus (555–539). The Book of Daniel depicts Belshazzar,
the son of Nabonidus, as the de facto king, since Nabonidus had spent ten
years in self-imposed exile in Arabia.[16] Apparently in anticipation of the

---

15. H. A. Storck, "The Lydian Campaign of Cyrus the Great in Classical and Cuneiform
Sources," *Ancient World* 19 (1989): 69–76.

16. Paul-Alain Beaulieu, *The Reign of Nabonidus, King of Babylon 556–539 B.C.*, Yale Near
Eastern Researches 10 (New Haven: Yale University Press, 1989).

Alternating Persians and Medes from the Apadana at Persepolis, 521–486 B.C. (height of each panel: 3′)   *Courtesy of Edwin M. Yamauchi*

growing Persian threat, Nabonidus returned to Babylon in 543 and in a desperate measure gathered all the gods from the neighboring cities into Babylon.

In order to attack Babylon, Cyrus had to outflank the Median Wall, which stretched from Sippar on the Euphrates to Opis on the Tigris. In September 539, according to the Nabonidus Chronicle, Cyrus battled the army of Akkad at Opis. By October 10 the Persians were able to capture Sippar without a fight. Herodotus (1:191) indicates that the Persians gained entrance into Babylon by diverting the Euphrates River, which ran through the city.[17]

The Nabonidus Chronicle confirms that the defector Gubaru and his troops entered Babylon "without a battle" on 12 October 539.[18] The inhab-

17. On Babylon, see Donald J. Wiseman, *Nebuchadrezzar and Babylon*, Schweich Lectures 1983 (London: Oxford University Press for the British Academy, 1985).

18. Gubaru is identified by some scholars with the enigmatic "Darius the Mede" of Daniel. On this issue see Lester L. Grabbe, "Another Look at the *Gestalt* of 'Darius the Mede,'" *Catholic Biblical Quarterly* 50 (1988): 198–213. Both William H. Shea ("Darius the Mede in His Persian-Babylonian Setting," *Andrews University Seminary Studies* 29 [1991]: 235–57) and Brian E. Colless ("Cyrus the Persian as Darius the Mede in the Book of Daniel," *Journal for the Study of the Old Testament* 56 [1992]: 113–26) support Donald J. Wiseman's proposal that "Darius the Mede" was another designation for Cyrus.

itants of Babylon greeted Cyrus not as a conqueror but as a liberator according to an important propaganda text now called the "Cyrus Cylinder."[19] This cylinder claims that Cyrus showed his concern for the people of Babylon, who resembled skeletons, and restored their "dilapidated dwellings." A fragment that has recently been identified as coming from the cylinder informs us that Cyrus restored the city's inner wall and moats.[20]

Cyrus instituted the enlightened policy of placating the gods of his subject peoples instead of carrying off their cult statues and peoples as most rulers had done. His generosity to the Jews was not unique but was paralleled by his benevolence to the Babylonians and to others. A Hebrew copy of his edict permitting the Jews to return to the Holy Land is found in Ezra 1:2–4 and an Aramaic memorandum of the same in Ezra 6:3–5.[21] Though earlier scholars questioned the authenticity of the decree, documents from the Persian period provide convincing evidence of its authenticity.[22]

In 530, though nearly seventy years old, Cyrus campaigned in the distant northeastern part of his realm against the nomadic Massagetae (Herodotus 1:201–4), where he was killed in battle toward the end of July. The body of the great monarch was transported a thousand miles to be placed in his splendid tomb at Pasargadae.[23]

Cambyses II (529–522)

Cambyses II succeeded his father Cyrus. His main achievement was the conquest of Egypt in 525. In this feat he was aided by an important Egyptian defector, Udjahorresnet. Under the Persians the latter was able to restore the temple of Neith in Sais as well as the medical colleges throughout Egypt. The role of Udjahorresnet parallels in some respects the roles of Ezra and Nehemiah.[24]

---

19. See Amélie Kuhrt, "The Cyrus Cylinder and Achaemenid Imperial Policy," *Journal for the Study of the Old Testament* 25 (1983): 83–94.

20. Christopher B. F. Walker, "A Recently Identified Fragment of the Cyrus Cylinder," *Iran* 10 (1972): 158–59.

21. See Edwin M. Yamauchi, "Ezra–Nehemiah," in *The Expositor's Bible Commentary*, ed. Frank E. Gaebelein (Grand Rapids: Zondervan, 1988), 4:601–2, 605, 641–42.

22. See Elias J. Bickerman, "The Edict of Cyrus in Ezra 1," *Journal of Biblical Literature* 65 (1946): 249–75; Roland de Vaux, "The Decrees of Cyrus and Darius on the Rebuilding of the Temple," in *The Bible and the Ancient Near East*, trans. Damian McHugh (Garden City, N.Y.: Doubleday, 1971), 63–96; C. Hensley, *The Official Persian Documents in the Book of Ezra* (Ph.D. diss., University of Liverpool, 1977).

23. See David Stronach, *Pasargadae* (New York: Oxford University Press, 1978).

24. Alan B. Lloyd, "The Inscription of Udjahorresnet: A Collaborator's Testament," *Journal of Egyptian Archaeology* 68 (1982): 166–80; Joseph Blenkinsopp, "The Mission of Udjahorresnet and Those of Ezra and Nehemiah," *Journal of Biblical Literature* 106 (1987): 409–21.

Herodotus ascribed all kinds of fiascoes to Cambyses, including an army that got lost in a sandstorm in the Sahara and a failed expedition to Nubia (the Sudan). His supposed killing of the Apis bull has been disproved by the evidence of a sarcophagus dedicated to the Apis by Cambyses. Although the Persians may have destroyed some temples as indicated by the Elephantine papyri and may have curtailed some donations to the temples, Cambyses favored others, such as the temple to Neith.[25]

In 522 Cambyses learned of a coup d'état and hastened home. On his way he accidentally stabbed himself in the thigh and died three weeks later. We have reason to believe that Cambyses had begun to prepare a tomb for himself prior to his departure for Egypt. Some ruins north of Persepolis, today called Takht-i Rustam, were identified by Ernst Herzfeld as the unfinished grave of Cambyses.[26] About 650 feet to the east, foundation slabs of limestone for column bases in two parallel rows were discovered in 1973. This building may have been part of an audience hall built by Cambyses.[27]

Darius I (522–486)

According to Darius's Behistun inscription, Cambyses had secretly murdered his brother before he invaded Egypt in 525. While Cambyses was away, an impostor named Gaumata (called Smerdis by Herodotus) seized control for seven months. Herodotus's account agrees in general with Darius's inscription. Though some historians doubt that the murder could have been concealed, the official account is far more credible than the proposed alternatives.[28]

Once it was discovered that the new king was not Cambyses' brother but his look-alike Gaumata, Darius and six other nobles banded together in a conspiracy to overthrow the usurper. Since Darius came from a collateral line and was not the obvious heir to the throne he had first to extinguish a fire storm of rebellions that broke out in almost every part of the empire. Darius's Behistun inscription is principally concerned with detailing the nine defeated rebels and the nineteen battles that ensued over the course of a year.

One of the areas that rebelled was Egypt. Darius himself arrived in Egypt late in 519 and stayed for six months. During a later visit (497–496) Darius

---

25. J. D. Ray, "Egypt 525–404 B.C.," in *CAH* 4:254–61.

26. Ernst Herzfeld, *The Persian Empire*, ed. Gerold Walser (Wiesbaden: Steiner, 1968), 36; W. Kleiss and P. Calmeyer, "Das unvollendete achaemenidische Felsgrab bei Persepolis," *Archäologische Mitteilungen aus Iran*, n.s. 8 (1975): 81–98.

27. A. B. Tilia, "Discovery of an Achaemenian Palace near Takht-i Rustam to the North of the Terrace of Persepolis," *Iran* 12 (1974): 200–204.

28. For a skeptical view of Darius's account, see J. Balcer, *Herodotus and Bisitun* (Stuttgart: Steiner, 1987).

built a temple to Amon at Hibis in the el-Khargeh oasis.[29] Darius also ordered the codification of the laws of Egypt.[30]

Herodotus's report that Darius completed a canal between the Nile and the Red Sea has been corroborated by the discovery of four steles inscribed in cuneiform and hieroglyphic. In 1972 the French excavators of Susa made a striking discovery, a larger than life-size statue of Darius, which unfortunately was lacking its head. The statue and base were inscribed in Old Persian, Elamite, Akkadian, and Egyptian. The text proclaims, "This is the statue of stone that Darius the King ordered made in Egypt in order that in the future whoever sees it will know that the Persian possesses Egypt."[31]

The Jews, who had returned under Cyrus, laid the foundation of the Second Temple to replace Solomon's Temple, which had been destroyed by Nebuchadnezzar II. But work was soon halted in the face of opposition (Ezra 4:1–5). In the reign of Darius, under the leadership of Zerubbabel and Jeshua the high priest and stirred by the prophets Haggai and Zechariah, the Jews renewed efforts to complete the work. Their enemies challenged their right to do this and complained to the Persian authorities. According to Ezra 6:1–4 Darius responded to the request as follows:

> King Darius then issued an order, and they searched in the archives stored in the treasury at Babylon. A scroll was found in the citadel of Ecbatana in the province of Media, and this was written on it:
>
> Memorandum:
>
> > In the first year of King Cyrus, the king issued a decree concerning the temple of God in Jerusalem. (NIV)

Darius then solemnly warned the enemies of the Jews against interfering with the rebuilding of the temple (Ezra 6:11), which was finished in 515 (Ezra 6:14–15), a little over seventy years after its destruction.

The Ionian Greeks, who had been subject to the Persians since the reign of Cyrus, erupted in a revolt against Darius in 499 and were not suppressed until 494. Angered by the aid proffered to the Ionian rebels by Athens and Eretria, Darius determined to punish these city-states. An initial expedition in 492 was shipwrecked in the northern Aegean at Mount Athos. The second expedition led to the capture of Eretria and the famous Battle of Marathon in 490. Led by Miltiades, the Athenians were able to defeat the Persians by

---

29. E. Cruz-Uribe, "Oasis of the Spirit," *Archaeology* 42.5 (1989): 48–53.
30. Edwin M. Yamauchi, *Persia and the Bible* (Grand Rapids: Baker, 1990), 149–51.
31. Ibid., 151–52.

the novel tactic of having their armed hoplites advance at a run against the Persian archers.[32]

Darius is credited with establishing the "pony express" courier system on the Royal Road that linked Susa in southwestern Persia to Sardis in western Anatolia (Herodotus 8:98). The route of 1,700 miles was covered by ordinary travelers in ninety days, but the royal couriers covered the same distance in a week.[33] Darius was also responsible for the organization of the empire into districts governed by satraps. Royal inspectors, called by the Greeks "the king's eyes" and "the king's ears," checked up on the satraps periodically.

Six listings of peoples are extant from the reign of Darius and one from the reign of Xerxes.[34] Herodotus (3:89) speaks of the organization of the empire by Darius into twenty satrapies, among whom are mentioned sixty-seven different tribes and nations. George Cameron concludes that all of the Old Persian lists under Darius are not of satrapies but of various groups of peoples.[35] Their purpose was to impress their readers with the great varieties of peoples represented in the Persian Empire.

Darius standardized weights and measures and began the minting of coins: silver coins known as *sigloi* and the famous gold *darics*.[36] Because of his various economic measures, Darius acquired the reputation of a huckster among the Greeks. According to Herodotus (3:89): "It is by reason of this fixing of tribute, and other like ordinances, that the Persians called Darius the huckster, Cambyses the master, and Cyrus the father; for Darius made petty profit out of everything, Cambyses was harsh and arrogant, Cyrus was merciful and ever wrought for their well-being."

Darius died at Persepolis, his new capital, in 486. He was buried in a tomb carved in a rock cliff at Naqsh-i Rustam just north of Persepolis. Like the other three tombs there, Darius's tomb is cut in the form of a large cross. The top section bears a relief, originally painted, which depicts the king standing on a platform upheld by two tiers of representatives from thirty nations whose identities are given in a trilingual inscription.[37]

---

32. William K. Pritchett, *Marathon* (Berkeley: University of California Press, 1960); A. Lloyd, *Marathon* (New York: Mentor, 1973).

33. Yamauchi, *Persia and the Bible*, 174–77.

34. Arnold J. Toynbee, *A Study of History* (London: Oxford University Press, 1954), 7:580–689; O. K. Armayor, "Herodotus' Catalogues of the Persian Empire in the Light of the Monuments and the Greek Literary Tradition," *Transactions of the American Philological Association* 108 (1978): 1–9.

35. George Cameron, "The Persian Satrapies and Related Matters," *Journal of Near Eastern Studies* 32 (1973): 47–56.

36. E. S. G. Robinson, "The Beginnings of Achaemenid Coinage," *Numismatic Chronicle* 18 (1958): 187–93.

37. See Erich F. Schmidt, *Persepolis*, vol. 3: *The Royal Tombs and Other Monuments*, Oriental Institute Publications 70 (Chicago: University of Chicago Press, 1970).

Treasury relief from Persepolis depicting Darius (or Xerxes) on the throne, 6th–5th century B.C.
(length: 20′)   *Courtesy of the Oriental Institute of the University of Chicago*

Xerxes I (485–465)

Xerxes I succeeded his father Darius. His name is rendered as Ahasuerus in the Book of Esther (the only other biblical reference is in Ezra 4:6). The most important source is Herodotus, who is primarily concerned about the Persian invasion of Greece and who therefore offers little information on the period after 479.

Before Darius died, a revolt had broken out in Egypt, and Xerxes went in person in 485 to suppress this revolt. There were also two short-lived revolts in Babylon, which were harshly repressed. As punishment the Persians destroyed the great ziggurat and the temple of Marduk in Babylon according to classical sources, although cuneiform sources indicate that the reprisals may not have been so severe.[38]

After the suppression of these revolts, Xerxes was ready for his massive invasion of Greece. Although there should be little doubt that he was able to amass the largest army and navy ever mustered in antiquity, the enormous numbers listed by Herodotus have aroused the greatest skepticism. He reports that the army contained 1.7 million infantry (7:60). More credible are his figures for the navy: twelve hundred triremes and three thousand penteconters (7:184).

As the huge Persian juggernaut advanced into northern Greece, many key Greek states such as Thessaly and Thebes "Medized," that is, they joined the

38. See Amélie Kuhrt, "Babylonia from Cyrus to Xerxes," in *CAH* 4:135.

Persian side. The gallant stand of the Spartans under Leonidas at the Thermopylae Pass (480) could slow but not stop the Persian advance. Panic stricken, the Athenians abandoned their city. However, under the brilliant leadership of Themistocles, the Greeks were able to lure the Persian fleet into the narrow waters of the Bay of Salamis for a decisive victory.[39] Concerned for his safety, Xerxes fled to Asia Minor, but still left behind a substantial force.

The final battle on the Greek mainland was fought in 479 at Plataea. The Spartans under the leadership of Pausanias won a great victory. Pausanias himself, however, became the victim of hubris, an overweening arrogance that led him into a treasonable correspondence with the Persians. His downfall in turn affected the fortunes of his Athenian friend, Themistocles, who ironically ended his life as a loyal Persian subject.

According to Herodotus (7:61), Xerxes' queen was a very powerful woman named Amestris; according to the Book of Esther her name was Vashti. Stafford Wright suggests that by assuming certain phonetic modifications an identification of Vashti with Amestris can be made—a conclusion accepted also by William H. Shea.[40] Shea works out a detailed synchronism to show how the events of Esther, which has a gap between the third year (Esth. 1:3) and the seventh year (Esth. 2:16), can be harmonized with Xerxes' absence in Greece in 480–479.[41]

Esther's guardian is named Mordecai, a name attested among the roster of Persian officials in the Elamite tablets of Persepolis, which come from the reigns of Darius and Xerxes.[42] Mordecai sat "in the gate" at Susa as an indication of his official status (Esth. 2:19, 21; 5:9, 13). Recently the French excavators have after many years of searching discovered the gate of the Achemenid palace at Susa. They are impressed by the detailed and accurate knowledge of Susa revealed by the author of Esther.[43]

The Book of Esther betrays a thorough knowledge of Persian customs and background; especially striking are thirty or more personal names of Persian and Elamite origin and twelve Persian loanwords in the text of Esther.[44] The

39. See Peter Green, *Xerxes at Salamis* (New York: Praeger, 1970).

40. J. Stafford Wright, "The Historicity of the Book of Esther," in *New Perspectives on the Old Testament*, ed. J. Barton Payne (Waco, Tex.: Word, 1970), 40–41; William H. Shea, "Esther and History," *Andrews University Seminary Studies* 14 (1976): 235.

41. Shea, "Esther and History," 231–40.

42. J. A. Delaunay, "Remarques sur Quelques Noms de Personne des Archives Élamites de Persépolis," *Studia Iranica* 5 (1976): 17; Edwin M. Yamauchi, "Mordecai, the Persepolis Tablets, and the Susa Excavations," *Vetus Testamentum* 43 (1992): 272–75.

43. See Yamauchi, *Persia and the Bible*, 298–300.

44. For other discussions of the Persian background of Esther see Henry S. Gehman, "Notes on the Persian Words in the Book of Esther," *Journal of Biblical Literature* 43 (1924): 321–28; Carey A. Moore, "Archaeology and the Book of Esther," *Biblical Archaeologist* 38 (1975): 62–79.

Hebrew text of Esther preserves the Persian names with remarkable accuracy, as Alan R. Millard demonstrates.[45] Many other parallels to the Persian names in Esther have now been provided by the Elamite Persepolis texts.[46]

After his return from the west, Xerxes was mainly preoccupied with completing the work of his father at Persepolis. After reigning for twenty years, Xerxes was killed in a palace plot in August 465 by Artabanus, the captain of the bodyguard. Xerxes' tomb is believed to be the one on the extreme right of the four tombs at Naqsh-i Rustam.

Artaxerxes I (464–424)

After killing Artabanus, Artaxerxes I began his long reign. Hostilities between the Persians and the Greeks continued, with the Greeks attempting to help liberate Cyprus and Egypt from Persian control. Finally in 449 the Peace of Callias was signed, requiring the Greeks and the Persians to desist from intervening in the other's territories.

It was under Artaxerxes I that first Ezra in 458 (Ezra 7:7) and then Nehemiah in 445 (Neh. 2:1) came to the Holy Land to serve there, the former as a preacher of the Torah and the latter as the governor of Judah. Though some scholars argue for a reversal of the traditional biblical order with Ezra following Nehemiah in the later reign of Artaxerxes II (404–359) in 398,[47] most now reject this revisionism.[48]

That Artaxerxes I commissioned Ezra the Scribe to administer the law to his people troubles some critics. But this fits in perfectly with Persian policy. A close parallel is the similar commission given by Darius to Udjahorresnet, an Egyptian priest and scholar. As Joseph Blenkinsopp observes, "In the light of the preceding, we can now see that the two goals of Ezra's mission correspond to the two phases of Udjahorresnet's activity: the restoration of the cult at the national and dynastic shrine of Sais; the reorganization of judicial institutions, for which the smooth functioning of the Houses of Life was a necessary precondition."[49]

Nehemiah had occupied the prestigious position of cupbearer before Artaxerxes I (Neh. 1:11), which meant that he had to taste the wine to make

45. Alan R. Millard, "The Persian Names in Esther and the Reliability of the Hebrew Text," *Journal of Biblical Literature* 96 (1977): 481–88.

46. Yamauchi, *Persia and the Bible*, 238.

47. William F. Stinespring, "Prolegomenon," to Charles C. Torrey's *Ezra Studies* (New York: Ktav, 1970), xiv.

48. U. Kellermann, "Erwägungen zum Problem der Esradatierung," *Zeitschrift für die Alttestamentliche Wissenschaft* 80 (1968): 55–87; Edwin M. Yamauchi, "The Reverse Order of Ezra/Nehemiah Reconsidered," *Themelios* 5.3 (1980): 7–13.

49. Blenkinsopp, "Mission of Udjahorresnet," 419.

certain there was no poison in it.[50] The province that Nehemiah came to govern had been greatly reduced in size. The archeological evidence of Yehud (Judah) coins and seals confirms the biblical boundaries.[51] Nahman Avigad uses recently recovered bullas (clay seal impressions) and coins to develop a list of the governors who preceded Nehemiah.[52]

Inscriptional evidence confirms the historicity of Nehemiah's various opponents: Sanballat the Samaritan, Tobiah the Ammonite, and Geshem the Arab.[53] Excavations reveal the situation in Jerusalem at the time that Nehemiah rallied the people to rebuild the walls about the city.[54] About 900 feet to the west of the temple area, Avigad discovered a 23-foot-thick wall, which he identified with "the broad wall" (Neh. 3:8) repaired by Nehemiah.[55] The diminished circuit of the city wall in his day helps to explain the rapidity in which the reconstruction was accomplished, once Nehemiah had aroused the people with his inspired leadership.[56]

The economic distress of the people of Judah, including inflation and indebtedness, caused in part by Persian taxation, is vividly illustrated by the fifth chapter of Nehemiah.[57] Though taxation did not produce a scarcity of

50. Edwin M. Yamauchi, "Was Nehemiah the Cupbearer a Eunuch?" *Zeitschrift für die Alttestamentliche Wissenschaft* 92 (1980): 132–42.

51. Ephraim Stern, *Material Culture of the Land of the Bible in the Persian Period, 538–332 B.C.* (Warminster: Aris & Phillips, 1982), chaps. 7–8.

52. Nahman Avigad, *Bullae and Seals from a Post-Exilic Judean Archive* (Jerusalem: Magnes, 1976). See also Hugh G. M. Williamson, "The Governors of Judah under the Persians," *Tyndale Bulletin* 39 (1988): 59–82.

53. On Sanballat, see Frank M. Cross, "The Discovery of the Samaria Papyri," *Biblical Archaeologist* 26 (1963): 110–21; idem, "A Reconstruction of the Judean Restoration," *Journal of Biblical Literature* 94 (1975): 4–18; idem, "The Historical Importance of the Samaria Papyri," *Biblical Archaeology Review* 4.1 (1978): 25–27. On Tobiah, see Benjamin Mazar, "The Tobiads," *Israel Exploration Journal* 7 (1957): 137–45, 229–38; C. C. McCown, "The 'Araq el-Emir and the Tobiads," *Biblical Archaeologist* 20 (1957): 63–76. On Geshem, see Frank M. Cross, "Geshem the Arabian, Enemy of Nehemiah," *Biblical Archaeologist* 18 (1955): 46–47; I. Rabinowitz, "Aramaic Inscriptions of the Fifth Century BCE," *Journal of Near Eastern Studies* 15 (1956): 1–9; William J. Dumbrell, "The Tell el-Maskhuṭa Bowls and the 'Kingdom' of Qedar in the Persian Period," *Bulletin of the American Schools of Oriental Research* 203 (1971): 33–44.

54. Kathleen Kenyon, *Jerusalem: Excavating Three Thousand Years of History* (London: Thames & Hudson, 1967), 107–11; idem, *Digging up Jerusalem* (New York: Praeger/London: Benn, 1974), 183–84; Yigal Shiloh, "City of David: Excavation 1978," *Biblical Archaeologist* 42 (1979): 168.

55. Nahman Avigad, "Excavations in the Jewish Quarter of the Old City, Jerusalem, 1970," *Israel Exploration Journal* 20 (1970): 129–40.

56. Hugh G. M. Williamson, "Nehemiah's Walls Revisited," *Palestine Exploration Quarterly* 116 (1984): 81–88.

57. Edwin M. Yamauchi, "Two Reformers Compared: Solon of Athens and Nehemiah of Jerusalem," in *The Bible World: Essays in Honor of Cyrus H. Gordon*, ed. Gary A. Rendsburg et al. (New York: Ktav, 1980), 269–92; Muhammad A. Dandamaev and Vladimir G. Lukonin,

cash, it did concentrate wealth in the hand of entrepreneurs who could take advantage of the situation.[58]

Aramaic papyri from Elephantine and Hermopolis in Egypt, dated to the fifth century, illuminate the linguistic, political, and cultural background of the Jews in the Persian Empire.[59] In Elephantine in Upper Egypt the Jews had built a temple of Yaho (Yahweh), which was destroyed in 411 by fanatical Egyptians. The Jews then asked for permission to rebuild the temple. The papyri reveal the incidence of mixed marriages, which led to syncretistic practices. Ostraca (inscribed potsherds) from Elephantine mention the Sabbath and the Passover.[60] Letters of Arsames, the satrap of Egypt, reveal him as an all too typical governor, greedy for wealth and power—a striking contrast to the selflessness of Nehemiah.[61]

Persian Architecture and Art

As the Persian Empire expanded under the Achemenian kings, Persian art developed a very cosmopolitan and eclectic style, infused by traits from many cultures and executed by skilled workers from many lands. With the exception of the frozen Persian rug at Pazarcik,[62] brilliantly colored and decorated textiles have perished. But some magnificent gems, all kinds of jewelry, and silver and gold vessels have survived to illustrate the Persian luxury that dazzled the Greeks.[63]

Only one statue in the round, that of Darius, has survived. But splendid reliefs, all originally colored, may still be seen at Pasargadae and Persepolis.[64] At the former site the most striking monument is the famous tomb of Cyrus, made of white limestone, which rests upon a six-level base for a total

---

The Culture and Social Institutions of Ancient Iran (Cambridge: Cambridge University Press, 1989), 177–95.

58. Matthew W. Stolper, *Entrepreneurs and Empire: The Murašû Firm and Persian Rule in Babylonia* (Leiden: Nederlands Historisch-Archaeologisch Instituut te Istanbul, 1985), 151, 154.

59. Bezalel Porten, *Archives from Elephantine: The Life of an Ancient Jewish Military Colony* (Berkeley: University of California Press, 1968).

60. André Dupont-Sommer, "L'Ostracon Araméen du Sabbat," *Semitica* 2 (1949): 29–39.

61. Godfrey R. Driver, *Aramaic Documents of the Fifth Century B.C.* (Oxford: Clarendon, 1954).

62. E. D. Phillips, *The Royal Hordes* (New York: McGraw-Hill, 1965), 85.

63. See Roman Ghirshman, *The Art of Ancient Iran* (New York: Golden, 1964).

64. J. A. Lerner, "A Painted Relief from Persepolis," *Archaeology* 26 (1973): 116–22; Erich F. Schmidt, *Persepolis*, vols. 1–2, Oriental Institute Publications 68–69 (Chicago: University of Chicago Press, 1953–57); A. Farkas, *Achaemenid Sculpture* (Istanbul: Nederlands Historisch-Archaeologisch Instituut in het Nabije Oosten, 1974); D. Wilber, *Persepolis: The Archaeology of Parsa, Seat of the Persian Kings*, rev. ed. (Princeton: Darwin, 1989).

height of about thirty-six feet. It was originally surrounded by a "paradise" or park.[65]

Persepolis was begun by Darius sometime after 520. The buildings were completed after sixty years of labor during the reigns of Xerxes and Artaxerxes I. A few additions were made by later Achemenid kings. Darius was responsible for building the fortifications, platform, monumental stairway, central building, his palace, the Apadana (audience hall), and part of the treasury. Xerxes completed the Apadana, the Gate of All Nations, his palace, harem, and treasury. He began the throne hall, which was completed by Artaxerxes I. Alexander the Great destroyed the site by fire in 330, according to some classical sources as an act of vengeance for the destruction of Athens by Xerxes in 480.[66]

The widely held view that Persepolis functioned primarily as a ritual city for the celebration of the Persian New Year has fallen into disfavor; it is now recognized that—like all monumental art—the reliefs and buildings at Persepolis were primarily expressions of kingship and empire.[67] Among the most important reliefs at the site are those on the eastern stairway of the Apadana, which pictures twenty-three delegations from all parts of the empire bearing gifts or tribute. Though these are not accompanied by texts, scholars are in general agreement about the identification of most of these delegations.[68]

Among the many groups who contributed to the execution of the Achemenid art and architecture were Greeks, especially from Ionia. Greek influence and artistic skill are quite evident at Pasargadae, the capital of Cyrus.[69] The Persepolis tablets explicitly refer to Ionians among the workers, and one tablet was written in Greek. Several Greek graffiti were incised in the quarries near Persepolis.[70] The overwhelming evidence of Greeks and Greek objects and influence in the Near East long before Alexander should end attempts to date Daniel to the Hellenistic era on the basis of the Greek words that occur in its text.[71]

Persian Religion

Early Iranian religion was very similar to the Indo-Aryan religion reflected in the Hindu Rig-Veda scriptures. The earliest written attestation of the

65. On Persian "paradises," see Yamauchi, *Persia and the Bible*, 332–34.

66. M. Wheeler, *Flames over Persepolis* (New York: Reynal, 1968).

67. See M. C. Root, *The King and Kingship in Achaemenid Art* (Leiden: Brill, 1979).

68. See Yamauchi, *Persia and the Bible*, 355.

69. Carl Nylander, *Ionians in Pasargadae* (Lund: Universitetsbiblioteke Uppsala, 1970).

70. G. P. Carratelli, "Greek Inscriptions of the Middle East," *East and West*, n.s. 16 (1966): 31–36.

71. Yamauchi, *Persia and the Bible*, chap. 11.

Indo-Aryan gods is found in a fourteenth-century treaty between the Hittite king Shuppiluliuma and Mattiwaza of Mitanni. Mitra (Iranian Mithra), who appears in this text, was worshiped by both the ancient Iranians and Indians.

The great founder of a new Persian religion was Zoroaster (Zarathushtra). As the only certainly contemporary source on Zoroaster is his Gathas, we have very little trustworthy data on the life of Zoroaster.[72] Scholars differ greatly on their estimates of the date of Zoroaster. Many place Zoroaster in the seventh or sixth century on the basis of late Iranian and Arabic traditions; at the other extreme Mary Boyce argues for a date prior to 1200; and other scholars favor an intermediate date, placing Zoroaster in the tenth or ninth century.[73] The evidence of the Gathas places the prophet in the area of northeastern Iran.

According to the Gathas, Zoroaster came from a background of cattle herders, who were menaced by nomads who stole and slaughtered cattle. He was a priest who preached the message of the worship of Ahura Mazda in spite of opposition from the nobles. When he was forty-two he gained his most notable convert, the ruler Vishtaspa and his queen Hutaosa. Those who favor the "late" date of Zoroaster identify the former with Hystaspes, the father of Darius I.

Zoroaster preached an ethical dualism, teaching that each person must choose between Righteousness and the Lie. He protested the violent, bloody sacrifices of the cattle by the "daeva" (demon) worshipers—probably not a proscription of animal sacrifices altogether, but of their abuse. In a similar fashion, Zoroaster condemned the use of the intoxicating haoma plant, which became the focus of the central ceremony of later Zoroastrianism. Boyce, who believes in the continuity of the major elements of the prophet and the later community rather than in a process of devolution, argues that Zoroaster simply attacked abuses in the cult rather than the haoma plant itself.[74]

Scholars disagree about whether the Achemenids were Zoroastrians. Though some scholars such as Boyce believe that all the Achemenians, including Cyrus II, were Zoroastrians, the evidence is quite inconclusive for Cyrus II and Cambyses II.[75] The strongest case for a Zoroastrian background can be made in the case of Darius I, who mentions the god Ahura Mazda repeatedly in his Behistun inscription. Though the king focused on Ahura Mazda, Persepolis texts from Darius's reign indicate that the court also rec-

72. M. Molé, *La Légende de Zoroastre selon les Textes Pehlevis* (Paris: Klincksieck, 1967).

73. Yamauchi, *Persia and the Bible*, 413–15.

74. Mary Boyce, *A History of Zoroastrianism* (Leiden: Brill, 1975), 1:216–17.

75. Dandamaev and Lukonin, *Culture and Social Institutions*, 34–48; T. Cuyler Young Jr., "The Consolidation of the Empire and Its Limits of Growth under Darius and Xerxes," in *CAH* 4:100–101.

ognized numerous other gods as well.[76] Both biblical and nonbiblical texts indicate that in general the Achemenian kings not only tolerated other religions but actively sought their prayers and devotions by granting subsidies.[77]

Zoroaster's message does not seem to have been an unqualified monotheism. One of the most original doctrines of Zoroaster was the association with Ahura Mazda of six Amesha Spentas ("Bounteous Immortals"), who are conceived of as semipersonal manifestations of this supreme god. They were more than personified abstractions, as they were separately venerated by Zoroaster.[78]

Many scholars believe that Zoroaster taught not a monotheism, but a dualism, with two primordial uncreated Spirits, a Good Spirit (i.e., Ahura Mazda) and an Evil Spirit (Angra Mainyu, later spelled Ahriman). The dualism implicit in the Gathas was made quite explicit in the later Sasanian period (A.D. 224–651). According to an important cosmological text, the *Bundahishn*, all things in creation belong either to one sphere or another: aligned with the Good Spirit are light, fire, summer, water, fertile land, health, growth, and domestic animals, especially the dog. Aligned with the Evil Spirit are darkness, night, winter, drought, infertile land, vermin, sickness, and death.

Numerous scholars assume that during the exilic period Zoroastrianism influenced Judaism's teachings on Satan, demonology, angelology, and especially eschatological beliefs such as judgment, resurrection, apocalypticism, a fiery trial, heaven, and hell. To sustain such claims one must assume (1) the chronological priority of the Iranian beliefs, (2) late dates for the Old Testament texts, (3) a close parallelism between the beliefs, and (4) reasons for dependence.

Critical analyses of these matters reveal that many of the parallels are drawn from late (ninth century A.D.) Pahlavi cosmological and eschatological Zoroastrian texts. Moreover many of the parallels are less than exact. There is therefore reason to believe that these doctrines can be better explained on the basis of an inner Jewish development without recourse to Persian influence.[79]

76. Richard N. Frye, "Religion in Fars under the Achaemenids," in *Orientalia J. Duchesne-Guillemin Emerito Oblata* (Leiden: Brill, 1984), 172.

77. H. Koch, *Die religiösen Verhältnisse der Dareiozeit* (Wiesbaden: Harrassowitz, 1977); idem, "Götter und ihre Verehrung im achämenidischen Persien," *Zeitschrift für Assyriologie* 77 (1987): 239–78.

78. Boyce, *History of Zoroastrianism*, 1:202.

79. Yamauchi, *Persia and the Bible*, 458–66; James Barr, "The Question of Religious Influence: The Case of Zoroastrianism, Judaism, and Christianity," *Journal of the American Academy of Religion* 53 (1985): 201–33.

Recommended Reading

Boardman, John, N. G. L. Hammond, D. M. Lewis, and M. Ostwald (eds.). *The Cambridge Ancient History*, vol. 4: *Persia, Greece and the Western Mediterranean, c. 525–479 B.C.* Cambridge: Cambridge University Press, 1988.

Boyce, Mary. *A History of Zoroastrianism.* 2 vols. Leiden: Brill, 1975–82.

Cook, John M. *The Persian Empire.* New York: Schocken, 1983.

Dandamaev, Muhammad A. *Persien unter den ersten Achämeniden.* Translated by H.-D. Pohl. Wiesbaden: Reichert, 1976.

———. *A Political History of the Achaemenid Empire.* Translated by W. J. Vogelsang. Leiden: Brill, 1990.

Dandamaev, Muhammad A., and Vladimir G. Lukonin. *The Culture and Social Institutions of Ancient Iran.* Cambridge: Cambridge University Press, 1989.

Davies, W. D., and Louis Finkelstein (eds.). *The Cambridge History of Judaism*, vol. 1: *Introduction; the Persian Period.* Cambridge: Cambridge University Press, 1984.

Frye, Richard N. *The History of Ancient Iran.* Munich: Beck, 1984.

Gershevitch, Ilya (ed.). *The Cambridge History of Iran*, vol. 2: *The Median and Achaemenian Periods.* Cambridge: Cambridge University Press, 1985.

Schmandt-Besserat, Denise (ed.). *Ancient Persia.* Malibu, Calif.: Undena, 1979.

Stern, Ephraim. *Material Culture of the Land of the Bible in the Persian Period, 538–332 B.C.* Warminster: Aris & Phillips, 1982.

Williamson, Hugh G. M. "Ezra and Nehemiah in the Light of the Texts from Persepolis." *Bulletin for Biblical Research* 1 (1991): 41–61.

Yamauchi, Edwin M. *Persia and the Bible.* Grand Rapids: Baker, 1990.

Zadok, Ran. *The Jews in Babylonia during the Chaldean and Achaemenian Periods.* Haifa: University of Haifa Press, 1979.

Part 2

Anatolia
Syria-Palestine
Egypt

Hittites

Harry A. Hoffner Jr.

*The Lord had caused the Arameans to hear the sound of chariots
and horses and a great army, so that they said to one another,
"Look, the king of Israel has hired the Hittite and Egyptian kings
to attack us!"*
—2 Kings 7:6

History

Historiography

Before discussing what is known about Hittite history from texts and archeological investigation, we should touch briefly on the question of how the Hittites recorded their own past.[1] The Hittites had no chronographic literature. The closest Hittite approximation to a king list does not record dates or lengths of reigns. Hittite kings left behind annalistic records of their military campaigns, beginning as early as the Old Hittite king Ḫattushili I.[2] Royal edicts, such as those of the Old Hittite kings Ḫattushili I and Telepinu and the New Hittite king Ḫattushili III, often contain historical narrative.[3] Treaties with historical prologues first appear in the so-called Middle Hittite period (ca. 1420–1344).

---

1. Annelies Kammenhuber, "Die hethitische Geschichtsschreibung," *Saeculum* 9 (1958): 136–65; Alfonso Archi, "La Storiografia Ittita," *Athenaeum* 47 (1969): 7–20; Harry A. Hoffner Jr., "Propaganda and Political Justification in Hittite Historiography," in *Unity and Diversity: Essays in the History, Literature, and Religion of the Ancient Near East*, ed. Hans Goedicke and J. J. M. Roberts (Baltimore: Johns Hopkins University Press, 1975), 49–62; idem, "Histories and Historians of the Ancient Near East: The Hittites," *Orientalia* 49 (1980): 283–332; Hans G. Güterbock, "Hittite Historiography: A Survey," in *History, Historiography, and Interpretation: Studies in Biblical and Cuneiform Literatures*, ed. Hayim Tadmor and Moshe Weinfeld (Jerusalem: Magnes/Leiden: Brill, 1983), 21–35.
2. Hoffner, "Histories and Historians." For English translations of Old Hittite historical texts see Trevor R. Bryce, *The Major Historical Texts of Early Hittite History* (Queensland, Australia: University of Queensland Press, 1982).
3. Hoffner, "Histories and Historians"; idem, "Propaganda and Political Justification."

There was a deliberate attempt at verification in the annals, emphasized by remarks like the following: "Whoever hears the narrative of this tablet (and doubts its description of the city of Ura), let him send and see for himself how the city of Ura was built."[4]

Pre–Old Kingdom

It is not known when or from where the Indo-European-speaking ancestors of the Hittites entered Anatolia.[5] Their presence cannot reliably be detected from nonlinguistic remains.[6] The first onomastic evidence for Hittite or Luwian speakers is in the Old Assyrian documents (dated from the nineteenth and eighteenth centuries) from the Anatolian trade centers (Old Assyrian *karûm*).[7] Since it is usually assumed that the speakers of the closely related Indo-European languages Hittite (Nesite), Luwian, and Palaic entered Anatolia as a single group and that their languages differentiated after they dispersed in Anatolia, it seems to follow that the passage of several centuries would have been required between the date of their immigration and the beginning of the Assyrian merchant colonies.[8]

The earliest Hittite kings who ruled at Ḫattusha identified their history with a city named Kushshar. This same city was the original seat of rule of a king named Anitta, who is attested in Old Assyrian commercial documents and is best known from a long narration of military conquest preserved in an Old Hittite tablet.[9] Based on its grammar and style, Erich Neu concludes that the Anitta text cannot be a translation into Old Hittite from another language.[10] It might follow from this that Anitta was himself a speaker of Hittite, but no Hittite king traced his lineage back to him.

Although Anitta destroyed the city of Ḫattusha and laid a curse on its resettlement, Hittite kings beginning with Ḫattushili I settled there, and this

4. Albrecht Goetze, *Die Annalen des Muršiliš*, Mitteilungen der Vorderasiatisch-Ägyptische Gesellschaft 38 (Leipzig: Hinrichs, 1933), 98.

5. James Mellaart, "Anatolia and the Indo-Europeans," *Journal of Indo-European Studies* 9 (1981): 135–49; Itamar Singer, "Hittites and Hattians in Anatolia at the Beginning of the Second Millennium BC," *Journal of Indo-European Studies* 9 (1981): 119–34; James G. Macqueen, *The Hittites and Their Contemporaries in Asia Minor*, 2d ed. (London: Thames & Hudson, 1986), 22–35; Oliver R. Gurney, *The Hittites*, 2d ed. (Baltimore: Penguin, 1990), 15–21.

6. Ronald A. Crossland, "Immigrants from the North," in *CAH* 1/2:824–76.

7. Louis L. Orlin, *Assyrian Colonies in Cappadocia* (The Hague: Mouton, 1970); Mogens T. Larsen, *The Old Assyrian City-State and Its Colonies* (Copenhagen: Akademisk Forlag, 1976).

8. Crossland, "Immigrants from the North."

9. Tahsin Özgüç, "The Dagger of Anitta," *Türk Tarih Kurumu Belleten* 20 (1956): 33–36.

10. Erich Neu, *Der Anitta-Text*, Studien zu den Boğazköy-Texten 18 (Wiesbaden: Harrassowitz, 1974).

city remained the political center of Hittite government until the state finally collapsed around 1180.

Old Kingdom

We now know the names of the kings who reigned during the Old Kingdom period, which stretches from ca. 1750 to 1600:[11]

Labarna I	Zidanta I	Alluwamna
Ḫattushili I	Ammuna	Ḫantili II
(= Labarna II)	Ḫuzziya I	Zidanta II
Murshili I	Telepinu	Ḫuzziya II
Ḫantili I	Taḫurwaili	Muwatalli I

Many of these names until quite recently were known only from lists compiled during the New Kingdom (ca. 1400–1180) for sacrifices to the images of deceased royalty.[12] Some scholars doubt the existence of Ḫantili II, Zidanta II, and Ḫuzziya II, but recent textual discoveries confirm their existence and justify their use by Albrecht Goetze and Michael B. Rowton to establish a "longer" chronology.[13] Surprisingly, the most recent attempts to establish a Hittite chronology still advocate a "short" chronology.[14]

Foreign expansion of the Hittite Kingdom during the Old Hittite period followed several stages. During the reign of Ḫattushili I, the armies cam-

---

11. Macqueen, *Hittites*, 36–45; Gurney, *Hittites*, 16–19.

12. Heinrich Otten, "Die hethitischen 'Königslisten' und die altorientalische Chronologie," *Mitteilungen der Deutschen Orientgesellschaft* 83 (1951): 47–71.

13. Albrecht Goetze, "The Problem of Chronology and Early Hittite History," *Bulletin of the American Schools of Oriental Research* 122 (1951): 18–25; idem, "Alalaḫ and Hittite Chronology," *Bulletin of the American Schools of Oriental Research* 146 (1957): 20–26; idem, "On the Chronology of the Second Millennium B.C.," *Journal of Cuneiform Studies* 11 (1957): 53–61; Michael B. Rowton, "Chronology, II: Ancient Western Asia," in *CAH* 1/1:193–238 (Hittite material on pp. 202, 211–17). The new finds are described in Heinrich Otten, *Das hethitische Königshaus im 15. Jahrhundert v. Chr.: Zum Neufund einiger Landschenkungsurkunden in Boğazköy* (Vienna: Verlag der Österreichischen Akademie der Wissenschaften, 1987). Scholars who deny the existence of these kings are Otten, "Die hethitischen 'Königslisten'"; idem, "Das Hethiterreich," in *Kulturgeschichte des alten Orient*, ed. Hartmut Schmökel (Stuttgart: Kröner, 1961), 313–447; idem, *Die hethitischen historischen Quellen und die altorientalische Chronologie* (Wiesbaden: Akademie der Wissenschaften und der Literatur in Mainz, 1968); Kammenhuber, "Die hethitische Geschichtsschreibung."

14. Gernot Wilhelm and J. Boese, "Absolute Chronologie und die hethitische Geschichte des 15. und 14. Jahrhunderts v. Chr.," in *High, Middle or Low? Acts of an International Colloquium on Absolute Chronology Held at the University of Gothenburg 20th–22nd August 1987*, ed. Paul Åström (Gothenburg: Åströms, 1987), 1:74–117; Michael Astour, *Hittite History and Absolute Chronology of the Bronze Age*, Studies in Mediterranean Archaeology and Literature 73 (Gothenburg: Åströms, 1989).

paigned in the far western Arzawa lands and in the southeast in north Syria. During the reign of Murshili I, a long march through Syria brought the Hittite armies into Babylonia, where they sacked the city of Babylon and brought to an end the First Dynasty of Babylon (ca. 1595). During the reigns of Murshili I's successors, Hittite control of lands to the east and southeast seems to have collapsed, for we hear of no further campaigning there.

New Kingdom

Although Hittite influence in western Asia Minor and north Syria declined at the end of the Old Kingdom and was then revived by Tudhaliya II (ca. 1420–1370), the founder of the New Kingdom, the greatest period of foreign expansion occurred during the hundred years from the accession of Shuppiluliuma I (ca. 1344) to the end of the reign of his grandson Hattushili III (ca. 1239). During this period the Hittites gained and retained control of Syria almost as far south as Damascus. Several battles with the Egyptians led to a diplomatic stabilization of the boundaries of their spheres of influence in Syria-Palestine. Hattushili III concluded a treaty with Ramesses II and gave him a Hittite princess in marriage.

The alliance with Egypt survived intact during the sixty years of the Hittite Empire (ca. 1239–1180) under the reigns of Tudhaliya IV, Arnuwanda III, and Shuppiluliuma II. But new forces were active that were to prove even more threatening to the stability of the Hittite state. Assyria under its rulers Shalmaneser I and Tukulti-Ninurta I was showing itself much more aggressive against its northern neighbors, as we learn not only from the annals of the Assyrian kings but also from the coordination of a previously obscure diplomatic letter from Tudhaliya IV (possibly to the king of Ishuwa) with a newly published letter from Ugarit.[15] In the west, the growing power of the Ahhiyawa kingdom is reflected in a passage from the treaty of Tudhaliya IV with the king of Amurru, where Ahhiyawa is listed with Egypt and Assyria as one of the great powers.[16]

Closer to home Tudhaliya IV had serious troubles with the kingdom of Tarhuntashsha to the south, which since the death of his grandfather Mu-

15. Sylvie Lackenbacher, "Nouveaux Documents d'Ugarit, I: Une Lettre Royale," *Revue d'Assyriologie* 76 (1982): 141–56; Itamar Singer, "The Battle of Nihriya and the End of the Hittite Empire," *Zeitschrift für Assyriologie* 75 (1985): 100–123; idem, "Dating the End of the Hittite Empire," in *Hethitica VIII: Acta Anatolica E. Laroche oblata*, ed. René Lebrun (Louvain/Paris: Peeters, 1987), 413–22; Harry A. Hoffner Jr., "The Last Days of Khattusha," in *The Crisis Years: The Twelfth Century* B.C., ed. William A. Ward and Martha S. Joukowsky (Dubuque, Iowa: Kendall/Hunt, 1992), 46–52.

16. Cord Kühne and Heinrich Otten, *Der Šaušgamuwa-Vertrag*, Studien zu den Boğazköy-Texten 16 (Wiesbaden: Harrassowitz, 1971), 14–15.

watalli II had been ruled by Muwatalli's own descendants: first Kurunta (written KAL), followed by Ulmi-Teshub. Important new evidence bearing on this kingdom came to light with the discovery in 1986 of an intact copy of a treaty between Tudḫaliya IV and Kurunta preserved on a bronze tablet.[17] Despite Tudḫaliya's self-serving description of undying love between Kurunta and him, it appears that relations between Tarḫuntashsha and Ḫattusha during this last century were strained, to say the least. An impression of Kurunta's royal seal, on which he styles himself "Great King," an unthinkable appropriation of the imperial title, has been found in the upper city at Ḫattusha. This, together with evidence for a destruction layer in the upper city that can be attributed to the reign of Tudḫaliya IV, has led both Peter Neve and Heinrich Otten to conclude that Kurunta for a time succeeded in wresting the throne from Tudḫaliya.[18]

Despite all the welcome new evidence bearing on the last years of Ḫattusha, we still cannot identify precisely what political or social forces (or combination of both) brought about the fall of Ḫattusha.[19] It is, however, now clear that what "fell" was not the entire Hittite Empire, but only the imperial capital Ḫattusha. There was a continuation of Hittite rule in other centers, particularly in the east at Carchemish[20] and in the south in the general area of the Tarḫuntashsha kingdom, as the Kızıldağ-Karadağ relief and inscription shows.[21]

Language and Writing System

Language

Indo-European Origin. The Indo-European character of the Hittite language was recognized at the time of its decipherment and has never been seriously questioned.[22] Hittite shares many linguistic features with the other Indo-

---

17. Heinrich Otten, *Die Bronzetafel aus Boğazköy: Ein Staatsvertrag Tuthalijas IV*, Studien zu den Boğazköy-Texten 1 (Wiesbaden: Harrassowitz, 1988).

18. Peter Neve, "Boğazköy-Hattusha: New Results of the Excavations in the Upper City," *Anatolica* 16 (1989–90): 7–20.

19. Hoffner, "Last Days of Khattusha."

20. Ibid.; J. David Hawkins, "Kuzi-Tešub and the 'Great Kings' of Karkamiš," *Anatolian Studies* 38 (1988): 99–108.

21. Sedat Alp, "Eine neue hieroglyphenhethitische Inschrift der Gruppe Kızıldağ-Karadağ aus der Nähe von Aksaray und die früher publizierten Inschriften derselben Gruppe," in *Anatolian Studies Presented to Hans Gustav Güterbock on the Occasion of His Sixty-fifth Birthday*, ed. Kurt Bittel, Philo H. J. Houwink ten Cate, and Erica Reiner (Istanbul: Nederlands Historisch-Archaeologisch Instituut in het Nabije Oosten, 1974), 17–27; and J. David Hawkins, "Light in the Dark Ages: Evidence for Hittite Continuity," paper read at a symposium entitled "The Eyes and Ears of the Ancient Near East," University of Pennsylvania, Philadelphia, 1989.

22. Gurney, *Hittites*, 97–101.

European languages of ancient Anatolia: Luwian (and its descendant Lycian) and Palaic.[23]

Non-Indo-European Features. Although the grammatical structure of Hittite, Luwian, and Palaic is Indo-European, when speakers of these languages arrived in Anatolia they adopted much vocabulary from the peoples they encountered.[24] This was particularly true of terms for native flora and fauna for which the Indo-Europeans had no corresponding terms from their earlier homeland,[25] and also of terms denoting social status and professions peculiar to the new land. While the terms for king and queen seem to be Indo-European, those for various kinds of priests and artisans are clearly not. Interestingly, the Hittite word for priest, *shankunnish,* was borrowed not from the local non-Indo-European Anatolians, but from Mesopotamia (Sumerian SANGA, Akkadian *šangû*) via the Hurrians (the suffix *-nni*). As usual, foreign elements appear rarely in verbs, but quite commonly in nouns and adjectives.

Development. The Hittite language was written over a period of several centuries, from ca. 1650 to 1180. From the early days of Hittitology, when texts of the earliest kings were edited, it was known that Old Hittite could be distinguished from the classical language of Shuppiluliuma I's successors. But at that time no criterion had yet been elaborated to distinguish Old Hittite originals from New Hittite copies of Old Hittite originals. The latter were likely to include many modernizations, making it very difficult to determine which linguistic features were genuinely old. New research and the publication of new texts (from ca. 1965 to the present) now allow this determination.[26] The *Chicago Hittite Dictionary,* edited by Hans Güterbock and me, indicates both the date of the original composition (Old Hittite, Middle Hit-

---

23. Pierro Meriggi, *Schizzo Grammaticale dell'Anatolico* (Rome: Accademia Nazionale dei Lincei, 1980); J. David Hawkins, Anna Morpurgo-Davies, and Günter Neumann, *Hittite Hieroglyphs and Luwian: New Evidence for the Connection,* Nachrichten der Akademie der Wissenschaften in Göttingen, Philologisch-historische Klasse 73/6 (Göttingen: Vandenhoeck & Ruprecht, 1974); Annelies Kammenhuber, "The Linguistic Situation of the Second Millennium B.C. in Ancient Anatolia," *Journal of the Royal Asiatic Society* (1975): 116–20; Calvert Watkins, "Questions Linguistiques Palaïtes et Louvites Cunéiformes," in *Hethitica VIII: Acta Anatolica E. Laroche oblata,* ed. René Lebrun (Louvain/Paris: Peeters, 1987), 423–26; Terumasa Oshiro, "Some Luwian Words of Indo-European Origin," *Orient* 24 (1988): 47–54.

24. Gurney, *Hittites,* 99.

25. Harry A. Hoffner Jr., *Alimenta Hethaeorum: Food Production in Hittite Asia Minor,* American Oriental Series 55 (New Haven: American Oriental Society, 1974).

26. Philo H. J. Houwink ten Cate, *The Records of the Early Hittite Empire (c. 1450–1380 B.C.)* (Istanbul: Nederlands Historisch-Archaeologisch Instituut in het Nabije Oosten, 1970) (see my review in *Journal of Near Eastern Studies* 31 [1972]: 29–35); Hans G. Güterbock and Harry A. Hoffner Jr., *The Hittite Dictionary of the Oriental Institute of the University of Chicago* (Chicago: Oriental Institute, 1989), vol. L–N (originally labeled vol. 3), pp. x–xi.

tite, or New Hittite) and the date of the copy (Old Script, Middle Script, or New Script).

Writing System

Derivation. Since the cuneiform script used on the tablets from Ḫattusha ultimately must have derived from Mesopotamia, where it was invented in the third millennium, the question remains, where was the more immediate source? Although during the period of the Old Assyrian trade colonies cuneiform was used to write Old Assyrian, it is thought that both the shapes of the individual signs and the choice of particular signs for specific syllabic values differed too radically between Old Assyrian and Hittite for the latter to have been directly derived from the former. For this reason the standard view is that the Hittites adopted their cuneiform writing system from a form of Old Babylonian used in Syria.[27] If such was the case, the initial contact may have occurred during one of the Hittite military forays into north Syria, perhaps during the reign of Ḫattushili I.

Adaptation. Since cuneiform was primarily intended for writing Sumerian and Akkadian, Hittite scribes had to make some changes in order to write Hittite. The z-series of syllabic signs (*za, zi, zu, az, iz,* etc.) was taken over not to represent a voiced sibilant, but the sound /ts/. Although the Hittite language possessed the voiced-unvoiced opposition in the occlusives (b/p, d/t, g/k), this distinction was not expressed by separate signs for *ba* and *pa* or for *gu* and *ku.* Certain signs were given new phonetic values; for example, since the Hittite word for wine was *wiyanaš,* Hittite scribes gave the syllabic value *wi* to the Sumerian word sign for wine (GEŠTIN).[28]

Diachronic Aspects. As the Hittite language itself—its grammar and lexicon—gradually changed over the five centuries of its written history, so also did the way of writing Hittite cuneiform. This affords a criterion for the dating of individual clay tablets. The first step was the recognition of the Old Hittite ductus. The determination of the date of this distinctive type of script was made possible by the recovery of the so-called Zukrashi tablet from an archeological stratum datable on other grounds to the Old Hittite period. On the basis of this single tablet it was then possible to identify other Old Hittite copies from the archives of thirteenth-century Ḫattusha. The first attempts—

27. Thomas V. Gamkrelidze, "The Akkado-Hittite Syllabary and the Problem of the Origin of the Hittite Script," *Archiv Orientální* 29 (1961): 406–18; J. David Hawkins, "The Origin and Dissemination of Writing in Western Asia," in *The Origins of Civilization,* ed. P. Roger S. Moorey (Oxford: Clarendon, 1979), 128–66.

28. The best current description of the Hittite writing system is Christel Rüster and Erich Neu's *Hethitisches Zeichenlexikon: Inventar und Interpretation der Keilschriftzeichen aus den Boğazköy-Texten,* Studien zu den Boğazköy-Texten 2 (Wiesbaden: Harrassowitz, 1989).

necessarily tentative and incomplete—to show the evolution of Hittite cune-iform paleography and to work out the development of this writing system were made by Christel Rüster and Erich Neu in 1972–75.[29] Some, notably Annelies Kammenhuber and her students, fundamentally challenged the con-cept;[30] others accepted it with modifications. The first volume of the *Chicago Hittite Dictionary* primarily followed the dating scheme advocated by Car-ruba, Otten, Houwink ten Cate, and Neu. With the appearance of Rüster and Neu's *Hethitisches Zeichenlexikon* there now exists a comprehensive register of sign forms used in Hittite texts.

Archeological Excavations

From the standpoint of Hittite history and culture, by far the most important excavated site is ancient Ḫattusha (modern Boğazköy or Boğaz-kale). The concession to excavate the massive ruins near Boğazköy was ob-tained for the German Oriental Society by Hugo Winckler, and excavations began in 1906. Winckler worked with Theodore Makridi in 1907, 1911, and 1912. After an interruption caused by the Balkan War, the First World War, and the Greco-Turkish War, excavations were resumed in 1931 under the joint auspices of the German Archeological Institute and the German Oriental Society. Nine consecutive annual campaigns (from 1931 to 1939) were conducted on the site under the direction of Kurt Bittel. After another hiatus, caused by World War II, excavations were resumed in 1952, with no interruptions since then. Since 1952, the epigraphy has been under the di-rection of Heinrich Otten, now emeritus professor at Philipps University in Marburg and director of the center for Hittitological research in Mainz. Bittel's successor, the current general director of the excavations, is Peter Neve.

The best general presentation of the results of the excavations at Ḫattusha through the 1960s is Bittel's *Ḫattusha: The Capital of the Hittites*.[31] No sin-gle published work gives a complete summary of the excavations of the 1970s and 1980s. For this, one must consult the annual reports by Neve in *Archäol-*

29. Christel Rüster, *Hethitische Keilschriftpaläographie*, Studien zu den Boghazköy-Texten 20 (Wiesbaden: Harrassowitz, 1972); Neu and Rüster, "Zur Datierung hethitischer Texte," in *Festschrift Heinrich Otten*, ed. Erich Neu and Christel Rüster (Wiesbaden: Harrassowitz, 1973), 221–42; Neu and Rüster, *Hethitisches Keilschrift-Paläographie II (14./13. Jh. v. Chr.)*, Studien zu den Boğazköy-Texten 21 (Wiesbaden: Harrassowitz, 1975).
30. Susanne Heinhold-Krahmer et al., *Probleme der Textdatierung in der Hethitologie*, Texte der Hethiter (Heidelberg: Carl Winter Universitätsverlag, 1979).
31. Kurt Bittel, *Ḫattusha: The Capital of the Hittites* (New York: Oxford University Press, 1970).

ogischer Anzeiger and the important archeological studies of Hittite Anatolia written in English that have appeared in the past twenty years.[32]

Textual Sources

Cuneiform Tablets (Including Inscriptions on Seals)

In the first season of digging at Ḫattusha (1906) the site yielded thousands of inscribed clay tablets. Many of these were in Akkadian and could be read immediately. The most important tablets, state treaties that gave information about political history and diplomacy, were published by Ernst F. Weidner in 1923.[33] Even before the decipherment of Hittite by Bedřich Hrozný, material from the newly discovered Sumero-Akkado-Hittite vocabularies was studied and exploited by leading Assyriologists. And within a few years of the decipherment, full-fledged Hittite grammars were written, some of which are still useful today, although the current standard grammar is Johannes Friedrich's *Elementarbuch*.[34]

In accordance with their agreement with the Turkish authorities, the Germans immediately set about copying, publishing, cleaning, and conserving the clay tablets excavated from Ḫattusha. Most of these were transported to Berlin for this purpose, although a small number remained in Istanbul. In Berlin, Hans Ehelolf was in charge of the Hittite material and under his direction a small group of skilled Assyriologist-Hittitologists began the work of making hand copies of the Hittite tablets. Among them were Hugo H. Figulla, Ernst F. Weidner, Albrecht Goetze, Arnold Walther, J. Schiele, Hans G. Güterbock, C. G. von Brandenstein, Josef Sturm, and Heinrich Otten. Ehelolf died during World War II and was succeeded in Berlin for a time by Otten, who continued the publication of Hittite tablets on loan to the Berlin museum in the KUB series (Keilschrifturkunden aus Boghazköi). After Otten emigrated to West Ger-

---

32. James Mellaart, *The Archaeology of Ancient Turkey* (London: Bodley Head, 1978); Tahsin Özgüç, *Excavations at Maşat Höyük and Investigations in Its Vicinity* (Ankara: Türk Tarih Kurumu, 1978); idem, *Inandıktepe: An Important Cult Center in the Old Hittite Period* (Ankara: Türk Tarih Kurumu, 1988); Maurits N. van Loon, *Anatolia in the Second Millennium* B.C., Iconography of Religions 15/12 (Leiden: Brill, 1985); Jeanny V. Canby, "Hittite Art," *Biblical Archaeologist* 52 (1989): 109–29; Neve, "New Results."

33. Ernst F. Weidner, *Politische Dokumente aus Kleinasien: Die Staatsverträge in akkadischer Sprache aus dem Archiv von Boghazköi*, Boghazköi-Studien 8–9 (Leipzig: Hinrichs, 1923).

34. Johannes Friedrich, *Hethitisches Elementarbuch*, vol. 1: *Kurzgefasste Grammatik*, 2d ed., Indogermanische Bibliothek: Lehr- und Handbücher (Heidelberg: Carl Winter Universitätsverlag, 1960). Earlier grammars include Emil Forrer, "Die Inschriften und Sprachen des Hatti-Reiches," *Zeitschrift der Deutschen Morgenländischen Gesellschaft* 76 (1922): 174–269; Johannes Friedrich, "Die hethitische Sprache," *Zeitschrift der Deutschen Morgenländischen Gesellschaft* 76 (1922): 153–73.

many, that task was assumed by Horst Klengel. In West Germany, Otten revived the old KBo series (Keilschrifttexte aus Boghazköi), which has become the vehicle for the publication of tablets found at Ḫattusha since World War II. At this writing there are sixty volumes in KUB and thirty-two in KBo.

Hieroglyphic Inscriptions

Although known for years as "hieroglyphic Hittite," it is now recognized that the language of the hieroglyphic texts composed by the Hittite kings is a dialect of Luwian. The corpus of Luwian texts written in cuneiform, first presented by Otten, has now been enlarged and updated by F. Starke.[35] A glossary of the cuneiform Luwian texts and an outline of their grammar was published by Emmanuel Laroche.[36]

Although the solid research of Ignace J. Gelb, Pierro Meriggi, and Emmanuel Laroche laid a substantial foundation for the reading and interpretation of hieroglyphic Luwian inscriptions, 1974 represented a watershed. In this year a joint publication of J. David Hawkins, A. Morpurgo-Davies, and G. Neumann proposed new readings of signs that allowed the close relationship between the grammar and lexicon of the cuneiform and hieroglyphic Luwian texts to be seen.[37] In the 1970s and 1980s several important new hieroglyphic inscriptions were identified and published, and known inscriptions were reexamined and reinterpreted. At this writing the most recent attempt at a comprehensive reassessment of the hieroglyphic Luwian texts is Marazzi's.[38] Scholars are awaiting the appearance of Hawkins's announced corpus of hieroglyphic Luwian inscriptions, which will doubtless set a new standard.[39] Also eagerly awaited is the official publication by Hawkins of the new inscription of Shuppiluliuma II from the southern fortress at Ḫattusha.[40]

35. Heinrich Otten, *Luvische Texte in Umschrift*, Deutsche Akademie der Wissenschaften zu Berlin, Institut für Orientforschung, Veröffentlichung 17 (Berlin: Akademie Verlag, 1953); F. Starke, *Die keilschrift-luwischen Texte in Umschrift*, Studien zu den Boğazköy-Texten 30 (Wiesbaden: Harrassowitz, 1985).

36. Emmanuel Laroche, *Dictionnaire de la Langue Louvite* (Paris: Adrien-Maisonneuve, 1959).

37. Hawkins, Morpurgo-Davies, and Neumann, *Hittite Hieroglyphs and Luwian*.

38. Massimiliano Marazzi, *Il Geroglifico Anatolico: Problemi di Analisi e Prospettive di Ricerca*, Biblioteca di Ricerche Linguistiche e Filologiche 24 (Rome: Dipartimento de Studi Glottoantropologici, Università "La Sapienza," 1990).

39. J. David Hawkins, *The Hieroglyphic Luwian Inscriptions of the Iron Age* (Berlin: de Gruyter, forthcoming).

40. Neve, "New Results"; and Hoffner, "Last Days of Khattusha." A provisional report was given in Heinrich Otten, "Die hieroglyphen-luwische Inschrift," *Archäologischer Anzeiger* 1989: 333–37.

Material Culture

Agriculture

The basic treatment of agriculture and food production among the Hittites remains my *Alimenta Hethaeorum*.[41] The texts show that several cereals and a wide variety of fruits and vegetables (beans, chick peas, lentils, cucumbers, onions, leeks, and garlic) were cultivated. Both honey and wax were obtained from bee-keeping. Beverage wine was produced from vineyards, as were raisins. The technique of beer-making was known and practiced. Various classes of wine are not distinguished in the texts, but at least three varieties of beer are. Other fermented beverages included "beer-honey," which could be either mead or regular beer made from barley and sweetened with honey; others remain only names to us: *walḫi*, *tawal*, and something called "beer-wine."

Livestock

Meat, lard, milk, butter, and cheeses were food products derived from raising livestock (cattle, sheep, goats, and pigs).[42] A list of standard prices for food commodities can be found in the Hittite laws.[43] The hides of certain animals were also sold.[44] The horns (Hittite *karawar*) of certain animals were used as containers, wall decorations, and musical instruments (Hittite *shawatar* or *shawitra*). Plowing was done with oxen. Donkeys were a common means of transporting loads. Oxen and mules drew carts, and horses pulled war chariots. Both mules and horses were used for riding.

Food Preservation

Texts mention the collection and storage of snow and ice in special houses for later use during the hot seasons.[45] These may have been used both for the cooling of beverages and for the preserving of fresh meat. But the preservation of both fruits and meat by drying is well attested in the texts.[46] Sugar-containing fruit juices were also preserved by the process of fermentation.

---

41. Hoffner, *Alimenta Hethaeorum*.

42. Ibid., 120–23.

43. ANET 195–96 §§178–86; Johannes Friedrich, *Die hethitischen Gesetze: Transkription, Übersetzung, sprachliche Erläuterungen und vollständiges Wörterverzeichnis*, Documenta et Monumenta Orientis Antiqui 7 (Leiden: Brill, 1959), 78–83; Harry A. Hoffner Jr., "The Hittites and Hurrians," in *Peoples of Old Testament Times*, ed. Donald J. Wiseman (Oxford: Clarendon, 1973), 207.

44. ANET 196 §185; the unit price of hides (or fleeces) ranged from one-twentieth of a shekel to four shekels. For comparison with prices of other commodities in the laws see Hoffner, "Hittites and Hurrians," 207.

45. Harry A. Hoffner Jr., "Hittite *Ega-* and *Egan-*," *Journal of Cuneiform Studies* 24 (1971): 31–36.

46. Hoffner, *Alimenta Hethaeorum*, 16–17.

Architecture and City Planning

Excavations at second-millennium Boğazköy, Alaca Hüyük, Beycesultan, Tarsus, Maşat, Norşuntepe, and Tepecik give evidence for a certain level of town planning.[47] Streets were usually straight and surfaced with a layer of coarse gravel. Sloping sites were terraced, with attention given to drainage. Many streets had stone-roofed drainage channels running down the middle, with smaller channels feeding into them from houses or side streets.

Private houses were by no means uniform in plan. Most had a courtyard, but often in front of the house, rather than in the center. Houses were constructed of mud brick with timber reinforcement (against earthquakes) on a foundation of stones. Mud-thatched roofs were flat rather than pitched. Both the mud-brick exterior and the thatched roofs required periodic renewal to prevent leakage. Columns on the ground level supported a second story. Floors were either of stamped earth or covered with plaster or stones. Windows, if they existed, were small and high up, not for looking out, but to permit sunlight in.

Metallurgy

There is no truth to the common misconception that the Hittites were the inventors of iron technology in the Near East and that they owed their military supremacy to this advantage.[48] Like other large states of the late second millennium with a need for metals with which to make weapons, the Hittites exclusively exploited bronze for that purpose. Bronze armor scales were found at Ḫattusha.[49] Textual evidence on the use of iron shows it to have been largely a luxury used for making small items, but almost never for weapons.[50] Other metals used were gold, silver, copper, lead, and tin. Gold was used for very small objects and as a plating on statues of deities. Prices and fines were measured in weights of silver. Copper was imported from the is-

---

47. Macqueen, *Hittites*, 79–96; Nilüfer Boysan-Dietrich, *Das hethitische Lehmhaus aus der Sicht der Keilschriftquellen*, Texte der Hethiter 12 (Heidelberg: Carl Winter Universitätsverlag, 1987).

48. Jane Waldbaum, "The First Archaeological Appearance of Iron and the Transition to the Iron Age," in *The Coming of the Age of Iron*, ed. Theodore A. Wertime and James D. Muhly (New Haven: Yale University Press, 1980), 69–98, esp. 83–84.

49. Macqueen, *Hittites*, 63, pl. 33.

50. Aharon Kempinski and Silvin Košak, "Hittite Metal 'Inventories' (CTH 242) and Their Economic Implications," *Tel Aviv* 4 (1977): 87–93; Jana Siegelová, "Gewinnung und Verarbeitung von Eisen im hethitischen Reich im 2. Jahrtausend v. u. Z.," *Annals of the Náprstek Museum* 12 (1984): 71–168; Silvin Košak, "The Gospel of Iron," in *Kaniššuwar: A Tribute to Hans G. Güterbock on His Seventy-fifth Birthday, May 27, 1983*, ed. Harry A. Hoffner Jr. and Gary M. Beckman, Assyriological Studies 23 (Chicago: Oriental Institute, 1986), 125–35.

King and queen from Alaca Hüyük, 14th–13th century B.C. (height: 4′ 2″)

Courtesy of the Museum of Anatolian Civilizations, Ankara

land of Cyprus (ancient Alashiya). Lead was sometimes employed in magical implements because of its supposed imperviousness to evil influences.[51]

Society

Structure

King. At the top of the social scale was the king.[52] Unlike Egyptian pharaohs or some Mesopotamian kings who claimed divinity during their lifetimes,

51. Harry A. Hoffner Jr., "Second Millennium Antecedents to the Hebrew *ʾôḇ,*" *Journal of Biblical Literature* 86 (1967): 398–99 and n. 33; idem, "Hittite *Tarpiš* and Hebrew *Terāphîm,*" *Journal of Near Eastern Studies* 27 (1968): 61–68.

52. Hans G. Güterbock, "Authority and Law in the Hittite Kingdom," in *Authority and Law in the Ancient Orient,* Journal of the American Oriental Society Supplement 17 (New Haven: American Oriental Society, 1954), 16–24; Oliver R. Gurney, "Hittite Kingship," in *Myth, Ritual and Kingship,* ed. Samuel H. Hooke (Oxford: Clarendon, 1958), 105–21; Albrecht Goetze, "State and Society of the Hittites," in *Neuere Hethiterforschung,* ed. Gerold Walser

Hittite kings were not considered to be divine while living. When a king died, however, it was said that he "became a god." This concept is reflected not only in the official cult for the spirits of deceased kings, but also in the pictorial representation of deceased kings, who are shown in reliefs standing on mountains (Tudhaliya IV in Yazılıkaya) or with horns coming from their heads or crowns (Shuppiluliuma II in the southern fortress of Hattusha)—just like the deities portrayed on reliefs or seals or as statuettes.[53] Living kings portrayed on their seals do not have these attributes.

According to tradition,

> The land belongs only to the Stormgod. Heaven and earth with the people belong to the Stormgod. He has made the Labarna, the king, his administrator, and gave him the whole land of Hatti. Let the Labarna keep administering the whole land with his hand![54]

Thus the king was the gods' appointed regent. The fate of the land and the people at the hand of the gods depended upon how well the king served the gods and executed his role as administrator. This at once secured great respect for the person of the king and placed upon him exacting requirements of behavior.

As the land's supreme priest, the king's person was sacred and had to be protected at all times from defilement. His presence at the major religious festivals was important enough to bring him back from distant battlefields. When presiding at religious ceremonies the king carried a crook (Hittite *kalmush*) and wore the robe and cap of the sun god. It is in this attire that we see him depicted on many reliefs, including those at Alaca Hüyük and Yazılıkaya.

As the land's supreme judge,[55] the king heard cases of the gravest nature, requiring the death penalty:

(Wiesbaden: Steiner, 1964), 23–33; Galya Kellerman, "The King and the Sun-god in the Old Hittite Period," *Tel Aviv* 5 (1978): 199–208; Philo H. J. Houwink ten Cate, "The Sun God of Heaven and the Hittite King," in *Effigies Dei: Essays on the History of Religions*, ed. Dirk van der Plas, Numen Supplement 51 (Leiden: Brill, 1987), 13–34.

53. For Tudhaliya IV, see Gurney, *Hittites*, 119, fig. 8, no. 64.; Kurt Bittel, *Die Hethiter: Die Kunst Anatoliens vom Ende des 3. bis zum Anfang des 1. Jahrtausends vor Christus* (Munich: Beck, 1976), 214. For Shuppiluliuma II, see Peter Neve, "Die Ausgrabungen in Boğazköy-Hattuša 1988," *Archäologischer Anzeiger* 1988: 317, pl. 40. For deities on reliefs, see Macqueen, *Hittites*, 25, 131; Bittel, *Die Hethiter*, 173, 179, 212, 214; on seals, see Gurney, *Hittites*, 172–73; Macqueen, *Hittites*, 48, pl. 23; Bittel, *Die Hethiter*, 168, 170, 172; as statuettes, see Bittel, *Die Hethiter*, 213.

54. Güterbock, "Authority and Law," 16.

55. Ibid., 16–24; Harry A. Hoffner Jr., *The Laws of the Hittites* (Ph.D. diss., Brandeis University, 1963), 325–26.

sorcery (§§44, 111)
adultery (§198)
sexual relations with certain animals (§§187–88, 199)
treason
serious dereliction of military duties
major theft (§102)
allowing a bull to escape from its corral (§176)
taxation (§47 and its late parallel)

Even stray livestock found in the vicinity of Ḫattusha had to be driven to "the king's gate" (i.e., a royal tribunal) in order for legal custody to be assigned to the finder (§71). Persons who believed themselves unjustly treated in lower courts could appeal to the king's court (§55). Refusal to comply with the king's or the magistrates' verdict brought extremely serious consequences (§173).

Queen. We know relatively little of the queen's power in the Old Kingdom.[56] During the New Kingdom she seems to have exercised great influence.[57] The king and queen used a joint seal that portrayed the king on the right and the queen on the left, both standing under the winged solar disk and facing each other across the hieroglyphs that identified them.[58] Some if not all queens held the office of chief priestess, corresponding to their husbands' office of chief priest. In this capacity they could control a substantial amount of temple wealth. On occasion this led to a conflict of interest with the king himself, as in the case of King Murshili II and his stepmother, the dowager queen Tawannanna.[59] Ḫattushili III's queen, Puduhepa, who was the daughter of a powerful priest of Kizzuwatna, was one of the most influential persons in the history of the New Kingdom.[60] During her husband's lifetime she corresponded independently with Pharaoh Ramesses II of Egypt, and as dowager queen she continued to issue decisions regarding matters of state in the southeastern dependencies.

56. Shoshanna R. Bin-Nun, *The Tawananna in the Hittite Kingdom*, Texte der Hethiter 5 (Heidelberg: Carl Winter Universitätsverlag, 1975).

57. Albrecht Goetze, *Kleinasien*, 2d ed., Handbuch der Altertumswissenschaft: Kulturgeschichte des Alten Orients (Munich: Beck, 1957), 92–95.

58. A good example is the seal of King Tudḫaliya IV and his queen; see Bittel, *Die Hethiter*, 171 (mistakenly labeled Shuppiluliuma I in Macqueen, *Hittites*, 77, pl. 48).

59. Gurney, *Hittites*, 54; Harry A. Hoffner Jr., "A Prayer of Muršili II about His Stepmother," *Journal of the American Oriental Society* 103 (1983): 187–92.

60. Heinrich Otten, *Eine hethitische Königin in ihren Textzeugnissen*, Akademie der Wissenschaften und der Literatur [Mainz]: Abhandlungen der Geistes- und Sozialwissenschaftlichen Klassen, Jahrgang 1975/1 (Mainz: Steiner, 1975).

Princes. By *prince* I do not mean only young sons of the king. Rather I include all male descendants of kings, regardless of age. Hittite princes are depicted on the rock reliefs at Hanyeri, Hemite, and Imamkulu.[61] In the former two, the prince is shown with a spear held vertically in his right hand, a bow slung over his left shoulder, and a sword or dagger in his belt.

At some point during his reign the king designated one of his sons, usually the oldest, as crown prince (Hittite *tuḫukantish*). This designation could always be changed, as in fact it was on a number of occasions. During the Old Kingdom, Ḫattushili I replaced his first choice with another son, only to replace this second with his grandson Murshili I. Ḫattushili III replaced his oldest son by the younger Tudḫaliya IV. Princes often held responsible positions in the government. Already in the earliest phase of the Old Kingdom, Labarna I and Ḫattushili I sent princes to govern the major provincial cities of their kingdoms. After the conquest of north Syria, Shuppiluliuma I installed two of his sons as hereditary kings of the major centers Carchemish and Aleppo. Ḫattushili III installed his nephew and adopted son Kurunta as hereditary king of Tarḫuntashsha.

Nobility. The term *Great Family* (Hittite *shalli ḫashatar*) already in the early Old Kingdom designated the extended family, that is, blood relatives, of the king. It was from this pool that the king supplied all the high officials of his realm. It was they who made up the *pankush* ("ruling class") that in the Old Kingdom constituted an advisory body for the king. They did not make law, but they did have the power to convict and execute a king for murdering a fellow member of the Great Family.[62] They were responsible for the safety and education of one who succeeded to kingship while still a child.[63] While a Hittite king should always be characterized by mercy, his judicial clemency was especially appropriate toward a member of this Great Family.

Free Persons. While the concept of freedom in the Hittite kingdom was much less comprehensive than the modern Western concept, the law distinguished between "free" and "unfree."[64] Very few persons were exempt from

---

61. Bittel, *Die Hethiter*, 180–82.

62. Edgar H. Sturtevant and George Bechtel, *A Hittite Chrestomathy* (Philadelphia: Linguistic Society of America, University of Pennsylvania, 1935), 190–91; Bryce, *Major Historical Texts*, 137–38, with comments on 153–55.

63. Ferdinand Sommer and Adam Falkenstein, *Die hethitisch-akkadische Bilingue des Hattusili I. (Labarna II.)*, Abhandlungen der Bayerischen Akademie der Wissenschaften: Philosophisch-historische Abteilung (Munich: Verlag der Bayerischen Akademie der Wissenschaften, 1938), 8–9 §8; Bryce, *Major Historical Texts*, 102–3; see also Harry A. Hoffner Jr., "Advice to a King," in *Festschrift for Sedat Alp*, ed. Hayri Ertem, Yaşar Coşkun, and Aygül Süel (Ankara: Türk Tarih Kurumu, 1992), 295–304.

64. Güterbock, "Authority and Law," 16–24; Goetze, *Kleinasien* 106–7; Gurney, *Hittites*, 57–58, 78–81; Goetze, "State and Society of the Hittites," 28–29; Hans G. Güterbock, "Be-

some form of compulsory payment or duty. Only a minority of the persons called free (Hittite *arawannis*) were also exempt (*arawash*) from the payment of the twin obligations *shaḫḫan* and *luzzi*. In the more general sense, free persons could buy and sell, enter into contracts, change their place of residence, and enter and leave marriage without need to secure the approval of some superior. This was not so for the unfree.

Domestic or Private Slaves. The most obvious type of unfree person was the private slave,[65] who was the property of a master. In the laws, if a slave caused damage, the master was required to make compensation to the injured party or else lose the slave. Reparations for injury inflicted on a slave went to the master. Occasionally we read of a slave making a payment to a free person to induce the latter to marry the slave's daughter—which implies the ability of slaves to acquire some private wealth. Whether they ever used this wealth to purchase their own freedom is not known. A kind of periodic remitting of debts and manumitting of debt slaves seems to have been known among the Hurrians, who constituted a major component of the Hittite population during the New Kingdom. To date, this custom is only known from a Hurro-Hittite bilingual literary text, where the practice is enjoined on the basis of a divine precedent.[66] We have no historical or legal text from Ḫattusha to show its application, although it is claimed that this practice is reflected in a Middle Hittite edict.[67]

Public Slaves. The *arnuwalash* (Sumerian NAM.RA) was essentially a displaced person, someone of foreign birth captured in battle and serving (in a community of similar persons) as migrant workers or farmer-settlers. The king could assign them wherever there was a need. The local provincial gov-

---

merkungen zu den Ausdrücken *ellum, wardum* und *asīrum* in hethitischen Texten," in *Gesellschaftsklassen im alten Zweistromland und in den angrenzenden Gebieten: XVIII. Rencontre Assyriologique Internationale*, ed. Dietz O. Edzard (Munich: Verlag der Bayerischen Akademie der Wissenschaften, 1972), 93–97. On the Hittite words for "free," see my "Review of *Hethitisches Wörterbuch* by Johannes Friedrich and Annelies Kammenhuber," *Bibliotheca Orientalis* 40 (1983): 409–11.

65. Sumerian ÌR; Hittite reading unknown.

66. Heinrich Otten, "Blick in die altorientalische Geisteswelt: Neufund einer hethitischen Tempelbibliothek," *Jahrbuch der Akademie der Wissenschaften in Göttingen* 1984: 50–60; idem, "Ebla in der hurritisch-hethitischen Bilingue aus Boğazköy," in *Wirtschaft und Gesellschaft in Ebla: Akten der Internationalen Tagung Heidelberg, 4.–7. November 1986*, ed. H. Waetzoldt and H. Hauptman (Heidelberg: Heidelberger Orientverlag, 1988), 291–92; Erich Neu, *Das Hurritische: Eine altorientalische Sprache in neuem Licht* (Stuttgart: Steiner, 1988); idem, "Varia Hurritica: Sprachliche Beobachtungen an der hurritisch-hethitischen Bilingue aus Ḫattuša," in *Documentum Asiae Minoris Antiquae*, ed. Erich Neu and Christel Rüster (Wiesbaden: Harrassowitz, 1988), 235–54.

67. Raymond Westbrook and Roger D. Woodard, "The Edict of Tudhaliya IV," *Journal of the American Oriental Society* 110 (1990): 641–59.

ernor would then provide them with food, shelter, seed, and equipment to do their job. The *ḫipparash* (Akkadian *asīrum*) is less clearly understood.[68] From the laws (§§48–49) it appears that they were not allowed to buy or sell (which suggests ownership by the state) and could not dispose of anything that they used.

Metics. At the capital city there would always be a small community of foreign ambassadors, or temporary foreign residents (Akkadian *ubārum*).[69] While not citizens of Hatti, these persons were from the upper class, often relatives of their king, and possessed certain rights and privileges, which included limited access to the Hittite temple precincts. This class of persons has some similarities to the Biblical Hebrew *gēr* and the Greek *metoikos* or *paroikos*.

Law

In illiterate societies, law is obviously unwritten. But also in some ancient societies where the ruling and administrative classes were literate no written (or codified) law has been preserved. For example, no collection of laws is known from the important kingdom of Ugarit. But among ancient Near Eastern societies who wrote on clay tablets, there are collections of laws from Sumer, Babylonia, Assyria, and Hatti.[70] The Hittite laws can be studied in critical editions and translations; in addition, there are discussions of the laws as a corpus.[71]

Formal codifications of case laws such as the Hittite collection are not the only written sources for law. Diplomatic law is illustrated in state treaties. Bureaucratic and administrative law is expressed in royal decrees and in what

68. Güterbock, "Bemerkungen zu den Ausdrücken," 96–97.

69. On *ubārum* in general, see Wolfram von Soden, *Akkadisches Handwörterbuch*, 3 vols. (Wiesbaden: Harrassowitz, 1965–81), 1399; on its use in Old Assyrian, see Larsen, *Old Assyrian City-State*, 279; on its use as a logogram in Hittite texts, see Einar von Schuler, "Hethitische Kultbräuche in dem Brief eines ugaritischen Gesandten," *Revue Hittite et Asianique* 21 (1963): 45–46 n. 17; Harry A. Hoffner Jr., "An English-Hittite Glossary," *Revue Hittite et Asianique* 25 (1967): 42 n. 56; Franca Pecchioli Daddi, *Mestieri, Professioni e Dignità nell'Anatolia Ittita*, Incunabula Graeca 69 (Rome: Ateneo, 1982), 575–78.

70. Translations in *ANET*, with discussions in the following monographs: Kenneth A. Kitchen, *Ancient Orient and Old Testament* (Chicago: InterVarsity, 1966), 134–35, 147–48; idem, *The Bible in Its World: The Bible and Archaeology Today* (Downers Grove, Ill.: InterVarsity, 1977), 79–85; Cyril J. Gadd, "Hammurabi and the End of His Dynasty," in *CAH* 2/1:177, 182–85, 187–95, 195–97, 202–6; John H. Walton, *Ancient Israelite Literature in Its Cultural Context* (Grand Rapids: Zondervan, 1989), 69–93 (with full anterior literature).

71. Friedrich, *Die hethitischen Gesetze*; Fiorella Imparati, *Le Leggi Ittite*, Incunabula Graeca 7 (Rome: Ateneo, 1964); Hoffner, *Laws of the Hittites*, 8–123; Albrecht Goetze, "The Hittite Laws," in *ANET* 188–97; Einar von Schuler, "Die hethitischen Gesetze," in *Texte aus der Umwelt des Alten Testaments*, vol. 1: *Rechts- und Wirtschaftsurkunden historisch-chronologische Texte* (Gütersloh: Mohn, 1978), 96–123. For discussions, see Güterbock, "Authority and Law"; Goetze, *Kleinasien*, 109–17; Hoffner, *Laws of the Hittites*.

Hittitologists call "instruction texts." The administration of Hittite law in the provinces and tributary states of the empire is illustrated in documents from Ugarit and Emar.[72] The general outline of how such cases would be heard is also described in the "Instructions to the District Commanders."[73] The conduct of inquests to determine guilt or innocence in cases affecting the Hittite state or royalty is portrayed in the genre of texts known as *Gerichtsprotokolle*. Serious cases that carried the death penalty (such as treason) were always referred to the king's court.[74]

Statecraft

Hittite government was above all a government of law. In addition to the corpus of laws that governed all citizens, there were "rule books" for the conduct of every major office of the government, only some of which have survived in the form of "instruction texts."[75] There were even instructions for the king.[76] It was fitting, therefore, that relations between Hittite kings and their equal-ranked and subordinate foreign counterparts should be formalized and regulated in writing. To this practice we owe the extensive collection of treaty documents in the Ḫattusha archives.

Hittite treaties have been the object of intensive investigation over the past half century—by Hittitologists themselves and by a number of outside scholars, some specializing in comparative law, others in Old Testament. Hittitologists have been principally interested in the content of the documents: what they have to say about Hittite history and the interrelations of the various states of the Hittite bloc and the outside powers.[77] Non-Hittitologists have

72. In Ugarit: Einar von Schuler, "Eine hethitische Rechtsurkunde aus Ugarit," *Ugarit-Forschungen* 3 (1971): 223–34; in Emar: Horst Klengel, "Die Keilschrifttexte von Meskene und die Geschichte von Astata/Emar," *Orientalistische Literaturzeitung* 83 (1988): 645–53.

73. Einar von Schuler, *Hethitische Dienstanweisungen für höhere Hof- und Staatsbeamte*, Archiv für Orientforschung Beiheft 10 (Osnabrück: Biblio-Verlag, 1957), 47–48 (iii 9–16); English translation by Goetze in *ANET* 211.

74. Hoffner, *Laws of the Hittites*, 325, 327.

75. Von Schuler, *Hethitische Dienstanweisungen*; idem, "Hethitische Königserlässe als Quellen der Rechtsfindung und ihr Verhältnis zum kodifizierten Recht," in *Festschrift Johannes Friedrich zum 65. Geburtstag*, ed. R. von Kienle et al. (Heidelberg: Carl Winter Universitätsverlag, 1959), 435–72; idem, "Staatsverträge und Dokumente hethitischen Rechts," in *Neuere Hethiterforschung*, ed. Gerold Walser (Wiesbaden: Steiner, 1964), 34–53; English translations by Goetze in *ANET* 207–11.

76. Hoffner, "Advice to a King."

77. Johannes Friedrich, *Staatsverträge des Ḫatti-Reiches in hethitischer Sprache*, vol. 2, Mitteilungen der Vorderasiatisch-Ägyptische Gesellschaft 34 (Leipzig: Hinrichs, 1930); Viktor Korošec, *Hethitische Staatsverträge*, Leipziger rechtswissenschaftliche Studien 60 (Leipzig: Weicher, 1931); von Schuler, "Staatsverträge und Dokumente hethitischen Rechts"; idem, "Sonderformen hethitischer Staatsverträge," *Jahrbuch für kleinasiatische Forschungen* 2 (1965): 445–64; Albrecht Goetze, "The Hittites and Syria (1300–1200 B.C.)," in *CAH* 2/2:252–73; Oliver R. Gurney, "The Hittite Empire," in *Power and Propaganda: A Symposium on An-*

compared these texts with similar documents from Mesopotamia and ancient Israel and have seen them as a valuable form-critical tool for dating and interpreting treaty and covenant documents.[78]

Earlier studies on the literary pattern of Hittite treaties were restricted to examples from the period after Shuppiluliuma I (ca. 1344). Subsequently published examples from the Middle Hittite period (ca. 1420–1344) revealed a different structure. The period during which the structure of Hittite treaties most closely resembles that of the Old Testament covenant form is ca. 1344–1271 (reigns of Shuppiluliuma I, Murshili II, and Muwatalli II). The elements of that literary form include the following:

1. introduction of the speaker
2. historical prologue
3. stipulations
4. statement concerning the document

---

cient Empires, ed. Mogens T. Larsen (Copenhagen: Akademisk Forlag, 1979), 151–65; FiorellaImparati, "La Politique Extérieure des Hittites: Tendances et Problèmes," in *Hethitica VIII: Acta Anatolica E. Laroche oblata*, ed. René Lebrun (Louvain/Paris: Peeters, 1987), 187–208; Onofrio Carruba, "Die Hajasa-Verträge Hattis," in *Documentum Asiae Minoris Antiquae*, ed. Erich Neu and Christel Rüster (Wiesbaden: Harrassowitz, 1988), 59–76; Heinrich Otten, *Die 1986 in Boğazköy gefundene Bronzetafel*, Innsbrucker Beiträge zur Sprachwissenschaft 42 (Innsbruck: Universität Innsbruck, 1988).

78. George E. Mendenhall, *Law and Covenant in Israel and the Ancient Near East* (Pittsburgh: Biblical Colloquium, 1955); idem, "Covenant Forms in Israelite Tradition," *Biblical Archaeologist* 17 (1954): 50–76 (repr. in *The Biblical Archaeologist Reader*, vol. 3, ed. Edward F. Campbell Jr. and David N. Freedman [Garden City, N.Y.: Doubleday, 1970], 25–53); idem, "The Suzerainty Treaty Structure: Thirty Years Later," in *Religion and Law: Biblical-Judaic and Islamic Perspectives*, ed. Edwin B. Firmage, Bernard G. Weiss, and John W. Welch (Winona Lake, Ind.: Eisenbrauns, 1990), 85–100; Klaus Baltzer, *The Covenant Formulary in Old Testament, Jewish, and Early Christian Writings*, trans. David E. Green (Philadelphia: Fortress, 1971); Dennis J. McCarthy, *Treaty and Covenant*, 2d ed., Analecta Biblica 21a (Rome: Pontifical Biblical Institute Press, 1981); Delbert R. Hillers, *Covenant: The History of a Biblical Idea* (Baltimore: Johns Hopkins University Press, 1969); Kitchen, *Bible in Its World*, 79–85; P. Kalluveettil, *Declaration and Covenant: A Comprehensive Review of Covenant Formulae from the Old Testament and the Ancient Near East* (Rome: Pontifical Biblical Institute Press, 1982); Walton, *Ancient Israelite Literature*, 95–110. Exceptions to this general dichotomy of interests are the studies of the treaties' literary form and specialized vocabulary by Korošec, *Hethitische Staatsverträge*; von Schuler, "Staatsverträge und Dokumente hethitischen Rechts"; idem, "Sonderformen hethitischer Staatsverträge"; Guy Kestemont, *Diplomatique et Droit International en Asie Occidentale (1600–1200 av. J.C.)*, Publications de l'Institut Orientaliste de Louvain 9 (Louvain-la-Neuve: Université Catholique de Louvain, Institut Orientaliste, 1974); G. F. del Monte, *Sulla Terminologia Hittita per la Restituzione de Fuggiaschi*, Studia Mediterranea 4 (Pavia: Aurora, 1983); Dietrich Sürenhagen, *Paritätische Staatsverträge aus hethitischer Sicht*, Studia Mediterranea 5 (Pavia: Aurora, 1985); Carruba, "Die Hajasa-Verträge Hattis"; and Theo van den Hout, *KBo IV-10 + (CTH 106): Studien zum spätjunghethitischen Texte der Zeit Tuthalijas I* (Ph.D. diss., University of Amsterdam, 1989).

5. divine witnesses
6. curses for noncompliance and blessings for compliance

Scholars differ on the derivation of the biblical covenant form with relation to the form evident in the Hittite treaties. A conservative Christian viewpoint is represented by Egyptologist Kenneth Kitchen (followed by John Walton), who gives a tentatively positive verdict with the *caveat* that there is still much that is unknown about this form in certain areas of the Near East during the first millennium.[79]

Military

Since many of the historical texts are concerned with the military expeditions of the king, Hittite texts yield valuable information about ancient warfare. The first cultural synthesis of the Hittites devoted a chapter to the subject.[80] Recent years have witnessed renewed interest in this subject, with the appearance of three lengthy articles, a chapter in a book, and a doctoral dissertation soon to be revised into a book.[81] Ahmet Ünal studies the technical

Warrior from the King's Gate at Ḫattusha (Boğazköy), 14th–13th century B.C. (height: 6′ 6″)   *Courtesy of the Museum of Anatolian Civilizations, Ankara*

79. Kitchen, *Ancient Orient and Old Testament*, 90–102; idem, *Bible in Its World*, 79–85; Walton, *Ancient Israelite Literature*, 106–7.

80. Goetze, *Kleinasien*, 122–29 ("Das Kriegswesen"). An English summary with the same perspective appeared six years later: idem, "Warfare in Asia Minor," *Iraq* 25 (1963): 124–30.

81. Ahmet Ünal, "Untersuchungen zur Terminologie der hethitischen Kriegsführung, I: 'Verbrennen, in Brand stecken' als Kriegstechnik," *Orientalia* 52 (1983): 164–80; idem, "Studien über das hethitische Kriegswesen, II: Verba Delendi *harnink-/harganu-* 'vernichten, zugrunde richten,'" *Studi Micenei ed Egeo-Anatolici* 24 (1984): 71–85; Philo H. J. Houwink ten Cate, "The History of Warfare according to Hittite Sources: The Annals of Hattusilis I (part II),"

terminology of warfare, Philo Houwink ten Cate investigates key texts dealing with warfare, and Richard Beal brings a vast amount of data from all kinds of written sources to bear on the question of the organization of the military. James G. Macqueen illustrates the technology and method of Hittite warfare, utilizing both texts and archeological remains.

Temples and Priesthood

It is well known that the Ḫattusha excavations revealed the foundations of several large temples.[82] The largest (temple I) was in the lower city and contained a double cella, indicating in all probability that the chief god Teshub and the chief goddess Ḫebat (identified with the sun goddess of Arinna) were the principal deities worshiped there. Up through the 1960s four other temples (nos. II–V) were found, all in the upper city. But in the past twenty years, Neve has discovered a veritable temple city in the previously unexcavated portions of the upper city. Not all of the structures Neve calls temples may eventually prove to be such. But even when such an allowance is made, there seem to have been at least twenty Hittite temples inside the city.

The famous outdoor galleries at Yazılıkaya undoubtedly served as part of a temple complex, although perhaps of a specialized type: a temple to deceased royalty.[83]

Anatolica 11 (1984): 47–83; Macqueen, *Hittites*, chap. 4; Richard Beal, *The Organization of the Hittite Military* (Ph.D. diss., University of Chicago, 1986), now published: Texte der Hethiter 20 (Heidelberg: Carl Winter Universitätsverlag, 1992).

82. Jacob Milgrom, "The Shared Custody of the Tabernacle and a Hittite Analogy," *Journal of the American Oriental Society* 90 (1970): 204–9; Rudolf Naumann, *Architektur Kleinasiens von ihren Anfängen bis zum Ende der hethitischen Zeit*, 2d ed. (Tübingen: Wasmuth, 1971); Hans G. Güterbock, "The Hittite Temple according to Written Sources," in *Le Temple et le Culte: Compte Rendu de la Vingtième Rencontre Assyriologique International* (Istanbul: Nederlands Historisch-Archeologisch Instituut te Istambul, 1975), 125–32; Viktor Korošec, "Einiges zur inneren Struktur hethitischer Tempel nach der Instruktion für Tempelleute (KUB XIII,4)," in *Anatolian Studies Presented to Hans Gustav Güterbock on the Occasion of his Sixty-fifth Birthday*, ed. Kurt Bittel, Philo H. J. Houwink ten Cate, and Erica Reiner (Istanbul: Nederlands Historisch-Archeologisch Instituut in het Nabije Oosten, 1974), 165–74; Horst Klengel, "Zur ökonomischen Funktion der hethitischen Tempel," *Studi Micenei ed Egeo-Anatolici* 16 (1975): 181–200; Kurt Bittel, "The Great Temple of Hattusha-Boğazköy," *American Journal of Archaeology* 80 (1976): 66–72; idem, "Hittite Temples and High Places in Anatolia and North Syria," in *Temples and High Places in Biblical Times*, ed. Avraham Biran (Jerusalem: Israel Exploration Society, 1981), 63–72; Sedat Alp, *Beiträge zur Erforschung des hethitischen Tempels: Kultanlagen im Lichte der Keilschrifttexte* (Ankara: Türk Tarih Kurumu, 1983) (see Gary M. Beckman's review in *Journal of the American Oriental Society* 104 [1984]: 583–84); Gary M. Beckman, "The Religion of the Hittites," *Biblical Archaeologist* 52 (1989): 98–108; Gurney, *Hittites*, 120–30.

83. Bittel, *Ḫattusha*, 91–112; Kurt Bittel et al., *Das hethitische Felsheiligtum Yazılıkaya*, Boğazköy-Ḫattuša 9 (Berlin: Mann, 1975); Hans G. Güterbock, *Les Hiéroglyphes de Yazılı-*

In addition, the texts tell us that every city and town in the Hittite domains had at least one temple, served by both male and female cult personnel. The texts that show this most clearly are the cult inventory texts prepared during the reign of Tudḫaliya IV.[84] I have elsewhere drawn up a list of Hittite cities and the deities known to have had temples there.[85]

The village priest was not of noble descent and occupied a relatively low rung in Hittite society. But chief priests of temples in major cities were sometimes of royal descent, younger brothers who were not eligible to succeed to the throne. Priests could marry and were exempted from many taxes and forced labor.

Temple servants included many occupations found also in the "secular" sphere: cooks, leather workers, potters and other artisans, musicians, augurs and other diviners, herders for the temple flocks, and farmers who tilled the temple lands.

Jacob Milgrom points out that the two classes of temple guards mentioned in Hittite instructions for priests correspond in function rather closely to the biblical priests and Levites,[86] which indicates greater antiquity for the tabernacle ritual in the Pentateuch than is often assumed by more critical scholars.

Religion

An overall view of Hittite religion can be had from chapters in handbooks on the Hittites and from separate books and essays on the subject.[87]

Mythology

Although the Hittite language is of Indo-European derivation, the Hittites as a large, mixed group were by no means Indo-European in every aspect of their culture. This is particularly apparent in the case of their myths, none of which is derived from an Indo-European type. In fact, Hittite mythological texts are usually classified in three groups (none of which is Indo-European per se): Hattian-Anatolian, Hurrian-Mesopotamian, and Asianic.

kaya: A Propos d'un Travail Récent, Institut Français d'Études Anatoliennes (Paris: Éditions Recherche sur les Civilisations, 1982); Macqueen, *Hittites*, 123–32; Gurney, *Hittites*, 116–17, 123–24, 165–70.

84. Charles Carter, *Hittite Cult Inventories* (Ph.D. diss., University of Chicago, 1962).

85. Hoffner, "Hittites and Hurrians," 211–12.

86. Milgrom, "Shared Custody."

87. Oliver R. Gurney, *Some Aspects of Hittite Religion*, Schweich Lectures 1976 (Oxford: Oxford University Press for the British Academy, 1977); Beckman, "Religion of the Hittites"; Harry A. Hoffner Jr., "Hittite Religion," in *Religions of Antiquity*, ed. Robert Seltzer (New York: Macmillan, 1989), 69–79.

We possess no example of a mythological text in the Old Hittite script, but certain myths in the Hattian-Anatolian category seem to have derived from the Old Hittite period, notably myths dealing with the vanishing god (the "Telepinu myth") and the slaying of the serpent ("Illuyanka").[88]

Myths derived from or by way of the Hurrians include the "Song of Kumarbi" (sometimes called "Theogony" or "Kingship in Heaven") and the songs of Hedammu, Ullikummi, the god LAMMA, and Silver.[89]

One myth of West Semitic origin is preserved in a Hittite translation: a myth about the god Elkunirsha (Semitic *ʾel qônēh ʾerṣi*, "El, Creator of earth"; cf. Gen. 14:19, 22), his wife Asherah, and the young storm god Baal-Haddu.[90] Its motif of a virtuous young male (Baal-Haddu) refusing the advances of a married female (Asherah) is the same as the Egyptian "Tale of Two Brothers" and the biblical account of Joseph and Potiphar's wife.

Since the Hebrew Bible does not contain "myths" as such, evangelical biblical scholars customarily only utilize the myths of surrounding peoples to compare with the passages in the Hebrew Bible dealing with creation.[91] But one type of Hittite myth, namely the vanishing-deity myth, illuminates the situation portrayed in 1 Kings 18:20–29, where the priests of Baal invoke their absent deity and are mocked by the prophet Elijah in terms that recall scenes from ancient myths about deities who have run off and must be brought back. The way such *evocatio* rituals were conducted is illustrated not only in the ritual portions of the myths themselves but also in the separate rogation rituals.[92]

Cult

Our knowledge of Hittite cult continues to grow.[93] That there was a calendar of cultic events for the capital city is suggested by the much more abbreviated

88. English translations by Goetze in *ANET* 125–28 and by Harry A. Hoffner Jr., *Hittite Myths*, ed. Gary M. Beckman; Writings from the Ancient World 2 (Atlanta: Scholars Press, 1990), 10–14. Surveys of their contents may be found in Hans G. Güterbock, "Hittite Mythology," in *Mythologies of the Ancient World*, ed. Samuel N. Kramer (Garden City, N.Y.: Doubleday, 1961), 139–79; Harry A. Hoffner Jr., "Hittite Mythological Texts: A Survey," in *Unity and Diversity: Essays in the History, Literature, and Religion of the Ancient Near East*, ed. Hans Goedicke and James J. M. Roberts (Baltimore: Johns Hopkins University Press, 1975), 136–45.

89. Cf. Hoffner, *Hittite Myths*, 38–61.

90. Goetze, *ANET* 519; Hoffner, *Hittite Myths*, 69–70.

91. For example, compare Walton, *Ancient Israelite Literature*, chap. 1.

92. Emmanuel Laroche, *Catalogue des Textes Hittites* (Paris: Klincksieck, 1971), nos. 422–23, 483–85; cf. English translation by Goetze in *ANET* 351–53.

93. Gurney, *Some Aspects of Hittite Religion*; Hoffner, "Hittite Religion," 74–76; Beckman, "Religion of the Hittites"; James Moyer, "Hittite and Israelite Cultic Practices: A Selected Comparison," in *Scripture in Context*, vol. 2, ed. William W. Hallo, James C. Moyer, and Leo G. Perdue (Winona Lake, Ind.: Eisenbrauns, 1983), 19–38; Nancy W. Leinwand, "Archaeological Evidence for Hittite Cult Statuary," *American Journal of Archaeology* 89 (1985): 338–39.

counterparts for the smaller provincial towns and cities included in the great cult inventory texts drawn up at the command of Tudḫaliya IV.[94] And although we have no copy of such a calendar, it is possible to reconstruct its broad lines from the large number of festival descriptions found in the royal archives.[95]

Much is known about festivals.[96] Although there was, of course, a daily cult for each of the temples, festivals were special times when the cult statue of the deity was transported in procession through the streets and "entertained" with music, dancing, acrobatics, and athletic events, as well as a wide variety of sacrifices and offerings.[97] In ancient Israel, in addition to the major festivals, solemn convocations marked the new moon and the Sabbath. The Hittites had no equivalent to the Sabbath. Their most frequently repeated festival was the "festival of the month," by which we are probably to understand a festival marking the new moon. Most Hittite seasonal festivals were celebrated in the spring and fall, marking the harvesting or planting of some crop.[98]

Magic Rituals

Considerable use was made of magical practices in Hittite rituals.[99]

Several Hittite rituals involve making offerings to chthonic deities, the offerings being lowered into specially prepared pits in the ground. The name of one pit is written *a-a-bi*, the precise phonetic interpretation of which is still unclear. Goetze advocates /ayabi/, while Friedrich and other Hittitologists normalize the word as *ābi*. Vieyra and I compare this to the Biblical Hebrew word ᵓôb, which represents either a being in the realm of the dead who is consulted by necromancy or the means for such consultation.[100] Influenced by

94. Carter, *Hittite Cult Inventories*.

95. Laroche, *Catalogue des Textes Hittites*, 103–44.

96. Gurney, *Hittites*, 126–30; Harry A. Hoffner Jr., "Religions of the Biblical World: Asia Minor," in *ISBE* 4:79–85; idem, "Hittite Religion," 75–76; Hans G. Güterbock, "An Outline of the Hittite AN.TAḪ.ŠUM Festival," *Journal of Near Eastern Studies* 19 (1960): 80–89; idem, "Some Aspects of Hittite Festivals," in *Actes de la XVIIᵉ Rencontre Assyriologique Internationale*, ed. André Finet (Brussels: Comité Belge de Recherches en Mésopotamie, 1970), 175–80; Goetze in *ANET* 346–61.

97. Güterbock, "Hittite Festivals."

98. Hoffner, *Alimenta Hethaeorum*, 18–20, 49–50.

99. David Engelhard, *Hittite Magical Practices* (Ph.D. diss., Brandeis University, 1970); Ahmet Ünal, "The Role of Magic in the Ancient Anatolian Religions according to the Cuneiform Texts from Bogazköy-Hattuša," in *Essays on Anatolian Studies*, ed. T. Mikasa (Wiesbaden: Harrassowitz, 1988), 52–85.

100. Maurice Vieyra, "Le Noms du 'Mundus' en Hittite et en Assyrien et la Pythonisse d'Endor," *Revue Hittite et Asianique* 69 (1961): 47–55; Hoffner, "Second Millennium Antecedents to the Hebrew ᵓôb̠"; idem, "Hittites and Hurrians," 216–17; and idem, "אוֹב ᵓôbh," in *TDOT* 1:130–34.

the Hittite parallel, I favor the second interpretation. Others dispute the connection of the Hurro-Hittite word with the Hebrew and Ugaritic.[101]

Cultural and Literary Parallels to the Old Testament

From the beginnings of Hittitology it was assumed that the Hittites mentioned in the Old Testament were the same people whose capital was at Boğazköy-Ḫattusha in central Anatolia.[102] There are two questions that must be addressed. First, was it the intention of the biblical writers to indicate that persons bearing the name *Hittite* or *sons of Heth* belonged to that foreign people from the north (Anatolia or north Syria)? Second, is it credible or plausible that such Hittites from the north actually were in Palestine in Old Testament times?

Many Old Testament scholars answer the first question "yes" and the second "no." They regard references to Hittites in the Old Testament, especially the references in the patriarchal narratives of Genesis, as anachronisms—a reading back into earlier times of the Hittites known from the period of the Israelite monarchy (ca. 950–700).

Others answer both questions "yes," the first one confidently, the second tentatively. Assyriologist-Hittitologist Emil Forrer takes this second point of view. Both Oliver R. Gurney and Aharon Kempinski seem to incline to this view.

I hold a third point of view, answering the first question "yes and no."[103] Passages referring to Hittites during the Israelite monarchy almost certainly refer to the Syrian kingdoms earlier controlled by the Hittite Empire during the fourteenth and thirteenth centuries and still referred to by the name *Hatti* in the annals of the Neo-Assyrian kings. But Hittites mentioned in the narratives of Genesis–Joshua are native Palestinians, members of a group mentioned alongside Canaanites, Jebusites, Amorites, etc. Their personal names are West Semitic and their customs (e.g., the purchase of the cave and field of Ephron in Gen. 23) offer no convincing evidence for an Anatolian connec-

---

101. Cf. literature cited in Johannes Friedrich and Annelies Kammenhuber, *Hethitisches Wörterbuch*, 2d ed., Indogermanische Bibliothek: Wörterbücher (Heidelberg: Carl Winter Universitätsverlag, 1975–84), 181.

102. Emil Forrer, "The Hittites in Palestine, I," *Palestine Exploration Quarterly* (1936): 190–203. This subject has been discussed in several publications: Gurney, *Hittites*, 1–11, 47–50; Harry A. Hoffner Jr., "Some Contributions of Hittitology to Old Testament Study," *Tyndale Bulletin* 20 (1969): 27–55; Ruth Mayer, "Die Hethiter und das Alte Testament," in *Mysterium der Gnade*, ed. H. Rossmann (Regensburg: Pustet, 1975), 65–73; Aharon Kempinski, "Hittites in the Bible: What Does Archaeology Say?" *Biblical Archaeology Review* 5.4 (1979): 20–45; Richard Beal, "The Hittites after the Empire's Fall," *Biblical Illustrator* (1983): 73–81.

103. Hoffner, "Some Contributions of Hittitology," 28–37.

tion. The tradition preserved in Genesis 10 of their descent from Heth, who with Canaan is descended from Ham, places them firmly in Palestine.

Archeological evidence for an Anatolian Hittite presence in ancient Palestine, as given by Kempinski, supports this "yes and no" answer: "Recent archaeological finds suggest that Hittite immigration at the end of the 13th century and at the beginning of the 12th century . . . extended into Canaan as well as into Syria."[104] But the only evidence that Kempinski adduces for a Hittite immigration southward into Palestine earlier than ca. 1200 is the well-known Hittite passage (originally adduced by Forrer) about the people of the city Kurushtamma, who prior to the reign of Shuppiluliuma I migrated from Hatti into Egyptian territory. Such a migration, the reverse of that mentioned in Judges 1:26, would hardly account for all the "Hittites" of the Genesis-to-Joshua period.

But whether or not the Hittites of the early parts of the Old Testament are products of the early imperial culture of Anatolia, it is possible to see influences from that distant northern culture in the Old Testament. Over the past twenty-five years many studies of the Hittites and the Old Testament have appeared.[105] Elsewhere I have proposed a number of Hittite parallels to institutions described in the Old Testament, some of which have been reviewed in the preceding discussion.[106]

Culture words (German *Kulturwörter*) common to Hittite and Biblical Hebrew include the following:

	Hittite	Hebrew
wine	*wiyanaš*	*yayin*
helmet, headgear	*kubaḫiš*	*kôbaᶜ*
sesame	*šapšama*	*šumšôm*

---

104. Kempinski, "Hittites in the Bible," 41.

105. Kitchen, *Ancient Orient and Old Testament*, 90–102, 154–56; Hoffner, "Some Contributions of Hittitology"; Milgrom, "Shared Custody"; Mayer, "Die Hethiter und das Alte Testament"; Kitchen, *Bible in Its World*, 71, 80–86; Kempinski, "Hittites in the Bible"; Beal, "Hittites after the Empire's Fall"; Herbert M. Wolf, *The Apology of Hattusilis Compared with Other Political Self-Justifications of the Ancient Near East* (Ph.D. diss., Brandeis University, 1967); J. B. Geyer, "Ezekiel 18 and a Hittite Treaty of Mursilis II," *Journal for the Study of the Old Testament* 12 (1979): 31–46; P. Kyle McCarter Jr., "The Apology of David," *Journal of Biblical Literature* 99 (1980): 489–504; Moyer, "Hittite and Israelite Cultic Practices"; Matitiahu Tsevat, "Two Old Testament Stories and Their Hittite Analogues," *Journal of the American Oriental Society* 103 (1983): 321–26; David P. Wright, *The Disposal of Impurity: Elimination Rites in the Bible and in Hittite and Mesopotamian Literature*, Society of Biblical Literature Dissertation Series 101 (Atlanta: Scholars Press, 1987).

106. Hoffner, "Some Contributions of Hittitology," 37–55; idem, "Hittites and Hurrians," 213–21.

oak	*allan* (in *allantaru*)	*ʾallôn*
glaze	*zapzigi*	*sipsîgîm*[107]
idol	*tarpiš* (a demon)	*tĕrāpîm*

A topos found in two Hittite texts is also reflected in Isaiah:

> Let the mountains be leveled before you, O gods!
>
> (KUB 15.34 i 45, iii 52)

> Before you, O god, let the rivers be bridged!
>   Before you let the valleys be leveled!
> Let the mountains betake themselves down to the vegetation!
>
> (KBo 15.25 obv. 13–15)

> In the desert prepare the road of Yahweh!
>   In the Arabah make a straight highway for our God!
> Let every valley be elevated;
>   let every mountain and hill be brought low!
> Let the crooked become straight
>   and the rough places level!
>
> (Isa. 40:3–4)

On the Hittite parallel to priests and Levites sharing the custody of the tabernacle see above under "Temples and Priesthood."

A close similarity exists between the scapegoat ritual of the Day of Atonement, as described in Leviticus 16, and the various magic rituals of the Hittites in which a small animal was dispatched bearing away sin or impurity.[108]

Recommended Reading

Bittel, Kurt. *Ḫattusha: The Capital of the Hittites.* New York: Oxford University Press, 1970.

Friedrich, Johannes. *Die hethitischen Gesetze: Transkription, Übersetzung, sprachliche Erläuterungen und vollständiges Wörterverzeichnis.* Documenta et Monumenta Orientis Antiqui 7. Leiden: Brill, 1959.

———. *Staatsverträge des Ḫatti-Reiches in hethitischer Sprache.* 2 vols. Mitteilungen der Vorderasiatisch-Ägyptische Gesellschaft 31, 34. Leipzig: Hinrichs, 1926–30.

107. Reading *kĕsapsîgîm* for the MT's *kesep sîgîm* in Prov. 26:23.
108. Gurney, *Some Aspects of Hittite Religion*, 47–52.

Friedrich, Johannes, and Annelies Kammenhuber. *Hethitisches Wörterbuch.* 2d edition. Indogermanische Bibliothek: Wörterbücher. Heidelberg: Carl Winter Universitätsverlag, 1975–84.

Goetze, Albrecht. "Hittite Rituals, Incantations, and Description of Festivals." Pp. 346–61 in *Ancient Near Eastern Texts Relating to the Old Testament.* Edited by James B. Pritchard. 3d edition. Princeton: Princeton University Press, 1969.

Gurney, Oliver R. *Some Aspects of Hittite Religion.* Schweich Lectures 1976. Oxford: Oxford University Press for the British Academy, 1977.

———. *The Hittites.* 2d edition. Baltimore: Penguin, 1990.

Güterbock, Hans G. "Hittite Mythology." Pp. 139–79 in *Mythologies of the Ancient World.* Edited by Samuel N. Kramer. Garden City, N.Y.: Doubleday, 1961.

Güterbock, Hans G., and Harry A. Hoffner Jr. *The Hittite Dictionary of the Oriental Institute of the University of Chicago.* Chicago: Oriental Institute, 1989–.

Hoffner, Harry A., Jr. "An English-Hittite Glossary." *Revue Hittite et Asianique* 25 (1967): 7–99.

———. "Histories and Historians of the Ancient Near East: The Hittites." *Orientalia* 49 (1980): 283–332.

———. *Hittite Myths.* Edited by Gary M. Beckman. Writings from the Ancient World 2. Atlanta: Scholars Press, 1990.

———. "The Hittites and Hurrians." Pp. 197–228 in *Peoples of Old Testament Times.* Edited by Donald J. Wiseman. Oxford: Clarendon, 1973.

———. "Some Contributions of Hittitology to Old Testament Study." *Tyndale Bulletin* 20 (1969): 27–55.

Macqueen, James G. *The Hittites and Their Contemporaries in Asia Minor.* 2d edition. Ancient Peoples and Places. London: Thames & Hudson, 1986.

Neve, Peter. "Boğazköy-Hattusha: New Results of the Excavations in the Upper City." *Anatolica* 16 (1989–90): 7–20.

Canaanites and Amorites

Keith N. Schoville

The ... Amorites live in the hill country; and the Canaanites live near the sea and along the Jordan.

—*Numbers 13:29*

Two ancient peoples figure largely in the early history of Israel—the Canaanites and the Amorites. An accurate portrayal of the Canaanites and their culture according to our current level of knowledge should lead to a clearer understanding of the distinctions between Canaanites and Israelites.

The Bible is replete with references to the land of Canaan and its inhabitants. The words *Canaan* and *Canaanite* occur some 160 times in the Bible.[1] The first appearance of the name is the reference to Canaan, the grandson of Noah. Canaan was cursed in the aftermath of the incident in Genesis 9:18–23 in which Ham, Canaan's father, looked upon the nakedness of the drunken Noah. Much later, the story of this ancient incident became the explanation for the Israelite enslavement of some of the Canaanites.[2]

The patriarch Abram was called by God to go into the land of Canaan. When he arrived at Shechem in the central hill country of Canaan west of the Jordan River, God promised to give the land of Canaan to Abram's descendants as a perpetual patrimony (Gen. 12:1–7).[3] That promise was repeated

---

1. Only three of these references are in the New Testament: Matt. 15:22 refers to the encounter of Jesus with a Canaanite woman from the region of Tyre and Sidon; in Acts 7:11 Stephen mentions the famine in Egypt and Canaan in the patriarchal period; and in Acts 13:19 Paul notes the destruction of seven nations in the land of Canaan.

2. The prehistoric story of Noah became a part of Israelite written literature after a long period of transmission as oral literature.

3. On the critical and ongoing importance of the promise of the land, see Harry M. Orlinsky, "The Biblical Concept of the Land of Israel: Cornerstone of the Covenant between God and Israel," *Eretz-Israel* 18 (1985; Nahman Avigad volume): 43*–55*.

to Isaac and Jacob (Gen. 26:3; 28:13; 35:12) and is referred to at the very end of Genesis, where the dying Joseph reminded his brothers of the promise and insisted that, when God moved to fulfill his pledge, they should carry his bones with them into the promised land (50:24).

At the call of Moses, God promised to deliver the Israelites from their affliction in Egypt and to bring them into "the land of the Canaanites, the Hittites, the Amorites, the Perizzites, the Hivites, and the Jebusites, a land flowing with milk and honey" (Exod. 3:8, 17 NRSV). Assuming that in this formulaic statement the order of names moves from the greatest to the least number of people, the major occupants of the land of promise were a people called the Canaanites.

Name

The origin of the name *Canaan* is obscure. Possibly the earliest written evidence for the name is from Ebla in central Syria, where Italian archeologists have recovered numerous clay tablets dating to approximately 2250.[4] In a list of offerings to various deities, the god Dagon is called "lord of Canaan (^d*be kà-na-na-im*)."[5] An eighteenth-century letter from Mari provides the next evidence for the name in a phrase that connects "thieves and Canaanites."[6] The *land of Canaan* is also attested in a fourteenth- or fifteenth-century text from Syria.[7] *Canaan* and *Canaanite* also occur in Egyptian on a stele of Amenhotep II (Dynasty 18, ca. 1450–1425) discovered at Memphis and on the "Israel Stele" of Pharaoh Merenptah (Dynasty 19, ca. 1227–1217).[8]

Many scholars used to relate *Canaan* to the Akkadian word *kinaḫḫu* ("red purple"), an explanation based on the purple dye that Canaanites living along the eastern Mediterranean coast produced from sea snails.[9] The derivation of the name from this source, however, has been largely disproved. The name more likely derives from a personal name, as indicated in the He-

4. Ebla is the ancient name of modern Tell Mardikh, south of Aleppo; see Paolo Matthiae, *Ebla: An Empire Rediscovered*, trans. Christopher Holme (Garden City, N.Y.: Doubleday, 1981).

5. Giovanni Pettinato, *The Archives of Ebla: An Empire Inscribed in Clay* (Garden City, N.Y.: Doubleday, 1981), 246, 248, 253 (the reference is to TM.75.G.1376 rev. ii 7–iii 3). The evidence is problematic; some scholars locate *ga-na-na-um* and its variants to the east of Ebla.

6. Jack M. Sasson, "The Earliest Mention of the Name 'Canaan,'" *Biblical Archaeologist* 47 (1984): 90.

7. In 1939 the statue of King Idrimi of Alalakh was discovered at Atchana in Syria; see *ANET* 557–58.

8. *ANET* 376, 378. This inscription is the earliest reference to Israel known outside the Bible. The telling phrase is, "Israel is laid waste, his seed is not."

9. Patrick E. McGovern, "A Dye for Gods and Kings," *Archaeology* 43:2 (1990): 33.

brew story of Noah and in Greek and Phoenician sources. *Canaan* combines the Semitic root *k-n-ᶜ* ("to sink, be low") with a common suffix -*(a)n*, but this gives little basis for the name as it stands. One attractive suggestion is that the root meaning could be applied to the movement of the sun sinking in the west. Thus the Canaanites would be the "Sundowners, Westerners."[10] (Interestingly, this is also the meaning of the name *Amorite*.) Whether the land took its name from the people or vice versa remains undetermined.

Defining the Land of Canaan

Biblical writers considered the Canaanites to be but one of a number of groups that occupied the land of Canaan at the time of the exodus and conquest—Canaanites, Hittites, Amorites, Perizzites, Hivites, Jebusites (Exod. 3:8).[11] It is not possible to establish exact dates for the exodus and the conquest (the historicity of these events is a matter of scholarly debate), but a general consensus is that they occurred near the end of the Late Bronze Age (ca. 1200). Israelite incursions into the land of Canaan, as well as Philistine and Aramean occupation of other areas once held by Canaanites, signaled the demise of Late Bronze Age Canaan.[12] But before the close of the Late Bronze Age, what territory did ancient Canaan occupy? The answer to this question is that territorial designations fluctuate over time and in relationship to the mighty powers of the ancient Near East—Egypt and Mesopotamia.

Egypt was inevitably and persistently interested in the Syro-Palestinian land bridge to its north between the Mediterranean Sea and the eastern desert. In Egyptian references dating to the Old Kingdom period (ca. 2700–2400), the inhabitants of this Asian region were called ᶜAamu, while the area along the Phoenician coast was known as Fenḫu (the meanings of these

10. Alan R. Millard, "The Canaanites," in *Peoples of Old Testament Times*, ed. Donald J. Wiseman (Oxford: Clarendon, 1973), 34; D. R. Ap-Thomas, "The Phoenicians," in *Peoples of Old Testament Times*, ed. Donald J. Wiseman (Oxford: Clarendon, 1973), 263. Cf. Michael C. Astour, "The Origin of the Terms 'Canaan,' 'Phoenician,' and 'Purple,'" *Journal of Near Eastern Studies* 24 (1965): 346–50.

11. For a discussion of other lists of people groups in Canaan, see Tomoo Ishida, "The Structure and Historical Implications of the Lists of Pre-Israelite Nations," *Biblica* 60 (1979): 461–90; Nadav Naʾaman, "Canaanites and Perizzites," *Biblische Notizen* 45 (1988): 42–47; and Kevin G. O'Connell, "The List of Seven People in Canaan," in *The Answers Lie Below: Essays in Honor of Lawrence Edmund Toombs*, ed. Henry O. Thompson (Lanham, Md.: University Press of America, 1984), 221–41.

12. Although Canaanite material culture continued to influence the cultures of both Israel and Philistia after the close of the Late Bronze Age, Canaan as a politico-geographical entity ceased. The end of the Late Bronze Age can conveniently be considered the close of the Canaanite era. Only the Phoenicians continued Canaanite culture in an unbroken stream.

names are unclear).[13] This Egyptian connection is confirmed by inscriptions discovered in the excavations at Byblos in Lebanon,[14] and the Canaanite link to Egypt is evident in Canaanite pottery found in Egyptian tombs of Dynasty 1 (ca. 3100–2890). The Egyptian presence in Syria is equally clear from the discovery at Ebla of fragments of Egyptian stone vases bearing titles of Pharaoh Khafre (Dynasty 4, ca. 2500), along with part of an Egyptian alabaster vase bearing the complete titles (in hieroglyphs) of Pepi I (Dynasty 6, 2300).[15]

Mesopotamian inscriptions from the third and second millenniums refer to all the country west of the Euphrates as far as the Mediterranean (the Sea of Amurru) as *the land of Amurru.* Because Mesopotamian experience with this region was primarily in Syria, references to the land of Amurru are primarily to that area, yet all of Syria-Palestine could be included in the expression. For example, during the Ur III period (ca. 2000), Canaanite Tyre on the Mediterranean coast was ruled by a local representative of the king of Ur in southern Mesopotamia.[16] Some scholars insist that Ebla was outside the region of Canaan,[17] but the native language (known as Paleo-Canaanite or Eblaite) found in approximately twenty percent of the texts thus far recovered from Ebla appears to have strong Northwest Semitic affinities.[18] This language exhibits a number of similarities to Biblical Hebrew, which was itself a dialect of Canaanite in use over a millennium later.

In the early second millennium, Canaan likely comprised the eastern Mediterranean coast from the River of Egypt northward past Carmel Head (modern Haifa) well into Lebanon.[19] A Late Bronze Age tradition in Joshua 13:3 extends the name to include the coastal plain all the way to the Shihor River

13. Yohanan Aharoni, *The Land of the Bible: A Historical Geography*, 2d ed., trans. and ed. Anson F. Rainey (Philadelphia: Westminster, 1979), 65.

14. These date back to Nebka (Khasekhemwy), the last king of Dynasty 2, ca. 2686, indicating an Egyptian interest and presence. Typical Egyptian materials from the same period were found also in an early temple on the site.

15. Matthiae, *Ebla*, 9.

16. William F. Albright, *Yahweh and the Gods of Canaan* (repr. Winona Lake, Ind.: Eisenbrauns, 1979), 113.

17. As an example of Ebla-Canaan connections, see Robert R. Stieglitz, "Ebla and the Gods of Canaan," *Eblaitica* 2 (1990): 79–89.

18. Pettinato, *Archives of Ebla*, 56. Alfonso Archi, however, refuses the designation *Early Canaanite* for the language of Ebla in "Ebla and Eblaite," *Eblaitica* 1 (1987): 8. Less adamant is the view of Igor M. Diakonoff in "The Importance of Ebla for History and Linguistics," *Eblaitica* 2 (1990): 29. The classification of Eblaite among the language groups of the Early Bronze Age is still problematic, as Cyrus H. Gordon notes: "Eblaite is indeed a border language, with isoglosses in both directions," that is, toward both East Semitic and West Semitic (*Eblaitica* 1 [1987]: 1). In fact, some scholars hold that Eblaite is an early form of Akkadian and not directly related to Northwest Semitic.

19. John Gray, *The Canaanites* (London: Thames & Hudson, 1964), 15.

on the border of Egypt.[20] The same passage in Joshua extends the territory of Canaan northward through the Philistine plain into the region of Sidon. Judges 5:19, reflecting an Iron Age I tradition, mentions "the kings of Canaan" whose forces under the command of Sisera fought against the Israelite tribes. These kings must have been rulers of small city-states in the plains of Jezreel, Megiddo, and Beth-shan as well as in Galilee, including Hazor. The king of Hazor is called "the king of Canaan" (Judg. 4:2, 23–24), and Hazor was called "the head of all those kingdoms" (Josh. 11:10).

In the Middle Kingdom (ca. 2000–1550), the Egyptians began to use the name *Retenu* for the regions of Syria-Palestine all the way to the Euphrates. Retenu continued in use in the New Kingdom (ca. 1550–1200), but two new names appeared as well: *Djahi* and *the land of Ḥurru*. The latter obviously refers to the Horites (Hurrians), a people mentioned in the Bible (Gen. 14:6; 36:20–30; Deut. 2:12, 22) who apparently entered Canaan during the period in which the Hyksos ruled Egypt and dominated Canaan (ca. 1750–1550).[21] Egyptian records from the fifteenth and fourteenth centuries, including the Amarna letters, contain the names of a number of rulers of Canaanite city-states who are clearly Hurrian.[22] Another name in full use during the New Kingdom is the *land of Canaan* (noted above). In the Amarna letters the Canaanite kings call themselves *Kinaḫu* or *Kinanu*. Also appearing on a stele of Pharaoh Amenhotep II recovered at Memphis (just south of modern Cairo),[23] this expression is clearly the equivalent of Northwest Semitic *Canaanite*.

Egyptians used *Retenu, Djahi, land of Ḥurru*, and *Kinanu* as general titles for the area of their dominance in Syria-Palestine during the Late Bronze Age (ca. 1550–1200).[24] They understood the name *Canaan* as referring to the full area: from the Brook of Egypt (south of Gaza) northward along the coast past Gebal/Byblos, then inland to the western fringe of the Syrian Desert, then southward to incorporate eastern Bashan down to the Yarmuk River, then down the Jordan Valley to the southern end of the Dead Sea, then westward through the Wilderness of Zin, and back to the Brook of Egypt. The

20. James K. Hoffmeier, "Shihor," in *ISBE* 4:476.

21. The Hyksos were chariot warriors out of Syria-Palestine who ruled the delta region of Egypt during the Second Intermediate period in Egyptian history.

22. The Amarna letters, discovered in Egypt in 1887, date to the fourteenth century and were written in Akkadian, the diplomatic language of the time. Of approximately 377 tablets, nearly 300 were from petty kings in Syria-Palestine to the Egyptian pharaoh. On ethnic and linguistic evidence from the Amarna letters, see Richard S. Hess, "Cultural Aspects of Onomastic Distribution in the Amarna Texts," *Ugarit-Forschungen* 21 (1989): 209–16.

23. Sabatino Moscati, *The World of the Phoenicians*, trans. Alastair Hamilton (London: Weidenfeld & Nicolson, 1965), 3.

24. Cf. Aharoni, *Land of the Bible*, 68–69.

territories of the Ammonites, Moabites, and Edomites were outside the Egyptian view of the land of Canaan, although the Transjordanian groups shared a common material culture with the neighboring Canaanite city-states.

The Late Bronze Age Egyptian province of Canaan is approximately the same region as the biblical land of Canaan.[25] A later biblical definition of the land of Israel occurs in the phrase *from Dan to Beer-sheba*, but the historical memory of the larger limits of Canaan were retained in the Bible.

Canaanite Origins

The origin of the Canaanites remains obscure. Struggling to integrate evidence from archeology and ancient texts in order to clarify Canaanite origins, experts confront these basic problems: Were the Canaanites native to the region or emigrants? If they emigrated, from where did they originate?

According to Donald Harden, Canaanites were not the aboriginal inhabitants of the region, but migrated into the area that was to bear their name. Unable to establish when the migration occurred, Harden thinks that they likely came northward out of Arabia or the Persian Gulf, perhaps as early as 2350.[26] The evidence from Byblos (noted above) perplexes him, however, for it indicates connections between that city and Egypt at a much earlier date. So Harden suggests the bare possibility that there might have been Semites dwelling at Gebal (the Semitic name of Byblos) who traded with the Egyptians as early as 3000.

John Gray also thinks that the Canaanites migrated, but from a nearby region—the north Arabian steppe—"from which its Semitic stock was constantly replenished when annual seasonal migrations of nomads for summer grazing after harvest became periodically mass settlement or armed invasion."[27]

It is unclear whether the Canaanites descended from Chalcolithic-era natives or entered the region from elsewhere. What is clear is that there are significant differences between the material culture of Chalcolithic Canaan and the subsequent Early Bronze culture, which many archeologists mark as the beginning of the Canaanite period. Kathleen Kenyon, for example, notes that the widespread Chalcolithic Ghassulian culture from the Jordan Valley "does not seem to have made any appreciable contribution towards what followed."[28] Groups entering Palestine in the last centuries of the fourth millen-

---

25. Ibid., 74, 77.

26. Donald Harden, *The Phoenicians* (New York: Praeger, 1962), 21.

27. Gray, *Canaanites*, 25.

28. Kathleen M. Kenyon, *Amorites and Canaanites*, Schweich Lectures 1963 (London: Oxford University Press for the British Academy, 1966), 6.

nium, likely from the east and northeast, were the people who established sites that became towns in the succeeding cultural phase. These sites ultimately became walled cities in the Early Bronze period.

Archeologists recognize that variations between the Chalcolithic and Early Bronze eras occur in terms of settlement patterns, population size and density, agricultural practices, trade relations, and artifact assemblages and forms.[29] At the same time, some elements of Early Bronze Age culture do exhibit continuity with the preceding period, and skeletal remains from the two periods fail to indicate the displacement of one population type by another. All this suggests a transition between the two periods, which is described by Amihai Mazar as "an intermingling of new features—originating in Syria, Anatolia, and Mesopotamia—with elements rooted in the local culture of the preceding period. . . . It is possible that new peoples arrived . . . mainly from Syria and mixed with the remnants of the autochthonous population."[30]

Previously, William F. Albright advocated a similar view: "It is clear that the ethnic identity of the people later known as 'Canaanites' was already established no later than the end of the fourth millennium B.C."[31] He bases this statement on the large number of towns with standard Semitic names established in the region before 3000—towns such as Beth-yerah, Megiddo, Jericho, and Arad. Additional evidence in support of this view comes from the Egyptian borrowing of Semitic words (e.g., *karmu* ["vineyard"] and *qamhu* ["wheat flour"]) no later than the early Pyramid Age (ca. 2700). Albright allows for the incursion of non-Semitic populations (e.g., from Anatolia) into the region who introduced the so-called Khirbet Kerak ware around 2500.

Between the twenty-third and twentieth centuries, Mesopotamian culture influenced the region, as reflected in the caliciform ware transmitted through Syria during this time. At the time Albright wrote, Ebla had not yet been discovered. Now this site supports his argument that a powerful Mesopotamian influence permeated Syria-Palestine during this period. Even more, however, Ebla testifies to a thriving center of culture in Syria with widespread connections to Anatolia, Egypt, and Mesopotamia.[32] The movement of a Syrian population into the southern adjacent region in the late third millennium is

29. Amihai Mazar, *Archaeology of the Land of the Bible 10,000–586* B.C.E. (New York: Doubleday, 1990), 104–5.

30. Ibid., 105.

31. Albright, *Yahweh and the Gods of Canaan*, 110–11. Moscati (*World of the Phoenicians*, 5) holds that the Phoenicians (descendants of the coastal Canaanites) were quite likely the result of a historical evolution in the Syro-Palestinian area and not a migration of people from outside.

32. Cf. Paolo Matthiae, "The Mature Early Syrian Culture of Ebla and the Development of Early Bronze Civilization in Jordan," in *Studies in the History and Archaeology of Jordan*, ed. Adnan Hadidi (Amman: Department of Antiquities, 1982), 1:77–91.

the most likely explanation for the arrival of the Amorites, who (as noted) were one of the predominant groups occupying the land of Canaan at the end of the Late Bronze Age.[33]

Amorite Origins

The urbanization of Canaan in the Early Bronze Age II (ca. 2900–2700), illustrated by sites such as Arad and Ai, declined during the Early Bronze Age III, which ended about 2300. Walled cities were destroyed or abandoned, and urban culture gave way to a pastoral, village way of life over the next two centuries, Early Bronze Age IV (about 2300–2000). The reasons for such drastic changes are unclear, but three possible causes may be suggested: (1) Egyptian military action, (2) changing environmental factors including overpopulation, or (3) an invading horde of Amorites. The Amorites would have destroyed the urban centers and established the variant lifestyle characteristic of the period until urbanization flowered in the subsequent Middle Bronze Age II. It is possible that all of these factors played a role in the changes that distinguish this transition from Early Bronze IV to Middle Bronze I.[34]

Numbers 13:29 states: "The Amalekites live in the land of the Negeb; the Hittites, the Jebusites, and the Amorites live in the hill country; and the Canaanites live by the sea, and along the Jordan" (NRSV). While the Amorites are here listed among the peoples of the land, the Bible provides scant evidence about them. By the time of the prophet Amos (2:9), the Amorites were vaguely remembered as a people of the heroic past. Extrabiblical texts, however, do provide a tentative basis for understanding the Amorites.

The word *Amorite* has ancient origins, deriving from Akkadian *Amurru*, the equivalent of the earlier Sumerian *Martu*. In both languages the word could designate a region, people, or direction. As a directional indicator, the

---

33. For a contrary opinion, see Thomas L. Thompson, *The Historicity of the Patriarchal Narratives: The Quest for the Historical Abraham*, Beiheft zur Zeitschrift für die Alttestamentliche Wissenschaft 133 (Berlin: de Gruyter, 1974), 89–96.

34. On the transition from the Early Bronze Age to the Middle Bronze Age, see William G. Dever, "New Vistas on the EB IV ('MB I') Horizon in Syria-Palestine," *Bulletin of the American Schools of Oriental Research* 237 (1980): 35–64; Suzanne Richard, "Toward a Consensus of Opinion on the End of the Early Bronze Age in Palestine-Transjordan," *Bulletin of the American Schools of Oriental Research* 237 (1980): 5–63; Mazar, *Archaeology of the Land of the Bible*, 151–73; John J. Bimson, "Archaeological Data and the Dating of the Patriarchs," in *Essays on the Patriarchal Narratives*, ed. Alan R. Millard and Donald J. Wiseman (Winona Lake, Ind.: Eisenbrauns, 1983), 53–89; Moshe Kochavi, "At That Time the Canaanites Were in the Land . . . ," in *Recent Archaeology in the Land of Israel*, ed. Hershel Shanks and Benjamin Mazar (Washington: Biblical Archaeology Society, 1981), 25–29.

name was already in use by about 2300. To the Mesopotamians, *Martu/ Amurru* referred to the west. Just as the north was called Subartu, the east Elam, and the south Sumer—after the peoples who lived in those directions— so too the west was named after the Amorites.[35]

Martu was employed as an ethnic expression as early as 2600. Numbers of Martu people of a later period are mentioned in texts recovered at Lagash, Umma, Adab, and Susa. These Martu apparently immigrated from the west into Mesopotamian cities before and during the Ur III period (ca. 2000). References to the Martu indicate that they were nomads and shepherds, supplying sheep and goats to the urban populace. Contact with and adaptation to urban environments inevitably brought changes: some Martu are mentioned as dealers in leather goods and others are named among the recipients of rations, probably for work done. Such references suggest that their assimilation to Mesopotamian urban society was in progress.

The Amorites (Martu) described in Mesopotamian records had their roots in Syria. The nomadic lifestyle noted and recorded in Mesopotamia, however, may not have been representative of all Amorites in Syria. We now know, thanks to archeological discoveries in Syria during the last two decades, that Amorite city-states existed in Syria in the last half of the third millennium. It is apparent that many westerners were urbanites. Texts from Mari clearly indicate that nomads (or seminomads practicing seasonal transhumance) together with farmers formed one ethnic unit rather than a dichotomy.[36]

It is evident that the home region of the Amorites was Syria. In fact, the Middle Bronze Age texts from Mari indicate a region of Amurru within Syria, and in the Late Bronze Age a kingdom of Amurru ruled by a certain Abdi-Ashirta existed in the mountainous part of Syria.[37] The problem, then, is to determine when the ancestors of the biblical Amorites migrated south into Canaan. At this point a definitive answer eludes us. Earlier archeologists posited the Amorite migration as the catalyst of the transition in Canaan from the Early Bronze Age IV to the Middle Bronze Age I (ca. 2250–2000). This transition coincided with the First Intermediate period in Egypt and a period

---

35. Compare Samuel N. Kramer, *Enmerkar and the Lord of Aratta: A Sumerian Epic Tale of Iraq and Iran* (Philadelphia: University Museum, 1952), lines 141–46, and his translation of the "Curse of Akkad" in *ANET* 648.

36. Cf. J. Tracy Luke, "'Your Father Was an Amorite' (Ezek. 16:3, 45): An Essay on the Amorite Problem in OT Traditions," in *The Quest for the Kingdom of God: Studies in Honor of George E. Mendenhall*, ed. Herbert B. Huffmon, Frank A. Spina, and Alberto R. W. Green (Winona Lake, Ind.: Eisenbrauns, 1983), 221–37. See also Mario Liverani, "The Amorites," in *Peoples of Old Testament Times*, ed. Donald J. Wiseman (Oxford: Clarendon, 1973), 107; and Victor H. Matthews, "The Role of the *Rabi Amurrim* in the Mari Kingdom," *Journal of Near Eastern Studies* 38 (1979): 129–34.

37. Liverani, "Amorites," 116.

of disruption in Mesopotamia,[38] and the Amorites were identified as the culprits. More recently, the connection of the Amorites to this transition is discounted because there is no supporting data from Canaan.[39] Rather, it is suggested that the Amorites arrived in Canaan at the start of the Middle Bronze Age II and that they were responsible for the renewed urbanization.[40]

For the Late Bronze Age (ca. 1550–1200),[41] Egyptian texts corroborate what the Bible clearly states: the population of Canaan was quite diverse in this time. Egyptian records document the following peoples: ʿApiru, Canaanites, Hurrians (Horites), Israelites, and Shasu (= Bedouin tribes);[42] the Bible refers to Amorites, Canaanites, Girgashites, Hittites, Jebusites, Kadmonites, Kenites, Kenizzites, Perizzites, and Rephaites (Gen. 15:19–21).

But the discernment of specific ethnic groups from archeological evidence is next to impossible. Excavations from Hazor in the north to Lachish in the south clearly indicate that throughout the region during the period of the Middle and Late Bronze Ages the material culture was uniform. In the absence of inscriptional material it is impossible to determine the relationship of particular material remains to a specific group. Nevertheless, Kathleen Kenyon begins with the biblical statement that "the Amorites live in the hill country; and the Canaanites live by the sea, and along the Jordan" (Num. 13:29 NRSV). Mapping the towns specifically designated as Amorite and Canaanite, she concludes that "the overall pattern, though it has gaps, accords well with the general location of the peoples of the land given in Numbers xiii.29. . . . The inhabitants of the hill country both to the east and the west of the Jordan were regarded by the Israelites as Amorites, and the inhabitants of the coastal plain, the valley of Esdraelon, and the valley of the Jordan as Canaanites. . . . The Amorites were hill dwellers, the Canaanites plain dwellers." Kenyon emphasizes that "the picture of two cultural provinces divided by the Jordan is that which in fact is given by the archaeological evidence."[43] Yet Amorites existed on both sides of the Jordan (Josh. 5:1; 10:6).

38. Kathleen Kenyon, *Archaeology in the Holy Land*, 3d ed. (New York: Praeger, 1971), 159–61.

39. William G. Dever, "The Patriarchal Traditions," in *Israelite and Judaean History*, ed. John H. Hayes and J. Maxwell Miller (Philadelphia: Westminster, 1977), 102–11; Kochavi, "At That Time," 28; Mazar, *Archaeology of the Land of the Bible*, 169–71.

40. William H. Stiebing Jr., "When Was the Age of the Patriarchs?—Of Amorites, Canaanites, and Archaeology" *Biblical Archaeology Review* 1.2 (1975): 17–20; Kochavi, "At That Time," 29. Cf. William G. Dever, "The Middle Bronze Age: The Zenith of the Urban Canaanite Era," *Biblical Archaeologist* 50 (1987): 148–77.

41. Albert Leonard Jr., "The Late Bronze Age," *Biblical Archaeologist* 52 (1989): 4–39.

42. The ʿApiru are mentioned in Amarna letter 271 (*ANET* 486), the Hurrians in the victory hymn of Merenptah (*ANET* 378), and the Shasu in a report of a frontier official (*ANET* 259).

43. Kenyon, *Amorites and Canaanites*, 3.

The distinctions between some of these population groups, however, indicates that they may be clans, rather than different ethnic groups. Mario Liverani argues that the biblical writers indiscriminately used *Amorite* or *Canaanite*. Alternatively, they used *Amorite* to refer to a geographical region that the term *Canaanite* did not fit.[44] This view is supported by William Stiebing, who suggests that "quite possibly, Amorites and Canaanites were ethnically and culturally identical, with the name Canaanite applied to those Amorites who inhabited the cities of the coastal plain, and specifically the merchant class that dominated those cities."[45] The ease with which the Bible intermingles *Amorite* and *Canaanite* is seen in Genesis 36:2–3. First we are informed in general terms that Esau married Canaanite women; then we are told specifically that his three wives were Hittite, Hivite, and Ishmaelite.

The close identity of the Amorites with the Canaanites is illustrated in Ezekiel's reprimand of the Jebusites living in Jerusalem: "Your origin and your birth were in the land of the Canaanites; your father was an Amorite, and your mother a Hittite" (16:3 NRSV).[46] In the prophet's view, ethnic identities are blurred and subsumed under the broader term *Canaanite*.

Canaanite Language

Canaanite is one of two main branches of the Northwest Semitic family of languages (the other is Aramaic). These languages and related dialects are distinguished from the Semitic languages of Mesopotamia, South Arabia, and Ethiopia. The oldest attested Semitic language is Akkadian, which is found in texts from the time of Sargon of Akkad (ca. 2300). Akkadian slowly displaced the earlier language of the Sumerians in the third millennium as Semites rose to power in Mesopotamia. While Akkadian appeared early, it continued to be spoken and written in Mesopotamia, evolving into Old Babylonian and Old Assyrian in the second millennium, when it was also in use at Mari. In the first millennium, Assyrian and Babylonian dialects prevailed until the rise of the Persian Empire.

Prior to the discovery of cuneiform texts at Ebla, a third-millennium Canaanite language was postulated but unproved.[47] Now Eblaite is tentatively identified as Old Canaanite because of its affinity with later Canaanite dialects. Eblaite was in use among urban peoples of Syria. Amorite was ap-

---

44. Liverani, "Amorites," 125.
45. Stiebing, "When Was the Age of the Patriarchs?" 21.
46. Luke, "Your Father Was an Amorite."
47. Pettinato, *Archives of Ebla*, 57.

parently the language of the rural people, and the only form of Amorite that has survived is known from personal names embedded in texts from Mesopotamia, Syria, and Egypt dating to the first half of the second millennium.[48] Eblaite likely differed only dialectically from Amorite, and linguistically there is little distinction between Amorite and Canaanite dialects until the middle of the second millennium, distinctions that might point to differences in ethnic origin or in time of arrival in Syria-Palestine.

Canaanite is derived from the Semitic language in use in Syria-Palestine in the third millennium. Early evidence of the language comes from Late Bronze inscriptions at Serabit el-Khadim in the Sinai Peninsula and in the slightly later Amarna letters.[49] The Amarna letters consist primarily of diplomatic correspondence between petty rulers of city-states in Syria-Palestine and the Egyptian pharaohs during the mid-fourteenth century. Surprisingly, in this period Akkadian rather than Egyptian was the language of diplomacy. As a reading aid for the Egyptian court officials who received the correspondence, Canaanite scribes frequently added Canaanite words written with cuneiform signs to explain Akkadian terms. These glosses provide a window through which to view scattered elements of the Canaanite language in the Late Bronze Age. Because of the direct relationship of Canaanite and Hebrew, the glosses are of particular interest to students of Hebrew.

The 1929 discovery of clay tablets at Ras Shamra, the site of ancient Ugarit, provided an important source of information on a language closely akin to Canaanite.[50] The find was made along the Mediterranean coast a few miles north of modern Latakia in Syria in a context datable to the Late Bronze Age. Written in a cuneiform script based on an alphabet rather than on a syllabic system of writing, the texts provide significant information on the social, political, economic, and religious ideas and practices of a city-state

48. Herbert B. Huffmon, *Amorite Personal Names in the Mari Texts* (Baltimore: Johns Hopkins University Press, 1965). Amorite names tended to consist of a verb and a subject or object.

49. On the Serabit el-Khadim materials, see William F. Albright, *The Proto-Sinaitic Inscriptions and Their Decipherment*, 2d ed., Harvard Theological Studies 22 (Cambridge: Harvard University Press, 1969); Benjamin Sass, *The Genesis of the Alphabet and Its Development in the Second Millenium* [sic] B.C., Ägypten und Altes Testament 13 (Wiesbaden: Harrassowitz, 1988); and Joseph Naveh, *Early History of the Alphabet* (Jerusalem: Magnes/Leiden: Brill, 1982), 23–27. Over 350 clay tablets were discovered in 1887 in the ruins of Tell el-Amarna in Egypt.

50. See Cyrus H. Gordon, "The Ugaritic Texts: Half a Century of Research," *Biblical Archaeology Today: Proceedings of the International Congress on Biblical Archaeology, Jerusalem, April 1984* (Jerusalem: Israel Exploration Society/Israel Academy of Sciences and Humanities/American Schools of Oriental Research, 1985), 492–501; W. Herrmann, "Ras Schamra—fünfzig Jahre Forschungen," *Das Altertum* 25.2 (1979): 99–102; Gordon D. Young (ed.), *Ugarit in Retrospect: Fifty Years of Ugarit and Ugaritic* (Winona Lake, Ind.: Eisenbrauns, 1981).

quite similar and related to southern Canaanite city-states.[51]

The Canaanite language had evolved by 1000 into several regional dialects: Phoenician, Hebrew, Edomite, Moabite, and Ammonite. Further north in Syria, Aramaic had developed from the earlier Northwest Semitic stock. In the course of time it would eclipse related languages to become the international language of the Persian Empire, to a large extent even displacing Hebrew as the language of the Jews.

Canaanite Religion

Religion is in part a human response to the environment. The environment exhibits powers—for example, sun, moon, sea, earthquakes, volcanoes, death, and reproductive power—that are greater than the individual and hence potentially destructive or beneficial. In the ancient world such powers were personified as deities, and ancient people responded to such powers with beliefs and practices that were the shared experiences and explanations of life in living communities. Religion is expressed, then,

Canaanite head from Ugarit (Ras Shamra), 14th–13th century B.C. (height: 6.3″)
Courtesy of the Direction Générale des Antiquités et des Musées, Damascus

51. Peter C. Craigie, *Ugarit and the Old Testament* (Grand Rapids: Eerdmans, 1983); Adrian Curtis, *Ugarit (Ras Shamra)* (Grand Rapids: Eerdmans, 1985); Rudolph H. Dornemann, "The Excavations at Ras Shamra and Their Place in the Current Archaeological Picture of Ancient Syria," in *Ugarit in Retrospect: Fifty Years of Ugarit and Ugaritic*, ed. Gordon D. Young (Winona Lake, Ind.: Eisenbrauns, 1981), 59–69; Gabriel Saadé, *Ougarit: Métropole Cananéenne* (Beirut: Imprimerie Catholique, 1979); Keith N. Schoville, *Biblical Archaeology in Focus* (Grand Rapids: Baker, 1978), 236–42.

as a pattern of human behavior in the face of life's difficulties. It is behavior shared by the group of people who trust in the beliefs and participate in the practices.

In attempting to describe the religion of the Canaanites, we must keep in mind that at best we can but speculate on the deeper nature of Canaanite religion. We cannot know what was in the heart and mind of a devotee of the Canaanite religious experience. Further, we can know little of the folk religion practiced by rural Canaanites, since they left no written records.

What can be known about the Canaanite religion derives from two general sources of information: written records and material remains. The Bible is an important source, but the biblical writers naturally present a somewhat biased point of view that deprecated the Canaanite religion (Deut. 18:9–14).[52] Of primary importance in providing insight into Canaanite religion are the Ugaritic texts—both literary (e.g., myths and legends) and nonliterary (e.g., offering lists).[53] Before the Ugaritic discoveries, scanty written information relating to the Canaanite/Phoenician religion was available: Phoenician and Punic inscriptions, references in Greek and Roman sources, and the writings of the Phoenician priest Sanchuniathon.[54] Archeological excavations in what was ancient Canaan have recovered evidence of sanctuaries, deity figurines, incense burners, altars, and related paraphernalia. At Phoenician colonies on Cyprus and further west on the coasts of the Mediterranean, evidences of the later Punic form of the Canaanite religion have been recovered, including

52. On Ugarit and the Old Testament, see Peter C. Craigie, "Ugarit and the Bible: Progress and Regress in Fifty Years of Literary Study," in *Ugarit in Retrospect: Fifty Years of Ugarit and Ugaritic*, ed. Gordon D. Young (Winona Lake, Ind.: Eisenbrauns, 1981), 99–111; idem, "Ugarit, Canaan, and Israel," *Tyndale Bulletin* 34 (1983): 145–68; C. Kloos, *Yhwh's Combat with the Sea: A Canaanite Tradition in the Religion of Ancient Israel* (Leiden: Brill, 1986); John Day, *God's Conflict with the Dragon and the Sea: Echoes of a Canaanite Myth in the Old Testament* (Cambridge: Cambridge University Press, 1985); and Jonas C. Greenfield, "The Hebrew Bible and Canaanite Literature," in *The Literary Guide to the Bible*, ed. Robert Alter and Frank Kermode (Cambridge: Harvard University Press, 1987), 545–60.

53. See Cyrus H. Gordon, *Ugaritic Textbook*, Analecta Orientalia 38 (Rome: Pontifical Biblical Institute Press, 1965); idem, "Poetic Legends and Myths from Ugarit," *Berytus* 25 (1977): 5–133; Michael D. Coogan, *Stories from Ancient Canaan* (Philadelphia: Westminster, 1978); John C. L. Gibson, *Canaanite Myths and Legends*, 2d ed. (Edinburgh: Clark, 1976); and John Gray, *The Legacy of Canaan: The Ras Shamra Texts and Their Relevance to the Old Testament*, 2d ed., Vetus Testamentum Supplement 5 (Leiden: Brill, 1965).

54. The original work, written in Phoenician in the sixth century, has been lost. What we have of it was transmitted through Philo of Byblos (who wrote in Greek ca. A.D. 100), and church historian Eusebius (265–339) in his *Praeparatio Evangelica*. We also have information on Sanchuniathon's work through Porphyry in his treatise *Against the Christians*. Born at Tyre in A.D. 234, Porphyry went to Athens to study in 254 and then to Rome in 263, where he died between 301 and 310. See also James Barr, "Philo of Byblos and His 'Phoenician History,'" *Bulletin of the John Rylands Library* 57 (1974): 17–68.

cemeteries (called *tophets*) that confirm the sacrifice of children; however, no *tophets* have been found in Canaan proper.[55] (Note, however, the recent discovery of a possible *tophet* at Tyre, mentioned by William A. Ward in the chapter on the Phoenicians in this volume.) The excavations at Ugarit also revealed cultic centers (i.e., temples) and related features.[56]

Any reconstruction of the Canaanite religion from these sources is ultimately inadequate, for the sources are fragmentary. Phoenician and Punic inscriptions give little more than the names of the gods being invoked, and only a part of Sanchuniathon's work survives. The Ugaritic texts provide authentic Canaanite records that contain firsthand expressions of Canaanite religious thought and practice, but the texts are incomplete and often damaged. And archeological remains are but the surviving remnant of what once existed. The meaning given to archeological remains is an educated guess. Nevertheless, a general picture of Canaanite religious beliefs and practices emerges from a study of these sources.[57]

Myths

A religious myth consists of words spoken in connection with ritual actions. The words are intended to help make the rites effective for the officiating priests and the people who follow their instructions in the rituals. The acts of the worshipers imitate the actions of the characters in the myths. In a magical way, the rituals are made effective by the recitation of the appropriate myths as the acts are performed.

The literary texts from Ugarit include both myths (in which the gods are the actors and the center of focus) and epics (in which mortals are the major characters, although the gods may be involved). The myths involve Baal (also known as Hadad, god of thunder and lightning), the most active god of the Ugaritic pantheon;[58] Yam, the god of the sea (Hebrew *yām* means "sea"); El, the patriarchal deity, and his spouse Athirath (Asherah = Astarte); Kothar-

55. Evidence suggesting human sacrifice was recovered in excavations at Gezer in Israel, according to Reuben Bullard, staff geologist (private communication).

56. The temples of Dagon and Baal were major buildings located on the acropolis of the site. Between them was the house of the chief priest containing a library from which religious texts were recovered.

57. André Caquot and M. Sznycer, *Ugaritic Religion* (Leiden: Brill, 1980); Patrick D. Miller Jr., "Ugarit and the History of Religions," *Journal of Northwest Semitic Languages* 9 (1981): 119–28.

58. Baruch Margalit, *A Matter of "Life" and "Death": A Study of the Baal-Mot Epic (CTA 4–5–6)*, Alter Orient und Altes Testament 206 (Kevelaer: Butzon & Bercker/Neukirchen-Vluyn: Neukirchener Verlag, 1980); Mark S. Smith, "Interpreting the Baal Cycle," *Ugarit-Forschungen* 18 (1986): 313–40.

wa-Khasis, the god of crafts; Mot, god of the underworld, death, and sterility (Hebrew *môt* means "death");[59] and Anat, the sister of Baal.[60]

There is some internal evidence in the texts to indicate that the main Baal myths were used in connection with rituals. The myths were possibly a part of a liturgy of the autumnal New Year festival, but they may also have been used during other parts of the agricultural year.[61] (Only faint hints of the Canaanite calendar remain.) The myths were not primarily esthetic nor speculative, but religiously functional.[62] The Canaanites, like their neighbors in Anatolia, Egypt, and Mesopotamia, were not detached onlookers but an integral part of their environment. No one at any stage in history can be completely detached from the cycle of nature; the Canaanites were emotionally involved with the realities of life as they perceived them, and the forces of nature were personified by the gods and perpetuated in the myths.

The Canaanites' view of life focused on the forces of nature, both benevolent and malevolent, against which they were helpless. The annual cycle of life in ancient Canaan was often tenuous, subject to periods of drought or inadequate rainfall in a land between the desert and the sea. The Canaanites knew the chaos of the raging sea and the disaster of a placid stream flowing from the mountains that could become a destructive torrent in minutes. They knew the importance of the winter rains and thunderstorms for the fertility of the soil, and Baal, the god of rain, was also recognized as the source of fertility for flock and family. In the myths, then, Baal fights against the chaotic forces that threaten life in the Levant—sea, river, death, and sterility.

But the annual cycle of life in Canaan included the dry summer months of the Mediterranean climate. So in their myths, Mot (Death) overcame Baal for a time, and Baal died, was buried, and revived. The most likely setting for the reenactment of Baal's myth was in late September when the fall rains returned to renew the agricultural year. The recitation of the myth at the turn of the agricultural New Year would have involved the worshipers in a drama that

59. Mark S. Smith and Elizabeth M. Bloch-Smith, "Death and Afterlife in Ugarit and Israel," *Journal of the American Oriental Society* 108 (1988): 277–84.

60. John Gray, "The Blood Bath of the Goddess Anat in the Ras Shamra Texts," *Ugarit-Forschungen* 11 (1979): 315–24; H. F. Van Rooy, "The Relation between Anat and Baal in the Ugaritic Texts," *Journal of Northwest Semitic Languages* 7 (1979): 85–95.

61. Lester L. Grabbe, "The Seasonal Pattern and the 'Baal Cycle,'" *Ugarit-Forschungen* 8 (1976): 57–63.

62. Robert Ratner and Bruce Zuckerman, "'A Kid in Milk': New Photographs of KTU 1:23, line 14," *Hebrew Union College Annual* 57 (1986): 15–60; T. L. Fenton, "The Claremont 'MRZḤ' Tablet: Its Text and Meaning," *Ugarit-Forschungen* 9 (1977): 71–75; Richard E. Friedman, "The MRZḤ Tablet from Ugarit," *Maarav* 2 (1979–80): 187–206; Baruch Margalit, "The Ugarit Feast of the Drunken Gods: Another Look at RS.24.258 (KTU.1.114)," *Maarav* 2 (1979): 65–120.

actualized the natural order. There would have been weeping and lamentation for the dead god and expressions of joy at his return. In a magical way, the enactment of the ritual and the recitation of the myth assured the continuation of life. And the god's subduing of chaos helped establish or maintain the natural order, the status quo. It served to relieve the tensions of humankind and to assure them of the future.

Besides the major gods who possessed temples at this place or that, there were other holy places without buildings where local deities and divine manifestations could be recognized and given due regard. And always there was the possibility of magic. Even El resorts to magic in one text. Thus, by myth and ritual at festivals, through the maintenance of temple and cult, and through the power of magic, the Canaanites sought to survive in the face of the multitude of forces that hedged their lives about.

Legendary Epics

In the epic about King Keret of Hubur, disasters leave him a widower without heirs.[63] He bewails his condition, and kindly El instructs him in a dream to mount a military campaign to Udom. There Huriya, the daughter of King Pabil, can be obtained as his wife. En route to Udom, Keret swears an oath to Asherah of Sidon that he will give the goddess gold and silver if she prospers his plan. She does, he brings Huriya home to Hubur, and she bears him sons. One will be nursed by the goddesses Asherah and Anat (and will therefore be able to succeed Keret). But trouble comes because Keret forgets his vow. He falls ill to the point of death. One of his sons questions his divine nature and immortality (in some cultures, kings in the ancient world became demigods at death). Mention is also made that the earth suffers because of the king's illness. With the help of El, Keret's health is restored. Meantime, one of Keret's sons, Yassib, who thought his father was dying and who wanted to succeed to the throne, came to his father's chambers to declare his intent. The end of the epic is missing, but the fragment ends with a terrible curse pronounced on Yassib. The Keret epic is likely a social myth, conserved because it was used regularly in the social life of Canaan, perhaps at royal weddings.[64]

Another epic presents the theme of the death and resurrection of the main character, Aqhat, the son of King Danel, who is promised to Danel by El himself.[65] Danel, a virtuous king who judges rightly the cause of the widow and the orphan, receives a guest one day, Kothar-wa-Khasis, the god of crafts. The

---

63. See *ANET* 142–49 for English translation.
64. Gray, *Legacy of Canaan*, 112.
65. See *ANET* 149–55 for English translation.

artisan god carries a bow and arrows destined for the goddess Anat, but Aqhat receives them. Anat, seeing the boy with the weapons, desires them and offers him much silver and gold, which he refuses, adding that she should have her own made like his. She then promises him immortality like Baal, if he will give the bow to her. He replies that she cannot give immortality to a human whose destiny is to die, and he adds that the bow is a man's weapon, not to be used by a woman. In a mishap, Aqhat is killed and the bow is lost. Anat, frustrated in her desire, weeps over the fallen Aqhat and announces that she will restore him to life so that he may give her the bow and arrows and so that fertility may be restored on the earth. Meantime, Danel becomes aware of the death of Aqhat, vows vengeance, mourns his dead, and curses three cities. The end of the tablet is missing.

In both these legends the close relations between rulers, their families, and the gods is indicated. The health and well-being of the king (and the heir apparent) are intricately involved with the natural order of things upon which the Canaanites were so desperately dependent. The myths and epics likely reflect Canaanite views in the Middle Bronze Age, although the extant copies belong to the Late Bronze period.

Other Sources

Additional evidence about Canaanite religion can be gleaned from Late Bronze administrative texts, among them lists of sacrifices to various gods, rituals for sacrifices and offerings, lists of gods, names of religious personnel.[66]

Two temples have been excavated at Ugarit, the largest of which is the temple of Baal, called the "son of Dagon." The other temple is associated with Dagon, a god of grain who is hardly mentioned in the extant mythic texts.[67] Originally a fertility god worshiped from earliest times in Mesopotamia, Dagon was the chief god of the city-state Tuttul east of Ugarit in the Balikh River region.

A temple was a monumental building that functioned as the dwelling place of the god, comparable to the palace of a king. It was not used for religious gatherings; its courts, however, might be used for festival assemblies. Of course, the god did not dwell in the earthly temple, but in the heavens, although his presence was assumed to be established in the earthly building. Proof of the deity's presence was the statue set up in the building. The temple

---

66. On administrative texts, see Michael Heltzer, *The Internal Organization of the Kingdom of Ugarit* (Wiesbaden: Reichert, 1982).

67. Ulf Oldenburg, *The Conflict between El and Baʿal in Canaanite Religion* (Leiden: Brill, 1969), 46–57; John F. Healey, "The Underworld Character of the God Dagan," *Journal of Northwest Semitic Languages* 5 (1977): 43–51.

personnel were there to minister to the needs of the god. Sacrifices, liquid offerings, incense, etc., were provided to the god by humans (servants of the gods) and, in return, humans might hope for divine rewards. The earliest Canaanite temples (ca. 3000–2000) were single rooms with a door in the long side of the room.[68] Middle and Late Bronze Age temples tended to be square, with a special vestibule or portico over the entrance.[69] In time, a third room was added to the rear of the large, square room. This cubicle, raised above the main room and reached by steps, is identified as the holy place, the inner sanctum. This was a prototype for later temples, such as the Solomonic temple built about 950 in Jerusalem,[70] which contained a porch, a long narrow hall, and the cubicle inner sanctum.

In the epics of Ugarit, the king assumes certain sacerdotal functions, for he was believed to have a continuing and close contact with the gods, and he represented his human community before the gods. One piece of carved ivory graphically depicts the relation of the royal family to the divine. Two young princes of the royal family are shown suckling from the breast of a goddess.

From the administrative texts, however, we find that there were twelve priestly families at Ugarit, and one text names a high priest. Among the cultic personnel listed at Ugarit are priests, consecrated persons,[71] singers, makers of vestments, and sculptors. At the end of one text the high priest Attenu the Diviner is cited as an authority for a version of the Baal myth, so priests probably functioned as scribes as well.

One text from Ugarit lists the names of many of the gods and the proper sacrifices for each of them. Along with the major pantheon some lesser gods are mentioned (e.g., "the lords of threshing"). Offerings included oxen, sheep, burnt offering (in which the entire sacrifice is burned to the god), and communion offering (where part of the sacrifice was eaten by the offerer); other sacrificial materials included grain, wine, oil, and other produce. Religious terminology included "gift," "vow," "to offer up the victim," "to prepare (for sacrifice)."

---

68. Mazar, *Archaeology of the Land of the Bible*, 125–7.

69. Ibid., 211–13.

70. On cultic structures, see William G. Dever, *Recent Archaeological Discoveries and Biblical Research* (Seattle: University of Washington Press, 1990), 110–17; Avraham Biran (ed.), *Temples and High Places in Biblical Times* (Jerusalem: Nelson Glueck School of Biblical Archaeology of the Hebrew Union College–Jewish Institute of Religion, 1981).

71. These may have been cultic prostitutes; see Edwin M. Yamauchi, "Cultic Prostitution— A Case Study in Cultural Diffusion," in *Orient and Occident: Essays Presented to Cyrus H. Gordon on the Occasion of His Sixty-fifth Birthday*, ed. Harry A. Hoffner Jr., Alter Orient und Altes Testament 22 (Kevelaer: Butzon & Bercker/Neukirchen-Vluyn: Neukirchener Verlag, 1973), 213–22; Mayer I. Gruber, "Hebrew *Qĕdēšāh* and Her Canaanite and Akkadian Cognates," *Ugarit-Forschungen* 18 (1986): 133–48.

Canaanite religious practices focused upon the myths and rituals connected with Baal and the lesser gods and goddesses of fertility. It is quite probable that the major festival was the New Year's festival in the fall, but other festivals likely existed at harvest times.

Canaanite Culture

Culture has been defined as a uniquely human system of learned habits and customs, transmitted by society, and used by humans as their primary means of adapting to their environment.[72] (Although here treated separately, religion is an integral part of culture.) The Canaanite culture that the Israelites confronted at the end of the Late Bronze Age was the result of a continuum that began around 1900 (following the Early Bronze Age IV–Middle Bronze Age I cultural interruption noted previously). Archeological and textual evidence provide a basis for understanding and appreciating the achievements of the Canaanites before they began to fade into history as the result of sociopolitical changes in Palestine at the beginning of the Iron Age.[73]

The Middle Bronze Age II Canaanites were exceptional engineers, building great fortified cities. The battered-earth ramparts that they constructed and that give the tells their characteristic form have been exposed at many sites.

Bronze plaque from Hazor, 14th–13th century B.C. (height: 3.7″)
Courtesy of the Hazor Excavations in Memory of Yigael Yadin, Institute of Archaeology, Hebrew University of Jerusalem

72. James Deetz, *Invitation to Archaeology* (Garden City, N.Y.: Natural History Press, 1967), 6–7.

73. For nontraditional views on the appearance of Israel in Canaan, see Norman K. Gottwald, "Two Models for the Origins of Ancient Israel: Social Revolution or Frontier Development," in *The Quest for the Kingdom of God: Studies in Honor of George E. Mendenhall*, ed. Herbert B. Huffmon, Frank A. Spina, and Alberto R. W. Green (Winona Lake, Ind.: Eisenbrauns, 1983), 5–24; and Gösta W. Ahlström, *Who Were the Israelites?* (Winona Lake, Ind.: Eisenbrauns, 1986).

At Tell Dan (ancient Laish) an earlier wall and a city gate with a stepped-street entrance were incorporated into and covered with the rampart. The new entrance to the city has not been discovered; however, at other Middle Bronze Age II sites, such as Hazor, a new gate design that could accommodate war chariots on its smooth surface and straight entrance replaced earlier stepped-street entrances. The rampart was constructed of alternating layers of occupational debris from within the site and wadi material from outside. The massive amount of material moved and the interlocked effect of the layering give evidence of careful planning and the sophisticated social organization required to complete such a project.[74]

Ramparted fortification apparently moved from the north, beginning in Syria, toward the south, eventually finding expression as far south as Gaza (Tell el-Ajjul). The development of effective battering rams may have stimulated the building of the battered-earth ramparts. Underground drainage systems carried water away from the imposing gate structures, palaces, and temples.

The Canaanites were also creative artisans, producing exceptionally beautiful pieces of jewelry—earrings, pendants, armlets, and signet rings—made from sheets of gold and golden wire as well as silver. The artisans used sophisticated techniques—engraving, filigree, inlay, and the like. Canaanite engravers carved

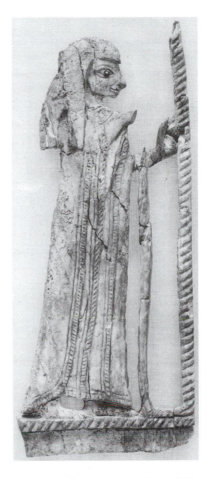

Woman in ivory from Megiddo, 1350–1150 B.C. (average thickness: 0.6″)
Courtesy of the Oriental Institute of the University of Chicago

74. In the seventeenth and sixteenth centuries (the Hyksos era), Hurrians from northern Syria migrated southward. Under the leadership of Indo-Aryan chieftains (as indicated by their names; see Albright, *Yahweh and the Gods of Canaan*, 114–15), these chariot warriors appear to have established themselves as a ruling class over the masses in a fruitful, symbiotic relationship. The construction of ramparted defenses may best be attributed to this group of elite leaders.

ivory and bone for inlays in decorative furniture and also worked semiprecious stone. Sculptors worked in stone and metal to produce images of deities and guardian lions. They drew inspiration from the artistic traditions of neighboring peoples in Egypt, Syria, Anatolia, the Mediterranean isles, and the Mesopotamian civilization, adding their own creative distinctives.

Canaanite metallurgists cast bronze mirrors, daggers, swords, tools, and figurines.[75] Molds have been discovered, indicating standardized production of some forms. The making of true bronze, a combination of tin and copper, became commonplace.[76]

Canaanite potters produced graceful yet practical domestic pottery—storage jars, cooking pots, bowls, jugs, juglets, and chalices—as well as the Canaanite jar, used for shipping products such as grain, wine, and olive oil by caravan or sea.[77] The use of a fast potter's wheel and firing at a high temperature produced strong, thin-walled ceramics. Special pieces were produced in the form of animals (zoomorphic), cultic incense burners, and masks likely used in religious ceremonies.

Canaanites were enterprising merchants; in fact, by the time of the prophet Isaiah the word *kĕna͑an* (normally "Canaan, Canaanite") could mean "merchant, trader" (Isa. 23:8) and a derivative word could signify "wares, bundle" (Jer. 10:17). A fourteenth-century Egyptian tomb painting, depicting Canaanite merchant ships unloading cargo, is illustrative of Canaanite commerce. Lovely decorated pottery imported from Crete and Cyprus testify to Canaanite interest in luxury items.

Canaanites were ingenious inventors. Caught between the cumbersome writing systems of Mesopotamian cuneiform and Egyptian hieroglyphs, the Canaanites invented a simplified form of writing that was destined to become the predominant means of written communication—the alphabet.[78] Our ability to write and read by means of alphabetic signs is traceable directly

---

75. Ora Negbi, *Canaanite Gods in Metal* (Tel Aviv: Institute of Archaeology, Tel Aviv University, 1976).

76. Michael Heltzer, "The Metal Trade of Ugarit and the Problem of Transportation of Commercial Goods," *Iraq* 39 (1977): 203–11.

77. Ruth Amiran, *Ancient Pottery of the Holy Land* (New Brunswick, N.J.: Rutgers University Press, 1969).

78. Robert R. Stieglitz, "The Ugaritic Cuneiform and the Canaanite Linear Alphabet," *Journal of Near Eastern Studies* 30 (1971): 135–39; Alan R. Millard, "The Canaanite Linear Alphabet and Its Passage to the Greeks," *Kadmos* 15 (1976): 130–44; idem, "The Ugaritic and Canaanite Alphabets—Some Notes," *Ugarit-Forschungen* 11 (1979): 613–16; Naveh, *Early History of the Alphabet*; Émile Puech, "Origine de l'Alphabet: Documents en Alphabet Liné et Cunéiforme du IIᵉ Millénaire," *Revue Biblique* 93 (1986): 161–213; Martin Bernal, *Cadmean Letters: The Transmission of the Alphabet to the Aegean and Further West before 1400 B.C.* (Winona Lake, Ind.: Eisenbrauns, 1990).

back to the Canaanite alphabet. The Canaanites were also intellectually so-phisticated, using their writing system not only for commercial and cultic purposes, but also to produce a body of literature that left its subsequent imprint on the authors of our Hebrew Bible. The prophet Isaiah identifies the speech of Judah with the language of Canaan (19:18).

Canaanites were intelligent, presumably developing from a tribal organization into a city-state form of government that was well adapted to the physical environment of the region. The terrain of fertile valleys separated by hills and mountains provided for such petty monarchies, each with a central fortified city and adjacent villages and hinterland. The surrounding agricultural and pastoral lands, through subsistence farming, made each kingdom essentially self-sufficient.[79] While Canaanite kings, as with the later kings of Israel, controlled the political and commercial enterprises as well as extensive property, the kings and their subject people were mutually obligated to each other. The people supported their kings, while the kings were charged with defending the widow and the orphan.[80]

Canaanites were religious, expressing their worldview through myths in which the forces of nature were personified and deified.[81] How Canaanites viewed life is also seen in legends in which epic human figures interacted with gods and goddesses, perhaps reflecting the tensions and turmoils that people experienced in life. They held religious festivals. They had temples and priests. They made offerings to their deities (similar to those that Israel offered to Yahweh). They prayed. So religious were they that they offered the fruit of their loins as offerings to the gods. Though there is little evidence in Syria-Palestine of child sacrifice among the Canaanites, ample evidence of the practice exists among their descendants, the Phoenicians, at Carthage in North Africa and at other colonies scattered around the Mediterranean basin.[82]

79. On farming see Michael Heltzer, *The Rural Community in Ancient Ugarit* (Wiesbaden: Reichert, 1976); Lawrence E. Stager, "Farming in the Judean Desert during the Iron Age," *Bulletin of the American Schools of Oriental Research* 221 (1976): 145–58.

80. Cf. Aqhat 2.5.6–8: "He [the king] decides the case of the widow, / he judges the suit of the orphan."

81. Richard J. Clifford, "Phoenician Religion," *Bulletin of the American Schools of Oriental Research* 279 (1990): 55–64.

82. Alberto R. W. Green, *The Role of Human Sacrifice in the Ancient Near East*, American Schools of Oriental Research Dissertation Series 1 (Missoula, Mont.: Scholars Press, 1975); P. G. Mosca, *Child Sacrifice in Canaanite and Israelite Religion: A Study of Mulk and Molech* (Ph.D. diss., Harvard University, 1975); Morton Smith, "On Burning Babies," *Journal of the American Oriental Society* 95 (1975): 477–79; and Lawrence E. Stager and Samuel R. Wolff, "Child Sacrifice at Carthage: Religious Rite or Population Control?" *Biblical Archaeology Review* 10.1 (1984): 30–51.

This, then, was the people the invading tribes of Israel set out to conquer in the name of the Lord under the leadership of Joshua. The biblical traditions indicate that Israel was supposed to utterly destroy the Canaanites and the other groups that occupied the land of Canaan (Deut. 7:1–5). The God of Israel called for this drastic treatment "because of the wickedness of these nations" (Deut. 9:4–5; cf. 12:29–31). They even burned their sons and daughters in the fire to their gods (Deut. 12:31). Thus the inhabitants of Canaan are depicted by the biblical writers as depraved and wicked because of the way in which they worshiped other gods (Deut. 7:4, 25; 9:5).

The command to destroy the Canaanites was never fully executed. The Israelite occupation of Canaan extended over a period of time, according to the Book of Judges. From the surviving Canaanites the Israelites learned dry-land farming, the digging of cisterns to hold water in the dry season—in short, adaptation to subsistence agriculture and animal husbandry. Ultimately, the remnant of the Canaanites in the region was absorbed into the Davidic kingdom. Particularly in the northern kingdom, the subtle influence of the Canaanites modified the Israelite culture in a process that reached a dramatic climax in the time of Ahab and Jezebel (ca. 850). In the aftermath of that period, the northern kingdom continued a decline that ultimately ended in the exile of its leading inhabitants. Judah, also under the influence of Canaanite culture, followed the same path in a decline broken by two reforms—that of Hezekiah and that of Josiah—before that kingdom, too, ended in exile away from the land of Canaan.

The Bible reflects the dangerous attraction of Canaanite culture for the Israelites. The distinctive features of official Israelite religion, with its exclusivistic monotheism, were in direct and continuing conflict with the religious views of the inclusivistic polytheists of Canaan, and archeology indicates that the monotheistic view did not completely conquer.[83] Israel inherited the ma-

---

83. On the relationship of Canaanite and Israelite religion, see Michael D. Coogan, "Canaanite Origins and Lineage: Reflections on the Religion of Ancient Israel," in *Ancient Israelite Religion: Essays in Honor of Frank Moore Cross*, ed. Patrick D. Miller Jr., Paul D. Hanson, and S. Dean McBride (Philadelphia: Fortress, 1987), 115–24; William G. Dever, "The Contribution of Archaeology to the Study of Canaanite and Early Israelite Religion," in *Ancient Israelite Religion: Essays in Honor of Frank Moore Cross*, ed. Patrick D. Miller Jr., Paul D. Hanson, and S. Dean McBride (Philadelphia: Fortress, 1987), 209–47; Elmer B. Smick, "Israel's Struggle with the Religions of Canaan," in *Interpretation and History*, ed. R. Laird Harris, S. H. Quek, and J. Robert Vannoy (Singapore: Christian Life, 1986), 123–33; Frank M. Cross, *Canaanite Myth and Hebrew Epic: Essays in the History of the Religion of Israel* (Cambridge: Harvard University Press, 1973); T. J. Lewis, *Cults of the Dead in Ancient Israel and Ugarit*, Harvard Semitic Monographs 39 (Atlanta: Scholars Press, 1989). A reference to Yahweh and his Asherah, recovered by Zev Meshel in 1978, has stimulated research on the Israelite-Canaanite religious interconnections; see *Kuntillet ʿAjrud: A Religious Centre from the Time of the Judaean Monarchy on the Border of Sinai*, Israel Museum Catalogue 175 (Jerusalem: Israel Mu-

terial culture of Canaan, along with the language of the Canaanites and their simplified writing system. It was difficult for Israel to resist the attraction of the Canaanite cult and worldview, with its emphasis on fertility.[84] Ultimately, the majority of the Israelites succumbed to Canaanite influences, despite the warning cries of the prophets of the Lord. Only a remnant survived in exile in Babylon, there to be purged of the fatal attraction that, according to the Bible (2 Kings 17; 23:4–27), had destroyed their forebears. From that time on Jews did not use idols.

Recommended Reading

Aharoni, Yohanan. *The Land of the Bible: A Historical Geography*. Translated and edited by Anson F. Rainey. Philadelphia: Westminster, 1979.

Albright, William F. *Yahweh and the Gods of Canaan*. Reprinted Winona Lake, Ind.: Eisenbrauns, 1979.

Coogan, Michael D. *Stories from Ancient Canaan*. Philadelphia: Westminster, 1978.

Craigie, Peter C., and Gerald H. Wilson. "Religions of the Biblical World: Canaanite (Syria and Palestine)." Vol. 4 / pp. 95–101 in *International Standard Bible Encyclopedia*. Edited by Geoffrey W. Bromiley et al. Grand Rapids: Eerdmans, 1988.

Dever, William G. *Recent Archaeological Discoveries and Biblical Research*. Seattle: University of Washington Press, 1990.

Gibson, John C. L. *Canaanite Myths and Legends*. 2d edition. Edinburgh: Clark, 1976.

Gray, John. *The Canaanites*. London: Thames & Hudson, 1964.

Kenyon, Kathleen M. *Amorites and Canaanites*. Schweich Lectures 1963. London: Oxford University Press for the British Academy, 1966.

---

seum, 1978); idem, "Did Yahweh Have a Consort?" *Biblical Archaeology Review* 5.2 (1979): 24–35; John Day, "Asherah in the Hebrew Bible and Northwest Semitic Literature," *Journal of Biblical Literature* 105 (1986): 385–408; David N. Freedman, "Yahweh of Samaria and His Asherah," *Biblical Archaeologist* 50 (1987): 241–49; Walter A. Maier III, ʿ*Asherah: Extrabiblical Evidence*, Harvard Semitic Monographs 37 (Atlanta: Scholars Press, 1986); Patrick D. Miller Jr., "The Absence of the Goddess in Israelite Religion," *Hebrew Annual Review* 10 (1986): 239–48; Mark A. Smith, "God Male and Female in the Old Testament: Yahweh and His 'Asherah,'" *Theological Studies* 48 (1987): 333–40; William G. Dever, "Asherah, Consort of Yahweh? New Evidence from Kuntillet ʿAjrûd," *Bulletin of the American Schools of Oriental Research* 255 (1984): 21–37; idem, *Recent Archaeological Discoveries and Biblical Research*, 140–49; and Mark S. Smith, *The Early History of God* (San Francisco: Harper & Row, 1990).

84. See Dever, *Recent Archaeological Discoveries and Biblical Research*, 119–66.

Kochavi, Moshe. "At That Time the Canaanites Were in the Land. . . ." Pp. 25–34 in *Recent Archaeology in the Land of Israel*. Edited by Hershel Shanks. Washington: Biblical Archaeology Society, 1984.

Liverani, Mario. "The Amorites." Pp. 100–133 in *Peoples of Old Testament Times*. Edited by Donald J. Wiseman. Oxford: Clarendon, 1973.

Mazar, Amihai. *Archaeology of the Land of the Bible 10,000–586 B.C.E.* New York: Doubleday, 1990.

Millard, Alan R. "The Canaanites." Pp. 29–52 in *Peoples of Old Testament Times*. Edited by Donald J. Wiseman. Oxford: Clarendon, 1973.

Pettinato, Giovanni. *The Archives of Ebla: An Empire Inscribed in Clay*. Garden City, N.Y.: Doubleday, 1981.

———. *Ebla: A New Look at History*. Translated by C. Faith Richardson. Baltimore: Johns Hopkins University Press, 1991.

Schoville, Keith N. *Biblical Archaeology in Focus*. Grand Rapids: Baker, 1978.

Phoenicians

William A. Ward

The glory of Lebanon will come to you,
the pine, the fir and the cypress together,
to adorn the place of my sanctuary.
— *Isaiah 60:13*

The word *Phoenician* comes from an ancient Greek nickname for the people and cities of the eastern Mediterranean littoral during the first millennium.[1] Phoenicia lies along a narrow coastal strip for roughly two hundred miles, from the island of Aradus (modern Arwad) in the north to Tyre in the south. The Lebanon mountain range to the east has throughout history created a political and cultural barrier between the coast and inland Syria. While rain falls in the region only during the winter months, mountain springs provide water the rest of the year for the rich agricultural land along the sea. The land is limited, however, and the cities founded around the natural harbors of the coast remained small. The great coniferous forests that once blanketed the mountains were the major natural resource of ancient Phoenicia and the basis for an active export trade in lumber, wood, oil, and resin.[2]

The present essay deals with the "classical" Phoenicians of the Iron Age (ca. 1200–332), though this civilization did not spring into history without antecedents.[3] The Iron Age Phoenicians represent a later phase of the general

---

1. For the theories on the origin of the Greek term, see Claude Vandersleyen, "L'Étymologie de Phoïnix, 'Phénicien,'" in *Phoenicia and the East Mediterranean in the First Millennium B.C.*, ed. Édouard Lipiński, Studia Phoenicia 5 (Louvain: Peeters, 1987), 19–22; Michael C. Astour, "Origin of the Terms 'Canaan,' 'Phoenician,' and 'Purple,'" *Journal of Near Eastern Studies* 24 (1965): 346–50; James D. Muhly, "Homer and the Phoenicians: The Relations between Greece and the Near East in the Late Bronze and Early Iron Ages," *Berytus* 19 (1970): 24–30.

2. See John P. Brown, *The Lebanon and Phoenicia: Ancient Texts Illustrating Their Physical Geography and Native Industries*, vol. 1: *The Physical Setting and the Forest* (Beirut: American University of Beirut Press, 1969), chap. 5.

3. Wolfgang Röllig, "On the Origins of the Phoenicians," *Berytus* 31 (1983): 79–93; Robert R. Stieglitz, "The Geopolitics of the Phoenician Littoral in the Early Iron Age," *Bulletin of the American Schools of Oriental Research* 279 (1990): 9–12.

Canaanite culture that goes back into the third millennium and beyond. They were still Canaanite, but are distinguished from their ancestors and neighbors by their own unique culture.

A true history of the Phoenician cities cannot be compiled since we lack sufficient written and archeological documentation. Most Iron Age texts from the Phoenician homeland are funerary in nature or treat the building and repair of temples and the dedication of objects to various deities. They yield very little of political import beyond the names of several kings of Byblos and Sidon.[4] Much of what is recorded about Iron Age Phoenicia comes from Greek and Roman historians, the Old Testament, Mesopotamian and Egyptian records, and myths and legends from Homer and later classical works, though the latter deal primarily with Phoenician westward expansion.[5] All of this material must be treated with varying degrees of caution since each source has its own bias and much of the information contained therein remains unverified by other evidence.

The archeological record is somewhat more informative, though very sparse for the earlier part of the period.[6] Of the major coastal cities, Aradus has not been excavated due to its dense population. There are a few objects from Byblos or Beirut, though no architectural remains at all for the period 1200–600. Excavations at Sidon over several decades have uncovered splendid remains of the Persian period, including the well-known stone sarcophagi and a temple to Eshmun, but nothing of the city itself. The extensive work at Tyre has been concerned primarily with the Roman and Byzantine periods, though a recent excavation has gone down to Early Bronze Age levels in one area of the ancient island city. Lesser known coastal sites have also produced Iron Age material. In the region of Aradus, house remains and objects have been found at Tabbat al-Hammam, Tell Kazel (ancient Simyra), and Tell ʿArqa. At Amrit in the same region a sixth-century temple of Melqart has been excavated. South of Beirut an extensive tenth- to eighth-century cemetery has been found at Khaldé, and substantial material from

---

4. Collections of inscriptions include Herbert Donner and Wolfgang Röllig, *Kanaanäische und aramäische Inschriften*, 3 vols. (Wiesbaden: Harrassowitz, 1962–64); and Pietro Magnanini, *Le Iscrizione Fenicie dell'Oriente* (Rome: Istituto di Studi del Vicino Oriente, 1973). Short texts naming owners of pottery vessels and the like continue to turn up in excavations from the Levant to Spain.

5. For a general orientation, see Guy Bunnens, *L'Expansion Phénicienne en Méditerranée: Essai d'Interprétation Fondé sur une Analyse des Traditions Littéraires* (Brussels: Institut Historique Belge de Rome, 1979).

6. Surveys of the archeological material include James B. Pritchard, *Recovering Sarepta: A Phoenician City* (Princeton: Princeton University Press, 1978), chap. 2; Patricia M. Bikai, "The Phoenicians," in *The Crisis Years: The Twelfth Century* B.C., ed. William A. Ward and Martha S. Joukowsky (Dubuque, Iowa: Kendall/Hunt, 1992), chap. 16.

several cemeteries in south Lebanon has now been published. A major excavation has been carried out at Sarepta (modern Sarafand, biblical Zarephath where Elijah visited; 1 Kings 17:8–24) south of Sidon where houses, shrines, and a number of pottery kilns (all tenth century and later) have been found. There is also a growing body of evidence for strong Phoenician influence along the northern coast of Israel from Acco to the Yarkon Valley.

History

In terms of political events, the history of Iron Age Phoenicia can be divided into two phases: (1) from the advent of the Sea Peoples in the twelfth century to the initial Assyrian assault on the region in 876 and (2) from 876 to the conquests of Alexander in 332. Following 332, the Phoenician cities were gradually absorbed into the new Hellenistic Orient, losing their unique native character.

The first phase is little known and much must be inferred from indirect evidence. There is much disagreement about the role played by the western Sea Peoples in fostering the Phoenician maritime dominance of the Iron Age.[7] To some, these invaders were instrumental in motivating the Phoenician cities to assume mastery of the sea after the collapse of a previous Late Bronze Age Mycenaean thalassocracy. Others argue that the Sea Peoples had little if anything to do with Phoenician enterprise; there is no hard evidence of the Sea Peoples in Phoenicia, the

Sarcophagus of King Eshmunazar II of Sidon, 5th century B.C. (height: 7' 6")
Courtesy of the Louvre Museum

7. Nancy K. Sandars, *The Sea Peoples: Warriors of the Mediterranean* (London: Thames & Hudson, 1978). The latest survey is Ward and Joukowsky, *Crisis Years*.

coastal cities already had a long history of dominance in East Mediterranean waters, and it is even possible that the Phoenicians became allies of these invaders from the west. Whatever their role, the arrival of the Sea Peoples was roughly concurrent with a series of major events that formed a watershed in the history of the Phoenician cities: the collapse of most empires and kingdoms around the Mediterranean and the appearance of new political entities such as the Philistines, Hebrews, and Arameans. The world order of the Late Bronze Age gave way to a time of readjustment, after which empires from the east established a new political orientation.

For Phoenicia, this time of readjustment began what many have called its "golden age." Its cities were now free of foreign interference and there was no external power to challenge internal development. This golden age appears to have emerged slowly. Of the initial two centuries, there is hardly any archeological material. Scant though the evidence is, however, it is apparent that some coastal cities in Phoenicia survived through this little-known period, though foreign trade was drastically curtailed.

Two well-known literary documents date to this period. The Egyptian "Story of Wenamon" recounts the commercial travels of a temple official to purchase timber at Byblos in approximately 1075.[8] Wenamon's journey took him to the Philistine towns of Dor, Tyre, Sidon, and Byblos, plus the isle of Cyprus. All the coastal cities are portrayed as active seaports, and since the papyrus preserving this account is almost contemporary to the events it describes, there is no reason to doubt its description of the region. The other contemporary document records the Mediterranean campaign of Tiglath-pileser I (1114–1076) during which he received tribute from Byblos, Sidon, and Aradus.[9] The text does not state what this tribute was, although it does note that Tiglath-pileser came to the Lebanon Mountains to obtain cedar for the construction of a temple in his capital. The two texts thus show that four of the primary Phoenician cities—Tyre, Sidon, Byblos, Aradus—were in existence at the beginning of the eleventh century and that the trade in coniferous woods was active at that time.

Under the Assyrians

The campaign of Tiglath-pileser was little more than a probing expedition, for he made no effort to create provinces from the "conquered" territories, mainly because for the next two centuries Assyrian rulers were busy at home with innumerable local wars. During this time of Assyrian quiescence, west-

8. *ANET* 25–29; Hans Goedicke, *The Report of Wenamon* (Baltimore: Johns Hopkins University Press, 1975).
9. *ANET* 274–75.

ward Phoenician expansion began and the archeological record in Phoenicia itself becomes somewhat more abundant. The coastal cities were free of external political pressures, were growing larger, and were looking to the west for much-needed raw materials.

In the early ninth century, Assyrian expansion began in earnest, and the royal annals, beginning with those of Ashurnasirpal II (883–859), record an ever-widening series of conquests that soon engulfed the Phoenician city-states.

Ashurnasirpal II marched through northern Syria and reached the seacoast in 876. While he speaks of military conquests inland, he notes only the collection of tribute from Tyre, Sidon, Byblos, the island kingdom of Aradus, and other coastal cities.[10] The tribute list includes precious metals and manufactured items, and probably the timber that Ashurnasirpal cut in the Amanus Range north of the Lebanon Mountains. Shalmaneser III (858–824) led several campaigns to the region and frequently notes that he received tribute from Tyre, Sidon, and Byblos and that he cut down cedar in the Amanus Mountains.[11] The first hint that any Phoenician city was involved in actual fighting is seen at the Battle of Qarqar in 853, when Aradus sent a small infantry company of two hundred to join a coalition against Shalmaneser.

Adad-nirari III (810–783) includes Tyre and Sidon among cities paying tribute,[12] and the annals of Tiglath-pileser III (744–727) record the names of Phoenician kings who paid tribute: Shipit-Baal of Byblos, Mattan-Baal of Aradus, and Mattan and Hiram II of Tyre. The town of ʿArqa now appears for the first time among the tribute cities.[13] With Sennacherib (704–681) comes the first recorded Assyrian siege and destruction of a Phoenician city: Sidon was taken along with its dependencies, including mainland Tyre and the north Palestinian towns of Achzib and Acco. The Sidonian ruler ʾIluʾili was forced into exile on Cyprus,[14] and a new king of that city was installed by Sennacherib.

Esarhaddon (680–669) speaks again of the destruction of the unhappy Sidon, the beheading of its king ʿAbdimilkut, and the construction of a new city there. He likewise describes the conquest of Tyre and the seizure of all Tyrian vassal towns. Baalu of Tyre, Milkʾasap of Byblos, and Mattan-Baal of Aradus are among a list of twenty-two rulers of the area forced to transport cedar logs to Nineveh.[15] The final Assyrian intervention in Phoenicia came under

10. *ANET* 276.
11. *ANET* 279–81.
12. *ANET* 281.
13. *ANET* 283.
14. *ANET* 287–88.
15. *ANET* 290–91.

Ashurbanipal (668–627) during his Egyptian campaign. This time it was the island stronghold of Tyre that surrendered after a siege in which its food and water supplies were cut off. Yakinlu of Aradus also submitted to the Assyrians, and, when he died shortly thereafter, Ashurbanipal installed one of Yakinlu's sons on the throne.[16]

It is not possible to correlate the history of Assyrian interference in the west with the archeological record of Phoenicia, which can do little more than confirm the existence of the main cities mentioned in the literary sources. While Iron Age Byblos, mentioned constantly by Assyrian kings, is not preserved, the sarcophagus of Ahiram, a series of local inscriptions, and three royal statues of the Egyptian Dynasty 22 indicate that the city was in existence in the tenth and early ninth centuries. Egyptian alabasters looted from Sidon by Esarhaddon have been found at Ashur, and a contemporary fragment of an Egyptian libation table was found long ago at Aradus.[17] Tyre shows continuous occupation up to the beginning of the seventh century. The constant reference to "Tyre, Byblos, and Aradus" by Assyrian kings, possibly a cliché meaning all of Phoenicia, is thus supported by the meager archeological material. Sarepta, mentioned but twice in the Assyrian annals and once in an Egyptian Ramesside composition, was a thriving town throughout this period.[18] ʿArqa, mentioned only by Tiglath-pileser III, shows occupation for much of the period. By the tenth and ninth centuries, sites such as Tabbat al-Hammam, Tell Kazel, Khaldé, and several southern cemeteries indicate growing habitation and settlement of the country.

It is clear from the Assyrian annals that the Phoenician cities were not destroyed or even occupied by Assyrian armies until the early seventh century with the siege of Sidon by Sennacherib. Prior to this, amid the constant theme in the Assyrian annals of the destruction, conquest, or punishment of Aramean and north Syrian states,[19] runs the counter-theme that tribute was collected from the Phoenician cities but they were not attacked. The distinction between the hinterland and the coast is that the small but powerful in-

---

16. *ANET* 295–96.

17. Jean Leclant, "Les Relations entre l'Égypte et la Phénicie du Voyage d'Ounamon à l'Expédition d'Alexandre," in *The Role of the Phoenicians in the Interaction of Mediterranean Civilizations*, ed. William A. Ward (Beirut: American University of Beirut Press, 1968), 12–13.

18. Sarepta was not ordinarily mentioned by the Assyrians since it was a dependency of Sidon, as stated in the Esarhaddon text and 1 Kings 17:9. For the Egyptian reference see *ANET* 477 and Hans-Werner Fischer-Elfert, *Die satirische Streitschrift des Papyrus Anastasi I* (Wiesbaden: Harrassowitz, 1986), 171–72.

19. Hélène S. Sader, *Les États Araméens de Syrie Depuis Leur Fondation jusqu'à Leur Transformation en Provinces Assyriennes* (Beirut: Orient-Institut der Deutschen Morgenländischen Gesellschaft, 1987).

land kingdoms presented a threat to Assyrian border security; the coastal cities did not. Furthermore, the latter provided both annual tribute and access to the rich Mediterranean commerce. Being merchants rather than warriors, the Phoenicians seem to have accepted a subordinate vassal-like role rather than threaten their far-flung shipping interests. It was a small price to pay for semiautonomy.[20]

Assyrian rule in Phoenicia was fairly mild. The internal administrative reforms of Tiglath-pileser III in the second half of the eighth century aimed at closer royal supervision over a far-flung empire, better communication between its parts, and above all the assurance of tribute payments.[21] Typically, the penalty for rebellion or nonpayment was destruction. Thus, in Sennacherib's third campaign (noted above), ꜂Iluꜣili of Sidon and Sidka of Ashkelon, both of whom had refused to pay tribute, were replaced, their cities destroyed, and the tribute reimposed. Sennacherib also names many kings who paid tribute and were left alone. In some cases, at least, Assyrian officials were resident at important cities to oversee the collection of tribute and the tax on Phoenician exports.[22]

Egyptian involvement in the affairs of Phoenicia during the Assyrian domination is documented but difficult to define. After the "Story of Wenamon" the next documents to prove contact are statue fragments of three pharaohs of early Dynasty 22 found at Byblos: Shoshenq I (945–924), Osorkon I (924–889), and Osorkon II (874–850).[23] Inscribed on the first two fragments are additional Phoenician texts of two rulers of Byblos, Abibaal and Elibaal. While none of these objects can be dated via its archeological context, the two inscribed pieces belong to a group of six Byblian texts that, on paleographical grounds plus the sparse related archeological material, can be placed in the tenth century.[24] The logical implication is that Egypt was still in contact with Byblos at this time. That this went beyond purely commercial ties is highly

20. Guy Kestemont, "Le Commerce Phénicien et l'Expansion Assyrienne du IXe–VIIIe S.," *Oriens Antiquus* 11 (1972): 137–44.

21. Harry W. F. Saggs, *The Might That Was Assyria* (London: Sidgwick & Jackson, 1984), 85–87.

22. For example, at Tyre: Harry W. F. Saggs, "The Nimrud Letters," *Iraq* 17 (1955): 127–28. The power over local economic affairs is clearly seen in the treaty between Esarhaddon and Baal of Tyre (*ANET* 533–34). The treaty is particularly concerned with shipping and trade goods.

23. Maurice Chehab, "Noms de Personnalités Égyptiennes Découvertes au Liban," *Bulletin du Musée de Beyrouth* 22 (1969): 38–40. He includes a fragment of an arm that names Osorkon I (but the fragment may belong to a second statue of this king).

24. P. Kyle McCarter Jr., *The Antiquity of the Greek Alphabet and the Early Phoenician Scripts*, Harvard Semitic Monographs 9 (Missoula, Mont.: Scholars Press, 1975), 31–39.

doubtful. Nor can the statue of Shoshenq I be related to his military campaign into Palestine, which did not reach the Phoenician cities and which created no new empire.[25]

Alabaster vessels that name kings of Dynasty 22 have been found in burials at Almuñécar and other Spanish sites, but they may not be evidence of Egyptian royal contacts with Phoenicia, as is generally supposed. It is suggested that many of these vessels were Phoenician imitations manufactured for export, as these objects seem to have been especially popular abroad. In this regard, on Egyptian alabaster vessels discovered at Ashur, cuneiform texts were added that stated they were taken from the palace of ʿAbdimilkut of Sidon when Esarhaddon destroyed that city.[26] It is thus probable that stores of such items, whether genuine or imitation, were maintained as trade goods in Phoenician emporiums such as Sidon. In any case, there is sufficient nonroyal Egyptian material in Iron Age Phoenician deposits to verify commercial ties with Egypt during this period, and objects made of coniferous Phoenician wood are known from Egyptian contexts.[27]

Throughout the ninth to sixth centuries, Egypt was intermittently engaged in warfare with Assyria, usually sending contingents of troops to join Syro-Palestinian coalitions, for example, at the Battle of Qarqar (853) against Shalmaneser III, to help Hoshea of Israel against Shalmaneser V,[28] and against Sennacherib in 701. Such coalitions were defeated and ultimately the Assyrians under Esarhaddon were able to invade Egypt itself. Of the Phoenician cities, we hear almost nothing from Egyptian sources since the battlefields lay outside Egypt and since Phoenicia was more aligned politically with Assyria. An Egyptian text of Psammetichus I, dating to about the same year as the fall of Nineveh to Babylon (612), may be significant. This text notes that the chiefs of Lebanon "were subjects of the [Egyptian] palace, with a royal courtier placed over them, and their taxes were assessed for the resi-

---

25. Kenneth A. Kitchen, *The Third Intermediate Period in Egypt* (Warminster: Aris & Phillips, 1973), 432–47. Shoshenq I is Shishak of 1 Kings 14:25–28, which refers to the same campaign.

26. William Culican, "Almuñécar, Assur and Phoenician Penetration of the Western Mediterranean," *Levant* 2 (1970): 28–36; Ingrid Gamer-Wallert, *Ägyptische und ägyptisierende Funde von der iberischen Halbinsel* (Wiesbaden: Reichert, 1978), 224–28. A few genuine Egyptian alabasters at Spanish sites date several hundred years before their archeological contexts, supporting the idea of Phoenician storehouses full of such goods. Such vessels could only have arrived in the west through Phoenician initiative.

27. For example, Anthony J. Spalinger, "The Foreign Policy of Egypt Preceding the Assyrian Conquest," *Chronique d'Égypte* 53 (1978): 26–27. Egyptian material in Iron Age Phoenicia is surveyed by Gabriella Scandoni, "Testimonianze Egiziane in Fenicia dal XII al IV sec. A.C.," *Rivista di Studi Fenici* 12 (1984): 133–63.

28. Under Pharaoh Osorkon IV (730–715), who is King So of 2 Kings 17:4.

dence," implying at least the Egyptian claim of rule over Phoenicia.[29] One should not read too much into this kind of offhand remark, though an Egyptian claim to control over the Phoenician coast seems reasonable, since Psammetichus I undertook an active policy in western Asia against the imminent Babylonian threat to Egyptian interests in Canaan.[30]

Under the Babylonians

With the fall of Nineveh in 612, the Assyrian Empire came to a close, except for its remnants in northern Syria, centered at Haran. In his closing years, Nabopolassar of Babylon (625–605), the conqueror of Assyria, fought a joint Assyrian and Egyptian army for control of Haran. Egyptian intervention in the north was finally stopped when the army of Pharaoh Neco II was defeated at Carchemish in 605, and Haran was taken by Nebuchadrezzar (biblical Nebuchadnezzar, 604–562) in the same year. That event sparked a series of western campaigns in which Nebuchadrezzar quickly brought Cilicia, Syria, Phoenicia, and Palestine under his control.[31] At some time during his early years, Nebuchadrezzar could boast in a text carved in the Wadi Brissa in north Lebanon that the region was now safe from its enemies[32]— meaning, of course, that Babylon had conquered the west. In another text, Nebuchadrezzar lists the kings of Tyre, Sidon, and Aradus, among other western rulers,[33] who presumably were now vassals of Babylon. That Nebuchadrezzar established a system like that of the Assyrians to maintain his control over foreign vassals is shown by a group of cuneiform tablets, three of which were written from Tyre. One of these mentions the Babylonian official responsible for Babylonian interests in that city.[34] Another text lists foreigners receiving rations in Babylon, among whom are Phoenician carpenters from Byblos and Aradus.[35] Babylonian supremacy in the west lasted little longer that the reign of Nebuchadrezzar, which spanned over four decades.

29. Cf. K. S. Freedy and Donald B. Redford, "The Dates in Ezekiel in Relation to Biblical, Babylonian and Egyptian Sources," *Journal of the American Oriental Society* 90 (1970): 477.

30. This policy is explored by Anthony J. Spalinger, "Egypt and Babylonia: A Survey (c. 620 B.C.–550 B.C.)," *Studien zur altägyptischen Kultur* 5 (1977): 223–25.

31. In his regnal years 1 through 11; A. Kirk Grayson, *Assyrian and Babylonian Chronicles* (Locust Valley: Augustin, 1975), 100–101. These campaigns were all directed against the land of Hattu, a broad geographical designation including all of northwest Syria, Phoenicia, and Palestine.

32. *ANET* 307.

33. *ANET* 308.

34. Eckhard Unger, "Nebukadnezar und sein Šandabakku (Oberkommissar) in Tyrus," *Zeitschrift für die Alttestamentliche Wissenschaft* 44 (1926): 314–17. A similar official residing at Qadesh is also mentioned.

35. *ANET* 308.

Following three short reigns taking up a mere four years came the last king of an independent Babylonia, Nabonidus (555–539), who presided over the defeat of Babylon by Cyrus II of Persia.

As previously with Assyria, a major problem for the Babylonians in Phoenicia and Philistia was Egyptian interference, now of Dynasty 26.[36] As noted above, one text of the founder of this dynasty, Psammetichus I, may indicate that Phoenicia was under his control. The statement of Herodotus (2:157) that this king laid siege to Ashdod for twenty-nine years certainly exaggerates the length of time but probably reflects a renewed Egyptian interest in the coastal cities. It is generally believed that the following Egyptian ruler, Neco II (610–595), built a short-lived empire in Canaan in the early years of his reign, though there is little evidence to support this. In any case, his defeat by Nebuchadrezzar at Carchemish in 605 put an end to any serious Egyptian ambitions in the north. Phoenicia was now in the hands of Babylon, and Philistia went the same way a short time later. It was Neco II who, according to Herodotus (4:42), sent a Phoenician fleet down the Red Sea and around the African continent, returning through the Straits of Gibraltar to Egypt. Since this account can be neither proved nor disproved, it has long been and will remain a matter of academic debate.[37] During the reign of Psammetichus II (595–589), there is nothing to indicate Egyptian activity in Phoenicia, though it has been suggested that he used Phoenician mercenaries in his Nubian campaign and there is mention of a Tyrian camp near Memphis.[38]

For the reign of Apries (589–570), Herodotus (2:161) notes almost in passing that Apries "sent an army against Sidon and fought a naval battle with the Tyrians." Whether this occurred before, during, or after the contemporary siege of Tyre by Nebuchadrezzar is still unknown, as is the reason for his attack.[39] A naval battle with Tyre, long experienced in sea-faring (as opposed to the Egyptians), was possible by Saïte times since there was now a new Egyptian Mediterranean fleet outfitted with triremes. One can perhaps see in Herodotus's enigmatic remark the attempt by Egypt to wrest Tyre from Babylonian dominance and reassert its own influence there.

---

36. Spalinger, "Egypt and Babylonia," 221–44; Abraham Malamat, "The Twilight of Judah: In the Egyptian-Babylonian Maelstrom," in *Congress Volume: Edinburgh 1974*, Vetus Testamentum Supplement 28 (Leiden: Brill, 1975), 123–45.

37. Alan B. Lloyd, "Necho and the Red Sea: Some Considerations," *Journal of Egyptian Archaeology* 63 (1977): 148–54. See also Mary Cary and Brian H. Warmington, *The Ancient Explorers* (Baltimore: Penguin, 1963), chap. 5.

38. A Tyrian camp or mercantile settlement (the Greek term can mean either) at Memphis is mentioned only by Herodotus (2:112). The Phoenician graffiti at Abu Simbel are dated to the Nubian campaign of Psammetichus II on indirect evidence only and probably represent foreign individuals living at Memphis; see Freedy and Redford, "Dates in Ezekiel," 476 n. 69.

39. Ibid., 481–84.

Under the Persians

With the fall of Babylon in 539, Phoenicia came under Persian dominance and, along with Cyprus and a newly acquired Egypt, belonged to the Fifth Satrapy (province) of the Persian Empire.[40] The most important city was Sidon, seat of the Persian governor and his administration. The Persians were interested both in the western commercial ties of the coastal cities as well as the Phoenician fleets that became part of the Persian military forces in the long and ultimately unsuccessful attempt to take Greece. The Persian dominance gave Phoenicia a period of relative peace and great prosperity, situated as it was in the center of a trade network stretching from Gibraltar to Persia, from the Caucasus to Nubia. The introduction of coinage, first at Sidon around 450, greatly facilitated this international commerce; Tyre, Aradus, and Byblos began minting coins within the next quarter century. Evidence of the wealth of the period is reflected in the numerous stone sarcophagi from upper-class burials and the construction of imposing temples at Amrit and Sidon that show strong Persian influence in their architecture. Eastern elements also appear in Phoenician art, Egyptian influence is still prominent, and Greek features appear in the later part of this age.

The prosperous and peaceful life of the Phoenician cities was interrupted from time to time, especially in the fourth century, with both Greek and Egyptian encouragement. Several cities saw this as an opportunity to rid themselves of Persian dominance in local affairs, though they were internally divided between their Greek and Persian sympathies. In 392, Tyre either joined with or submitted to Evagorus I of Salamis, aided by Athens and Egypt, during his war to unite Cyprus and free the island from Persia. This failed, and, though Evagorus retained his throne, Tyre reverted to Persian authority. In 362, Straton I of Sidon joined a general revolt in the west, and Sidon revolted again under Tennes (Tannit) in 347. Each time, the rebellion was put down, in the latter case with the destruction of the city.[41] Persia was thus able to maintain an uneasy control over the continuing unrest, but rising pro-Greek sentiments, the interference of Egypt, and the desire to escape Persian

40. For a general orientation of Phoenicia during the Persian period, see Josette Elayi, "The Phoenician Cities in the Persian Period," *Journal of the Ancient Near Eastern Society* 12 (1980): 13–28; idem, "The Relations between Tyre and Carthage during the Persian Period," *Journal of the Ancient Near Eastern Society* 13 (1981): 15–29; idem, "Studies in Phoenician Geography during the Persian Period," *Journal of Near Eastern Studies* 41 (1982): 83–110.

41. Dan Barag, "The Effects of the Tennes Rebellion on Palestine," *Bulletin of the American Schools of Oriental Research* 183 (1966): 6–9. On the various uprisings of the fourth century against the Persians, see Muhammad A. Dandamaev, *A Political History of the Achaemenid Empire* (Leiden: Brill, 1989), chaps. 35–37.

domination made this increasingly difficult and helped pave the way for the Macedonian conquest.

Overseas Expansion

During the past quarter century, investigation of the Phoenician interest in the west Mediterranean has produced an extraordinary amount of new material.[42] Dozens of archeological sites have been discovered there, and the massive amount of information gained is still being studied and analyzed. Any present attempt to assess the Phoenician colonial movement must therefore be a tentative one. Classical sources suggest that Phoenician colonization began in the twelfth or eleventh century, though intensive archeological work over the past few decades failed to produce evidence of settlement earlier than the eighth century.[43] Hints of earlier Phoenician penetration in the area suggest that there was a period of "precolonialization" without actual settlement. True colonies, including the building of towns, an agricultural base, and the like, began at the end of the ninth century, a short time before the Greek colonial movement got under way in the early eighth.[44]

The reasons for the vast Phoenician movement toward the west have been variously given: pressure from the Neo-Assyrian Empire, an impetus from the arrival of the Sea Peoples, or simply to fill the vacuum left by the collapse of Mycenaean control of east Mediterranean waters at the close of the Bronze Age. But none of these adequately explain the expansion. Overpopulation may have been a contributing factor since the narrow coastal strip of agricultural land would not support much population growth.[45] Phoenician overseas interests were stimulated above all by a search for new sources of metal, both for their customers throughout the Orient and for their own rapidly growing industries in manufactured goods.[46] Hence, the initial objectives

42. Sabatino Moscati (ed.), *The Phoenicians* (New York: Abbeville, 1988), 46–53, 152–242.

43. On the chronological statements of classical writers, see Bunnens, *L'Expansion Phénicienne*, chap. 3.

44. One important object that belongs to the earliest phase of Phoenician westward expansion is the stele fragment from Nora, Sardinia, not to be confused with the later Nora Stone. While this fragment preserves only four words, paleographical considerations show that it can date no later than the eleventh century; Frank M. Cross, "The Oldest Phoenician Inscription from Sardinia: The Fragmentary Stela from Nora," in *"Working with No Data": Semitic and Egyptian Studies Presented to Thomas O. Lambdin*, ed. David M. Golomb and Susan T. Hollis (Winona Lake, Ind.: Eisenbrauns, 1987), 65–74. This and objects such as Phoenician bronzes (p. 71) indicate an early Phoenician presence in the west long before actual colonies were established.

45. C. R. Whittaker, "The Western Phoenicians; Colonialization and Assimilation," *Proceedings of the Cambridge Philological Society* n.s. 20 (1974): 58–79.

46. Wolfgang Röllig, "Die Phönizier des Mutterlands zur Zeit der Kolonisierung," in *Phönizier im Westen*, ed. Hans G. Niemeyer, Madrider Beiträge 8 (Madrid: Deutsches Archäologisches Institut, 1982), 15–30.

were the rich copper mines of Cyprus and the silver, tin, and copper of Spain. Between Phoenicia and Spain, then, we must think more in terms of a series of landing and victualing stations to support the westward sea routes running along the northern and southern coastal regions of the Mediterranean Sea. By the eighth century, many such stations had become permanent settlements, with colonists from the homeland bringing their material and spiritual culture to the west.

Phoenician settlement on Cyprus began somewhat earlier, as attested by archeological material from at least the ninth century, though there are clear indications that a strong Phoenician presence on the island began even before that[47]—primarily at Kition (modern Larnaca), but also at Paphos, Amathus, and Idalion. Kition appears to have been under Tyrian rule, and it is probable that this important city became a staging point for journeys to the west.[48] The most active period for Phoenician settlement farther west was the eighth century, for which period there is ample archeological material from North Africa, Spain, Malta, Sicily, and Sardinia. By the seventh century, Phoenician settlements had spread as far as Mogador on the Atlantic coast of Morocco. Some of the original colonies established by the homeland Phoenicians mounted similar efforts of their own. Gadir (modern Cadiz) established settlements around the southern Spanish coast and in the Balearic Islands, notably Ibiza. From at least the fifth century, Carthage founded its own network of colonies on Sardinia, Sicily, and elsewhere. Colonies like these were the moving force behind the growth and spread of Punic culture in the west.[49]

It has recently been proposed that in the eleventh century the Phoenicians invaded and settled the north Palestinian coast from Acco (near Tyre) to the Yarkon Valley (the northern border of Philistine territory). Ephraim Stern, who bases his views primarily on his excavations at Dor, forcefully defends

47. Patricia M. Bikai, "Trade Networks in the Early Iron Age: The Phoenicians at Palaepaphos," in *Western Cyprus Connections*, ed. D. W. Rupp, Studies in Mediterranean Archaeology 77 (Göteborg: Åströms, 1987), 125–28; idem, "Cyprus and the Phoenicians," *Biblical Archaeologist* 52 (1989): 203–9; Ora Negbi, "Evidence for Early Phoenician Communities on the Eastern Mediterranean Islands," *Levant* 14 (1982): 179–82.

48. Vassos Karageorghis, *Kition: Mycenaean and Phoenician Discoveries in Cyprus* (London: Thames & Hudson, 1976), 95–96. On Phoenicians in Cyprus in general, see Einer Gjerstad, "The Phoenician Colonization and Expansion in Cyprus," *Reports of the Department of Antiquities, Cyprus* 1979: 230–54.

49. The term *Punic* is an anglicized adjective from Latin *poeni*, itself taken from Greek *phoinikē*. Punic refers to the western Phoenician culture established during the colonizing period that soon took on its own character through separate development and influences from the native cultures of the region. While Punic civilization is usually equated with Carthage, it is found throughout the western Mediterranean coastal areas and islands.

Phoenician nobleman from Dor, 9th–
8th century B.C. (height: 4″)
*Courtesy of Ephraim Stern and
the Tel Dor Project;
photograph by Ilan Stulman*

the doubtful thesis of Phoenician rule from around 1050 to 1000, at which time the region passed into the kingdom of David.[50] Within the framework of this southern Phoenician expansion, probably commercial rather than military, we find the first strong ties with the Hebrews: the agreements of Hiram I of Tyre (ca. 969–936) with David and Solomon of the then newly established kingdom at Jerusalem.[51] The initial contact was under King David, who contracted with Hiram to send cedar wood, carpenters, and stonemasons to build his palace (2 Sam. 5:11). David also began collecting materials from Tyre and Sidon for the construction of the temple of Yahweh (1 Chron. 22:2–5), though it was left to Solomon to actually build it (1 Kings 5). Hiram supplied the usual coniferous woods and artisans, and Solomon provided the labor force and paid for the services of the Tyrian king in annual

50. Ephraim Stern, "New Evidence from Dor for the First Appearance of the Phoenicians along the Northern Coast of Israel," *Bulletin of the American Schools of Oriental Research* 279 (1990): 27–34. Phoenician influence is certainly present at many sites, but an invasion and settlement remains unproved.

51. On relations between the Phoenicians and Israel, see Brian Peckham, "Israel and Phoenicia," in *Magnalia Dei, the Mighty Acts of God: Essays on the Bible and Archaeology in Memory of G. Ernest Wright*, ed. Frank M. Cross, Werner E. Lemke, and Patrick D. Miller Jr. (Garden City, N.Y.: Doubleday, 1976), 224–48; Herbert Donner, "The Interdependence of Internal Affairs and Foreign Policy during the Davidic-Solomonic Period (with Regard to the Phoenician Coast)," in *Studies in the Period of David and Solomon and Other Essays*, ed. Tomoo Ishida (Winona Lake, Ind.: Eisenbrauns, 1982), 205–14; Christopher J. Davey, "Temples of the Levant and the Building of Solomon," *Tyndale Bulletin* 31 (1980): 107–46.

shipments of wheat and olive oil.[52] The export of Phoenician artisans is also evidenced in the well-known ivories from palaces at Samaria and Nimrud, where ivory decorative panels of Phoenician style have been found in profusion.[53] The other cooperative venture of Hiram and Solomon was maritime, from the Red Sea port of Elath (Ezion Geber) to Ophir, probably the Somali coast (1 Kings 9:26–27).[54] The mention of *tarshish* ships (which belonged to Hiram, not Solomon) in these joint trading efforts refers to large cargo ships named after the smelting installations, from whence they carried raw materials to the Levant.[55] The biblical narrative must refer to the use of these ships on the Ophir run due to the cargoes carried (1 Kings 10:22).

Culture

Phoenician culture must be viewed from two perspectives, that of the homeland and that of the western colonies. In the Levant, it is clear that while there is much that is new in Iron Age Phoenician culture, its roots are firmly planted in the older Canaanite traditions. In general, it is characterized by a synthesis of elements of the surrounding oriental cultures with that of the coast. A major feature in the west from the eighth century on was the integration of the homeland culture with the native cultures wherever colonies were established and (later) with the classical civilizations of the region.

Language and Writing

Phoenician is a later dialect of Canaanite or West Semitic, akin to Aramaic and Biblical Hebrew, all being descendants of older Semitic languages of the region.[56] Inscriptions are known around the east Mediterranean from the

52. The tradition was maintained in later times: cedar from Tyre and Sidon was again imported for the repair of the temple after the Babylonian captivity (Ezra 3:7).

53. Cf. Richard D. Barnett, *A Catalogue of the Nimrud Ivories*, 2d ed. (London: British Museum, 1975).

54. André Lemaire, "Les Phéniciens et le Commerce entre la Mer Rouge et la Mer Méditerranée," in *Phoenicia and the East Mediterranean in the First Millennium* B.C., ed. Édouard Lipiński, Studia Phoenicia 5 (Louvain: Peeters, 1987), 49–60; see also Robert R. Stieglitz, "Longdistance Seafaring in the Ancient Near East," *Biblical Archaeologist* 47 (1984): 134–42; Patricia M. Bikai, "Rich and Glorious Traders of the Levant," *Archaeology* 43.2 (1990): 22–30.

55. Michael Koch, *Tarschisch und Hispanien*, Deutsches Archäologisches Institut, Madrider Forschungen 14 (Berlin: de Gruyter, 1984).

56. For a general orientation, see Sabatino Moscati (ed.), *An Introduction to the Comparative Grammar of the Semitic Languages* (Wiesbaden: Harrassowitz, 1964). Recent works dealing specifically with Phoenician are the following: Corinne Baurain, Claude Bonnet, and V. Krings (eds.), *Phoinikeia Grammata*, Studia Phoenicia 13 (Brussels: Société des Études Classiques, forthcoming); J. Brian Peckham, *The Development of the Late Phoenician Scripts* (Cambridge: Harvard University Press, 1968); Stanislav Segert, *A Grammar of Phoenician and Punic* (Munich: Beck, 1976); Richard S. Tomback, *A Comparative Semitic Lexicon of the Phoenician and Punic Languages* (Missoula, Mont.: Scholars Press, 1977).

eleventh to first centuries and in the west from the ninth to fifth centuries. From the latter date, the language is known in the west as Punic, used into late Roman times. While there are several thousand inscriptions preserved, the great bulk are Punic funerary texts of very repetitive nature, hence generally uninformative and often uncertain in meaning. Reflecting the language as spoken in different regions, several dialects of Phoenician can be discerned: for example, Byblian, Sidonian, Cypriot, Cilician, and Punic.

At one time, a considerable Phoenician literature existed: Menander of Ephesus (second century) is said to have written a history of the Phoenician kings using the official annals of Tyre, and Philo of Byblos (first century A.D.) reportedly translated Sanchuniathon's history of Phoenicia into Greek.[57] Of this literary tradition, nothing is extant save that quoted by later authors. Only rare historical texts are presently known, but these deal with affairs outside Phoenicia proper (e.g., from Zenjirli and Karatepe).[58]

Phoenician is written in a consonantal alphabet, and it is for the transmission of this alphabet to Europe that the Phoenicians are most remembered. Around the mid-eighth century, inscriptions begin to appear in Greek in a script obviously borrowed from that of the Phoenicians, with a few changes to accommodate the phonemes of the Greek language.[59] It has become apparent in recent years that the origin and early history of the alphabet is not at all as straightforward as it was once thought to be, and scholars are now in the process of reassessing the scattered and often ambiguous evidence.[60] That the Iron Age Phoenicians transmitted alphabetic writing to the West is fairly certain, though the actual invention and early history of the alphabet may lie further south. Texts in what is incorrectly called the "Phoenician alphabet," usually consisting of only a few letters, go back to the seventeenth or eighteenth century in Palestine and are more properly designated Proto-Canaanite. The earliest known texts in the Phoenician language date to the eleventh century. This is not a reliable guide, however, since all these texts are

57. On Menander, see Bunnens, *L'Expansion Phénicienne*, 139–42. The information about Philo is provided by Eusebius and Porphyry; see Albert I. Baumgarten, *The Phoenician History of Philo of Byblos*, Études Préliminaires aux Religions Orientales dans l'Empire Romain 89 (Leiden: Brill, 1981), 41–42.

58. *ANET* 653–55.

59. McCarter, *Antiquity of the Greek Alphabet*, 65–66. Others suggest a date about a century earlier; note Joseph Naveh, "The Greek Alphabet: New Evidence," *Biblical Archaeologist* 43 (1990): 22–25. The great innovation of the Greeks was the assignment of some of the signs to represent vowels; Semitic alphabets were all consonantal.

60. See, e.g., Giovanni Garbini, "The Question of the Alphabet," in *The Phoenicians*, ed. Sabatino Moscati (New York: Abbeville, 1988), 92–102; Benjamin Sass, *The Genesis of the Alphabet and Its Development in the Second Millenium* [sic] B.C., Ägypten und Altes Testament 13 (Wiesbaden: Harrassowitz, 1988).

inscribed on durable materials such as stone or bronze. Alphabetic writing in Phoenicia, or elsewhere for that matter, may have been used much earlier on a perishable material like papyrus that has not survived the wet climate of the region.

Art and Crafts

Phoenician art is characterized by its blending of styles borrowed from all the foreign traditions with which Phoenician artists came into contact.[61] The true genius of Phoenician art is that, while many designs and motifs can be traced to foreign origins, it combined what it took from others into a distinct, new art form. Few artistic traditions have as successfully joined such diverse art forms as, for example, the free-flowing circular movement of Minoan and Mycenaean art with the static cubism of Egypt. It is this inventive syncretism that makes Phoenician art truly creative.

Phoenician art was popular in antiquity, and the products of Phoenician artisans are found throughout the Mediterranean. These, in turn, were copied by local artisans trained by Phoenician artists who had moved abroad. The complaint is sometimes leveled that Phoenician emphasis on manufacture for export fostered the mass production of trinkets. But while the Phoenicians were basically a mercantile people and needed a large and continuing inventory of objects for trade, many of these objects are technically superb and are genuine works of art in their own right. Phoenician artists excelled in making gold jewelry, metal dishes, ivories, and small varicolored glass bottles and flasks. They adopted the Egyptian scarab tradition, and one of their best products is the "Phoenician" (or Greco-Phoenician) scarab, a miniature masterpiece of engraving. All of these objects, made of expensive materials, were easily transported abroad for sale in the international marketplace. In the west, once the initial trade contacts and settlements had been established, local workshops carried on the artistic traditions of the homeland.

Funerary steles, known by the thousands from Punic sites, generally show the clumsy crafting of Phoenician stonework. These steles, as well as innumerable terra-cotta figurines, are characteristic of Punic art and show the Greek influence that features in Punic art from the seventh century on. In modeling, style, and iconography, such objects illustrate the international network of artistic influences that underlay the design and production of objects of all kinds. International commercial and political relationships created a kind of cultural *koine*, though local variations are quite in evidence. Cypriot art, for example, played a significant role in the origins of Punic art.

61. In general, see Moscati, *Phoenicians*, part 3.

Gold funerary mask from Phoe-
nicia, 4th century B.C.
*Courtesy of the Louvre
Museum*

The Phoenician Iron Age artistic tradition had long antecedents, since metal vessels, ivory carving, and fine jewelry were luxury items produced by Bronze Age Canaanite artists.[62] The purple-dye industry also originated in the Bronze Age. A thirteenth-century dye works has been found at Sarepta, and imported purple (or red) cloth is mentioned in the contemporary Mycenaean texts. Purple-dyed fabrics are also mentioned in Ugaritic texts, though there is no evidence that they were manufactured there. During the Iron Age, this industry too was taken westward and dye factories were established at coastal sites in North Africa, Malta, Sicily, and Spain. This indelible—hence highly prized—dye ranges in color from deep red to violet and was made from mollusks of the *Murex* genus found in the shallow waters of the Mediterranean coastal region.[63]

62. Glenn E. Markoe, "The Emergence of Phoenician Art," *Bulletin of the American Schools of Oriental Research* 279 (1990): 13–26.
63. Lloyd B. Jensen, "Royal Purple of Tyre," *Journal of Near Eastern Studies* 22 (1963): 104–18; J. Doumet, *A Study on the Ancient Purple Color* (Beirut: Imprimerie Catholique, 1980); I. Irving Ziderman, "Seashells and Ancient Purple Dyeing," *Biblical Archaeologist* 53 (1990): 98–103.

Religion

Although there are now over six thousand Phoenician and Punic inscriptions extant and the corpus of archeological material grows larger each year, there is relatively little in this material that defines Phoenician religious concepts.[64] We know the major deities, but have little idea of their nature. There are temples in the homeland and colonies, but the cultus practiced there is practically unknown. Without appropriate native written sources, then, Phoenician religious practice can only be described in the broadest terms.

There is, of course, some descriptive material in the works of classical writers and the Old Testament. But these express the Hellenized viewpoint of Greek and Latin authors or the openly anti-Phoenician bias of the Hebrew prophets. The Late Bronze Age literature of Ugarit is of limited value except as a general background, since it represents the pantheon, ritual, and beliefs of an earlier time that does not always apply to Iron Age Phoenicia. The one native author whose work is partially preserved is likewise of doubtful value. Philo of Byblos, writing in the first century A.D., is known only from quotations, almost exclusively in Eusebius. Philo is said to have translated from Phoenician an earlier history by Sanchuniathon; what little is preserved is concerned with creation, the early history of the gods, and the discovery of the necessities of life such as food, fire, boats, and medicine. There is probably some basis for believing that Philo does record a few genuine Phoenician beliefs, but his work is heavily overlaid with Hellenistic, especially euhemeristic, thought.[65]

The deities honored in Iron Age Phoenicia are a mixture of gods and goddesses known from earlier Canaanite times and new ones who are evidenced only from the early first millennium. In some cases, the relative importance of the older deities has changed. For example, El, creator and king of the gods at Ugarit, is mentioned only once in texts from the homeland. Astarte, of minor importance at Ugarit, plays a dominant role in Iron Age Tyre and

---

64. For general orientation, see Sergio Ribichini, "Beliefs and Religious Life," in *The Phoenicians*, ed. Sabatino Moscati (New York: Abbeville, 1988), 104–27; Richard J. Clifford, "Phoenician Religion," *Bulletin of the American Schools of Oriental Research* 279 (1990): 55–64; Paolo Xella, Giovanni Garbini, and Mitchell Dahood (eds.), *La Religione Fenicia*, Studi Semitici 53 (Rome: Centro di Studio per la Civiltà Fenicia e Punica, 1981); Corinne Bonnet, Édouard Lipiński, and Patrick Marchetti (eds.), *Religio Phoenicia*, Studia Phoenicia 4 (Brussels: Société des Études Classiques, 1986). The present essay generally omits references in the classical sources.

65. On Philo of Byblos, in addition to Baumgarten, *Phoenician History of Philo of Byblos*, see also James Barr, "Philo of Byblos and His 'Phoenician History,'" *Bulletin of the John Rylands Library* 57 (1974): 17–68; Harold W. Attridge and Robert A. Oden (eds.), *Philo of Byblos: The Phoenician History*, Catholic Biblical Quarterly Monograph Series 9 (Washington, D.C.: Catholic Biblical Association, 1983).

Sidon. While the extant texts are full of references to numerous deities, it is not possible to trace a national Phoenician pantheon. This should be expected since there was no national Phoenician state that would have required one. At Tyre, Melqart ("King of the City") was the chief deity, perhaps its dynastic god, while El may have been considered the head of the local pantheon. Other Tyrian deities include Baal-Shamem, Baal-Ṣaphon, Astarte, and Eshmun, though the latter two are principally associated with Sidon. Other Sidonian deities are Baal-Sidon, Astarte/Face-of-Baal, and perhaps Reshep. The most important deity of Byblos was Baalat Gubla ("Mistress of Byblos") (= Anat or Astarte), with a long history at that city. Baal ("the Lord") and Baal-Shamem ("Lord of Heavens") also appear at Byblos. Shadrapa ("Shad the Healer") and Tannit are mentioned in texts from Sarepta, and Melqart, Eshmun, and Shadrapa were worshiped as gods of healing in the temple at Amrit. Even from this partial list, it is evident that an individual deity may be primarily associated with one city, as well as be prominent elsewhere.

The frequent term *baal* simply means "lord," and it is difficult to determine which deity is meant in any given case. Baals are often associated with mountains: Baal-Ṣaphon, Baal-Lebanon, Baal-Ḥammon (= Amanus), Baal-Shamem (usually identified as Hadad, though on uncertain evidence), Baal-Addir, Baal-Marqod, and Baal-Malage. In each instance, the meaning is "lord of" a place or attribute, though the deity involved can only be surmised. Baal-Sidon, for example, is probably Eshmun and Baal-Tyre is probably Melqart, but there is no conclusive proof to support this.

Wherever the Phoenicians established settlements or colonies, they took their deities with them. A well-known example is the construction at Samaria of a temple to Baal-Tyre by Ahab of Israel when he married Jezebel, a princess of Tyre (1 Kings 16:31–32, which refers to her father as king of the "Sidonians," used interchangeably with "Tyrians" in several traditions). In so doing, Ahab followed the example of Solomon who worshiped Astarte of Sidon (1 Kings 11:5) in shrines that were not torn down until the reforms of Josiah over two centuries later (2 Kings 23:13).

The spread of Phoenician cults and temples followed the path of Phoenician colonization. The list of Phoenician shrines in foreign places is impressive; many are known by actual remains, others from references in classical sources.[66] In Cyprus, the most imposing is the temple of Astarte at Kition, built in the mid-ninth century and the center of religious life of that city for

---

66. C. Grottanelli, "Santuari e Divinità della Colonie d'Occidente," in *La Religione Fenicia*, ed. Paolo Xella, Giovanni Garbini, and Mitchell Dahood; Studi Semitici 53 (Rome: Centro di Studio per la Civiltà Fenicia e Punica, 1981), 109–33.

the next five centuries.[67] Another temple of Astarte was used for many centuries at Palaepaphos. Phoenician texts from Kition mention the deities Eshmun, Baal-Shamem, and Reshep-MKL (who was especially popular at Idalion).[68]

While many Phoenician deities appear at Carthage, by the fifth century Baal-Ḥammon and Tannit took the leading role. Baal-Ḥammon is identified as "[El], Lord of (Mount) Amanus," and Tannit is perhaps the Canaanite Asherah, rather than Astarte with whom she is usually identified.[69] Both deities are known in the Phoenician homeland.[70] From Carthage, these two cults spread throughout the Punic world along with those of many other deities, though the original expansion from Phoenicia itself had established Phoenician deities like Melqart, Eshmun, and Astarte everywhere in the west.

Textual evidence is sparse on the ritual and theology of the Phoenicians, and one should treat with some caution the statements in non-Phoenician sources. Religious practice in Phoenicia probably differed somewhat from that in the west. For example, kings were the high priests of the major city gods in Phoenicia, but this function was exercised by important families in the west. The few Phoenician documents dealing with religious practice may not apply generally. A partial roster of temple personnel of the Astarte temple of Kition includes artisans, sacrificers, cultic barbers, and temple prostitutes;[71] two "tariffs" of the Hellenistic period from Carthage and Marseilles list numerous sacrificial animals, the cost of each, and the disposition of the

---

67. Karageorghis, *Kition*, chap. 5.

68. The Apollo Amyklos of Idalion; André Caquot and Olivier Masson, "Deux Inscriptions Phéniciennes de Chypre," *Syria* 45 (1968): 295–313.

69. Frank M. Cross, *Canaanite Myth and Hebrew Epic: Essays in the History of the Religion of Israel* (Cambridge: Harvard University Press, 1973), 24–34.

70. This accepts Cross's thesis that Baal-Ḥammon is an epithet of the old Canaanite El. Tannit was worshiped in Phoenicia from at least the seventh century; James B. Pritchard, "The Tanit Inscription from Sarepta," in *Phönizier im Westen*, ed. Hans G. Niemeyer, Madrider Beiträge 8 (Madrid: Deutsches Archäologisches Institut, 1982), 83–92; Pierre Bordreuil, "Tanit du Liban," in *Phoenicia and the East Mediterranean in the First Millennium* B.C., ed. Édouard Lipiński, Studia Phoenicia 5 (Louvain: Peeters, 1987), 79–85. Tannit is also mentioned on the new funerary steles from the *tophet* at Tyre, now published by Hélène Sader, "Phoenician Stelae from Tyre," *Berytus* 39 (1991): 101–24; idem, "Phoenician Stelae from Tyre (Continued)," *Studi Epigrafici e Linguistici* 9 (1992): 53–79.

71. Mathias M. Delcor, "Le Personnel du Temple d'Astarté à Kition d'après une Tablette Phénicienne (CIS 86A et B)," *Ugarit-Forschungen* 11 (1979): 147–64. On the possible role of Phoenicians in the diffusion of temple prostitution, see Edwin M. Yamauchi, "Cultic Prostitution—A Case Study in Cultural Diffusion," in *Orient and Occident: Essays Presented to Cyrus H. Gordon on the Occasion of His Sixty-fifth Birthday*, ed. Harry A. Hoffner Jr., Alter Orient und Altes Testament 22 (Kevelaer: Butzon & Bercker/Neukirchen-Vluyn: Neukirchener Verlag, 1973), 213–22.

animal parts after the sacrifice has been made.[72] Because such documents are so rare, one is tempted to use them to interpret Phoenician religious practice in general, but since they apply to specific places at specific times, they may not describe the cultus elsewhere.

Two categories of gods appear to have played an important role throughout the region influenced by the Phoenicians. Healing deities (Melqart, Eshmun, and Shadrapa) can be verified for Phoenicia itself as well as in the west. Dying and reviving gods (Melqart, Eshmun, and Adonis) related to the seasonal pattern have been postulated, though here the evidence is all from classical sources.

Burial in Phoenicia was generally by inhumation with the usual grave goods: pottery, amulets, beads, and other small objects. Royal and upper-class tombs probably contained richer grave goods, though these were largely plundered in antiquity. Cremation was practiced alongside inhumation in both the homeland and in the west. At present, we cannot define the beliefs that lay behind the use of these two forms of burial, which sometimes occur at the same time and in the same (family?) tomb. Upper-class inhumation burials of the later period are known from Punic sites, with occasional evidence of embalming, though this was not a widespread practice. It is possible that burial rites included the *marzēaḥ* ("funerary feast"), known at Ugarit, in the Old Testament, and elsewhere.[73]

The subject of burial raises the most discussed question in the Phoenician-Punic religious sphere, that of the *tophet*, or child cemetery. The largest and best known is that of Carthage, which originally contained some twenty thousand cinerary urns with the remains of infant children and animals. Other *tophets* have been found at several sites in Sardinia and Sicily. Such cemeteries are outside the city walls and contain, besides the cinerary urns, many votive images and large numbers of stone steles that commemorate a rite called *mlk* to Tannit and Baal-Ḥammon. The long controversy over the significance of these *tophets* revolves around a single issue: is this evidence of purposeful child sacrifice? The debate has been fueled by remarks of classical authors who speak of the Punic practice of sacrificing children in times of calamity and by numerous Old Testament injunctions against Hebrew participation in the practice of "passing (children) through fire." There has been much contentious argument over this question simply because neither the archeological nor the linguistic evidence is conclusive. There is, for example, little agreement on the meaning of the key technical terms used in the pertinent

---

72. *ANET* 656–57.

73. Marvin H. Pope, "The Cult of the Dead at Ugarit," in *Ugarit in Retrospect: Fifty Years of Ugarit and Ugaritic,* ed. Gordon D. Young (Winona Lake, Ind.: Eisenbrauns, 1981), 176–79.

texts.[74] The remarkable 1991 discovery of a possible *tophet* near Tyre, the first to be found in Phoenicia itself, will introduce a whole new dimension into the debate and may offer evidence leading to a solution of this problem.[75]

The Phoenicians probably shared the general concepts of an underworld as conceived by the Canaanites and other western Asiatic societies, but there is little trace of these beliefs. Which deity presided over this underworld cannot be determined; the general opinion is that, by analogy to Ugarit, it would be Môt. A "Mistress of the Underworld" has been seen in a Punic text, though this is uncertain and the phrase involved is also rendered "mistress of the bridal tent."[76] The latter is an excellent example of the many difficulties in understanding precise meanings of Phoenician words and phrases. There is no reference to the underworld itself in Phoenician texts, nor is there any clear allusion to the state of existence after death. There are certain hints, however, in the earlier funerary texts that regularly offer curses against any who desecrate or rob a tomb. These include the threat that such violators will be cut off with no offspring of their own, will have no tomb of their own, and will have no "resting place with the *rpʾm*," the inhabitants of the netherworld.[77] One violation noted several times is the removal of the owner's name from the tomb or from a structure someone else has built. And in the funerary texts of kings and commoners alike is the wish for a long life. Now all this is reminiscent of the general belief prior to Hellenistic times that humans received what reward was due them in this life and that they had only the gloomy netherworld to look forward to in the next.[78] It therefore seems safe to assume that the earlier Phoenicians shared this grim view of life after death. However, the curses more or less disappear in Hellenistic times to be replaced by simple requests for a divine blessing, perhaps under the influence of the so-called salvation cults. This would appear to indicate that Phoenician

74. For the present state of the debate, see Lawrence A. Stager and Samuel R. Wolff, "Child Sacrifice at Carthage—Religious Rite or Population Control?" *Biblical Archaeology Review* 10.1 (1984): 30–51; Moshe Weinfeld, "The Worship of Molech and of the Queen of Heaven and Its Background," *Ugarit-Forschungen* 4 (1972): 133–54; C. Picard, "Les Sacrifices Molk chez les Puniques: Certitudes et Hypothèses," *Semitica* 39 (1990): 67–76; Michael Gras, Pierre Rouillard, and Javier Teixidor, "The Phoenicians and Death," *Berytus* 39 (1991): 127–76.

75. Several articles in *Berytus* 39 (1991) present the initial studies on this *tophet*.

76. Donner and Röllig, *Kanaanäische und aramäische Inschriften*, #83 (vol. 2, p. 100); H. Stocks, "Adoniskult in Nordafrika," *Berytus* 3 (1936): 31–32.

77. The *rpʾm*, best known from Ugarit and the Old Testament, represent a somewhat complicated theology. At Ugarit, they seem to be mainly deceased ancestors or the like, which explains the Phoenician contexts admirably. Of the more recent studies, note Manfried Dietrich, Oswald Loretz, and Joaquín Sanmartín, "Die ugaritischen Totengeister *rpu(m)* und die biblischen Rephaim," *Ugarit-Forschungen* 8 (1976): 45–52; Pope, "Cult of the Dead at Ugarit."

78. Clearly expressed in such works as the Babylonian "Poem of the Righteous Sufferer" and "Gilgamesh Epic," the Canaanite "Aqhat Epic," and the Old Testament Book of Job.

theology, like that of so many of its Hellenistic-Roman contemporaries, developed the idea of reward and punishment in the next life, which accordingly now consisted of a heaven and a hell.

Recommended Reading

In addition to the items listed below, special issues of two journals contain many articles on the Phoenicians: *Archaeology* 43.2 (1990) and *Bulletin of the American Schools of Oriental Research* 279 (1990). The items by Jidejian and Moscati, plus the special issue of *BASOR*, include extensive bibliography. Detailed annual bibliographies are published in the journal *Rivista di Studi Fenici* (Rome).

Bunnens, Guy. *L'Expansion Phénicienne en Méditerranée: Essai d'Interprétation Fondé sur une Analyse des Traditions Littéraires.* Brussels: Institut Historique Belge de Rome, 1979.

Culican, William. *The First Merchant Venturers.* London: Thames & Hudson, 1966.

———. *Opera Selecta: From Tyre to Tartessos.* Göteborg: Åströms, 1986.

Gubel, Eric, et al. *Les Phéniciens et le Monde Méditerranéen.* Brussels: Générale de Banque, 1986.

Harden, Donald. *The Phoenicians.* 3d ed. Harmondsworth: Penguin, 1980.

Jidejian, Nina. *Beirut through the Ages.* Beirut: Dar el-Mashreq, 1973.

———. *Byblos through the Ages.* Beirut: Dar el-Mashreq, 1968.

———. *Sidon through the Ages.* Beirut: Dar el-Mashreq, 1971.

———. *Tyre through the Ages.* Beirut: Dar el-Mashreq, 1969.

Katzenstein, H. Jacob. *The History of Tyre.* Jerusalem: Schocken, 1973.

Lipiński, Édouard (ed.). *Phoenicia and the East Mediterranean in the First Millennium B.C.* Studia Phoenicia 5. Louvain: Peeters, 1987.

Moscati, Sabatino. *The World of the Phoenicians.* Translated by A. Hamilton. New York: Praeger, 1968.

——— (ed.). *The Phoenicians.* New York: Abbeville, 1988.

Muhly, James D. "Phoenicia and the Phoenicians." Pp. 177–91 in *Biblical Archaeology Today: Proceedings of the International Congress on Biblical Archaeology, Jerusalem, April 1984.* Jerusalem: Israel Exploration Society/Israel Academy of Sciences and Humanities/American Schools of Oriental Research, 1985.

Niemeyer, Hans G. (ed.). *Phönizier im Westen.* Madrider Beiträge 8. Madrid: Deutsches Archäologisches Institut, 1982.

Pritchard, James B. (ed.). *Ancient Near Eastern Texts Relating to the Old Testament.* 3d ed. Princeton: Princeton University Press, 1969.

Ward, William A. (ed.). *The Role of the Phoenicians in the Interaction of Mediterranean Civilization.* Beirut: American University of Beirut Press, 1968.

Arameans

Wayne T. Pitard

Now Ben-hadad king of Aram mustered his entire army. Accompanied by thirty-two kings with their horses and chariots, he went up and besieged Samaria and attacked it.

—1 Kings 20:1

The Arameans were a large group of linguistically related peoples who spoke dialects of a West Semitic language known as Aramaic and who lived over a substantial part of the Fertile Crescent during the first millennium, largely in Mesopotamia and Syria. The Arameans in south Syria had numerous contacts with biblical Israel and appear quite often in the Hebrew Bible. This is especially the case with the Aramean state that had its capital at Damascus. Although never a unified political power like the Assyrians or Babylonians, the Arameans came to have a major cultural influence on the Near East, as their language slowly became the *lingua franca* of the Persian Empire and eventually replaced many of the local languages of the area, including Hebrew.

Origins

The Bible preserves some legendary material concerning the origins of the Arameans and their relationship to the Israelites. The genealogies in Genesis, apparently created to indicate the relation between the Israelites and their Near Eastern neighbors, provide two distinct traditions as to the place of the Arameans in the political makeup of the Near East. In the earlier genealogical notice (Gen. 22:21), Aram, the eponymous ancestor of the Arameans, is a grandson of Abraham's brother Nahor. This suggests that at one time Aram was basically considered an equal of Israel (= Jacob, grandson of Abraham). But in the priestly table of nations (Gen. 10:22), dating to a time when Aramean influence was widespread across the Near East, Aram is listed as a son of Shem, along with Elam, Ashur (Assyria), Arpachshad, and Lud. A third tradition about Aramean origins occurs in Amos 9:7, where Yahweh is said to have brought the Arameans (probably here particularly referring to the Arameans of Damascus) to their present homeland from an unknown location called Qir or Kir.[1]

Biblical traditions attested largely in Genesis (25:20 and 31:20, where Abraham's relatives Bethuel and Laban are identified as Arameans) and Deuteronomy (26:5, where Jacob himself is called an Aramean) assume a close relationship between Israel and the Arameans. Such traditions fit well with the overall worldview evident in Israelite literature that there was a blood relation with most of the Semitic-speaking nations surrounding them, whether those nations were usually hostile or friendly toward Israel (e.g., Edom = Esau, Jacob's brother; Moab and Ammon, descendants from Lot, Abraham's nephew; Ishmaelites, descendants of Isaac's half-brother). These traditions, however, provide little historical insight into the origins of the various ethnic groups of Syria-Palestine.

The early development of the Arameans is, in fact, shrouded in obscurity. They make their first incontestable appearance in ancient documents only in the late twelfth century,[2] in the years following a period of general collapse and chaos throughout the ancient Near East that began around 1250. Scholars have normally assumed that the Arameans represent a new population influx into northern Syria and Upper Mesopotamia during this period of collapse. They are viewed as nomadic hoards from the Syrian desert that swept northward and invaded the lands where they are found in the twelfth and eleventh centuries, conquering the native populations and quickly Aramaizing the area. From their new foothold along the Middle Euphrates, according to the common reconstruction, the Arameans began to spread out, moving southwest into Syria and southeast into Babylonia.[3] This view, while

---

1. Ran Zadok points out that, in a thirteenth-century document from Emar on the Middle Euphrates, one Pilsu-Dagan, a king of Emar, is also called "king of the people of the land of *Qiri*" ("Elements of Aramean Pre-History," in *Ah, Assyria . . . : Studies in Assyrian History and Ancient Near Eastern Historiography Presented to Hayim Tadmor*, ed. Mordechai Cogan and Israel Eph'al, Scripta Hierosolymitana 33 [Jerusalem: Magnes, 1991], 114). This may locate Qir along the course of the Middle Euphrates.

2. For a discussion of possible earlier references to Aram, see Roland de Vaux, *The Early History of Israel*, trans. David Smith (Philadelphia: Westminster, 1978), 200–205.

3. See, e.g., J. Nicholas Postgate, "Some Remarks on Conditions in the Assyrian Countryside," *Journal of the Economic and Social History of the Orient* 17 (1974): 234–37; J. D. Hawkins, "The Neo-Hittite States in Syria and Anatolia," in *CAH* 3/1:380–82; Hayim Tadmor, "The Decline of Empires in Western Asia ca. 1200 B.C.E.," in *Symposia Celebrating the Seventy-Fifth Anniversary of the Founding of the American Schools of Oriental Research*, ed. Frank M. Cross (Cambridge, Mass.: American Schools of Oriental Research, 1979), 11–14.

still the predominant one in the scholarly literature, may be called into question by recent anthropological studies concerning pastoral nomadism and the role of nomads in the rise and fall of civilizations. The scenario described above falls into a pattern of scholarly reconstructions of transitional periods in ancient Near Eastern history, characterized by the notion that urban cultures are often destroyed by invading hordes of nomadic barbarians. The nomads subsequently take over the land and eventually settle into villages, which then develop into cities. This scenario has been proposed to explain several such transitions: the collapse of the Early Bronze Age civilization in Palestine around 2300, the renewal of urbanization at the beginning of the Middle Bronze Age in the same area around 2000, the collapse of the Neo-Sumerian culture in southern Mesopotamia around 2000, and the collapse of Mycenaean civilization in Greece (the so-called Dorian invasion) around 1200. In recent studies there has been an increasing recognition that pastoral nomads in the Near East played only a minor role in the collapse of these cultures and that the archeological evidence gives no indication of major population shifts at these junctures. Economic, climatic, and social causes seem to have had a much more significant role in the changes evident in the collapses of the cultures.[4] Although, to my knowledge, no substantial discussion has related these new anthropological/sociological insights to the origins of the Arameans, it would seem that the traditional invasion model is also inadequate as an explanation for the appearance of these peoples. The early sources give no clear hint that the Arameans were newcomers into Upper Mesopotamia. They are portrayed as large, tribally oriented groups with substantial pastoral components and also large numbers of members living in towns and villages. This description is quite similar to that of the large tribes that inhabited this area during the eighteenth century, as known from the Mari archives.[5] It seems quite unlikely that the Arameans were immigrants into Syria and Upper Mesopotamia at all, but rather that they were the West Semitic–speaking peoples who had lived in that area throughout the second

4. The literature in this area is now quite substantial. A good place to begin looking at the issues is Kathryn A. Kamp and Norman Yoffee, "Ethnicity in Ancient Western Asia during the Early Second Millennium B.C.: Archaeological Assessments and Ethnoarchaeological Prospectives," *Bulletin of the American Schools of Oriental Research* 237 (1980): 85–104. See also Niels P. Lemche, *Early Israel*, Vetus Testamentum Supplement 37 (Leiden: Brill, 1985), 80–163; and Norman Yoffee, "The Collapse of Ancient Mesopotamian States and Civilization," in *The Collapse of Ancient States and Civilizations*, ed. Norman Yoffee and George L. Cowgill (Tucson: University of Arizona Press, 1988), 44–68.

5. See Victor H. Matthews, *Pastoral Nomadism in the Mari Kingdom (ca. 1830–1760 B.C.)*, American Schools of Oriental Research Dissertation Series 3 (Cambridge, Mass.: American Schools of Oriental Research, 1978); and Giorgio Buccellati, "The Kingdom and Period of Khana," *Bulletin of the American Schools of Oriental Research* 270 (1988): 43–61.

millennium, some as pastoralists and some in villages, towns, and cities. During the period following the collapse of the Hittite Empire, this West Semitic element of the population slowly became politically dominant in several areas, and it is this element, then, that begins to appear in the sources in the late twelfth century.[6]

The traditional understanding of the origins of the Aramean tribes in southern Mesopotamia, which views these tribes as migrating slowly down the Euphrates into Babylonia and especially into the land along the southern end of the Tigris, seems quite plausible. But even here, as John Brinkman points out, the Aramean tribes are located basically in the same area where the Amorite tribes are known to have lived in the early second millennium, which suggests the possibility that these Arameans are actually the descendants of the Amorites who had long since been part of the Babylonian population.[7] The preserved documentary evidence is simply too ambiguous at this point to draw conclusions about the origins of the Arameans in Babylonia.

Arameans in Northern Syria and Upper Mesopotamia (Eleventh to Eighth Centuries)

The first clear references to Arameans are found in the royal Assyrian inscriptions of the late twelfth and eleventh centuries. Tiglath-pileser I (1114–1076) came into conflict with Aramean tribes during his campaigns of expansion to the southwest of Assyria.[8] In one campaign, Tiglath-pileser claims to have fought the Arameans from Suḫu on the Babylonian border northward to Carchemish on the Euphrates. After they had been defeated, the Arameans retreated southward across the Euphrates to the Mount Bishri area. But Tiglath-pileser pursued them, destroyed six Aramean towns in the region,

6. A similar reconstruction may be found in Glenn M. Schwartz, "The Origins of the Aramaeans in Syria and Northern Mesopotamian: Research Problems and Potential Strategies," in *To the Euphrates and Beyond*, ed. O. Haex, H. Curvers, and P. Akkermans (Rotterdam/Brookfield: Balkema, 1989), 281–86. It is likely that some degree of population displacement did occur in northern Syria and Upper Mesopotamia. The Neo-Hittite kingdoms of northern Syria show a stratum of society that had clearly migrated from central Turkey after the fall of Hatti. This may have caused some further migrations of groups in north Syria. But this migration remains largely unconnected to the supposed Aramean invasions, which are most often viewed as coming from the desert to the south. There is simply no evidence that the populations of Upper Mesopotamia and northeast Syria were displaced by large groups of Aramean tribes that had been living previously in the desert.

7. See John A. Brinkman, *A Political History of Post-Kassite Babylonia 1158–722 B.C.* (Rome: Pontifical Biblical Institute Press, 1968), 281–85.

8. English translations of the Assyrian inscriptions from Tiglath-pileser I through Ashurnasirpal II may be found in A. Kirk Grayson, *Assyrian Royal Inscriptions*, vol. 2 (Wiesbaden: Harrassowitz, 1976).

and returned to his capital with considerable booty.[9] It is clear from a study of Tiglath-pileser's overall military strategy that his desire was to control the major trade routes from the Mediterranean and Anatolia to Babylonia. The Aramaic pastoral nomads of the Middle Euphrates and the Habur River region clearly proved to be a problem for Tiglath-pileser in keeping the routes open, since the nomads often supplemented their income by raiding caravans. This probably explains Tiglath-pileser's being forced to attack the Arameans almost yearly throughout his reign. In one inscription he states, "I have crossed the Euphrates twenty-eight times, twice in one year, in pursuit of the *aḫlamu* Arameans."[10]

Tiglath-pileser's reign appears to have ended during a period of serious drought in the Near East. A fragmentary part of a Middle Assyrian chronicle is interpreted as describing a large-scale Aramean invasion of Assyria during the famine, which led to the Aramean capture of Nineveh and the flight of Tiglath-pileser and his army.[11] It should be pointed out, however, that this reconstruction of the text remains uncertain, and it is not clear what the role of the Arameans actually was and whether they were involved in a capture of Nineveh at all.

Whatever the actual situation was during the time of this famine, the Aramean tribes along the Habur River and the Middle Euphrates continued to be a problem for Assyria through the eleventh and tenth centuries. Ashur-bel-kala (1073–1056), Tiglath-pileser's son and second successor, carried out campaigns against Aramean groups located to the northwest of Assyria, in the Habur triangle region, and westward to the Euphrates.[12] Following Ashur-bel-kala's reign, there is a period of about a century during which Assyria went into eclipse. Very little is known of this period or the causes that led to the sharp decline in the fortunes of the state. Some scholars propose that the situation was largely due to the increased pressure of the Aramean groups spreading along the Euphrates,[13] but other factors are likely to have played significant roles as well.

The inscriptions of Tiglath-pileser I and Ashur-bel-kala suggest that the Arameans they encountered were largely pastoralists and villagers, with no evidence of developed political centralization. However, by the late eleventh and early tenth centuries, sources indicate that a number of more centralized states had come into existence in Syria and Upper Mesopotamia under

9. Ibid., #34.
10. Ibid., #97.
11. Tadmor, "Decline of Empires," 12–13.
12. Grayson, *Assyrian Royal Inscriptions*, ##235–47.
13. For example, A. Kirk Grayson, "Assyria: Ashur-dan II to Ashur-nirari V (934–745 B.C.)," in *CAH* 3/1:248.

Aramean control, alongside other similar states whose ruling elites were culturally related to the older Hittite realm (the "Neo-Hittite" states, such as Patina, Hamath, Que, and Gurgum). These Aramean states were limited in size and never became a consolidated power like Assyria or Babylonia, under a single native ruler. Each state appears to have been ruled by a member of the dominant tribe, and several of the states came to be called after the eponymous founder of the dynasty, using the form *bīt*-PN ("the house of PN").[14]

In Upper Mesopotamia, the major Aramean states attested in the sources include Bit-Zamani, Bit-Bahiani, Bit-Halupe, and Laqu in a north-south line along the Upper Tigris and the Habur River to its junction with the Euphrates. These states lay directly on the western border of Assyria. To the west, in the Great Bend of the Euphrates River, was Bit-Adini, a formidable opponent to Assyrian expansion during the early ninth century. To the west of the Euphrates was Yahan, which later came to be known as Bit-Agusi, and Arpad. To the northwest of Bit-Agusi was a small Aramean state called Samʾal, known largely because of the numerous local inscriptions found at its capital (modern Zenjirli). To the south of Bit-Agusi was the important state of Hamath, which was ruled in the tenth and ninth centuries by kings bearing Anatolian names, but by the early eighth century had rulers with Aramaic names. Hamath, like most of the states in northern Syria, presumably had a mixed population of Arameans and Anatolians; thus the alternation of rulers with Anatolian and Aramaic names probably has little to do with major population shifts in the state and may not even identify the ethnic background of the ruler. To the south of Hamath, we know of two important Aramean states: Aram Zobah, located in the northern Baqaʿ Valley of Lebanon and extending into the Plain of Homs in central Syria, which was a substantial political power in the early tenth century; and Aram Damascus, which succeeded Zobah politically and became one of the most important of the Aramean states. The Bible also mentions other smaller Aramean states, including Aram Beth-rehob, Aram Maacah, and Geshur. In addition to all these more organized states, there were numerous minor Aramean tribes and towns throughout Syria and Mesopotamia that maintained their own identities, but were usually dominated by the larger tribes and were rarely mentioned in the texts.

The little historical information preserved about the Aramean states in Upper Mesopotamia is largely concerned with their conflicts with Assyria and their eventual incorporation into the Assyrian Empire. The Assyrian drive for control of the Aramean lands along the Habur River began again with the reign of Ashur-dan II (934–912) and picked up steam during the fol-

---

14. PN is an abbreviation used frequently in Assyriological studies for "personal name."

lowing reigns of Adad-nirari II (911–891) and Tukulti-Ninurta II (890–884).[15] But the decisive period came with the appearance of Ashurnasirpal II (883–859), the first of the great Neo-Assyrian monarchs.[16] Ashurnasirpal's campaigns effectively subdued the Aramean states of Bit-Zamani, Bit-Baḫiani, Bit-Ḫalupe, and the area of Laqu. Bit-Adini was involved in a number of anti-Assyrian intrigues during this time, at one point supporting a rebellion in Bit-Ḫalupe (883) by aiding in the assassination of the pro-Assyrian governor and replacing him with a man from Bit-Adini.[17] Sometime between 877 and 867 it also gave aid to a rebellion in Laqu, Ḫindanu, and Suḫu. A prince of Laqu took refuge in Bit-Adini, and Ashurnasirpal ravaged many towns of the latter in retaliation.[18] But Bit-Adini did not fully submit to the Assyrian king.

During the reign of Shalmaneser III (858–824), Assyrian domination stretched further westward.[19] Following a bitter four-year struggle, Bit-Adini was finally incorporated into the Assyrian provincial system, so that Assyrian control now reached all the way to the Euphrates.[20] Further west, Shalmaneser made vassals of the several Aramean and Neo-Hittite states, such as Bit-Agusi (called Yaḫan during the reign of Ashurnasirpal), Samʾal, and the Neo-Hittite Carchemish, Patina, Kummuḫu, Gurgum, Que, and others.[21] Shalmaneser's military goals in the west were not, however, limited to northern Syria. He was intent on expanding Assyrian domination into central and southern Syria as well. In 853 he marched his troops southward into Hamath, where he met a huge coalition of Syro-Palestinian states and fought them near the Hamathite royal city of Qarqar (discussed below).[22]

From 853 through the rest of Shalmaneser's reign, northern Syria and Upper Mesopotamia appear to have remained largely subject to Assyria. During the last few years of Shalmaneser's reign and during the subsequent years of Shamshi-Adad V (823–811), Assyria was besieged with problems and, ac-

15. For texts from Ashur-dan II, see Grayson, *Assyrian Royal Inscriptions*, ##361, 363, 391; for Adad-nirari II, ##421, 424–34; and for Tukulti-Ninurta II, ##467, 474–75.

16. For his reign, see Grayson, "Assyria," 253–59.

17. Grayson, *Assyrian Royal Inscriptions*, #547.

18. Ibid., ##578–80.

19. For a brief summary of this reign, see Grayson, "Assyria," 259–69. The major texts of Shalmaneser's reign were edited and translated in a series of articles by Ernst Michel: "Die Assur-Texte Salmanassars III. (858–824)," *Die Welt des Orients* 1 (1947–52): 5–20, 57–71, 205–22, 255–71, 385–96, 454–75; 2 (1954–59): 27–45, 137–57, 221–33, 408–14; 3 (1964): 146–55; 4 (1967–68): 29–37. An older, but generally good translation of the major texts into English is Daniel D. Luckenbill, *Ancient Records of Assyria and Babylonia*, 2 vols. (Chicago: University of Chicago Press, 1926–27), 1:200–252.

20. Luckenbill, *Ancient Records of Assyria and Babylonia*, 1:559–61, 599–609.

21. Ibid., 601, 610

22. Ibid., 611.

Prince from ʿAin et-Tell in North Syria, 9th century B.C. (height: 6′ 7″)

Courtesy of Alan R. Millard

cording to an inscription of Adad-nirari III,[23] the states of northern Syria began to pull away from Assyrian control. Adad-nirari III (810–783) was able to stabilize the situation somewhat. After a campaign (808) to subdue Guzanu in Bit-Baḫiani, which had rarely been out of the Assyrian orbit during most of the century, Adad-nirari spent the campaigns of 805 and 804 fighting a coalition of states led by Bit-Agusi under its king Attarshumki. Adad-nirari was able to break the rebellion and return northern Syria to Assyrian control.[24]

Most of the first half of the eighth century saw a steady decline of Assyrian power in northern Syria. The Assyrian governor for the area, Shamshi-ilu, whose administration lasted virtually the entire half-century, seems to have been more influential in the politics of Syria than the Assyrian kings. Shamshi-ilu led a number of the campaigns listed in the Assyrian eponym canon as royal campaigns.[25] But by the mid-760s the Assyrian government was being wracked by internal rebellion, and Arpad and other western states had once again declared independence.

The exact political situation in northern Syria during the 760s and 750s is unclear and problematic. One of the most enigmatic aspects of this period is related to the well-known Sefire treaties and the identification of the dominant member of those treaties. These stone inscriptions, containing a treaty between Matiʿel (son

23. Alan R. Millard and Hayim Tadmor, "Adad-nirari III in Syria: Another Stela Fragment and the Dates of His Campaigns," *Iraq* 35 (1973): 61.

24. Ibid., 58–62.

25. See Hawkins, "Neo-Hittite States," 404–5.

of Attarshumki), king of Arpad, and Bir-gaʾya, king of a land called *ktk*, were found early this century at Sefîre, a town that belonged to Arpad/Bit-Agusi in the mid-eighth century. What makes this treaty so enigmatic is that Arpad, the major political power in northern Syria earlier in the eighth century, is the subordinate member in the treaty, being dominated by the king of the otherwise unknown *ktk*. This is particularly mysterious in view of an extant vassal treaty between Matiʿel and Ashur-nirari V of Assyria.[26] Where was the land of *ktk* located, and how did it develop enough power to briefly subject Arpad? Why is it not mentioned in Assyrian inscriptions, and what happened to it after the mid-eighth century? In spite of numerous proposed identifications of *ktk*, no scholarly consensus has developed over the interpretation of this episode in north Syrian history.[27]

In 744 Tiglath-pileser III came to power and began a process of consolidation that allowed him to regain full control over the north within a few years. The leader of the Syrian alliance against Tiglath-pileser was Matiʿel of Arpad, who had been the vassal in the Sefîre treaties. With the support of Urartu and the states of Melid, Gurgum, and Kummuḫu to the north, Matiʿel fought against Tiglath-pileser in 743 and was defeated. Tiglath-pileser besieged Arpad for three years and finally captured it. Bit-Agusi caused no further problems for Tiglath-pileser. In 738 the king fought and defeated Unqi and Hamath, and by 737 all of northern Syria had been constituted into Assyrian provinces, as had part of Hamath.[28]

Arameans in Central and Southern Syria (Tenth to Eighth Centuries)

The earliest historical information so far preserved concerning the Aramean states in southern Syria is found in 2 Samuel 8 and 10, which recount three battles fought between the Aramean state of Zobah, under its ruler Hadadezer, son of Rehob (this might better be translated "the Rehobite," since Hadadezer also appears to have been the ruler of another small Aramean state called Beth-rehob), and Israel, under the leadership of

---

26. For the Assyrian treaty, see Ernst Weidner, "Der Staatsvertrag Assurniraris VI. von Assyrien mit Matiʾilu von Bit-Agusi," *Archiv für Orientforschung* 8 (1932–33): 17–34. For an English translation, see Luckenbill, *Ancient Records of Assyria and Babylonia*, 1:749–60.

27. The literature on the Sefîre inscriptions is considerable. See, most importantly, Joseph A. Fitzmyer, *The Aramaic Inscriptions of Sefîre* (Rome: Pontifical Biblical Institute Press, 1967); André Lemaire and Jean-Marie Durand, *Les Inscriptions Araméenes de Sfiré et l'Assyrie de Shamshi-ilu* (Geneva/Paris: Droz, 1984); and Hélène S. Sader, *Les États Araméens de Syrie* (Beirut: Steiner, 1987), 138–42.

28. On the Syrian campaigns of Tiglath-pileser, see Hawkins, "Neo-Hittite States," 410–13.

David.[29] It appears from these texts that Zobah was the dominant political power in southern Syria during the early part of the tenth century. Following an outbreak of war between Ammon and Israel, Hadadezer came to the support of Ammon, along with a number of vassals, and fought to a stalemate with the Israelites (2 Sam. 10:6–14 ‖ 1 Chron. 19:6–15). Hadadezer returned to Zobah, where he gathered new troops and prepared to meet Israel again (2 Sam. 10:15–19 ‖ 1 Chron. 19:16–19). But David marched his army northward and met Hadadezer at Helam, where the army of Zobah was decisively defeated. Several of Hadadezer's allies and vassals subsequently sued for peace and became David's vassals.

A further confrontation between David and Hadadezer is described in 2 Samuel 8:3–8 ‖ 1 Chronicles 18:3–8. Although some scholars argue that this is simply a variant account of the Battle of Helam, most view it as a separate battle, which, however, is usually thought to have occurred after those described in 2 Samuel 10. First Chronicles 8:3 places this final battle near Hamath in central Syria, and it is described as a decisive defeat for Hadadezer. It is during the course of this conflict that Aram Damascus makes its first appearance in the Hebrew Bible. According to 2 Samuel 8:5–6, troops from Damascus were sent to aid Hadadezer, but David defeated them as well and went on to place Israelite garrisons in Damascus, apparently making it an occupied territory.

Aram Damascus, usually called simply Aram in the Hebrew Bible ("Syria" in many translations) was the part of the Aramean world that had the greatest effect on biblical Israel. It was regularly the most powerful state that bordered on Israel, and the two nations had a close and complex relationship from the tenth through the eighth centuries. Unfortunately, historical information about this kingdom is limited almost exclusively to external sources, most especially the Hebrew Bible and the Assyrian inscriptions. With the exception of a few very short inscriptions that may have originated from there, no documents from Aram Damascus itself have yet been discovered,[30] and no

---

29. On Zobah, see Abraham Malamat, "Aspects of the Foreign Policies of David and Solomon," *Journal of Near Eastern Studies* 22 (1963): 1–6, revised in *Das davidische und salomonische Königreich und seine Beziehungen zu Ägypten und Syrien: Zur Entstehung eines Grosreichs* (Vienna: Österreichischen Akademie der Wissenschaften, 1983), 31–39. See also Wayne T. Pitard, *Ancient Damascus* (Winona Lake, Ind.: Eisenbrauns, 1987), 89–95.

30. The only probable inscriptions from Damascus are two ivories with brief inscriptions of Hazael on their backs, found among the booty taken by the Assyrians and left at Til Barsip in one case and at Calah in the other. The most famous inscription attributed to a Damascene king is the Melqart of Bir-Hadad Stele, a late ninth- or early eighth-century inscription found just north of Aleppo in the 1930s. New examination of that inscription, however, makes it doubtful that it can be attributed to a king of Aram Damascus; see Wayne T. Pitard, "The Identity of the Bir-Hadad of the Melqart Stela," *Bulletin of the American Schools of Orient Research* 272

excavations in Damascus have yet reached the Iron Age levels of the Aramean city. Thus, like the northern Aramean states, our knowledge of this nation is largely limited to its international relations in the period from approximately 1000 to 732, when it was incorporated into the Assyrian Empire and ceased to be an independent state.

Following David's defeat of Aram Damascus, we hear nothing further from Damascus until the period of Solomon. Sometime during Solomon's reign, a former officer of Hadadezer of Zobah named Rezon, son of Eliada, gathered together an army, seized Damascus, and proclaimed himself king (1 Kings 11:23–24). Solomon was either unwilling or unable to dislodge this rebel, and Damascus became an independent state.

Following Solomon's death, the united Israelite kingdom collapsed and its empire faded away. The rulers in Damascus took advantage of the power vacuum that followed to become a significant influence in the region. By the early ninth century, Aram, under King Bir-Hadad I (biblical Ben-Hadad) was powerful enough (in league with Judah) to stage an attack on the northern kingdom of Israel and temporarily capture a number of important towns in the northern part of the country (1 Kings 15:16–22).[31]

The peak of Damascus's political power came during the middle and final years of the ninth century. As the Assyrian threat expanded during the early days of Shalmaneser III (858–824), a defensive coalition was formed by twelve western states, led by Hadad-ʿidr of Aram Damascus, along with Irḫulena of Hamath and Ahab of Israel. In 853 Shalmaneser marched into the territory of Hamath, where he met this coalition near Qarqar. The two sides appear to have fought to a stalemate, since Shalmaneser did not proceed any further south, but turned westward briefly and then returned to Assyria.[32] Only after four years did Shalmaneser attempt to march again into central

---

(1988): 3–21; Émile Puech, "La Stèle de Bar-Hadad à Melqart et les Rois d'Arpad," *Revue Biblique* 99 (1992): 311–34; and Joseph A. Fitzmyer and Stephen A. Kaufman, *An Aramaic Bibliography*, part 1: *Old, Official, and Biblical Aramaic* (Baltimore: Johns Hopkins University Press, 1992), 11. See below on two recently published possible Hazael inscriptions. As this book goes to press, preliminary reports have appeared concerning a fragmentary Aramaic stele found at Tell Dan (northern Israel) during the summer of 1993. The script has been dated to the ninth century, and the broken lines make reference to "the king of Israel," "the house of David," the god Hadad, and chariotry. There is a strong possibility that it was a victory stele of a king of Aram Damascus, placed at Dan during one of the periods when Damascus controlled that area (cf., e.g., 1 Kings 15:17–22). If so, this becomes the first monumental inscription from a Damascene ruler. The stele is scheduled for publication in *Israel Exploration Journal*.

31. On the reign of this king, see Pitard, *Ancient Damascus*, 107–14. The newly discovered stele from Tell Dan may refer to this event.

32. Luckenbill, *Ancient Records of Assyria and Babylonia*, 1:611.

Syria, and he was again met and held back by the coalition under Hadad-ʿidr. Shalmaneser's inscriptions describe two further campaigns to that region in 848 and 843, but Hadad-ʿidr's coalition kept the Assyrians out of central Syria on each occasion. Hadad-ʿidr's continued leadership in this alliance indicates that Aram was the predominant political power of central Syria and Palestine during this period.[33]

A substantial controversy exists concerning the relation between Hadad-ʿidr of the Assyrian inscriptions and the king of Aram called Ben-Hadad in 1 Kings 20 and 22. These two chapters describe a series of conflicts between Israel and Aram that are said to have taken place during the last five years of the reign of Ahab of Israel, that is, between 858 and 853, the years just preceding the Battle of Qarqar. If these chapters are reliable, it would be necessary to conclude that the Ben-Hadad in 1 Kings 20 (called Ben-Hadad II by many scholars) should be identified with Hadad-ʿidr, and that a serious state of war existed between these two nations, even during the year of the Battle of Qarqar.

However, there are a number of indications in these chapters that they do not actually describe events of the reign of Ahab, but rather belong to the time of Joash, some fifty years later.[34] For example, the description of the political situation in 1 Kings 20, in which the king of Israel is portrayed as having been completely dominated by Aram Damascus, is quite different from the conditions that other biblical passages and extrabiblical sources indicate existed during Ahab's reign. Shalmaneser's Monolith Inscription, which gives the most complete account of the Battle at Qarqar, in which Ahab took part, reports that Ahab furnished two thousand chariots and ten thousand foot-soldiers for the battle. This is the largest contingent of chariots provided by any member of the coalition, and even if the figure is an exaggeration (as it probably is) this contrasts dramatically to the portrait of the weak king of Israel in 1 Kings 20. In addition, while the king and his father in 1 Kings 20 are portrayed as vassals of the king of Aram (see esp. 20:34), biblical and extrabiblical sources indicate that Omri and Ahab were two of the most powerful kings of Israel. The Mesha Stele from Moab indicates that Omri had reduced

---

33. On the reign of Hadad-ʿidr, see Pitard, *Ancient Damascus*, 125–38.

34. For a detailed discussion of the position taken here, see ibid., 114–25. See also J. Maxwell Miller, "The Elisha Cycle and the Accounts of the Omride Wars," *Journal of Biblical Literature* 85 (1966): 442–43, where it is proposed that the king of Israel should be identified with Joahaz, the father of Joash, rather than Joash. For an influential reconstruction of this period, which assumes the identity of Hadad-ʿidr and the Ben-Hadad of 1 Kings 20 and 22, see Benjamin Mazar, "The Aramean Empire and Its Relations with Israel," trans. Ben-zion Gold, *Biblical Archaeologist* 25 (1962): 106–16. The traditional interpretation may also be found in John Bright, *A History of Israel*, 3d ed. (Philadelphia: Westminster, 1981), 242–43.

Moab to vassaldom, something quite unlikely if he himself were under Aramean domination.[35] The biblical accounts of the building of Samaria as the new Israelite capital during Omri's reign (1 Kings 16:24) and the wealth of Ahab's court (1 Kings 22:39) also contrast significantly with the portrayal of the kings in 1 Kings 20. Further, the archeological evidence of major public building projects throughout Israel during Ahab's reign demonstrates that Israel was economically prosperous during this time.[36]

While 1 Kings 20 seems out of place in the reigns of Omri and Ahab, it fits perfectly into the period of Joahaz and Joash (814–782), when Israel was dominated by Aram under kings Hazael and his son, another Bir-Hadad (Hebrew Ben-Hadad; see 2 Kings 13:22–25). During the reign of Bir-Hadad, a greatly weakened Israel was able to overthrow Aramean overlordship in a decisive battle near the town of Aphek (2 Kings 13:17). In 1 Kings 20:26–30, the decisive battle also takes place at Aphek, and the description in 20:34 of the king's father as having been under the domination of Ben-Hadad's father fits perfectly into this period. It thus appears that the account in 1 Kings 20 should not be used to illuminate the relations between Ahab and the kingdom of Aram. In a similar way, the account of the battle at Ramoth Gilead in 1 Kings 22 seems problematic as well and should also be considered highly suspect.[37] It appears unlikely that there was a major war between Aram and Israel during the reign of Ahab. Rather, Ben-Hadad of 1 Kings 20 should be identified with Bir-Hadad, son of Hazael, from the early eighth century, not with Hadad-ʿidr of the mid-ninth century.

Thus there does not appear to have been a Bir-Hadad on the throne in Damascus during the middle part of the ninth century. Hadad-ʿidr was succeeded (most likely) by Hazael, a usurper, around 842.[38] At this point the coalition that had successfully held back the Assyrians for eleven years fell apart. Hamath, the major member of the coalition to the north, appears to have reached a separate agreement with Assyria, while to the south a border war broke out between Aram and Israel. During the course of this war, a conspiracy against King Joram of Israel came to fruition when the general, Jehu, assassinated the king and wiped out the family of Omri (2 Kings 9–10). This

35. *ANET* 320–21.

36. For a summary of the finds of this period, see Amihai Mazar, *Archaeology of the Land of the Bible 10,000–586 B.C.E.* (New York: Doubleday, 1990), 406–16. On new evidence for substantial public works during the reign of Ahab at Dor, see Ephraim Stern, "Hazor, Dor and Megiddo in the Time of Ahab and under Assyrian Rule," *Israel Exploration Journal* 40 (1990): 16–22.

37. Miller, "Elisha Cycle," 444–46; idem, "The Rest of the Acts of Jehoahaz (I Kings 20, 22:1–38)," *Zeitschrift für die Alttestamentliche Wissenschaft* 80 (1968): 340–41.

38. On the complexities surrounding the rise of Hazael, see Pitard, *Ancient Damascus*, 132–38.

revolution, on top of the animosity between Aram and Israel over the border, apparently led Israel to drop out of the alliance as well. So when Shalmaneser returned to Syria in 841, he found only Hazael of Damascus prepared to oppose him.[39] In a battle near Mount Senir (probably Jebel ez-Zabadani or Jebel esh-Sharqi to the north of Damascus, rather than the Mount Hermon region, which is the usual identification of Senir),[40] Hazael was defeated and forced to retreat into Damascus. Shalmaneser besieged Damascus briefly and ravaged its fertile fields, but was unable to capture the city. Instead he marched westward to the coast, where he received the submission of several kings, including Jehu.[41]

Shalmaneser apparently returned twice, in 838 and 837, to subdue Aram, but was unable to do so. Virtually no information has been preserved concerning these two confrontations.[42] But after 837, Shalmaneser turned his attention to lands in the north, and southern Syria and Palestine had thirty years of peace from Assyria. Once the Assyrian threat subsided, Hazael began a policy of expansion into Palestine. He was able to annex Israel's Transjordanian territories (2 Kings 10:32–33) and to apparently force Israel into vassaldom. According to the Lucianic texts of the Septuagint (following 2 Kings 13:22), Hazael also conquered Philistia and then turned eastward toward Judah. King Jehoash of Judah sent Hazael a large tribute, thereby presumably becoming a vassal, after which Hazael withdrew from Jerusalem (2 Kings 12:17–18 [MT 12:18–19]).

Thus, during the reign of Hazael, Aram became a significant empire that covered much if not all of southern Syria and Palestine. Some scholars also argue that Hazael gained hegemony over much of northern Syria as well, but until recently there was very little evidence of Hazael's influence in the north.[43] A bronze ornament for a horse's forehead, found on the Greek island of Samos, has an Aramaic inscription of the late ninth or early eighth century: *zy ntn hdd lmrᵓn ḥzᵓl mn ᶜmq bšnt ᶜdh mrᵓn nhr* ("that which Hadad gave our lord Hazael from the Valley [ᶜmq] in the year our lord crossed the river").[44] Part of booty carried off from the Near East to Samos

39. Ibid., 146–48.

40. Cf. Sader, *Les États Araméens de Syrie*, 265.

41. Luckenbill, *Ancient Records of Assyria and Babylonia*, 1:672.

42. Pitard, *Ancient Damascus*, 148–50.

43. Alfred Jepsen, "Israel und Damaskus," *Archiv für Orientforschung* 14 (1941–45): 168; Mazar, "Aramean Empire," 108–16. See also Pitard, *Ancient Damascus*, 152–58.

44. See Israel Ephᶜal and Joseph Naveh, "Hazael's Booty Inscriptions," *Israel Exploration Journal* 39 (1989): 192–200; François Bron and André Lemaire, "Les Inscriptions Araméennes de Hazael," *Revue d'Assyriologie* 83 (1989): 35–44. A second Aramaic inscription, on a blinker that was found early this century at Eretria (in Greece) but only recently published, may have a very similar text, but it is badly damaged. See the above articles.

at some later date, the inscription is interpreted as an indication that Hazael of Aram Damascus campaigned in northern Syria, took booty from Umqi (ᶜmq) = Patina, and probably marched his army across the Euphrates ("the River").

A certain amount of caution is worthwhile in dealing with this inscription. First, nothing on the inscription assures that the Hazael of this inscription is Hazael of Damascus (Hazael was a popular West Semitic name). Second, if *mn ᶜmq* is to be understood as the location whence the ornament came, the noun *ᶜmq* ("the Valley") is ambiguous. The assumption has been that it refers to the state of Umqi or Unqi in northern Syria, and this may be correct. However, note should be made that the valley between the Lebanon Mountains and the Anti-Lebanon Mountains directly west of Damascus was known as ᶜAmqi in the Late Bronze Age and may have retained that name into the first millennium (cf. Judg. 18:28). Third, it is not certain which river is referred to here. Although the Euphrates is the river *par excellence* in Near Eastern inscriptions, the term can be used for other rivers as well. Finally, there are clear indications that Bit-Agusi was the dominant power in northern Syria at least during the reign of Shamshi-Adad V (823–811) and the early years of the reign of Adad-nirari III (810–783). This was the state that led the important anti-Assyrian coalition that met Adad-nirari in 805. There is no hint that At-tarshumki was a vassal to anyone at this time. For these reasons, the new inscription must be used with great caution in reconstructing the extent of Hazael's empire.

Hazael was succeeded, probably around 800, by his son Bir-Hadad (often called Ben-Hadad III in the literature, since Hadad-ᶜidr was usually identified as a Ben-Hadad as well). The events of Bir-Hadad's reign are known from several sources: 1–2 Kings, Assyrian inscriptions of Adad-nirari III, and an Aramaic inscription of King Zakkur of Hamath and Luash. Each of these sources describes a different military defeat of Bir-Hadad, and together they clearly suggest a steep decline of Aram's power during this reign. Although there are no clear indications of the chronological order in which the events from the three sources occurred, one may speculate that those described in the Zakkur inscription occurred first.[45] The inscription describes an attack made on Zakkur by a coalition of states to the north and south of Hamath, led by Bir-Hadad of Damascus and apparently the king of Bit-Agusi in the north. The coalition attempted to capture Zakkur's capital in Luash, but was unable to do so. There is some indication in the broken part of the inscription

---

45. For a convenient translation, see *ANET* 655–56. The name of the king has traditionally been vocalized as Zakir. However, recently discovered cuneiform texts show that it was pronounced Zakkur.

that Zakkur was saved by the timely arrival of Assyrian troops to support him, but this is not certain.

Whether or not the Assyrians were responsible for Bir-Hadad's first defeat, they were responsible for his second one. Inscriptions of Adad-nirari III report that the Assyrian king personally entered Damascus, following a siege of the city, and received a substantial booty from the king of Aram, who is called Mar'i in the Assyrian inscriptions. Mar'i, which in Aramaic means "my lord," is almost certainly a title of Bir-Hadad.[46]

Bir-Hadad's third major defeat came at the hands of the Israelites, who regained their autonomy during this time, following decades of domination by Damascus (2 Kings 13:22–25). As mentioned above, 1 Kings 20 should probably be understood as a more detailed account of the battles between Joash and Bir-Hadad that led to Israelite independence.

There is no information about the rest of the Aramean Empire during Bir-Hadad's reign. If it had stretched to northern Syria, all of that was surely lost after the campaigns of Adad-nirari. In the south, the breaking away of Israel may have been followed by the collapse of the rest of the southern empire. No sources are preserved from the latter part of Bir-Hadad's reign, and it is not known how long he ruled. It is clear that the first half of the eighth century was a bad period for Aram. In 773 the Assyrians once again attacked Damascus, whose king, an otherwise unknown Ḥadianu, was forced to pay a large tribute.[47] Israel experienced a significant political revival during the reign of Jeroboam II (782–748) and appears to have actually placed Aram under vassaldom for a while (2 Kings 14:25–28).

Damascus's final moment of political influence began about the middle of the eighth century, with the reign of Aram's last king, called Rezin in the Bible, but pronounced more like Radyan in Aramaic. It is not certain when Radyan came to the throne, but he was king by 740 or 739, when his name occurs in a tribute list of Tiglath-pileser III of Assyria. During the years 737–735, while Tiglath-pileser was occupied elsewhere in his empire, Radyan formed a new anti-Assyrian coalition of Syro-Palestinian states, including the Phoenician city-state of Tyre, Ashkelon, and Israel.[48] Apparently in an attempt to force Judah to join the coalition, Radyan and Pekah of Israel at-

---

46. See Hayim Tadmor, "The Historical Inscriptions of Adad-nirari III," *Iraq* 35 (1973): 141–50.

47. The Pazarcik Stele, upon which this information is inscribed, is published in Veysel Donbaz, "Two Neo-Assyrian Stelae in the Antakya and Kahramanmaraş Museums," *Annual Review of the Royal Inscriptions of Mesopotamia Project* 8 (1990): 5–18.

48. On this reign, see Pitard, *Ancient Damascus*, 179–89. A more speculative reconstruction of the reign of Radyan may be found in J. Maxwell Miller and John H. Hayes, *A History of Ancient Israel and Judah* (Philadelphia: Westminster, 1986), 323–26.

tacked Judah and besieged Jerusalem (2 Kings 15:37; 16:5–9). Their plan, according to Isaiah 7:6, was to depose the young king Ahaz and replace him with a (presumably anti-Assyrian) puppet ruler named Tabeel, who would do their bidding. Ahaz, who apparently was not a vassal of Assyria at this point, immediately appealed to Tiglath-pileser for help. Tiglath-pileser marched into Syria in 734 and appears to have captured the coastal regions that belonged to the anti-Assyrian coalition (including Tyre and Philistia) during that campaign. The campaigns of 733 and 732 were directed largely at Aram Damascus, the leader of the coalition, and finally Damascus was captured in 732. Tiglath-pileser devastated the country, Radyan was executed, and the state of Aram was annexed into the Assyrian Empire as a province. This brought an end to the independent state of Aram.

Thus, from the reign of Tiglath-pileser III, virtually all of the Aramean states were part of the Assyrian provincial system, and by early in the reign of Sargon II (721–705), when the latter crushed a rebellion led by Hamath and including the recently annexed provinces of Arpad, Simirra, and Damascus, all of Syria was under Assyrian sovereignty.[49] During most of the seventh century, the height of Assyrian power, the Aramean provinces remained under tight control. By the time of the Neo-Babylonian Empire, very little trace of the old state structure remained.

Arameans in Southern Mesopotamia

Information concerning the Arameans in Babylonia is limited, but the available sources indicate that Aramean groups existed in Babylonia from the beginning of the first millennium and that they were largely organized as nomadic pastoral groups. Several texts indicate that these pastoralists often resorted to raiding and plundering caravans and towns. During the reign of the Babylonian king Adad-apla-iddina (1068–1047), Aramean and Sutian brigands apparently raided the Babylonian shrine cities of Sippar and Nippur. Other references to Aramean assaults and belligerence are found in later sources as well.[50]

But eighth-century documents also show that large numbers of Arameans lived in cities and towns, some in specifically Aramean domains and others in the major Babylonian cities.[51] References to disputes between Arameans and others over ownership of fields are found from the eighth century as well.

49. Luckenbill, *Ancient Records of Assyria and Babylonia*, 2:55.
50. See Brinkman, *Political History*, 279.
51. Ibid., 268–81.

By the ninth century, the Aramean tribal groups were often allied with the Babylonians against the Assyrians, and although Tiglath-pileser III defeated thirty-six Aramean tribes during his campaigns in Babylonia, the tribes apparently maintained a fiercely independent streak, for they are listed as rebels during the succeeding reigns of Sargon II and Sennacherib. They also played a role in the great rebellion of Babylonia against Ashurbanipal in 652–648.[52]

In all, it appears that the Arameans played a supplementary role in Babylonia rather than a dominant one, with the political dominance falling to the Chaldean tribes. But their cultural influence was quite significant in the realm of language, in that by the late eighth century Aramaic had become the predominant language in Babylonia, while Akkadian was relegated largely to government and literary use. There are a large number of loanwords and a few institutions that came into Babylonian culture from the Arameans during this period.[53]

Civilization

It is in many ways impossible with our current sources of information to produce more than a vague sketch of Aramean culture. In fact, one cannot refer to a single "Aramean culture," since each of the major Aramean groups was distinctive and rose in a specific context and set of circumstances.

The Arameans seem to have made few major contributions to political structure or practice in the Near East. This is not surprising, since in spite of the extent of their presence throughout the Fertile Crescent, they were never linked into a single political unit. The small state structure and the use of alliances and coalitions with other small states cannot be considered specifically Aramean. There is no indication that the Arameans ever attempted to set up alliances based strictly on their ethnic relationships.[54] A few elements of Aramean (and perhaps West Semitic) statecraft were, however, adopted eventually by the Assyrians, including the loyalty oath, called *adê* in Akkadian, which is a loanword from the Aramaic *ʿdy*.[55]

52. See John A. Brinkman, *Prelude to Empire: Babylonian Society and Politics, 747–626 B.C.* (Philadelphia: University Museum, 1984), 45–65, 94–101.
53. See ibid., 13–14; and Jonas C. Greenfield, "Babylonian-Aramaic Relationship," in *Mesopotamien und seine Nachbarn: Politische und kulturelle Wechselbeziehungen im alten Vorderasien vom 4. bis 1. Jahrtausend v. Chr.*, ed. Hans Jörg Nissen and Johannes Renger, 2d ed., 25th Rencontre Assyriologique Internationale (Berlin: Reimer, 1987), 471–82.
54. See the discussion in Sader, *Les États Araméens de Syrie*, 278–81.
55. See Hayim Tadmor, "The Aramaization of Assyria: Aspects of Western Impact," in *Mesopotamien und seine Nachbarn: Politische und kulturelle Wechselbeziehungen im alten Vorderasien vom 4. bis 1. Jahrtausend v. Chr.*, ed. Hans Jörg Nissen and Johannes Renger, 2d ed., 25th Rencontre Assyriologique Internationale (Berlin: Reimer, 1987), 455–58.

Nor was Aramean art and architecture very influential in the ancient world. It appears that much of north Aramean art was adopted and adapted from the surviving Hittite traditions that continued to exist in the Neo-Hittite states. As soon as Assyria began to take control of the west, art in the vassal states became an imitation of Assyrian styles. South Aramean (i.e., Damascene) art is even less well known. Only a few pieces of ivory and one stone relief can be identified as such so far. These pieces show major stylistic borrowing from Phoenicia, mixed with certain aspects of north Syrian styles. Little study has been done on determining specifically Aramean characteristics of architecture, but there seems to be little major contribution in this area as well. Little is known of Aramean art and architecture in Babylonia, either. It appears to have been largely swallowed up by the Mesopotamian tradition.[56]

Aramean religion seems to have been the descendant of the West Semitic religion of the second millennium.[57] The gods of the Arameans are the West Semitic gods, supplemented in

Tell Fekheriyeh statue with bilingual Assyrian-Aramaic inscription, 9th century B.C. (height: 5′ 5″)

Courtesy of Wayne T. Pitard

56. On Aramean and Syrian art in general, see Richard D. Barnett, *A Catalogue of the Nimrud Ivories* (London: British Museum, 1957), 31–62; Irene J. Winter, "Phoenician and North Syrian Ivory Carving in Historical Context: Questions of Style and Distribution," *Iraq* 39 (1976): 1–22; idem, "Is There a South Syrian Style of Ivory Carving in the Early First Millennium B.C.?" *Iraq* 43 (1981): 101–30; and Ekrem Akurgal, "Aramaean and Phoenician Stylistic and Iconographic Elements in Neo-Hittite Art," in *Temples and High Places in Biblical Times*, ed. Avraham Biran (Jerusalem: Nelson Glueck School of Biblical Archaeology, Hebrew Union College–Jewish Institute of Religion, 1981), 131–39. Note also the brief discussion of Babylonian art and architecture in Brinkman, *Prelude to Empire*, 120–21.

57. See Jonas C. Greenfield, "Aspects of Aramean Religion," in *Ancient Israelite Religion: Essays in Honor of Frank Moore Cross*, ed. Patrick D. Miller Jr., Paul D. Hanson, and S. Dean McBride (Philadelphia: Fortress, 1987), 67–78.

some cases with the gods of the neighboring cultures. From the surviving Aramaic inscriptions, it seems clear that Hadad was the preeminent deity of many of the Aramean tribes. He was the recipient of special praise in the Tell Fekheriyeh inscription of Haddyit'i, the subject of the giant Hadad statue erected by Panamu of Sam'al, and the national deity of Aram Damascus under the name Hadad-Rimmon (probably pronounced *rammān*, "Hadad the Thunderer"), according to 2 Kings 5:18 (cf. Zech. 12:11). The moon god, Sin/Shahar, the Lord of Haran, is prominent in several inscriptions, as are El, Rakib-el, Shamash, and Reshep.

The major legacy of the Aramean civilization was its language and script. In these areas, the Arameans had an extraordinary impact on the Near East, well beyond their political legacy. Aramaic was the most widely spoken language in Syria and Upper Mesopotamia during the first centuries of the first millennium. As full-fledged states began to appear, it is natural that monumental inscriptions should also be forthcoming. The earliest Aramaic inscriptions found thus far date to the mid-ninth century.[58] The script of the early inscriptions in Syria indicates that it was borrowed from the Phoenicians. This borrowing probably occurred as early as the late eleventh or early tenth century, although very little is known about this process. The most significant clue to the date of the borrowing is the recently discovered statue of Haddyit'i, a ninth-century Aramean governor of Guzanu and Sikanu in Bit-Baḥiani, which has a bilingual, Assyrian-Aramaic inscription incised on the skirt of the ruler.[59] The Aramaic inscription on this statue is written in an archaic form of the script that looks much like eleventh-century Phoenician script, in spite of the statue's almost certain dating to the ninth century. Other Aramaic inscriptions from the ninth century show a much more developed script, one that is very similar to ninth-century Phoenician script. This situation reflects a continued influence from the Phoenician coast among the western Aramean and Neo-Hittite states that appears not to have extended into the area of Bit-Baḥiani.[60] It is only in the eighth century when substan-

---

58. The new inscription from Tell Dan may date to the early ninth century, but this is as yet uncertain. A convenient translation of the major early Aramaic inscriptions may be found in John C. L. Gibson, *Textbook of Syrian Semitic Inscriptions*, vol. 2: *Aramaic Inscriptions* (Oxford: Clarendon, 1975). See also the recent survey by Scott C. Layton, "Old Aramaic Inscriptions," *Biblical Archaeologist* 51 (1988): 172–89.

59. On this statue, see Ali Abou-Assaf, Pierre Bordreuil, and Alan R. Millard, *La Statue de Tell Fekherye et Son Inscription Bilingue Assyro-Araméenne* (Paris: Éditions Recherche sur les Civilisations, 1982); and Alan R. Millard and Pierre Bordreuil, "A Statue from Syria with Assyrian and Aramaic Inscriptions," *Biblical Archaeologist* 45 (1982): 135–41.

60. For a discussion of the Phoenician cultural and economic presence in northern Syria during the ninth century, see Pitard, "Identity of Bir-Hadad," 13–16.

tial characteristics that may be called specifically Aramean begin to emerge in the script.[61]

The Arameans were the first to begin using some of the alphabetic letters to indicate long vowel sounds (the so-called *matres lectionis*). This important contribution to writing was slowly adopted by other cultures, including Israel. Eventually, the Aramaic script itself came into common use throughout Syria-Palestine as the older national scripts declined. The square script that was commonly used in Judea by the third century and is the ancestor of the modern Hebrew book script, is actually a descendent of Aramaic, rather than the archaic Israelite script.[62]

But it is the language itself that had the most wide-ranging impact on the Near East. Because of the Assyrian policy of deporting large numbers of people from their homelands into Assyria, a substantial part of the Assyrian population by the eighth century was Aramean, and this had an enormous impact on Assyria from that time onward.[63] By the mid-eighth century, Aramaic was being used for official communication between Assyria and the west. The Assyrians made regular use of Aramean scribes who wrote in Aramaic on papyrus. It has also become increasingly apparent that during the Neo-Babylonian period Aramaic was the most common spoken language in Babylonia, while Akkadian was largely a literary language.[64] By the time of the Persian Empire, Aramaic, as the most widespread language in the Near East, became the *lingua franca* of the empire. The dialect used by the Persian chancellery became widespread throughout the Near East and was used not only for official Persian documents, but for numerous literary purposes. It is this official Aramaic that is found in the Aramaic sections of Ezra and (in a later form) Daniel, as well as in numerous papyrus documents discovered in Egypt, including the famous Elephantine texts, which include the records of a Jewish military colony of the fifth century.[65] In Palestine, Aramaic documents of the

61. On the Aramaic script, see Joseph Naveh, "The Development of the Aramaic Script," *Proceedings of the Israel Academy of Sciences and Humanities* 5 (1971): 1–69.

62. On the Jewish scripts of the third century B.C. through the first century A.D., see Frank M. Cross, "The Development of the Jewish Scripts," in *The Bible and the Ancient Near East: Essays in Honor of William Foxwell Albright*, ed. G. Ernest Wright (Garden City, N.Y.: Doubleday, 1961), 131–202.

63. On the deportations into Assyria, see Bustenay Oded, *Mass Deportations and Deportees in the Neo-Assyrian Empire* (Wiesbaden: Reichert, 1979), 18–32.

64. On the Aramaic influence on Mesopotamian culture, see Tadmor, "Aramaization of Assyria"; Alan R. Millard, "Assyrians and Arameans," *Iraq* 45 (1983): 101–8; and Greenfield, "Babylonian-Aramaic Relationship."

65. On Elephantine, see Bezalel Porten, *Archives from Elephantine: The Life of an Ancient Jewish Military Colony* (Berkeley: University of California Press, 1968); and Bezalel Porten and Jonas C. Greenfield, *Jews of Elephantine and Arameans of Syene* (Jerusalem: Academon, 1974).

fourth century have been found in the Wadi ed-Daliyeh, and the discoveries in the Qumran caves produced a significant number of Jewish Aramaic literary works.[66] Aramaic inscriptions and texts are known from widely dispersed areas such as Egypt, Arabia, Syria-Palestine, central Turkey, Mesopotamia, Iran, and even as far east as Afghanistan.[67]

By Hellenistic times, Aramaic had replaced many of the local languages—including Hebrew—that had survived the Assyrian, Babylonian, and Persian empires. As Aramaic became the primary language of Judea, translations of the biblical texts, called targumim, were produced and read alongside the original Hebrew texts in the synagogue.[68] Aramaic was probably the primary language used by Jesus of Nazareth[69] and came to be an important language for Jewish literature. The Syriac dialect of Aramaic played a significant role in eastern Christianity as well. Descendant dialects of Aramaic still survive as living languages in a few isolated towns of Syria.

Recommended Reading

During the past forty years, no one has attempted a full-scale history of all the Arameans. The last such work, by Dupont-Sommer, is still valuable. Recent histories deal with more restricted subjects. The Aramean states of Syria are discussed in the fine study by Sader, who covers Bit-Bahiani (Guzanu), Bit-Adini, Bit-Agusi, Sam'al, Hamath, and Aram Damascus. The same area is also discussed by Hawkins. A detailed study of Damascus is provided by Pitard. Reinhold also deals extensively with Aram-Damascus. On Aram Zobah, see Malamat. No general study of the Arameans of southern Meso-

66. On the ed-Daliyeh documents, see the following works by Frank M. Cross: "Papyri of the Fourth Century B.C. from Dâliyeh," in *New Directions in Biblical Archaeology*, ed. David N. Freedman and Jonas C. Greenfield (Garden City, N.Y.: Doubleday, 1969), 41–62; "The Papyri and Their Historical Implications," in *Discoveries in the Wâdī ed-Dâliyeh*, ed. Paul W. Lapp and Nancy L. Lapp (Cambridge, Mass.: American Schools of Oriental Research, 1974), 17–29, esp. 25–29; "A Report on the Samaria Papyri," in *Congress Volume: Jerusalem 1986*, ed. John A. Emerton, Vetus Testamentum Supplement 40 (Leiden: Brill, 1988), 17–26; and "Samaria Papyrus 1: An Aramaic Slave Conveyance of 335 B.C.E. Found in the Wâdī ed-Dâliyeh," *Eretz Israel* 18 (1985): 7*–17*. On the Qumran texts, see Geza Vermes, *The Dead Sea Scrolls: Qumran in Perspective* (Cleveland: Collins & World, 1978).

67. For an introduction to the dialects of Aramaic from the earliest period to modern times, see Eduard Y. Kutscher, "Aramaic," in *Encyclopaedia Judaica* (Jerusalem: Keter, 1971), 3:259–87.

68. A good introduction to the targumim may be found in Philip S. Alexander, "Jewish Aramaic Translations of Hebrew Scriptures," in *Mikra: Text, Translation, Reading and Interpretation of the Hebrew Bible in Ancient Judaism and Early Christianity*, ed. Martin J. Mulder (Assen/Maastricht: Van Gorcum/Philadelphia: Fortress, 1988), 217–53.

69. On the complex linguistic situation of the first century A.D., see Joseph Fitzmyer, "The Languages of Palestine in the First Century A.D." *Catholic Biblical Quarterly* 32 (1970): 501–31.

potamia is available, but considerable information can be found in Brinkman's two works.

Very little has been written about Aramean culture, since so little is known of it. Translations of major Old Aramaic inscriptions may be found in Donner and Röllig and in Gibson. An excellent recent survey of Old Aramaic inscriptions with helpful bibliography is Layton. A comprehensive bibliography for Old, Official, and Biblical Aramaic has been compiled by Fitzmyer and Kaufman. A good general description of the Aramaic language may be found in Kutscher. On the religion of the Arameans, very little has been written; see, however, Greenfield, "Aspects of Aramean Religion." On the impact of Aramaic studies on the study of the Old Testament, see Greenfield, "Aramaic Studies and the Bible." For their impact on New Testament studies, see Fitzmyer.

Brinkman, John A. *A Political History of Post-Kassite Babylonia, 1158–722 B.C.* Rome: Pontifical Biblical Institute Press, 1968.

———. *Prelude to Empire: Babylonian Society and Politics, 747–626 B.C.* Philadelphia: University Museum, 1984.

Donner, Herbert, and Wolfgang Röllig. *Kanaanäische und aramäische Inschriften.* 3 vols. Wiesbaden: Harrassowitz, 1962–64.

Dupont-Sommer, André. *Les Araméens.* Paris: Maisonneuve, 1949.

Fitzmyer, Joseph A. *A Wandering Aramean: Collected Aramaic Essays.* Society of Biblical Literature Monograph Series 25. Missoula, Mont.: Scholars Press, 1979.

Fitzmyer, Joseph A., and Stephen A. Kaufman. *An Aramaic Bibliography,* part 1: *Old, Official, and Biblical Aramaic.* Baltimore: Johns Hopkins University Press, 1992.

Gibson, John C. L. *Textbook of Syrian Semitic Inscriptions,* vol. 2: *Aramaic Inscriptions.* Oxford: Clarendon, 1975.

Greenfield, Jonas C. "Aramaic Studies and the Bible." Pp. 110–30 in *Congress Volume: Vienna 1980.* Edited by John A. Emerton. Vetus Testamentum Supplement 32. Leiden: Brill, 1981.

———. "Aspects of Aramean Religion." Pp. 67–78 in *Ancient Israelite Religion: Essays in Honor of Frank Moore Cross.* Edited by Patrick D. Miller Jr., Paul D. Hanson, and S. Dean McBride. Philadelphia: Fortress, 1987.

Hawkins, J. David. "The Neo-Hittite States in Syria and Anatolia." Pp. 372–441 in *The Cambridge Ancient History,* vol. 3/1. Edited by John Boardman et al. Cambridge: Cambridge University Press, 1982.

Kutscher, Eduard Y. "Aramaic." Pp. 259–87 in *Encyclopedia Judaica,* vol. 3. Jerusalem: Keter, 1971.

Layton, Scott C. "Old Aramaic Inscriptions." *Biblical Archaeologist* 51 (1988): 172–89.

Malamat, Abraham. "Aspects of the Foreign Policies of David and Solomon." *Journal of Near Eastern Studies* 22 (1963): 1–17.

Pitard, Wayne. *Ancient Damascus: A Historical Study of the Syrian City-State from Earliest Times until Its Fall to the Assyrians in 732 B.C.E.* Winona Lake, Ind.: Eisenbrauns, 1987.

Reinhold, Gotthard G. G. *Die Beziehungen Altisraels zu den aramäischen Staaten in der israelitisch-judäischen Königzeit.* Frankfort am Main: Lang, 1989.

Sader, Hélène. *Les États Araméens de Syrie depuis leur Fondation jusqu'à leur Transformation en Provinces Assyriennes.* Beirut/Wiesbaden: Steiner, 1987.

Philistines

David M. Howard Jr.

*Now the rulers of the Philistines assembled to offer a great sacri-
fice to Dagon their god and to celebrate, saying, "Our god has
delivered Samson, our enemy, into our hands."*

—*Judges 16:23*

The Philistines are well known to readers of the Bible as adversaries
of Israel during the days of the judges and the early monarchy. Archeology
provides additional insights through literary texts (especially Egyptian), as
well as material remains. The picture that emerges, particularly in recent
scholarship, is one of a mixed group composed of peoples with different origins and whose material culture incorporated many different influences.

Name

The term *Philistine* (as well as *Palestine*) comes from the Hebrew *pĕ-
lištî(m)*, which occurs 288 times in the Old Testament; the term *pĕlešet* ("Philistia") occurs eight times. *Pĕlištî(m)* is usually rendered as *allophuloi*
("strangers, foreigners") in the Greek versions and less frequently as *phulis-
tiim*; it is found in Egyptian sources as *prst* ("Peleset") and in Assyrian sources
as *pilisti* and *palastu*. Its original derivation or meaning is unknown. In modern English, *philistine* has come to mean "boorish" or "uncultured," in an exaggerated extrapolation from the biblical presentation of the Philistines.

Origins

Biblical Evidence

The Philistines first appear on the world stage in texts from the Bible, which
place them in Canaan sometime around the end of the third millennium or

231

the beginning of the second millennium. The Book of Genesis tells of several encounters with the Hebrew patriarchs Abraham and Isaac at Gerar.

According to the Bible, the Philistines came to Canaan from the islands and coastlands of the Aegean Sea, including the island of Crete. In Ezekiel 25:15–16 and Zephaniah 2:4–5, the term *Cherethites* (i.e., Cretans) occurs in poetic parallel with *Philistines.*[1] In Jeremiah 47:4 and Amos 9:7, the Philistines are specifically associated with *Caphtor*, a term that occurs in cuneiform documents in several languages as *Kaptara* and in Egyptian texts as *Keftiu* and that can be identified with Crete or its environs.[2] That Caphtorites are to be identified closely with Cherethites is also indicated by Deuteronomy 2:23, which mentions the former settling in the areas south of Gaza, the same region that the latter occupied in David's day (1 Sam. 30:14).

Amos 9:7 speaks of Yahweh's bringing up the Philistines out of Caphtor in the same way that he brought the Israelites out of Egypt. This raises the possibility that Caphtor may not have been the Philistines' ultimate place of origin, since Egypt was not the place of the Israelites' ultimate origin either. This fits the datum in Genesis 10:13–14, which has the Philistines originating from the Egyptians, through the "Casluhites." The little-known Casluhites may have been the Philistines' progenitors before the Philistines went to Caphtor, and the reference to their origin from Egypt may reflect that their progeny was later settled in Canaan by the Egyptians under Ramesses III or else that they went to Caphtor from Egypt.[3]

However, we should note that Genesis 10 links the Philistines with various Hamitic peoples, including Canaanites (vv. 6–20), and not with the Indo-European descendants of Japheth from the coastlands or islands (vv. 2–5). This suggests that the Philistines actually were an amalgamation of several different peoples and that the Philistines descended from the Casluhites were different from those who came from Caphtor.[4]

---

1. On the Cherethite = Cretan equation, see Kenneth A. Kitchen, "The Philistines," in *Peoples of Old Testament Times*, ed. Donald J. Wiseman (Oxford: Clarendon, 1973), 56 and n. 15.

2. On the Caphtor = Crete equation, see ibid., 54, 56; Frederick W. Bush, "Caphtor," *ISBE* 1:610–11; Richard S. Hess, "Caphtor," in *ABD* 1:869–70; Gary A. Rendsburg, "Gen 10:13–14: An Authentic Hebrew Tradition concerning the Origin of the Philistines," *Journal of Northwest Semitic Languages* 13 (1987): 90 n. 3. That the term *Caphtor* may be broader than just one island is suggested by, among other evidence, the Septuagint version of Jer. 29:4, which reads "the islands" for the Masoretic Text's "the island of Caphtor" (at 47:4).

3. On the latter, see Rendsburg, "Gen 10:13–14."

4. John F. Brug, *A Literary and Archaeological Study of the Philistines*, British Archaeological Reports, International Series 265 (Oxford: British Archaeological Reports, 1985), 10–15, 46–50. For a similar suggestion, see also Roland K. Harrison, "Philistine Origins: A Reappraisal," in *Ascribe to the Lord: Biblical and Other Studies in Memory of Peter C. Craigie*, ed. Lyle Eslinger and Glen Taylor, Journal for the Study of the Old Testament Supplement 67 (Sheffield: JSOT Press, 1988), 11–19.

Egyptian Evidence

Outside the Bible, the Philistines are first mentioned by Egyptian Pharaoh Ramesses III (1184–1153) in connection with great land and sea battles in his eighth year between the Egyptians and people they called "the peoples of the sea."[5] Among these "Sea Peoples" was a group known as the "Peleset," whom most scholars identify with the biblical Philistines.

The Sea Peoples as a group first appear a few years earlier, in the fifth year of Pharaoh Merenptah (1208), as allies of a powerful group of Libyans who opposed the Egyptian king.[6] Five groups of Sea Peoples are mentioned: Sherden and Lukka (both previously known) and Ekwesh, Teresh, and Shekelesh (all previously unknown). They were foreign to northern Africa, and they appear to have been called "Sea Peoples" because many of them came to the eastern Mediterranean by sea and because they seem to have come from island or coastal areas in the Aegean or Anatolia (i.e., Asia Minor).[7] These (and other) peoples also are called "northerners coming from all lands" and foreigners from the "islands" in Egyptian texts.[8]

The Philistines themselves do not appear until the events of Ramesses' eighth year (1176). At the beginning of the twelfth century, the entire eastern Mediterranean basin was being shaken to its foundations: large-scale migrations were taking place here and to the west as a result of disturbances throughout the Aegean and the Mediterranean shortly after 1200. It is not clear exactly what the initial cause of the unrest and dislocation was; indeed, it probably had no single cause. However, evidence from Italy, Greece, the Aegean islands, Asia Minor, northern Syria, Canaan proper, Cyprus, and Egypt indicates that empires were threatened from within and without, economies were collapsing, societies were breaking apart, political stability was nonexistent, and even natural disasters were contributing to the general collapse of civilizations.[9]

5. The Egyptian dates used here are the "low" dates laid out by Kenneth A. Kitchen in "The Basics of Egyptian Chronology in Relation to the Bronze Age," in *High, Middle or Low?*, ed. Paul Åström (Gothenburg: Åströms, 1987–89), 1:37–55; 3:152–59. There is near unanimity now among Egyptologists concerning a low dating scheme, particularly after the accession of Ramesses II (1279).

6. James H. Breasted, *Ancient Records of Egypt* (1906; repr. New York: Russell & Russell, 1962), 3:§§569–617; John A. Wilson in *ANET* 376–78.

7. Richard D. Barnett, "The Sea Peoples," in *CAH* 2/2:360–69; Nancy K. Sandars, *The Sea Peoples* (London: Thames & Hudson, 1978), 105–15, 198–201.

8. Breasted, *Ancient Records of Egypt*, 3:§574; 4:§§64, 75.

9. See Vincent R. D. Desborough, *The Last Mycenaeans and Their Successors* (Oxford: Clarendon, 1964); *The Mycenaeans in the Eastern Mediterranean* (Nicosia: Department of Antiquities, 1972) [no editor listed]; Barnett, "Sea Peoples," 359–71; Frank H. Stubbings, "The Recession of Mycenaean Civilization," in *CAH* 2/2:338–58; William H. Stiebing, "The End of

The resultant chaos sent many peoples migrating in search of new home-lands. Some retreated from urban centers into hills and desert fringe areas, and some set out on longer migrations.[10] The Sea Peoples were part of the great upheavals, but by no means were they the primary cause of the unrest. For example, the picture reliefs of Ramesses III from Medinet Habu show slow-moving oxcarts, women, and children traveling alongside the warriors and chariots.[11] Since women, children, and oxcarts did not normally go into battle in the ancient Near East, it may have been that the warriors were migrating in search of new lands in which to settle, taking their families along with them, and that they were surprised by the Egyptians in their camps or on the march.[12] Alternatively, some Sea Peoples may have already been resident in Palestine long enough to have established households of their own there. Or, it may have been that there was a warrior class and confederation that merely happened to travel among migrating peoples, but with no real relationship to them.[13]

In Ramesses' eighth year, the great land and sea battles took place between the Sea Peoples and the Egyptians in southwestern Canaan and the Nile Delta. The Sea Peoples coalition was composed of the "Peleset, Tjeker, Shekelesh, Denyen and Weshesh," according to Ramesses, and it also included the Sherden.[14] The Shekelesh and Sherden had been among the earlier adversar-

the Mycenean Age," *Biblical Archaeologist* 43 (1980): 7–21; George E. Mendenhall, *The Tenth Generation* (Baltimore: Johns Hopkins University Press, 1973), 142–73; Sandars, *Sea Peoples*; Vassos Karageorghis, "Exploring Philistine Origins on the Island of Cyprus," *Biblical Archaeology Review* 10.2 (1984): 16–28; Ronald L. Gorny, "Environment, Archaeology, and History in Hittite Anatolia," *Biblical Archaeologist* 52 (1989): 78–96; Trude Dothan, "The Arrival of the Sea Peoples: Cultural Diversity in Early Iron Age Canaan," in *Recent Excavations in Israel: Studies in Iron Age Archaeology*, ed. Seymour Gitin and William G. Dever, Annual of the American Schools of Oriental Research 49 (Winona Lake, Ind.: Eisenbrauns, 1989), 1–14.

10. On the Sea Peoples' migrations, see Lawrence E. Stager, "When Canaanites and Philistines Ruled Ashkelon," *Biblical Archaeology Review* 17.2 (1991): 24–43, esp. 35 and n. 9. Stager argues forcefully for seeing Aegean, specifically Mycenaean, origins for the Sea Peoples, including the Philistines.

11. The plates of Ramesses III's reliefs were published in H. H. Nelson, *Medinet Habu*, vols. 1–2 (Chicago: University of Chicago Press, 1930–32). For convenient sketches and discussion of the land and sea battles, see Yigael Yadin, *The Art of Warfare in Biblical Lands in the Light of Archaeological Study*, 2 vols. (New York: McGraw-Hill/London: Weidenfeld & Nicolson, 1963), 248–51, 336–43; Trude Dothan, *The Philistines and Their Material Culture* (New Haven: Yale University Press, 1982), 5–13.

12. So Sandars, *Sea Peoples*, 120–21.

13. George E. Mendenhall, "Cultural History and the Philistine Problem," in *The Archaeology of Jordan and Other Studies Presented to Siegfried H. Horn*, ed. Lawrence T. Geraty and Larry G. Herr (Berrien Springs, Mich.: Andrews University Press, 1986), 542, 544. See also the evidence below that some of the Sea Peoples were mercenaries.

14. Breasted, *Ancient Records of Egypt*, 4:§§59–82, esp. §§64, 403; William F. Edgerton and John A. Wilson, *Historical Records of Ramses III: The Texts in "Medinet Habu," Volumes*

ies of Egypt (the mercenary Sherden had appeared as allies, as well), but the other four are new names. Very little is known of the Tjeker and the Weshesh, more of the Denyen and the Peleset.[15] As noted above, most scholars identify the Peleset with the biblical Philistines, mainly because of the linguistic similarities in their names and because the Peleset of the Egyptian texts settled in the areas in which the biblical Philistines were later found. We should note, however, that the Peleset are never specifically associated with the islands or the sea, as some other Sea Peoples are; nor in the Bible are the Philistines a seafaring people. Indeed, there is evidence that some of the Sea Peoples may not have come from distant lands at all.[16]

The land battle apparently came first. The Sea Peoples had come by land and sea from the north into southwestern Canaan, where their presence threatened Egyptian interests. The accounts of Egyptian preparations for this battle describe the Sea Peoples as having overwhelmed cities in Asia Minor and Cyprus, heading east and then south toward Egypt.[17] Ramesses met them at the Egyptian frontier. The battle was fierce, but Ramses claimed total victory.[18] The dramatic relief of the battle shows a frenzied tangle of warriors and chariots, dead and dying Sea Peoples, and women and children in oxcarts.

The sea battle apparently came after the land battle, against the same groups. It appears to have taken place in the Nile Delta itself, and here, too, Ramesses claimed a great victory.[19] The relief showing this battle is as chaotic as that showing the land battle: it depicts four Egyptian ships overwhelming five enemy ships, one of which has capsized, also in a furious jumble of ships, warriors, weapons, and prisoners.

Ramesses boasted of these and other conquests in several texts and mentioned the Peleset among the other Sea Peoples that he overwhelmed, although he undoubtedly exaggerated here and elsewhere.[20] Eventually he allowed the Peleset, along with other groups, to settle in southwestern

---

I and II, Studies in Ancient Oriental Civilization 12 (Chicago: University of Chicago Press, 1936), 53; Wilson in *ANET* 262–63.

15. For brief discussions, see Sandars, *Sea Peoples*, 158, 170 (on the Tjeker); 158, 163, 201 (on the Weshesh); 161–64 (on the Denyen); and 164–70 (on the Peleset).

16. Brug, *Philistines*, 18–20.

17. Breasted, *Ancient Records of Egypt*, 4:§§64–66; Edgerton and Wilson, *Historical Records of Ramses III*, 53–56; Wilson in *ANET* 262–63.

18. Breasted, *Ancient Records of Egypt*, 4:§§66–68; Edgerton and Wilson, *Historical Records of Ramses III*, 38–39, 55–58.

19. Edgerton and Wilson, *Historical Records of Ramses III*, 41–43.

20. Ibid., 30–31, 47, 48; Breasted, *Ancient Records of Egypt*, 4:§§44, 403. On Ramesses' historical accuracy, see Barnett, "Sea Peoples," 378; Brug, *Philistines*, 27–28 and n. 84; Barbara Cifola, "Ramses and the Sea Peoples," *Orientalia* 57 (1988): 275–306.

Captives of Ramesses III displayed at Medinet Habu, including a Philistine (second from right), 12th century B.C. (height: 3′ 9″)

Courtesy of the Oriental Institute of the University of Chicago

Canaan, which was precisely the area in which the biblical Philistines were to be found in the following years.[21]

Other Extrabiblical Evidence

Cuneiform and other Semitic documents provide some limited, general information concerning various Sea Peoples.[22] Worthy of note here is a Ugaritic reference to Shikels (i.e., Shekelesh or, possibly, Tjeker) who were mercenaries "liv[ing] in ships" and who were allied with Ugarit. The Amarna letters refer to Sherden and others who also appear as mercenaries in Canaan.[23] All of these are earlier than Ramesses III's time.

21. Breasted, *Ancient Records of Egypt*, 4:§410. In other Egyptian texts, Sherden, Tjeker, and Peleset are found in southwestern Canaan after Ramesses III; see Kitchen, "Philistines," 57 and n. 28; and the references in n. 27 below. Bryant G. Wood argues that the Philistines settled in southwestern Canaan as conquerors, not as vassals; "The Philistines Enter Canaan: Were They Egyptian Lackeys or Invading Conquerors?" *Biblical Archaeology Review* 17.6 (1991): 44–52, 89–90, 92.

22. See Brug, *Philistines*, 29–37. On Greek sources and the Philistine = Pelasgian problem, see pp. 40–43 and Kitchen, "Philistines," 56 and nn. 18–19.

23. See Brug, *Philistines*, 30–33; Itamar Singer, "The Origin of the Sea Peoples and Their Settlement on the Coast of Canaan," in *Society and Economy in the Eastern Mediterranean (c. 1500–1000 B.C.)*, ed. Michael Heltzer and Édouard Lipiński (Louvain: Peeters, 1988), 239–50.

Biblical and Extrabiblical Evidence Compared

The evidence for Philistine origins is complex. Ultimately, it points to different peoples from different times, all of whom came to be called "Philistines." Biblical and extrabiblical data concur in assigning some Philistine origins to coastal areas or islands in and around the Aegean Sea, although neither set of data is very specific. The extrabiblical data also point to the eastern Mediterranean.

The two sets of data diverge somewhat concerning the date that Philistines entered Canaan. According to the Bible, some Philistines already were resident in Canaan at the beginning of the second millennium, while most of the Egyptian evidence places their entry near the end of that millennium. Accordingly, many scholars dismiss the Genesis evidence as anachronistic or erroneous in some way.[24] However, there are other alternatives since some Egyptian and Semitic evidence places some Sea Peoples (if not Philistines per se) in Canaan prior to the twelfth century.

The data also present divergent glimpses of Philistine life and culture. For example, the early biblical Philistines were centered in and around Gerar under a "king" and were not organized into a pentapolis, as later. They were relatively peaceful, in contrast to the Philistines of the Egyptian or later biblical texts. Their names in Genesis (esp. 26:26) are a combination of Semitic names (Abi-melek and Ahuzzath) and non-Semitic ones (Phicol), which may reflect the mixed nature of the group.

Were these earlier and later groups of Philistines related to each other? Theoretically, the early ones could have been the direct progenitors of all of the later ones. This seems unlikely, however, given what we know about the entry of later ones into Canaan. However, earlier and later Philistines may very well have traced at least some of their roots back to Aegean or Anatolian groups. Aegean and Anatolian contacts with the eastern Mediterranean are known from at least the Middle Bronze Age (ca. 2000–1550), and contacts such as the Hebrew patriarchs had are not at all unreasonable.[25]

Furthermore, it is very possible that the biblical term *Philistine* encompassed more groups from overseas than just the Peleset of the Egyptian texts, and it may very well have included Canaanite groups.[26] Their being called "Philistines" in the Bible may simply reflect the political dominance of the Peleset among those who did settle in Canaan. Indeed, excavations

24. For example, R. A. S. Macalister, *The Philistines: Their History and Civilization* (London: Oxford University Press, 1913), 39; John A. Van Seters, *Abraham in History and Tradition* (New Haven: Yale University Press, 1975), 52–54. Cf. Dothan, *Philistines*, 15 n. 52.

25. Kitchen, "Philistines," 56–57.

26. Ibid., 57; Dothan, *Philistines*, 25; Brug, *Philistines*, 46–50; Harrison, "Philistine Origins."

in southwestern Canaan reveal hints of the presence of other peoples besides the Peleset/Philistines, such as the Tjeker at Dor and the Sherden at Acco.[27]

Thus, the Philistines in Genesis and those in the later biblical texts may not have been related genetically.[28] Their common features may have been that both had their origins in remote island or coastal areas to the north and west and that both were to be found in southwestern Canaan, in a region that received its name from a dominant later group, or perhaps even from an early substratum of the population.[29]

History

The most complete written records about the Philistines come from the Hebrew Bible, where they usually appear as adversaries of Israel. No clearly Philistine writings survive, and other extrabiblical references to them are random and incidental.

Early Philistines

Abraham and his son Isaac had several encounters with Philistines (Gen. 20:1–18; 21:22–34; 26:1–33). On different occasions in Philistine territory at Gerar, each one tried to pass off his wife as his sister, for fear that the Philistine king would take her for himself.[30] Instead, in each case the Philistine king acted honorably, the Hebrew patriarch appeared somewhat foolish, and the outcome of each incident was amicable. Conflicts later arose between both patriarchs and the Philistines concerning water rights, but these too were resolved.

27. Avner Raban, "The Harbor of the Sea Peoples at Dor," *Biblical Archaeologist* 50 (1987): 118–26; Moshe Dothan, "Archaeological Evidence for Movements of the Early 'Sea Peoples' in Canaan," in *Recent Excavations in Israel: Studies in Iron Age Archaeology*, ed. Seymour Gitin and William G. Dever, Annual of the American Schools of Oriental Research 49 (Winona Lake, Ind.: Eisenbrauns, 1989), 59–70.

28. Although genetic connections between some should not be ruled out a priori.

29. That is, the term *Philistine* may have come from the Egyptian *prst* ("Peleset") and may have been applied inclusively (if somewhat anachronistically) to earlier groups, or else the term *Philistine* existed in Canaan early and the later Peleset and Philistines somehow became associated with it. See Brug, *Philistines*, 15, 46–50; Harrison, "Philistine Origins."

30. Critical scholars usually see the episodes in Genesis 20 and 26 as variants of one event; e.g., Ephraim A. Speiser, *Genesis*, Anchor Bible 1 (Garden City, N.Y.: Doubleday, 1964), 150–52, 203–4; and Claus Westermann, *Genesis 12–36*, trans. John J. Scullion (Minneapolis: Augsburg, 1985), 423–24. I assume that they are separate events, written about in such a way as to maximize the similarities between the stories; see also John H. Sailhamer, *Genesis*, Expositor's Bible Commentary (Grand Rapids: Zondervan, 1990), 2:185–89. In either case, however, the information garnered about Philistines is essentially the same.

Philistines and the Israelite Judges

During the period around 1150–1000, the Philistines were Israel's major adversaries.[31] The "five lords of the Philistines" were among the nations that Yahweh left to test Israel (Judg. 2:6–3:6). Shamgar the judge killed six hundred of them with an oxgoad (Judg. 3:31). The Philistines were among the pagan nations to whose gods the Israelites turned, to whom Yahweh sold them, and from whom he delivered them (Judg. 10:6–7, 11).

Their major conflict with Israel came against Samson, around the beginning of the eleventh century. Despite Samson's less-than-exemplary character, Yahweh used him for his own purposes against the Philistines, who were ruling over Israel at that time (Judg. 13:5; 14:4). Samson's exploits fall into two segments (Judg. 14–15 and 16), each built around a cycle of offense and retaliation and climaxing with a mass destruction of Philistines.

Despite their setbacks at the hands of Samson, the Philistines soon were engaged in oppressing Israel again. By the middle of the eleventh century, they held a decided military superiority over Israel that lasted for decades. Among other things, they maintained control of metalworking and weapons (1 Sam. 13:19–21).[32]

After Samson, the first of the Philistines' recorded struggles with Israel took place between Aphek and Ebenezer in the northeastern portion of Philistine territory, and it was a fateful encounter, since the Israelites were defeated and the ark was captured (1 Sam. 4). The ark's presence among the Philistines had a deadly effect upon them, so, in response, they returned the ark to the Israelites on the advice of their priests and diviners (1 Sam. 5–6). The Philistines appear to have been aware of the reputation of Israel's God, since they referred to his victory in the exodus over the Egyptians (1 Sam. 6:6) and to the "gods" who had struck the Egyptians with the plagues (1 Sam. 4:8).

The last Israelite judge, Samuel, led the nation in repelling another Philistine incursion near Mizpah (1 Sam. 7:7–11). After a stunning victory, the

31. The date 1150 reflects Kitchen's low dates for Ramesses III and Amihai Mazar's judgments concerning the dates for the appearance of actual Philistine material remains; see Mazar, "Emergence of the Philistine Material Culture," *Israel Exploration Journal* 35 (1985): 95–107; idem, "Some Aspects of the «Sea Peoples'» Settlement," in *Society and Economy in the Eastern Mediterranean (c. 1500–1000 B.C.)*, ed. Michael Heltzer and Édouard Lipiński (Louvain: Peeters, 1988), 251–60.

32. This does not mean that the Philistines introduced iron to the Near East, nor that iron was exclusive to Philistia in 1150–1000, but rather that they—and not the Israelites—controlled metalworking technology and finished-metal products during this period. See James D. Muhly, "How Iron Technology Changed the Ancient World," *Biblical Archaeology Review* 8.6 (1982): 40–54; Dothan, *Philistines*, 20, 91–93; Brug, *Philistines*, 165–68.

land was pacified, and Israel recovered the cities and territory that the Philistines had taken.

Philistines and the Israelite Kings

The next recorded Philistine-Israelite conflict came after Israel asked for and received a king (1 Sam. 13–14). Saul's son Jonathan initially defeated a Philistine garrison at Geba, near his hometown of Gibeah (1 Sam. 13:2–4). The Philistines then amassed a large, well-equipped, and well-organized army to oppose Israel, but they were routed in the ensuing battle at the pass at Michmash (1 Sam. 14:13–23). Saul had continuing conflicts with Philistines throughout his reign (1 Sam. 14:52), and Israel was not to be free from them until David arose as its deliverer.

David's first encounter with Philistines was with Goliath, the Philistine champion who challenged Israel to a one-on-one duel in the Elah Valley west of Bethlehem (1 Sam. 17). He killed Goliath and the Philistines were routed, retreating toward their cities of Gath and Ekron.[33]

David's fortunes rose in Israel as a result, and he had continuing success against the Philistines (1 Sam. 18:20–30; 19:8). They continued for many years as a threat, however. David saved Keilah from a Philistine attack (1 Sam. 23:1–5), and Saul later fought them when they made a raid on Israelite territory (1 Sam. 23:27–28). David twice fled to Philistine territory to escape Saul (1 Sam. 21:10–15 [MT 21:11–16]; 27; 29). Saul died at the hands of the Philistines (1 Sam. 31), and they desecrated his body: his head was cut off, his body exposed upon the wall of Beth-shan, and his armor hung in the temple of the goddess Ashtoreth (1 Sam. 31:8–10).

David then continued the struggle against the Philistines. After he consolidated his power and took Jerusalem from the Jebusites, the Philistines came against him, perceiving him to be a threat. He defeated them in two separate encounters in the Rephaim Valley, just west of Jerusalem and Bethlehem (2 Sam. 5:17–25). In what likely were later encounters, he succeeded in almost completely subjugating them, taking much of their territory (2 Sam. 8:1, 12). Later, he and his mighty men defeated them again—along with four of their giants—in several encounters (2 Sam. 21:15, 18–22).

David used mercenaries from among the Cherethites (who were either Philistines or a group closely allied with them), the Pelethites, and Gath, a Philistine city (2 Sam. 15:18). Even one of his loyal commanders was from Gath

---

33. 2 Sam. 21:19 states that Elhanan killed Goliath. For a solution to this problem, see Carl F. Keil, *Biblical Commentary on the Books of Samuel* (1872; repr. Grand Rapids: Eerdmans, 1975), 465–66.

(2 Sam. 15:19–22). The list of David's heroes attests to the continuing struggles with the Philistines over his entire lifetime (2 Sam. 23:9–16).

Despite their survival in later centuries, David effectively eliminated the Philistines' threat. The five-city coalition was broken: later appearances of Philistine cities show them isolated and on their own. We see them as adversaries of Hezekiah (2 Kings 18:8), Jehoshaphat (2 Chron. 17:11), Jehoram (2 Chron. 21:16–17), Uzziah (2 Chron. 26:6–7), and Ahaz (2 Chron. 28:18). They appear occasionally in the records of Mesopotamian and Egyptian kings who invaded Canaan,[34] but they never figured again as a significant political or military force.

Society and Culture

When the Philistines of the Late Bronze Age entered southwestern Canaan sometime after 1200, they brought with them several distinctives, some of which their neighbors adopted. The Philistines quickly borrowed from and adapted to their surroundings, as well. Philistine society and culture was never purely foreign (i.e., Aegean), but always a mixture of various foreign and local Canaanite influences.

Military

The Bible provides some glimpses of Philistine military capacities; for example, the detailed description of Goliath's battle gear (1 Sam. 17:5–7):

> He had a bronze helmet on his head and wore a coat of scale armor of bronze weighing five thousand shekels; on his legs he wore bronze greaves, and a bronze javelin was slung on his back. His spear shaft was like a weaver's rod, and its iron point weighed six hundred shekels. His shield bearer went ahead of him. (NIV)

Goliath's spear, helmet, coat of mail, and particularly his leg greaves were typical for Aegean warriors.[35] His spear being "like a weaver's rod" probably refers to a leash of cord wrapped around the spear shaft, with a loop into

---

34. See Hayim Tadmor, "Philistia under Assyrian Rule," *Biblical Archaeologist* 29 (1966): 86–102; Nadav Naʾaman and Ran Zadok, "Sargon II's Deportations to Israel and Philistia," *Journal of Cuneiform Studies* 40 (1988): 36–46; H. J. Katzenstein, "Philistines (History)," in *ABD* 5:326–28.

35. See Edwin M. Yamauchi, *Greece and Babylon: Early Contacts between the Aegean and the Near East* (Grand Rapids: Baker, 1967), 43–46; Yadin, *Art of Warfare*, 354–55; cf. A. M. Snodgrass, *Arms and Armour of the Greeks* (Ithaca, N.Y.: Cornell University Press, 1967), 14–34.

which the warrior inserted one or more fingers.[36] When the spear was thrown, it would spin, thus flying farther and truer. Goliath's spear tip was made of iron, as the Philistines then controlled metalworking and weapons. However, by the early tenth century, the military and technological tide had shifted: Samuel, Saul, and David subdued the Philistines, and blacksmiths from northern Palestine began producing carburized iron (steel). Philistine sites show no corresponding technological advances.[37]

Goliath is called a "champion" (NIV), literally "a man of the between" (1 Sam. 17:4). This term refers to a designated warrior from each side who would step out between the armies and do battle; the winner's side would be declared the victor, without an all-out conflict. The practice is not widely attested in the ancient Near East, but clear examples do occur.[38]

We know little else of Philistine military organization from the Bible, except that their forces included chariotry, cavalry, infantry, and archers (1 Sam. 13:5; 31:3). Their officers are called *śārîm* ("commanders") (1 Sam. 18:30; 29:3).

The Egyptian reliefs of Ramesses III also show impressive Philistine personal armor and weapons. Their headgear appears to have been a distinctive headband that held the hair in a stiff, upright arrangement, which some have called a "feathered" headdress.[39] This was by no means unique to the Philistines, however: similar headgear or hairstyles appear from various parts of the Mediterranean, including Jerusalem and other parts of Canaan. Many of the Sea Peoples—Philistines presumably among them—had ribbed body armor that covered their torsos. They also wore tasseled kilts that did not quite reach the knees.

The Sea Peoples fought with infantry, ships, and chariots. Each foot soldier carried two spears, a round shield, and a long, straight sword, and they fought in groups of four. The chariots were pulled by two horses, had two

---

36. A weaver's rod was the block of wood attached to a cord that would separate the threads of the warp so that the threads of the woof could pass through; see Yigael Yadin, "Goliath's Javelin and the מנור ארגים," *Palestine Exploration Quarterly* 86 (1955), 58–69; idem, *Art of Warfare*, 354–55.

37. T. Stech-Wheeler et al., "Iron at Taanach and Early Iron Metallurgy in the Eastern Mediterranean," *American Journal of Archaeology* 85 (1981): 245. See also Dothan, *Philistines*, 91–93.

38. See Roland de Vaux, "Single Combat in the Old Testament," in *The Bible and the Ancient Near East*, trans. Damian McHugh (Garden City, N.Y.: Doubleday, 1971), 122–35; Robert P. Gordon, *I and II Samuel* (Grand Rapids: Zondervan, 1986), 154 and n. 12; P. Kyle McCarter Jr., *I Samuel*, Anchor Bible 8 (Garden City, N.Y.: Doubleday, 1980), 290–91.

39. An inscription over a picture of prisoners wearing such headdresses reads: "Words spoken by the fallen ones of Peleset." On this headgear, see Sandars, *Sea Peoples*, 132–37; and Brug, *Philistines*, 146–47, 150–52.

six-spoked wheels, and were operated by crews of three who were also armed with two long spears. They could only have engaged in short-range combat, a disadvantage against the Egyptian charioteers equipped with bow and arrows. The Sea Peoples' ships were powered by oars, whereas the Egyptian ones had both oars and sails, lending them greater maneuverability, as well.[40]

Cities

The Bible mentions five cities that were part of a unified Philistine pentapolis in southwestern Canaan: Gaza, Ashdod, Ashkelon, Gath, and Ekron (Josh. 13:2–3).[41] Each one was headed by a "lord" (*seren*).[42] Philistine rulers were also simply called "kings."[43] Under these lords or kings were the Philistine commanders (*śārîm*) mentioned above.

40. On their ships (and much more), see Avner Raban, "The Constructive Maritime Role of the Sea Peoples in the Levant," in *Society and Economy in the Eastern Mediterranean (c. 1500–1000 B.C.),* ed. Michael Heltzer and Édouard Lipiński (Louvain: Peeters, 1988), 261–94; Avner Raban and Robert R. Stieglitz, "The Sea Peoples and Their Contributions to Civilization," *Biblical Archaeology Review* 17.6 (1991): 34–42, 92–93. Cf. also the evidence from Tell Acco in this period: Michal Artzy, "On Boats and Sea Peoples," *Bulletin of the American Schools of Oriental Research* 266 (1987): 75–84.

41. For *entrée* into discussion of the excavations at these sites, see the following. For Ashdod: Moshe Dothan, "Ashdod at the End of the Late Bronze Age and the Beginning of the Iron Age," in *Symposia Celebrating the Seventy-Fifth Anniversary of the Founding of the American Schools of Oriental Research,* ed. Frank M. Cross (Cambridge, Mass.: American Schools of Oriental Research, 1979), 125–34. For Ashkelon: Stager, "When Canaanites and Philistines Ruled Ashkelon." For Ekron (Tel Miqne): Seymour Gitin and Trude Dothan, "The Rise and Fall of Ekron of the Philistines," *Biblical Archaeologist* 50 (1987): 197–222; Trude Dothan, "Ekron of the Philistines," *Biblical Archaeology Review* 16.1 (1990): 26–35. On the limited excavations made at Gaza (Tell Ḥarube) in 1922, see Asher Ovadiah, "Gaza," in *Encyclopedia of Archaeological Excavations in the Holy Land,* ed. Michael Avi-Yonah and Ephraim Stern (Englewood Cliffs, N.J.: Prentice-Hall, 1977), 408–17; and H. J. Katzenstein, "Gaza," in *ABD* 2:912–15. Trude Dothan has now excavated the burial ground at Deir el-Balaḥ, near Gaza, where she uncovered a large cache of anthropoid clay coffins; see *Philistines,* 252–60. The location of Gath is uncertain, but scholarly consensus now places it at Tell eṣ-Ṣafi; see Anson F. Rainey, "The Identification of Philistine Gath," *Eretz-Israel* 12 (1975): 63*–76*. However, no excavations have been carried out there since 1899; see Ephraim Stern, "Eṣ-Ṣafi, Tell," in *Encyclopedia of Archaeological Excavations in the Holy Land,* ed. Michael Avi-Yonah and Ephraim Stern (Englewood Cliffs, N.J.: Prentice-Hall, 1977), 1024–27; Joe D. Seger, "Gath," in *ABD* 2:908–9.

42. The word appears to have come from Neo-Hittite *tarwanas* (or *sarawanas*), a title borne by the Neo-Hittite kings, which seems to have formed the basis for Greek *turannos* ("tyrant"); see A. Andrewes, *The Greek Tyrants* (New York: Harper & Row, 1963), 22; Kitchen, "Philistines," 67; Sandars, *Sea Peoples,* 166; Brug, *Philistines,* 197.

43. The Philistine rulers in Genesis are called "kings," and Achish is "king" of Gath in David's time (1 Sam. 21:10, 12 [MT 21:11, 13]). Assyrian records later refer to Philistine kings, as well; Kitchen, "Philistines," 77 n. 125; Katzenstein, "Philistines (History)."

Along with the cities of the pentapolis, many other Canaanite cities were "Philistinized" over time to one degree or another.[44] The cities were well planned and laid out; some were walled (e.g., Gaza, Ashdod, Ashkelon, Ekron),[45] while others were not. Several were very large: Ashkelon, for example, was a thriving seaport more than 150 acres in size. One distinctive building feature was the free-standing hearth (found at Tell Qasile and Tel Miqne [Ekron]), which is otherwise unknown in Canaan but well known in the Aegean and Anatolian worlds.[46] For the most part, however, these were typical Canaanite cities, with short life cycles as Philistine cities: by 1000, they had been completely Canaanized. None rivaled the great cities of the Late Bronze Age, such as Ugarit.

Pottery

Philistine pottery is usually identified as the most distinctive part of their material culture. It flourished around 1150–1000[47] and was influenced by a number of styles, including Mycenaean, Egyptian, Cypriot, and Canaanite.

The most prominent influence was the delicate and beautifully crafted and painted Mycenaean pottery that found its way across most of the Mediterranean basin around 1400–1200. The clay was selected carefully, levigated, and fired to an exceptional hardness at higher-than-average temperatures. The pots were often covered with a fine slip before firing, to make them impermeable. Most were expertly wheel made and very thin walled. The fired vessels were normally buff colored, upon which patterns were painted in glossy red, brown, or black paint. Decorations were mostly carried out on the potter's wheel: characteristic features included concentric circles laid out as horizontal bands, with any pictorial decoration occurring on the shoulder or handle-zone. Typical shapes included the globular pilgrim jar, the delicate high-stemmed kylix, the large pyriform jar, the squat pyxis, and the popular stirrup jar.[48]

---

44. For a convenient survey of all excavations in Philistine territory up to the early 1980s, see Dothan, *Philistines*, 25–93; more briefly, Amihai Mazar, *Archaeology of the Land of the Bible: 10,000–586 B.C.E.* (Garden City, N.Y.: Doubleday, 1990), 308–13.

45. On Gaza, see Judg. 16:2–3; Trude Dothan, "What We Know about the Philistines," *Biblical Archaeology Review* 8.4 (1982): 30–35; and Stager, "When Canaanites and Philistines Ruled Ashkelon," 29.

46. Mazar, *Archaeology of the Land of the Bible*, 317–19. Kitchen also mentions the three-roomed house and the round houses from Ashdod as distinctive; "Philistines," 77 nn. 120–21; cf. Dothan, *Philistines*, 42.

47. Although its influence can be traced in Philistia beyond this time; see Mazar, *Archaeology of the Land of the Bible*, 533–36.

48. The definitive work on Mycenaean pottery is A. Furumark, *The Mycenaean Pottery* (Stockholm: n.p., 1941). See, more briefly, Ruth Amiran, *Ancient Pottery of the Holy Land* (New Brunswick, N.J.: Rutgers University Press, 1970), 179–81; W. Taylour, *The Mycenaeans* (London: Thames & Hudson, 1964), 48–52.

There was a sudden cutoff of Mycenaean imports in the eastern Mediterranean at the beginning of the twelfth century, at the time of the great upheavals mentioned above. In its place is found locally made pottery (known as Mycenaean IIIc) that imitates the Mycenaean style. In fact, even before the disruptions, imitation Mycenaean pottery was being made in Cyprus and Canaan, much of it fairly close in quality to the true product. After the disruptions, the quality deteriorated visibly: the vessels had thicker walls, with cruder decorations, and were often unfinished.[49]

Because the Philistines settled into the areas in which this imitation pottery was especially concentrated, its derivatives have come to be called "Philistine pottery." However, several cautions must be sounded here.[50] First, features of this pottery were extant in the eastern Mediterranean before the wave of Sea Peoples that included Peleset arrived around 1176. Second, it was an eclectic mix of several styles, not just Mycenaean. Third (and not often noted in this regard), despite its distinctiveness, this pottery represents only a small fraction of the total pottery inventories found at Philistine sites—less than thirty percent even where it is the most abundant (Ashdod and Tell Qasile). These data urge us not to focus on too limited a portion of the pottery styles and not to correlate the pottery too directly with the arrival of the Peleset and other Sea Peoples. Indeed, it is a difficult task to correlate directly any particular peoples with material remains (of whatever sort).[51]

Nevertheless, an eclectic Philistine style can be identified.[52] Philistine distinctives include the use of two colors—usually red and black, on a white slip—as opposed to the single-colored earlier Mycenaean or later Canaanite

49. V. M. Hankey, "Mycenaean Pottery in the Middle East: Notes on Finds since 1951," *Annual of the British School in Athens* 62 (1967): 107–47; F. Asaro and Isadore Perlman, "Provenience Studies of Mycenaean Pottery Employing Neutron Activation Analysis," in *The Mycenaeans in the Eastern Mediterranean* (Nicosia: Department of Antiquities, 1972), 213–24; G. Cadogan, "Patterns in the Distribution of Mycenaean Pottery in the East Mediterranean," in *The Mycenaeans in the Eastern Mediterranean* (Nicosia: Department of Antiquities, 1972), 166–74; Jan Gunneweg, Trude Dothan, Isadore Perlman, and Seymour Gitin, "On the Origin of Pottery from Tel Miqne–Ekron," *Bulletin of the American Schools of Oriental Research* 264 (1986): 3–16.

50. See especially Brug, *Philistines*, 53–144; cf. also Mazar, "Emergence."

51. See Carol Kramer, "Pots and Peoples," in *Mountains and Lowlands*, ed. Louis D. Levine and T. Cuyler Young (Malibu, Calif.: Undena, 1978), 91–112; Peter J. Parr, "Pottery, Peoples and Politics," in *Archaeology in the Levant: Essays for Kathleen Kenyon*, ed. Peter R. S. Moorey and Peter Parr (Warminster: Aries & Phillips, 1978), 202–9; W. Y. Adams, "On the Argument from Ceramics to History," *Current Anthropology* 20 (1979): 727–44.

52. W. A. Heurtley, "The Relationship between 'Philistine' and Mycenaean Pottery," *Quarterly of the Department of Antiquities in Palestine* 5 (1936): 90–110; Furumark, *Mycenaean Pottery*, 118–22; Desborough, *Last Mycenaeans*, 207–14; Amiran, *Ancient Pottery*, 266–68; Dothan, *Philistines*, 94–219; idem, "What We Know about the Philistines," 36–38; Brug, *Philistines*, 53–144.

pottery and the division of decorations into discrete areas (metopes).[53] Philistine pottery continued traditional Mycenaean-like bell-shaped bowls, large elaborately decorated kraters (i.e., large, two-handled bowls), and stirrup jars.[54] Decoratively, Mycenaean motifs carried on in Philistine pottery included stylized birds, spiral loops, concentric half-circles, and scale patterns.[55] Cypriot influence can best be seen in the bottle and the elongated, horn-shaped vessel.[56] Egyptian influence is most visible in the tall, long-necked jug, which was often decorated with a stylized lotus that is typical of Egyptian art.[57] Canaanite influence came to be more prominent as the years went by, such that Philistine ware eventually disappeared, replaced by local styles. Local styles that are found in Philistine pottery include the pilgrim flask, the large jar, small jugs, and variations of other jugs.[58]

Language

Despite many isolated possibilities, no clear examples of Philistine language or writing have survived. In the Old Testament, no language barrier appears to have existed between Philistines and Israelites. Thus, whatever their original language may have been, it seems that they spoke a dialect of Canaanite after they settled in Canaan. Only one word in the Bible—*seren* ("lord")—is clearly Philistine and non-Semitic.[59]

Religion

The forms of Philistine religion that we know conformed closely to common Canaanite religion, and their gods were common Semitic gods.

Pantheon. We know of only three Philistine deities, all with Semitic names: Dagon, Ashtoreth, and Baal-zebub.

---

53. Stager proposes (against the prevailing consensus) that even the earlier phase of single-colored pottery should be called "Philistine"; see "When Canaanites and Philistines Ruled Ashkelon," 35–36.

54. Another type of clay object (although not pottery per se) that reflects strong Mycenaean roots is the cylindrical "loom weight," more than 150 of which have been found at Ashkelon and Tel Miqne (Ekron); these were common in the Mycenaean homeland; see Stager, "When Canaanites and Philistines Ruled Ashkelon," 36–37.

55. Dothan, "What We Know about the Philistines," 37; idem, *Philistines*, 96–160.

56. Dothan, "What We Know about the Philistines," 37; idem, *Philistines*, 160–72.

57. Dothan, "What We Know about the Philistines," 37–38; idem, *Philistines*, 172–85.

58. Dothan, "What We Know about the Philistines," 38; idem, *Philistines*, 185–91; Amiran, *Ancient Pottery*, 266–68.

59. See n. 42 above. For a survey of attempts to link other words, names, and inscriptions with the Philistines, see Brug, *Philistines*, 193–200; Joseph Naveh, "Writing and Scripts in Seventh-Century Philistia," *Israel Exploration Journal* 35 (1985): 8–21; Aharon Kempinski, "Some Philistine Names from the Kingdom of Gaza," *Israel Exploration Journal* 37 (1987): 20–24. Cf. Stager's predictions that unambiguously Philistine texts that use Mycenaean Greek scripts eventually will be discovered; "When Canaanites and Philistines Ruled Ashkelon," 36.

Dagon was the principal Philistine god, whose temple figured in several episodes in the Bible (Judg. 16:23–25; 1 Sam. 5:1–5; 1 Chron. 10:10). This god was not unique to the Philistines: he was widely known in the ancient Near East, from Early Bronze Age Ebla to Middle Bronze Mari to Late Bronze Ugarit to Early Iron Philistia to Roman Gaza. In portions of the Baal mythology from Ugarit, Dagon is said to have been Baal's father. Little is known of Dagon's nature or character, however, since there are no mythological texts about him per se.[60]

Ashtoreth was a goddess for whom the Philistines also erected a temple (1 Sam. 31:10). She too was a common Semitic deity, known in Babylonia and Ebla as the goddess of love and war (Ishtar or Ashtar) and in Egypt as the goddess of war. She was also known at Ugarit as a consort of Baal (though his primary consort was Anat) and is seen many times in the Bible as a Canaanite goddess. The Greek form of her name was Astarte.[61]

Baal-zebub was the god of Ekron (2 Kings 1:2–3, 6, 16). His name means "lord of the flies," and it is unknown elsewhere in the ancient Near East. However, it is possible that the name was actually "Baal-zebul," meaning "Lord Baal" or "lord of the (heavenly) dwelling," and that he was called "Baal-zebub" derisively by the biblical writer. The form *zbl* is attested in the Ugaritic texts, and the New Testament preserves the form "Baal-zebul" (as *Beelzeboul*).[62]

Temples. Few Philistine temples are extant. At Tell Qasile three superimposed Philistine temples have been uncovered, as have two cultic buildings at Tel Miqne (Ekron).[63] At each site, at least two support pillars have been found, reminiscent of those mentioned in the Samson story (Judg. 16:25–29). The most distinctive feature of the latest temple at Tell Qasile (stratum X) is that its entrance was at a right angle to the axis of its two rooms: to approach the altar, one had to turn right after entering. The buildings at Tel Miqne each

60. Terence C. Mitchell, "Dagon," in *ISBE* 1:851; McCarter, *I Samuel*, 121–22; Robert R. Stieglitz, "Ebla and the Gods of Canaan," *Eblaitica* 2 (1990): 79–89; Lowell K. Handy, "Dagon," in *ABD* 2:1–3.

61. John Gray, "Ashtoreth," in *IDB* 1:255–56; Archibald H. Sayce and Kurt G. Jung, "Ashtoreth," in *ISBE* 1:319–20; Stieglitz, "Ebla and the Gods of Canaan"; John Day, "Ashtoreth," in *ABD* 1:491–94.

62. Matt. 10:25; 12:24, 27; Mark 3:22; Luke 11:15, 18–19. See Mordechai Cogan and Hayim Tadmor, *II Kings*, Anchor Bible 11 (Garden City, N.Y.: Doubleday, 1988), 25; John Gray, *I and II Kings*, 2d ed., Old Testament Library (Philadelphia: Westminster, 1970), 463; Duncan McIntosh, "Baal-zebub," in *ISBE* 1:381; Theodore J. Lewis, "Beelzebul," in *ABD* 1:638–40; Walter A. Maier III, "Baal-zebub," in *ABD* 1:554.

63. On Tell Qasile, see Dothan, *Philistines*, 63–67; Amihai Mazar, *Excavations at Tell Qasile*, part 1, Qedem 12 (Jerusalem: Hebrew University Press, 1980). On Tel Miqne, see Gitin and Dothan, "Rise and Fall of Ekron of the Philistines," 200–5; Dothan, "Ekron of the Philistines," 28–33.

consisted of a large hall with several small rooms adjoining it; some of the rooms had cultic platforms (*bāmôt*) in them. Such plans clearly set these buildings apart from typical Canaanite temples, which were built with the entrance along the same axis as the rooms. Also, Canaanite *bāmôt* tended to be in free-standing buildings, not as parts of larger complexes. Recent discoveries from Mycenae, the Aegean, and Cyprus show parallels with these plans, supporting the Philistines' links with these areas.[64] Other than these features, extant Philistine temples show no differences from typical Canaanite temples.[65]

Religious Customs. Today, we do not know many specifics of Philistine cultic practices. It appears that they had soothsayers and diviners, like most people around them (Isa. 2:6; cf. 2 Kings 1:2). They celebrated in the temples of their gods, like those around them. They were uncircumcised, which clearly set them apart from their neighbors and made them an object of derision among some.[66]

Philistine cultic apparatus give hints as to some of their religious practices.[67] The most distinctive type of object is the "Ashdoda," a cult figurine found complete at Ashdod and in fragments at other Philistine sites and incorporating Mycenaean, Cypriot, and Canaanite styles. This seated female figurine is molded into a four-legged throne. The figurine's flat torso forms the back of the throne, and it is decorated with typical Philistine art forms.[68] A distinctive cult vessel is the *kernos*, a hollow pottery ring found in several Philistine sites (e.g., Beth-shan and Beth-shemesh), although it is most commonly found in Cyprus. About ten inches in diameter, with small objects such as birds, fruits, and bowls set on its outer ring, it may have been used during a religious ceremony, in which liquid was poured into the ring and then poured out.[69] Another cultic vessel is the *rhyton*, a one-handled ritual or drinking cup with a lion's head decoration. It has been found at several Philistine sites, as well as at Mycenae and Knossos (on Crete) and is pictured on New Kingdom tomb walls in Egypt.[70]

Philistine mourning and burial customs are reflected in the archeological

---

64. Dothan, *Philistines*, 66 and nn. 214–15; Mazar, *Excavations at Tell Qasile*, 61–73.

65. Brug, *Philistines*, 189–91.

66. Judg. 14:3; 15:18; 1 Sam. 14:6; 17:26, 36; 31:4; 2 Sam. 1:20; 1 Chron. 10:4; cf. 1 Sam. 18:25. See also Brug, *Philistines*, 13–14 and n. 41.

67. See Mazar, *Excavations at Tell Qasile*, 78–121; Dothan, *Philistines*, 219–51; Brug, *Philistines*, 184–88.

68. Dothan, "What We Know about the Philistines," 39–40; idem, *Philistines*, 234–37; Brug, *Philistines*, 185–86.

69. Dothan, "What We Know about the Philistines," 38–39; idem, *Philistines*, 222–24; Brug, *Philistines*, 184–85.

70. Dothan, "What We Know about the Philistines," 38, 40; idem, *Philistines*, 229–34.

remains.[71] No cemeteries have been found in the major Philistine cities, but several elsewhere can be related to Philistine culture on the basis of tomb contents. One characteristic mourning custom is reflected in several figurines that have a long open dress revealing the naked body; most Canaanite figurines were completely naked. The raised arm positions are related to those of several Mycenaean figurines, either both above the head or one in the front of the body. The "naturalistic" style is more Canaanite, however.[72] The use of anthropoid clay coffins has been cited as a distinctive Philistine burial custom. However, this was an Egyptian practice, and it has been found in many non-Philistine sites; it was not unique to Philistines by any means. These coffins were similar to large storage jars, into which bodies were placed. The top third or half of the coffin was cut away so that the body could be inserted and the top replaced. Over the face a rough and somewhat grotesque likeness of the deceased was molded in the clay. A few of these coffins (from Beth-shan) are decorated with the distinctive fluted or "feathered" headgear known from the Egyptian reliefs of the Sea Peoples.[73]

Conclusion

In summary, the Philistines were a complex people, incorporating groups and cultural influences from different times and places. Their zenith in world history was a brief period around 1150–1000, during which they were settled in southwestern Canaan. They left an indelible impression on Israelite society and history of the pe-

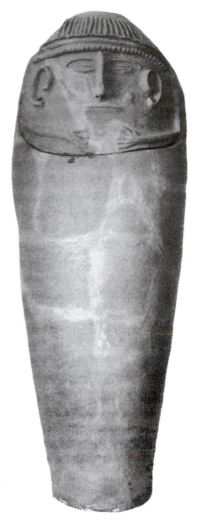

Beth-shan anthropoid coffin, 11th century B.C. (height: 6′ 1″)

Courtesy of the Israel Antiquities Authority

71. Dothan, "What We Know about the Philistines," 41–44; idem, *Philistines*, 252–88; Brug, *Philistines*, 148–64.

72. Dothan, "What We Know about the Philistines," 41, 44; idem, *Philistines*, 237–49; Brug, *Philistines*, 186.

73. Dothan, "What We Know about the Philistines," 41–44; idem, *Philistines*, 252–88; Brug, *Philistines*, 149–52.

riod. To the degree that the Philistine threat was a factor in the Israelites' ill-considered request for a king "like the nations," their influence remained in Israel many years after they themselves had disappeared. The archeological record in recent years has complemented the biblical record by illuminating their life and flourishing culture in ways that the biblical record did not.[74]

Recommended Reading

Bierling, Neal. *Giving Goliath His Due: New Archaeological Light on the Philistines*. Grand Rapids: Baker, 1992.

Brug, John F. *A Literary and Archaeological Study of the Philistines*. British Archaeological Reports, International Series 265. Oxford: British Archaeological Reports, 1985.

Dothan, Trude. *The Philistines and Their Material Culture*. New Haven: Yale University Press, 1982.

Dothan, Trude, and Moshe Dothan. *People of the Sea: The Search for the Philistines*. New York: Macmillan, 1992.

Sandars, Nancy K. *The Sea Peoples: Warriors of the Ancient Mediterranean, 1250–1150 B.C.* London: Thames & Hudson, 1978.

---

74. After this essay was completed, two books on the Philistines appeared: Neal Bierling, *Giving Goliath His Due: New Archaeological Light on the Philistines* (Grand Rapids: Baker, 1992); and Trude Dothan and Moshe Dothan, *People of the Sea: The Search for the Philistines* (New York: Macmillan, 1992). Both are popular overviews of the Philistines, the latter by two archeologists who have directed digs at several Philistine sites. See my review of both books in *Archaeology in the Biblical World* 2.2 (1993).

Egyptians

James K. Hoffmeier

Moses was educated in all the wisdom of the Egyptians.
—Acts 7:22

Egypt, "the gift of the Nile," is strategically located at the northeastern tip of Africa, bordering on Sinai and Palestine. Surrounded by deserts on the east and west and naturally defended by a series of cataracts in the south, Egypt is an oasis sustained by the Nile and somewhat cut off from the rest of the world.[1]

Strange as it may seem, the Egyptians had no single proper name for their land. Of their several expressions for Egypt, *t3.wy* ("the Two Lands") is one of the most common, and the title *Lord of the Two Lands* was regularly used by the pharaoh. Northern Egypt, including the delta, is known as Lower Egypt, while southern Egypt, moving upstream along the Nile, is Upper Egypt. In predynastic Egypt (before 3100), Upper Egypt and Lower Egypt had varying material cultures and worshiped different deities. The Memphite Theology, containing a tradition about the unification of Egypt by a southern king, says that the new capital, Memphis, was the " 'Balance of the Two Lands' in which Upper and Lower Egypt had been weighed."[2] The striking contrast between the rich soil of the Nile Valley and its delta and the vast stretches of desert resulted in the names *kmt* ("the Black Land") and *dšrt*

---

1. For further information on Egyptian geography, see William C. Hayes, *Most Ancient Egypt* (Chicago: University of Chicago Press, 1960); Hermann Kees, *Ancient Egypt: Geographical History of the Nile* (Chicago: University of Chicago Press, 1961); Karl W. Butzer, *Early Hydraulic Civilization in Egypt: A Study in Cultural Ecology* (Chicago: University of Chicago Press, 1976); John Baines and Jaromír Málek, *Atlas of Ancient Egypt* (New York: Facts on File, 1980).

2. Miriam Lichtheim, *Ancient Egyptian Literature*, 3 vols. (Berkeley: University of California Press, 1973–80), 1:53.

("the Red Land"). *Kmt* is probably the most frequently used expression by the indigenous population for Egypt.

The duality found in these terms is also reflected in the Old Testament name for Egypt: *miṣrayim*, which is dual in form. *Miṣrayim* occurs early in Genesis (10:6) as the name of the son of Ham, son of Noah, and is also used of Egypt by other Semitic-speaking peoples in Ugaritic texts, the Amarna letters, and Assyrian records.[3] The present-day Arabic word for Egypt is *miṣr*, a survival of the ancient Semitic root. The Egyptians also called their country *t3-mri* ("the Beloved Land"), which says something about their notoriously ethnocentric attitude toward their country.

The word *Egypt* has an interesting history, deriving from the name of the temple of the patron deity of Memphis: *ḥw(t) k3 ptḥ* ("the temple of the Ka (spirit) of Ptah").[4] The earliest usage of this term for Egypt is found in the Amarna letters (fourteenth century) as *ḥikuptaḥ*.[5] It came into Greek as *Aigyptos* in the writings of Homer and Herodotus and then into English as *Egypt*.[6] The term *Coptic* (Arabic *gibt*) is a survival of the same word.[7]

Egypt's ideal location between the great cultures of western Asia and Africa meant that it was destined to give to and take from these cultures, and thus it had significant impact on the history and culture of a vast region. While the Egyptians might well have been content to mind their farms and build their tombs for eternity, the richness of the Nile and the lush delta made it too attractive to Libyans in the west, Nubians to the south, and Semitic-speaking peoples in Syria-Palestine. Therefore, from the dawn of history, the pharaohs were called upon to defend Egypt. As early as Dynasty 1, Pharaoh Den is pictured bashing the head of a foreigner; an accompanying inscription reads, "The first occasions of smiting the easterners" (i.e., tribes from the Sinai).[8] Throughout Egyptian history, the pharaoh was responsible for the defense of the two lands: pharaohs from the earliest dynasties down to the Hellenistic period are regularly pictured in this defensive posture. Perhaps the last king to be shown defending Egypt in this manner is the Roman emperor Titus (A.D. 79–81). The king's role as warrior, as the incarnation of the god Horus (the "son of Re"), and as high priest of the ma-

---

3. William S. LaSor, "Egypt," in *ISBE* 2:29.

4. Ptah was the creator/artisan god of that region; see M. Sandman Homberg, *The God Ptah* (Lund: Gleerup, 1946).

5. Kenneth A. Kitchen, "Egypt," in *The Illustrated Bible Dictionary*, ed. James D. Douglas et al. (Leicester: Inter-Varsity/Wheaton, Ill.: Tyndale, 1980), 414.

6. Alan H. Gardiner, *Egypt of the Pharaohs* (Oxford: Oxford University Press, 1961), 2.

7. The word *Gypsy* was mistakenly applied to a people originally from India under the faulty notion that they were from Egypt.

8. Emma S. Hall, *The Pharaoh Smites His Enemies*, Münchner Ägyptologische Studien 44 (Berlin: Deutscher Kunstverlag, 1986), fig. 9.

jor cult centers made the pharaoh extremely powerful, especially in the Old Kingdom (2700–2200).[9]

History

Prehistory (before 3100)

The final century of the fourth millennium saw the introduction of writing, thus demarcating history from prehistory. The Nile Valley was home to hunter-gatherers before 7000, and humans in the western oases of Egypt can be traced back as early as the Lower Paleolithic period (ca. 250,000–90,000).[10] These people left behind only stone implements (e.g., hand axes) as evidence of their presence in an area that was by no means a desert then. Middle Paleolithic times saw the introduction of the spear. The bow and arrow likely appeared toward the end of the Paleolithic (ca. 12,000–10,000), preceding its appearance in Europe by at least three thousand years.[11] Ecological changes may have forced these hunter-foragers to migrate toward the Nile Valley to establish the Neolithic farming communities of the succeeding period.[12] In the late 1960s, evidence of the latest phase of Paleolithic humans in the Nile Valley was discovered at present-day el-Kab (ancient Nekheb). Carbon-14 dates for its three levels range from 6400 to 5980.[13]

The Neolithic revolution, marked by the introduction of animal husbandry, agriculture, and ceramics, burst on the scene in seventh-millennium Egypt around the same time as it did at Jarmo in Mesopotamia and at Jericho in Canaan. The next millennium saw the appearance of diverse cultures: from Merimde (at the base of the delta) and Fayum (just south of Cairo, along the shores of Lake Moeris or Birket el-Qarun) to the important sites of el-Badara and Naqada in Upper Egypt. The presence of flint sickle blades, querns, domestic architecture, distinctive pottery, and burials witness a developing culture. Circular, oval, and square pits, sometimes covered by a small mound of sand or dirt, served as the final resting place for the early Egyptians. A wide

9. Henri Frankfort, *Kingship and the Gods* (Chicago: University of Chicago Press, 1948). On the divine nature of the pharaoh, see W. Barta, *Untersuchungen zur Göttlichkeit des regierenden Königs: Ritus und Sacralkönigtum in Altägypten nach Zeugnissen der Frühzeit und des Alten Reiches*, Münchner Ägyptologische Studien 32 (Munich: Deutscher Kunstverlag, 1975); David Lorton, "Towards a Constitutional Approach to Ancient Egyptian Kingship," *Journal of the American Oriental Society* 99 (1979): 460–65.

10. M. A. Hoffman, *Egypt before the Pharaohs* (London: Ark, 1984), 53.

11. Ibid., 67.

12. Robert J. Wenke, *Patterns in Prehistory*, 3d ed. (New York: Oxford University Press, 1990), 376.

13. Hoffman, *Egypt before the Pharaohs*, 99–100.

range of grave goods—the basics for life—were placed with the dead. Most of the pottery, flints, jewelry, and other artifacts now in museums come from the cemeteries of this period.

The predynastic period, comprised of the Naqada II (Amratian) and III (Gerzean) periods (ca. 4000–3100), was a formative period, shaping cultural, religious, and political concepts that would appear fully developed at the dawn of history (e.g., divine kingship). Rudimentary writing began to appear on artifacts toward the end of the fourth millennium.

The cultural differences between the north and south may have taken on hostile dimensions toward the end of this period, perhaps because of differences over irrigation rights. Karl Butzer argues that the emergence of a chieftain was due to a community's need to build, maintain, and control canals and irrigation projects.[14] The Scorpion Macehead illustrates the agricultural ceremonies over which the king, shown wearing the so-called White Crown of Upper Egypt, presides.[15] Sometime around 3100, Narmer, perhaps the legendary Menes, the chieftain (or king) of Nekhen (Hierakonopolis), conquered the northern chieftain. The Narmer Palette may provide a pictorial record commemorating this event, although recent study of the macehead and palette questions this interpretation.[16] Even if these objects do not commemorate Egypt's unification, there is little doubt that the south subdued the north, resulting in the apparent founding of Memphis by Menes.[17]

The political unification of Egypt marks the beginning of Dynastic or Pharaonic Egypt. According to Manetho (a third-century Egyptian priest-historian), Menes was the founder of Dynasty 1, a tradition that finds some support in earlier inscriptions. The name *Meni* occurs first on king lists at Seti II's temple in Abydos (1294–1279).[18] The problem with determining whether Menes and Narmer are one and the same king lies in the use of two different royal names for the pharaoh as early as Dynasty 1. *Pharaoh*, familiar to readers of the Bible, is a title deriving from the expression *pr ꜥꜣ* meaning "great house" (i.e., the palace). Attested in the Old Kingdom, it is not applied to the king as a title until the New Kingdom (fifteenth century).[19]

14. Butzer, *Early Hydraulic Civilization*.

15. John Wilson, *The Culture of Ancient Egypt* (Chicago: University of Chicago Press, 1951), fig. 5a.

16. N. B. Millet, "The Narmer Macehead and Related Objects," *Journal of the American Research Center in Egypt* 27 (1990): 53–59.

17. Memphis in Egyptian is *mn-nfr*, which may contain a vestige of Menes' name in the term *mn*.

18. Gardiner, *Egypt of the Pharaohs*, 49, fig. 8.

19. Adolf Erman and Hermann Grapow, *Wörterbuch der ägyptischen Sprache* (Leipzig: Hinrichs, 1926), 1:516.

Archaic Period, Dynasties 1–2 (3100–2700)

The archaic period, comprised of Dynasties 1–2 (ca. 3100–2700), witnessed the beginnings of significant royal cemeteries at Sakkara (the necropolis at Memphis) and Abydos (the traditional spot of Osiris's burial). The burial structures, called "mastabas" after the Arabic word for mud benches, were large, single-floor buildings, likely fashioned after domestic architecture.[20] The superstructure served as a chapel to preserve the cult of the dead, while shafts contained the burial and vessels with food and other necessities for the afterlife. Writing is found on palettes, labels, seals, pots, and stone and wooden objects during the archaic period.

Contact between Egypt and Palestine is attested as early as Dynasty 1,[21] and Narmer's name has been found on potsherds at Tell Arad and Tell Erani.[22] On the Egyptian side, there is considerable inscriptional and pictorial evidence to show Egyptian interest in the Levant during Dynasties 1–6.[23] Scholars continue to debate the nature of this contact: some regard it as military in nature;[24] others maintain it was purely economic and peaceful.[25] The latter stance dismisses as unhistorical Egyptian militaristic motifs (e.g., those on the Narmer Palette) and attaches no significance to epithets such as *Conqueror of Asia*.[26] However, the two positions are not mutually exclusive. Ensuring Egypt's economic interest in Sinai and Palestine may well have required the use of military force, which for propagandistic purposes could be stretched a bit. This same combination of military and economic interest existed in Nubia during this same time.[27] And during the Middle Kingdom,

20. W. B. Emery, *Archaic Egypt* (Baltimore: Penguin, 1961), 128–64.

21. Shemuel Yeivin, "Early Contacts between Canaan and Egypt," *Israel Exploration Journal* 10 (1960): 193–205; R. Gophna, "Egyptian Immigration into Canaan during the First Dynasty?" *Tel Aviv* 3 (1976): 31–37; Amnon Ben-Tor, "New Light on the Relations between Egypt and Southern Palestine during the Early Bronze Age," *Bulletin of the American Schools of Oriental Research* 281 (1991): 3–10.

22. For Tell Arad, see Ruth Amiran, "An Egyptian Jar Fragment with the Name of Narmer from Arad," *Israel Exploration Journal* 24 (1974): 4–12; idem, "The Narmer Jar Fragment from Arad: An Addendum," *Israel Exploration Journal* 26 (1976): 45–46. For Tell Erani, see Amihai Mazar, *Archaeology of the Land of the Bible 10,000–586 B.C.E.* (New York: Doubleday, 1990), 106–7.

23. A review of all the sources is Donald B. Redford, "Egypt and Western Asia in the Old Kingdom," *Journal of the American Research Center in Egypt* 23 (1986): 125–43.

24. In addition to sources in nn. 21–22, see Yigael Yadin, "The Earliest Record of Egypt's Military Penetration into Asia?" *Israel Exploration Journal* 5 (1955): 1–16.

25. See recently William A. Ward, "Early Contacts between Egypt, Canaan, and Sinai: Remarks on the Paper by Amnon Ben-Tor," *Bulletin of the American Schools of Oriental Research* 281 (1991): 11–26.

26. Ibid., 12.

27. Bruce G. Trigger et al., *Ancient Egypt: A Social History* (Cambridge: Cambridge University Press, 1983), 61–63. On Egypt's interest in Nubia during the Old Kingdom, see G. E.

the height of Egyptian economic interest in Nubia coincided with a great military buildup, to judge from the dozen or so massive forts in the second cataract area.[28]

Dynasty 2 appears to have been marred by a rebellion in the north, which resulted in warfare that was resolved when a northern princess, Nemathap, married Khasekhemwy, the last king of Dynasty 2.[29] Resistance to political unity in Egypt arose periodically in the following centuries, resulting in the establishment of competing dynasties in the north, followed by warfare and then reunification.

Old Kingdom, Dynasties 3–6 (2700–2200)

The transition from the archaic period to the Old Kingdom remains problematic since the lengths of the various dynasties remain subject to debate. The date 2700 is commonly conjectured for the beginning of Dynasty 3.[30] Manetho's 214 years for this dynasty have been reduced to 138 years by recent investigations.[31]

The Old Kingdom, Dynasties 3–6 (ca. 2700–2200), the pyramid era, saw Egypt rise to its cultural apex, to judge from the execution of the massive pyramids and accompanying complexes for the burial of the pharaoh. The concept of divine kingship had been shaped in the predynastic period, and from Dynasty 1 onward, the king bore a Horus name, Horus being the son of Re, the sun.[32] During Dynasty 5 a further development on the royal titulary occurred: *Son of Re* became the new appellation that continued throughout and beyond pharaonic history.[33] Because of the divine nature of the king, it is not surprising that the monarch could initiate massive building projects for the gods and for himself.

With the reign of Pharaoh Netjerkhet, better known as Djoser, Egypt entered the pyramid age. His vizier Imhotep is credited with supervising the

Kadish, "Old Kingdom Egyptian Activity in Nubia: Some Reconsiderations," *Journal of Egyptian Archaeology* 52 (1966): 23–33.

28. Bruce G. Trigger, "The Reasons for the Construction of the Second Cataract Forts," *Journal of the Society for the Study of Egyptian Antiquities* 12 (1982): 1–6. Trigger shows that there is a link between the military (i.e., the forts) and trade.

29. Hoffman, *Egypt before the Pharaohs*, 351.

30. Gardiner, *Egypt of the Pharaohs*, 433; Wilson, *Culture of Ancient Egypt*, 319.

31. Nabil M. A. Swelim, *Some Problems on the History of the Third Dynasty*, Archaeology and Historical Studies 7 (Alexandria: Archaeological Society of Alexandria, 1983), 224.

32. Frankfort, *Kingship and the Gods*, 148–61; A. Rosalie David, *The Egyptians: Religious Beliefs and Practices* (London: Routledge & Kegan Paul, 1982); David Silverman, "Divinity and Deities in Ancient Egypt," in *Religion in Ancient Egypt: Gods, Myths, and Personal Practice*, ed. B. E. Shafer (Ithaca: Cornell University Press, 1991), 58–87.

33. Wilson, *Culture of Ancient Egypt*, 84–85.

transition of Djoser's original mastaba into a pyramid.[34] Surrounded by a wall that measures 1,800 feet by 900 feet, the six-stepped, limestone pyramid stands 204 feet high.[35] Many impressive chambers and chapels still stand within the funerary complex. Subsequent monarchs in Dynasty 3 built stepped-pyramids, but none approached that of Djoser's in size or quality (several are incomplete).[36] While Djoser was believed by many to have been the founder of Dynasty 3,[37] it now appears that at least one or more monarchs preceded him and experimented with pyramid structures.[38]

The development of the true pyramid came about in Dynasty 4, possibly during the reign of Sneferu, although it is conceivable that the last monarch of Dynasty 3, Huni, Sneferu's father-in-law, built the first true pyramid.[39] Sneferu constructed two large pyramids (and several subsidiary pyramids) at Dashur (south of Memphis). The southern pyramid is known as the "bent" pyramid because around half-way up the angle shifts from 54°31' to 43°21' (it stands just over 310 feet high). This somewhat experimental pyramid yielded to a second one, about the same height and approximately the same angle as the top of the bent pyramid.[40]

The Palermo Stone (an early Egyptian king list) records that during Sneferu's reign of twenty-four years he conducted military campaigns against Libya and Nubia and that forty ships bearing cedar (probably from Byblos) reached Egypt.[41] This and other evidence shows that Egypt continued to assert its interests in international affairs in the Mediterranean and Africa throughout the Old Kingdom.[42]

Sneferu's successor, Khufu (Hellenized as Cheops by Herodotus), moved the royal burial site from Dashur to Giza, where Egyptian pyramid building reached its apex. The great pyramids of Giza display the full development of

---

34. Imhotep was deified in later history; see J. B. Hurry, *Imhotep the Egyptian God of Medicine* (repr. Chicago: Ares, 1978); D. Wildung, *Imhotep und Amenhotep* (Munich: Deutscher Kunstverlag, 1977); idem, *Egyptian Saints: Deification in Pharaonic Egypt* (New York: New York University Press, 1977).

35. On this pyramid and the reconstruction of the complex, see J. P. Lauer, *Sakkara* (London: Thames & Hudson, 1976); I. E. S. Edwards, *The Pyramids of Egypt* (Penguin: Baltimore, 1961), 55.

36. Swelim, *Some Problems*, chaps. 2–3.

37. Gardiner, *Egypt of the Pharaohs*, 72.

38. W. Stevenson Smith, "The Old Kingdom in Egypt and the Beginning of the First Intermediate Period," in *CAH* 1/2:145–46; Swelim, *Some Problems*, 17–40.

39. Ahmed Fakhry, *The Pyramids* (Chicago: University of Chicago Press, 1961), 63–70; Edwards, *Pyramids of Egypt*, 90–97.

40. Fakhry, *Pyramids*, 71–97; Edwards, *Pyramids of Egypt*, 109.

41. Gardiner, *Egypt of the Pharaohs*, 78.

42. Donald B. Redford, "The Acquisition of Foreign Goods and Services in the Old Kingdom," *Scripta Mediterranea* 2 (1981): 5–16.

the pyramid complex of valley temple, causeway, upper (or funerary) temple, and pyramid proper. The function and purpose of these structures, especially the valley and upper temples, continue to be discussed by Egyptologists.[43] A funerary, cultic function seems most likely, despite recent theories suggesting that the function of the upper temple was to celebrate "the rituals of divine kingship."[44] The great pyramid stood 481 feet high and its base covered 13.1 acres.[45] One of the treasured discoveries from Khufu's complex is an impressive boat measuring 143 feet in length and 19.5 feet wide. It was probably used during the king's lifetime, but could have had afterlife functions too.[46]

The recent discovery of tombs, living quarters, bakery, and various workshops sheds new light on the workers who built the pyramids.[47] Such information helps us understand the human dimension of these massive building projects.

The arrangement of the Giza pyramids—moving southward from Khufu's tomb to those of Khafre and Menkaure (Hellenized, respectively, as Chephren and Mycerinus by Herodotus)—might lead one to think that these latter kings were the immediate successors of Khufu. However, some inscriptional evidence and the Turin Canon (an Egyptian king list) suggest that Redjedef succeeded Khufu for eight years before the accession of Khafre.[48] The appearance of Redjedef's name on the roofing blocks of Khufu's boat pit suggests that he presided over the interment of his father, which is the role of the successor.[49] But the hasty abandonment of his pyramid site at Abu Roash (five miles north of Giza) and the battered condition of his statues suggest that a rival party supporting Khafre was responsible for the damage and perhaps for Redjedef's demise.[50]

Khafre's pyramid complex is the best preserved of the Giza group. Its valley

43. For a thorough study of the Giza group that reviews the literature and proposes a different interpretation, see Zahi Hawass, *The Funerary Establishments of Khufu, Khafre, and Menkura during the Old Kingdom* (Ph.D. diss., University of Pennsylvania, 1987).

44. Ibid., xxv; James K. Hoffmeier, "The Use of Basalt in Floors of Old Kingdom Pyramid Temples," *Journal of the American Research Center in Egypt* 30 (1993): 117–23.

45. Edwards, *Pyramids of Egypt*, 118.

46. Christine Hobson, *The World of the Pharaohs* (New York: Thames & Hudson, 1987), 76–77. On the boat, see also Ahmed Kadry, "Finding a Pharaoh's Funeral Bark," and Peter Miller, "The Riddle of the Pyramid Boats," both in *National Geographic* 173.4 (April 1988): 513–33, 534–50.

47. Presently only press reports are available. Although she examines the workforce of the Twelfth Dynasty pyramid builders, A. Rosalie David's *The Pyramid Builders of Ancient Egypt: A Modern Investigation of Pharaoh's Workforce* (London: Routledge & Kegan Paul, 1986), also provides an accurate picture of conditions in Dynasty 4.

48. Smith, "Old Kingdom in Egypt," 172; Gardiner, *Egypt of the Pharaohs*, 434.

49. Smith, "Old Kingdom in Egypt," 173.

50. Ibid., 174.

temple is constructed of massive red granite blocks from Aswan, and it stands in the shadow of the sphinx, which is likely the work of Khafre's artisans. Statues of Khafre and Menkaure are among the most magnificently executed in ancient Egypt. Beyond these impressive burial complexes, little can be said about their accomplishments. Herodotus (2:124, 128) preserves the tradition that these two kings were tyrannical, but this may be the result of belief that Khufu employed one hundred thousand slaves to build his pyramid—an assessment that the Egyptian evidence does not support.

After Bakare's brief reign (two years according to the Turin Canon), Menkaure, generally thought to be a usurper, succeeded. His twenty-eight-year reign[51] is marked by the construction of the third and smallest pyramid at Giza, standing only 204 feet in height.[52] Some of Menkaure's famous statues, including the triads showing the king in the company of two deities, were found in his valley temple.[53]

Menkaure's death signaled the virtual end of Dynasty 4. His successor, Shepseskaf, ruled but four years (so the Turin Canon) and was buried in a mastabalike structure located between Dashur and Sakkara.[54] What led to the demise of this once powerful dynasty and the establishment of Dynasty 5 is not certain. There may be a link between the dynasties:

Triad of King Menkaure (Mycerinus) and two goddesses, 2548–2530 B.C. (height: 32.9"; width: 15.5")
Courtesy of the Museum of Fine Arts, Boston

51. Ibid., 175. Manetho's 63 years is likely exaggerated.

52. Edwards, *Pyramids of Egypt*, 161.

53. George A. Reisner, *Mycerinus: The Temples of the Third Pyramid at Giza* (Cambridge, Mass.: Harvard University Press, 1931), 41–47.

54. Gustave Jéquier, *Le Mastabat Faraoun* (Cairo: IFAO, 1928).

Userkaf, the founder of the new dynasty, appears to have been the son of Neferhetepes, the daughter of the usurper king Redjedef, but the identity of his father remains a mystery.[55]

Since Userkaf's claim to the throne was questionable, a number of steps were taken to legitimize the new king. He married Khentkawes, probably the daughter of Menkaure; she in turn became the mother of two succeeding kings of Dynasty 5: Sahure and Neferirkare.[56] Although it is not beyond dispute, the "Tale of Three Wonders" (Papyrus Westcar) might have been composed as propaganda to authenticate Userkaf's rule.[57] In the tale, the sage Djedi informs Khufu that a women is pregnant with triplets sired by Re. Djedi assures Khufu that these children will not come to the throne until Khufu's grandson has ruled. Because Papyrus Westcar is written in good Middle Egyptian, William K. Simpson believes it dates to Dynasty 12,[58] the early kings of which were masters of propagandistic literature.[59] Since Papyrus Westcar would have little political advantage for these kings, one is inclined to think that the section of Papyrus Westcar that legitimizes Fifth Dynasty monarchs is based on an Old Kingdom tradition.

Userkaf built his pyramid, which was poorly constructed and is not well preserved, at Sakkara near the funerary complex of Djoser. After only a seven-year reign (according to the Turin Canon),[60] he was succeeded by Sahure, who reigned twelve years.[61] Sahure, Neferirkare, Neferefre, and Neuserre all built their pyramid complexes at a new site, Abu Sir, situated between Giza and Sakkara. Neferirkare's pyramid originally stood around 228 feet in height and was the largest at that site.[62] Poorer construction techniques and irregular sizes of blocks contributed to the dilapidated condition

---

55. Smith, "Old Kingdom in Egypt," 178.

56. Ibid., 178–79.

57. Translations are found in William K. Simpson (ed.), *The Literature of Ancient Egypt: An Anthology of Stories, Instructions, and Poetry*, rev. ed. (New Haven: Yale University Press, 1973), 16–30; Lichtheim, *Ancient Egyptian Literature*, 1:215–22.

58. Simpson, *Literature of Ancient Egypt*, 15.

59. Adriaan de Buck, "La Littérature et la Politique sous la Douzième Dynastie Égyptienne," in *Symbolae ad Jus et Historian Antiquitatis pertinente Julio Christiano van Oven Dedicatae*, ed. M. David, B. A. van Groningen, and E. M. Meijers (Leiden: Brill, 1946), 1–28; E. Otto, "Weltanschauliche und politische Tendenzschriften," in *Handbuch der Orientalistik* 1/2, ed. B. Spuler (Leiden: Brill, 1952), 111–19; G. Posener, *Littérature et Politique dans l'Egypte de l'Egypte de la XIIe Dynastie* (Paris: Bibliothèque de l'École des Hautes Études, 1956); Ronald J. Williams, "Literature as a Medium of Political Propaganda in Ancient Egypt," in *The Seed of Wisdom: Essays in Honour of T. J. Meek*, ed. W. S. McCullough (Toronto: University of Toronto Press, 1964), 14–30.

60. Gardiner, *Egypt of the Pharaohs*, 435.

61. Ibid.

62. Edwards, *Pyramids of Egypt*, 186.

of the pyramids. Comparing the pyramids of Dynasties 4 and 5 might lead one to think that the power and prestige of the pharaoh had been somehow diminished. In one sense, this is true. John Wilson says, "In the Fourth Dynasty the pharaoh had dominated Re; in the Fifth Dynasty Re dominated the pharaoh."[63] Wilson believes that the Re priesthood at Heliopolis was jealous for their patron deity, whose power was being overshadowed by the pharaoh.[64] Evidence for this theory comes from two areas. Beginning with Userkaf, at least six of the nine monarchs built impressive sun temples near Abu Sir. And every king from Dynasty 5 onward used the epithet *son of Re* (*s3 r*c), perhaps signaling a more humble status for the king.[65]

Only two of these six sun temples have been discovered and excavated (those built by Userkaf and Neuserre, the other four are known only from contemporary textual evidence).[66] Neuserre's sun temple is situated at Abu Gurob, about a mile north of Abu Sir. Built completely of limestone, its focal point was a "ben-ben" or truncated obelisk erected on a raised platform (the "ben-ben" stone was the sacred symbol of the shrine of Re at Heliopolis).[67] The surviving reliefs from the sun temple are well executed. It is fair to say that the cost and energy of erecting the sun temples resulted in the smaller pyramid complexes for the royal burials. Concerning this economic reality of building both a personal burial structure and a sun temple, Sir Alan Gardiner says,

> The strain upon his [the king's] resources must have been enormous, the more so since there is good evidence that the predecessors' foundations were not abandoned at their demise. It is not surprising that the cumulative responsibility proved too much for Izozi [Isesi, Dynasty 5, king 8], in whose time such enterprises came to an end.[68]

Isesi abandoned both Abu Sir as a burial site and the practice of building sun temples. His humble pyramid complex was built closer to Sakkara[69]

---

63. Wilson, *Culture of Ancient Egypt*, 88.
64. Ibid., 87–88.
65. This epithet is used earlier by Khafre, but with Dynasty 5 its use is regular, not an option; see Smith, "Old Kingdom in Egypt," 179–80; Gardiner, *Egypt of the Pharaohs*, 84–85.
66. Edwards, *Pyramids of Egypt*, 171.
67. The temple at Heliopolis was called *hwt bnbn* ("Mansion of the Benben"); see Cyril Aldred, *The Egyptians*, rev. ed. (London: Thames & Hudson, 1984), 108. This same name was later used by Akhenaten for one of his solar temples at Thebes and then at Amarna; see Donald B. Redford, *Akhenaten: The Heretic King* (Princeton: Princeton University Press, 1984), 63, 71–78.
68. Gardiner, *Egypt of the Pharaohs*, 86.
69. Fakhry, *Pyramids*, 180–81.

and betrays his lengthy reign (probably more than the twenty-eight years assigned him in the Turin Canon). One text indicates that this king celebrated a Heb Sed, or renewal of kingship jubilee, which normally occurs on the thirtieth year.[70]

The last king of Dynasty 5, Unas, like Userkaf, the founder of the dynasty, moved his pyramid complex close to that of Djoser at Sakkara. The pyramid complexes of Dynasties 5 and 6 continued to use the layout established by Dynasty 4 at Giza. Unas's complex has two additional features: a 2,190-foot-long causeway and inscriptions engraved within the pyramid itself. Prior to the time of Unas, texts were likely recorded on papyri and have not survived.[71] The walls of Unas's pyramid, along with those of a number of Sixth Dynasty kings and queens, are covered with what Egyptologists call Pyramid Texts.[72] Comprising the most important corpus of Egyptian religious literature from the Old Kingdom, the Pyramid Texts include liturgical spells used in the funerary cult and magical incantations for the king in his journey through the netherworld.

In contrast to Wilson's view, some believe that the power of the king was not reduced during Dynasty 5.[73] However, funerary establishments of high-ranking Fifth Dynasty officials rival Old Kingdom royal tombs in size and quality (e.g., the mastaba of Vizier Ptahshepses at Abu Sir).[74] During Dynasty 4, the viziership and other top administrative posts were held by the king's sons. But this practice comes to an end during Dynasty 5.[75] Thus, while the king ideally was still the mythic son of Re and incarnation of Horus, power was no longer completely in the grasp of the royal family. This trend continues in Dynasty 6, as the kings continue to build humble pyramid establishments in the Memphite region, still the seat of power.

Officials could build their mastabas near the kings they served or in their home districts or nomes. Two Sixth Dynasty officials, Weni and Harkhuf,

---

70. Smith, "Old Kingdom in Egypt," 186.

71. An important discovery of several funerary-liturgical papyri from Dynasty 5 may hold the clue to the origin of the Pyramid Texts and provide other spells not attested in the standard critical edition (see n. 72). These papyri are being studied by Jean Leclant of Paris.

72. A critical edition of the Pyramid Texts was published by Kurt Sethe, *Die altaegyptischen Pyramidentexten*, vols. 1–2 (Leipzig: Hinrichs, 1908). A complete translation in English is contained in Raymond O. Faulkner, *The Egyptian Pyramid Texts* (Oxford: Clarendon, 1969).

73. R. Anthes, "Egyptian Theology in the Third Millennium B.C.," *Journal of Near Eastern Studies* 18 (1959): 180; D. O'Connor, "Political Systems and Archaeological Data on Egypt: 2600–1780 B.C.," *World Archaeology* 6.1 (1974): 16.

74. Z. Žaba, M. Verner, et al., *Preliminary Report on Czechoslovak Excavations in the Mastaba of Ptahshepses at Abu Sir* (Prague: Charles University Press, 1976).

75. Trigger et al., *Ancient Egypt,* 77.

chose to be buried in their home districts. These and other officials recounted in tombs and on steles their careers and service for their sovereign.

Weni traces his elevation from rather humble beginnings in Nekheb, modern el-Kab (south of Thebes), where he started as "custodian of the storehouse," moved on to the robing room of king Pepi I, and finally to chief justice and vizier. He boasts of hearing the case of Queen Weret Yamtes, who was implicated in a harem conspiracy against the king, but he is so preoccupied with relating the king's confidence in him that he never tells the outcome of the case. He led five military campaigns against troublesome nomads in the Sinai and quarrying expeditions to Hatnub (in Middle Egypt), Elephantine (at the first cataract), and Nubia to obtain stone for the funerary estate of King Merenre.

A scout who led trade expeditions to Nubia, Harkhuf also records an informative biography. He became the seal bearer of the king, making him something akin to the secretary of commerce. He was specially decorated by the youthful Pharaoh Pepi II for bringing an African pygmy to Egypt. Included in Harkhuf's tomb as part of his biography, the king's letter instructs Harkhuf to ferry the pygmy safely to Egypt:

> Come north to the residence at once! Hurry and bring with you this pygmy whom you brought from the land of the horizon-dwellers live, hale, and healthy, for the dances of the god, to gladden the heart, to delight the heart of King Neferkare [Pepi II] who lives forever! When he goes down with you into the ship, get worthy men to be around him on deck, lest he fall into the water! When he lies down at night, get worthy men to lie around him in his tent. Inspect [him] ten times at night![76]

This somewhat humorous anecdote shows the human side of the young king.

As we move through Dynasty 6, the influence of the governors increased. In part, because the nomarch's office became hereditary rather than being by royal appointment (which usually guaranteed loyalty to the crown).[77]

The reign of Pepi II, the last significant ruler of Dynasty 6, exacerbated the problem.[78] When crowned, he was but a child, and in his final years he was a senile old man. Both ends of his near-century-long reign, when royal power was weak, provided golden opportunities for the nomarchs to assert their power.[79] Further influence was gained when the Sixth Dynasty kings made

76. Lichtheim, *Ancient Egyptian Literature*, 1:27.

77. William A. Ward, *The Spirit of Ancient Egypt* (Beirut: Khayats, 1965), 36.

78. The Turin Canon assigns 90+ years to him, which makes Manetho's 99 years possible; see Gardiner, *Egypt of the Pharaohs*, 436.

79. Ward, *Spirit of Ancient Egypt*, 36.

various temple estates tax exempt.[80] While this may have had a short-term benefit of currying favor with nomarchs and regional cult centers, it weakened the economic and political base of the crown. Pepi II's long reign posed another serious dilemma: he outlived his heirs. The reign of Nitocris, a woman, marked the end of both Dynasty 6 and the Old Kingdom.[81]

First Intermediate Period, Dynasties 7–10 (2200–2000)

Egypt then plunged into a dark age known as the First Intermediate period.[82] Manetho's description of Dynasty 7 suggests confusion and uncertainty: "Seventy kings of Memphis, who reigned for seventy days."[83] The little knowledge we have of Manetho's Dynasty 8 comes from the names of its monarchs recorded by the Abydos King List. It is customary to allot forty to fifty years for Dynasties 7 and 8, but this is by no means certain.[84] Tombs and funerary steles surviving from this period furnish little historical information.[85]

The Turin Canon shows no separation between Dynasty 9 and Dynasty 10, together commonly called the Heracleopolitan period. During these dynasties, several kings bear the name *Khety*, the apparent founder of the dynasty. Little is known about Heracleopolis, which has been minimally excavated in recent years.[86] The dark age did not end until Dynasty 11, when Montuhotep II, a Theban king, reunited Egypt under his rule.

Middle or classical Egyptian replaced Old Egyptian as the vernacular during the First Intermediate period, and it remained the standard well into Dynasty 18 (ca. fourteenth century) when Late Egyptian began to emerge.[87] One

---

80. Hans Goedicke, *Königliche Dokumente aus dem alten Reich*, Ägyptische Abhandlungen 14 (Wiesbaden: Harrassowitz, 1967). A translation of a decree of Pepi I found at the temple of Min at Coptos is found in Lichtheim, *Ancient Egyptian Literature*, 1:28.

81. Manetho records Nitocris's reign as twelve years in duration; her reign (but not its length) is attested on the reliable Turin Canon. See Gardiner, *Egypt of the Pharaohs*, 436.

82. Recent historians avoid the term *dark age* for the First Intermediate period since some of the finest ancient Egyptian literature comes from this time. Consequently, *dark age* should be used to describe our lack of knowledge about the political or royal history, not the culture of this period.

83. Gardiner, *Egypt of the Pharaohs*, 437.

84. Smith, "Old Kingdom in Egypt," 197.

85. See, e.g., H. G. Fischer, *Denderah in the Third Millennium B.C. down to the Theban Dominion* (Locust Valley, N.Y.: Augustin, 1969); idem, *Inscriptions of the Coptite Nome*, Analecta Orientalia 40 (Rome: Pontifical Biblical Institute Press, 1964); J. Clère and J. Vandier, *Textes de la Première Période Intermédiare et de la XIième Dynastie*, Bibliotheca Aegyptiaca 10 (Brussels: Fondation Égyptologique Reine Élisabeth, 1948).

86. Baines and Málek, *Atlas of Ancient Egypt*, 129.

87. W. V. Davies, *Egyptian Hieroglyphs*, Reading the Past 6 (Berkeley: University of California Press/London: British Museum, 1987), 6–9.

piece of literature composed in this era is "The Eloquent Peasant," which portrays a resident of the Wadi en-Natrun oasis coming to Heracleopolis to trade at the capital.[88] En route, the peasant is robbed of his goods, and he lodges a complaint with the high steward, Rensi, who in turn makes Pharaoh Nebkaure aware of the situation.[89] The peasant's eloquent speeches on justice (*maat*) may have more to do with Egyptian rhetoric than with a historical description of the state of affairs.[90]

"Wisdom for Merykare," a didactic work by Merykare's father, Meryibre Khety, provides further evidence of civil strife between Heracleopolis and Thebes, the new emerging power.[91] The king confesses,

> Lo, a shameful deed occurred in my time;
> The Nome of This was ravaged;
> Though it happened through my doing,
> I learned it after it was done.[92]

This event is probably what prompted the king to say earlier:

> Egypt fought in the graveyard,
> Destroying tombs in vengeful destruction.
> As I did it, so it happened,
> As is done to one who strays from god's path.
> Do not deal evilly with the Southland. . . .
> I attacked This ⌐straight to⌐ its southern border ⌐at Taut⌐,
> I engulfed it like a flood;
> King Meriyebre, justified, had not done it;
> Be merciful on account of it,
> ——— renew the treaties.[93]

While caution is needed in extracting history from ancient literature, it is hard to believe that the king would admit wrongdoing if it were not true.[94] That a monarch would make such a confession shows how far the power and prestige of kingship had fallen. Accepting the historicity of Meryibre's state-

---

88. Lichtheim, *Ancient Egyptian Literature*, 1:169–84.

89. William C. Hayes, "The Middle Kingdom in Egypt," in *CAH* 1/2:465, suggests that this is Khety II, the fourth king of this dynasty.

90. William W. Hallo and William K. Simpson, *The Ancient Near East: A History* (New York: Harcourt Brace Jovanovich, 1971), 240–41.

91. For a translation see Lichtheim, *Ancient Egyptian Literature*, 1:97–109.

92. Ibid., 105.

93. Ibid., 102.

94. Gun Björkman, "Egyptology and Historical Method," *Orientalia Suecana* 13 (1964): 9–33.

ment that his troops penetrated south to the area of Abydos, possibly desecrating the monuments of the sacred city of pilgrimage, suggests that the Heracleopolitans were able to wield considerable clout well into Upper Egypt.

The reasons for the hostility could have been economic. Gardiner suggests that trade from the south was able to flow north because of this incursion.[95] The Heracleopolitan kings certainly would have felt squeezed between powerful southern nomarchs and a significant Asian population in the delta that apparently had infiltrated the region during the waning years of Dynasty 6. In "Wisdom for Merykare" there is specific reference to the foreign presence to the north.[96] The instruction may reflect a push north and south to provide the Middle Egyptian kingdom with breathing room.

One of the most important developments in the First Intermediate period is the rise of Thebes (in modern Luxor).[97] In the Old Kingdom, it was "no more than an insignificant village stretching along the eastern bank of the Nile."[98] During the New Kingdom, it rivaled Memphis in political and religious power. Under the energetic leadership of several nomarchs, Thebes engaged Heracleopolis and emerged as the winner.

Middle Kingdom, Dynasties 11–13 (2000–1700)

The fifth king of Dynasty 11,[99] Montuhotep II Nebhepetre, either began or continued a movement north to secure Middle Egypt under his control. Bearing the name of the Theban war god Montu, this king had three different Horus names, indicating his aspirations and accomplishments as the "uniter of the Two Lands": Sankhibtawy ("He who makes the heart of the Two Lands live"), used at his coronation in 2033; Netjerhedj ("Lord or possessor of the White Crown"; year 14), which may have signaled his northward march to gain control of Upper Egypt;[100] and Sematawy ("Uniter of the Two Lands"; year 39), indicating the reunification of Egypt and the end of the First Inter-

---

95. Gardiner, *Egypt of the Pharaohs*, 116.

96. Lichtheim, *Ancient Egyptian Literature*, 1:104.

97. On the history of Thebes and its development as the imperial city, see James K. Hoffmeier, "Thebes," in *Major Cities of the Biblical World*, ed. Roland K. Harrison (Nashville: Nelson, 1985), 249–57.

98. Gardiner, *Egypt of the Pharaohs*, 116.

99. The time from Montuhotep I through Intef III is approximately 2106–2033, according to Kenneth A. Kitchen, "Supplementary Notes on 'The Basics of Egyptian Chronology,'" in *High, Middle or Low? Acts of an International Colloquium on Absolute Chronology Held at the University of Gothenberg 20th–22nd August 1987*, ed. Paul Åström (Gothenberg: Åströms, 1989). I thank Prof. Kitchen for providing me with a prepublication typescript of this article.

100. Hayes, "Middle Kingdom in Egypt," 479–80.

mediate period. Thus, a little after the midpoint in his lengthy fifty-one-year reign, around 2000, the Middle Kingdom began.

Montuhotep II followed the lead of his predecessors in establishing his funerary estate in the area of western Thebes at Deir el-Bahri. The size of his magnificent funerary temple is testimony to the success of his reign and the revitalization of Egypt. Epigraphic evidence suggests that he moved south below the first cataract, Egypt's southern border, and possibly into Sinai to reassert Egyptian influence.[101]

An expedition to quarry stone for the sarcophagus of Montuhotep IV Nebtawyre left inscriptions at Wadi Hammamat, east of Coptos.[102] Heading up the expedition was the mayor of Thebes and Montuhotep IV's vizier, Amenemhet, who is almost certainly the founder of Dynasty 12.[103] Nothing suggests that Amenemhet usurped the throne; rather, this energetic official seemed most qualified to fill a vacancy. Aware of his nonroyal pedigree, Amenemhet (ca. 1963–1934)[104] took a number of steps to secure his throne and the place of his successors:

1. He utilized propagandistic literature to ensure his legitimacy. The "Prophecy of Neferti," set in the court of Sneferu (Dynasty 4), proclaims that after a period of instability and chaos, Ameny (short for Amenemhet) would become king, dispel the anarchy, and establish *maat* (order and justice).[105]

2. He secured Egypt's frontiers by building forts in Nubia and on Egypt's northeastern frontier. Neferti prophesied that Ameny would build "the Walls of the Ruler," which is the name given to the military posts mentioned in the "Tale of Sinuhe" that comes from the reign of Senusert I.[106]

3. He initiated the practice of coregency with the crown prince to secure dynastic succession.[107]

---

101. Ibid., 480.

102. For a translation, see Lichtheim, *Ancient Egyptian Literature*, 1:113–15.

103. Hallo and Simpson, *Ancient Near East*, 244.

104. Dates for Dynasties 12 and 18–20 follow Kitchen's chronology in "Supplementary Notes."

105. Lichtheim, *Ancient Egyptian Literature*, 1:143. Concerning the use of literature for political propaganda, see note 59.

106. For a translation of Sinuhe, see Lichtheim, *Ancient Egyptian Literature*, 1:222–35; and *ANET* 18–22. The mention of the "Walls of the Ruler" is found in line B/15. For the Nubian evidence, see Gardiner, *Egypt of the Pharaohs*, 136; and Trigger, "Reasons for the Construction."

107. William K. Simpson, "Single-dated Monuments of Sesostris I: An Aspect of the Institution of Coregency in the Twelfth Dynasty," *Journal of Near Eastern Studies* 15 (1956): 214–19.

4. He established a new capital at Itjtawy ("Seizer [i.e., Amenemhet] of the Two Lands") (modern Lisht). It remained the capital into Dynasty 13.[108]

5. He reduced the power of the powerful nomarchs and reassigned nome boundaries to their previous position. The office of nomarch remained hereditary, but now allegiance was clearly to the crown, and the governors were obliged to gather taxes in their district for the king.[109]

These policies contributed to making Dynasty 12 one of Egypt's most stable, peaceful, and prosperous periods. Thanks to vigorous international trade, the Middle Kingdom was a period of considerable wealth, and Egypt began to wield more influence in the Levant.[110] As early as the second half of Dynasty 11, trade via the Red Sea was reopened.[111] There was significant contact with the Levant (principally Byblos) and the Aegean. Mining expeditions to Sinai were a regular feature of the Middle Kingdom.[112]

At his death after a reign of nearly thirty years, Amenemhet was laid to rest in a pyramid at Lisht.[113] The pyramid complexes of Dynasty 12 follow the pattern popular at the end of Dynasty 6. In fact, Senusert I's establishment has been called "a near facsimile of that of Pepy II."[114]

Senusert I, the second king of Dynasty 12, is portrayed as an effective ruler and warrior in the "Tale of Sinuhe," probably written on his behalf for propagandistic purposes.[115] Although Karnak temple in Thebes may have its origin in Dynasty 11, its beautifully preserved White Chapel of Senusert I stands as a tribute to the god Amon, who emerged during this period as the preeminent deity in Egypt.[116] The name *Amenemhet* ("Amon is foremost"), borne by four monarchs during Dynasty 12, reflects this new status. Of the

---

108. Hallo and Simpson, *Ancient Near East*, 244–45; Trigger et al., *Ancient Egypt*, 149, 160; Stephen Quirke, "Royal Power in the 13th Dynasty," in *Middle Kingdom Studies*, ed. Stephen Quirke (Surrey, Kent: SIA, 1991), 123–40.

109. Hallo and Simpson, *Ancient Near East*, 245.

110. James M. Weinstein, "Egyptian Relations with Palestine in the Middle Kingdom," *Bulletin of the American Schools of Oriental Research* 217 (1975): 1–16; William A. Ward, *Egypt and the East Mediterranean World* (Beirut: American University of Beirut Press, 1971); idem, "Egyptian Relations with Canaan," in *ABD* 2:399–403.

111. Hayes, "Middle Kingdom in Egypt," 491–92.

112. Ronald J. Leprohon, "History of Egypt: Middle Kingdom—2d Intermediate Period (Dyn. 11–17)," in *ABD* 2:346–47; Trigger et al., *Ancient Egypt*, 116–48.

113. Edwards, *Pyramids of Egypt*, 218–19.

114. Hallo and Simpson, *Ancient Near East*, 246.

115. Lichtheim, *Ancient Egyptian Literature*, 1:222–35.

116. W. S. Smith, *The Art and Architecture of Ancient Egypt*, rev. ed. by William K. Simpson (New York: Penguin, 1981), 168–69.

new temple built in Heliopolis by Senusert, today only a single obelisk stands surrounded by corn fields as a memory of its past glory.[117] Senusert I won a complete victory in Lower Nubia in his eighteenth year and established an Egyptian military presence as far south as Buhen near the second cataract and perhaps as far south as Kerma at the third cataract.[118]

Under Senusert III (1862–1843), the fifth pharaoh of Dynasty 12, the fortress building in Nubia reached its zenith.[119] His stele from the Semna fortress near the third cataract indicates that he considered this spot Egypt's southern boundary.[120] More than a dozen massive forts in this area defended Egypt's southern frontier and safeguarded its economic interests.[121]

Amenemhet III ruled nearly a half-century (1843–1798). With Egypt militarily secure and economically prosperous, Amenemhet ruled Egypt during its greatest prosperity, surpassed perhaps only by the New Kingdom. No fewer than fifty-nine Sinai inscriptions attest to his acquisition of turquoise for jewelry.[122]

To Amenemhet III goes the credit for completing a land-reclamation project begun under Senusert II.[123] Some 17,000 acres of marshland were drained and made arable in the Fayum by diverting the Nile via channels. Amenemhet built energetically in this area: several temples, colossal statues of himself, and two pyramids. While this enduring and vibrant reign was a boon for Egypt in many ways, the long life of the monarch, as happened with Pepi II in Dynasty 6, contributed to the demise of the dynasty. Amenemhet IV must have been an old man when he came to the throne, for he reigned only nine years and was succeeded by Sobeknofru, a female coregent, who ruled independently for three years.[124]

Historians debate whether the following dynasty (13) was the end of the Middle Kingdom or the beginning of the Second Intermediate period. While a cultural continuity is evident and the royal family that succeeded the house of Amenemhet remained at Lisht, the power of the court began to wane toward the end of Dynasty 13, when rival kings arose in opposition to

117. Aldred, *Egyptians*, 130.
118. Hayes, "Middle Kingdom in Egypt," 499–500.
119. Gardiner, *Egypt of the Pharaohs*, 134–35.
120. Lichtheim, *Ancient Egyptian Literature*, 1:118–20.
121. Trigger, "Reasons for the Construction." On the size of these forts, see W. B. Emery, H. S. Smith, and Anne Millard, *The Fortress Buhen: The Archaeological Report* (London: Egypt Exploration Society, 1979); the fortified area is about 1,650 feet by 575 feet.
122. Alan H. Gardiner and T. Eric Peet, *The Inscriptions of Sinai*, 2d edition by Jaroslav Černý, 2 vols. (London: Egypt Exploration Society, 1952–55).
123. Hayes, "Middle Kingdom in Egypt," 510–11.
124. Gardiner, *Egypt of the Pharaohs*, 141.

Itjtawy.[125] A contributing factor may have been hard economic times brought on by inconsistencies in the Nile, as Cyril Aldred observes:

> Fluctuating climatic conditions seem to have returned to Egypt and caused ir-regularities in the flow of the Nile. High floods, slow to fall and allow seed to be sown at the proper time, were as disastrous in their effects as feeble inun-dations. The manifest inability of the pharaoh to control the Nile may have been the chief reason for another slump in the prestige of the kingship, which is apparent throughout the Thirteenth Dynasty, with a host of pharaohs each ruling in obscurity for a short time and leaving few monuments behind him.[126]

Second Intermediate Period, Dynasties 14–17 (1700–1540)

By the end of Dynasty 13, Egypt had slipped into its second major period of political turmoil, an "intermediate" period between the Middle Kingdom and New Kingdom, also described as the "Hyksos period" because Dynas-ties 15–17 were ruled by the Hyksos according to Manetho. "Who are the Hyksos?" and "where did they come from?" are questions that have vexed historians for centuries. Jewish historian Josephus (*Against Apion* 1:75, 78) quotes Manetho:

> Tutimaeus. In his reign, I know not why, a blast of God's displeasure broke upon us. A people of ignoble origin from the east, whose coming was unfore-seen, had the audacity to invade the country, which they mastered by main force without difficulty or even a battle. . . . Having discovered in the Sethroite nome a city very favorably situated on the east of the Bubastis arm of the river, called after some ancient theological tradition Auaris.

Manetho interpreted the term *Hyksos* to mean "king-shepherds," which re-flects a garbled understanding of *ḥḳȝ ḫȝswt* ("foreign ruler[s]"), which indeed they were. Manetho's claim of a Hyksos invasion and subjugation of Egypt is commonly interpreted this way: owing to the presence in the delta of Asi-atics (i.e., Semitic-speaking people from Syria-Palestine) and the breakdown of Egypt's defenses, more people infiltrated from the Levant and eventually took over.[127] For example, Manfred Bietak, the excavator of Tell ed-Dabʿa (most likely Avaris), suggests "a kind of exodus by Byblites to the Eastern

125. Quirke, "Royal Power," 125–26.
126. Aldred, *Egyptians*, 131.
127. This scenario is espoused by William C. Hayes, "Egypt: From the Death of Ammen-emes III to Seqenenre II," in *CAH* 2/1:54–60; John Van Seters, *The Hyksos: A New Investigation* (New Haven: Yale University Press, 1966); T. Säve Söderbergh, "The Hyksos Rule in Egypt," *Journal of Egyptian Archaeology* 37 (1951): 53–71; Gardiner, *Egypt of the Pharaohs*, 157.

Delta, particularly to Tell ed-Dabᶜa, where their own people had already strongly established themselves on most advantageous terms against the background of the declining 13th Dynasty." On the other hand, Donald B. Redford vigorously argues for a genuine foreign invasion that swept the Hyksos to power, thus supporting the Manethonian tradition.[128]

The nature of the Hyksos arrival remains unresolved, but there is a growing consensus that their place of origin was Syria-Palestine.[129] Based on ceramic evidence, Bietak believes it could be Phoenicia (i.e., the Byblos region).[130] And whether they came by force or by default, the precise date of the beginning of Hyksos rule also remains problematic. However, the dating of their expulsion from Egypt is well established. Ahmose I acceded to the throne in Thebes around 1550,[131] but his defeat of Avaris did not occur until his fifteenth regnal year (1535).[132] According to Redford's understanding of the Turin Canon, only 108 years can be accounted for and only eight true kings can be correlated between the king lists and epigraphic remains.[133] Thus it appears that the Hyksos domination of Egypt during the Second Intermediate period was just over a century in length.

New Kingdom, Dynasties 18–20 (1550–1100)

The liberation of Egypt and its eventual reunification under Ahmose I appear to go back to the Seventeenth Dynasty Theban ruler Seqenenre Tao II. The Late Egyptian "Story of Apophis and Seqenenre" suggests that hostilities toward the north began with this king. This may be confirmed by the shattered remains of Seqenenre's skull, careful investigation of which reveals wounds consistent with those caused by Hyksos weapons.[134] His legacy as a freedom

---

128. Manfred Bietak, "Canaanites in the Eastern Nile Delta," in *Egypt, Israel, Sinai: Archaeological and Historical Relationships in the Biblical Period*, ed. Anson F. Rainey (Jerusalem: Tel Aviv University Press, 1987), 52; Donald B. Redford, "The Hyksos Invasion in History and Tradition," *Orientalia* 39 (1970): 1–51; idem, *Egypt, Canaan, and Israel in Ancient Times* (Princeton: Princeton University Press, 1992), 101–6; and idem, "Hyksos (History)," in *ABD* 3:341–44.

129. Redford, *Egypt, Canaan, and Israel*, 114–15.

130. Bietak, "Canaanites in the Eastern Nile Delta," 46–55. James M. Weinstein ("Hyksos (Archaeology)," in *ABD* 3:345) is not compelled by the Syrian/Byblian origin averred by Bietak.

131. Kitchen, "Supplementary Notes," 42; Redford, "Hyksos (History)," 343–44.

132. Claude Vandersleyen, *Les Guerres d'Amosis* (Brussels: Foundation Egyptologique Reine Elisabeth, 1971), 34.

133. Redford, *Egypt, Canaan and Israel*, 106–11.

134. Thomas G. H. James, "Egypt: From the Expulsion of the Hyksos to Amenophis I," in *CAH* 2/1:289; George Steindorff and Keith C. Seele, *When Egypt Ruled the East*, rev. ed. (Chicago: University of Chicago Press, 1957), 27–29; J. E. Harris and K. R. Weeks, *X-Raying the Pharaohs* (New York: Scribner, 1973), 29; Manfred Bietak and E. Strouhal, "Die Todesumstände des Pharaos Seqenenre (17. Dynastie)," *Annual of the Natural History Museum, Vienna* 78 (1974): 29–52.

fighter was passed to his son Kamose: Karnak steles boast of Kamose's success against Apophis at Avaris.[135] Since it was left to Ahmose to dislodge the Hyksos from Avaris, it appears that Kamose had only marginal success, perhaps reclaiming areas of Middle Egypt under Hyksos control.[136] If Claude Vandersleyen is correct in allotting four years until Ahmose achieved victory,[137] then the time from Seqenenre's initial attempts until the Hyksos defeat might have taken decades.[138] Because of his successful conquests, Ahmose is generally credited with being the founder of Dynasty 18 (even though he is related to the Theban Dynasty 17) and the New Kingdom.

For the past half century it has been thought that Ahmose and his successors, especially Amenhotep I and Thutmose I, were largely responsible for bringing the Middle Bronze Age in Palestine to a conclusion, with the devastation of twenty or more major city-states.[139] However, in the past decade serious questions have been raised about this interpretation of the Egyptian historical records and the Palestinian archeological record.[140] While the traditional explanation for the end of Middle Bronze Age in Palestine is certainly plausible, it lacks the support of Egyptian sources. My challenge of the generally accepted understanding of the end of the Middle Bronze Age touched off a heated discussion.[141] The general consensus is that the Egyptians tried to

135. L. Habachi, *The Second Stela of Kamose and His Struggle against the Hyksos Ruler and His Capital* (Glückstadt: Augustin, 1972).

136. James, "Egypt," 289–93. For the military aspects of this campaign, see Alan R. Schulman, "Chariots, Chariotry and the Hyksos," *Journal of the Society for the Study of Egyptian Antiquities* 10 (1980): 105–53.

137. Vandersleyen, *Les Guerres d'Amosis*, 40.

138. Donald B. Redford, "Contact between Egypt and Jordan in the New Kingdom," in *Studies in the History and Archaeology of Jordan*, ed. Adnan Hadidi (Amman: Department of Antiquities, 1982), 1:117.

139. See James M. Weinstein, "The Egyptian Empire in Palestine: A Reassessment," *Bulletin of the American Schools of Oriental Research* 241 (1981): 1–28.

140. James K. Hoffmeier, "Reconsidering Egypt's Part in the Termination of the Middle Bronze Age in Palestine," *Levant* 21 (1989): 181–93. My article provides a historical review of this debate and offers a new analysis of key Egyptian terms describing sieges and demolition of cities.

141. William G. Dever, "'Hyksos,' Egyptian Destructions, and the End of the Palestinian Middle Bronze Age," *Levant* 22 (1990): 75–81; James K. Hoffmeier, "Some Thoughts on William G. Dever's '"Hyksos," Egyptian Destructions, and the End of the Palestinian Middle Bronze Age,'" *Levant* 22 (1990): 83–89; James M. Weinstein, "Egypt and the Middle Bronze IIC/Late Bronze IA Transition," *Levant* 23 (1991): 105–15; and James K. Hoffmeier, "James Weinstein's 'Egypt and the Middle Bronze IIC/Late Bronze IA Transition,'" *Levant* 23 (1991): 117–24. In support of my position see Piotr Bienkowski, "The Division of Middle Bronze IIB–C in Palestine," *Levant* 21 (1989): 176 n. 7; Manfred Bietak, "The Middle Bronze Age of the Levant—A New Approach to Relative and Absolute Chronology," in *High, Middle or Low? Acts of an International Colloquium on Absolute Chronology Held at the University of Gothenburg 20th–22nd August 1987*, ed. Paul Åström (Gothenburg: Åströms, 1989), 3:107 n. 133; and Redford, *Egypt, Canaan and Israel*, 138–40.

control the coastal areas (which permitted the empire-minded monarchs of Dynasty 18 to have access to key ports) and the Via Maris (the coastal highway) up to Phoenicia and points east into Syria. There is little archeological and no epigraphic evidence to place Egyptian military actions in the hill country of Ephraim and Judea.[142] Thutmose I and Thutmose III campaigned north to the Euphrates, and the latter crossed the great river to take on the Mitannians, whose rising power posed a threat to Egyptian hegemony in the Levant.[143]

Egypt's empire extended south into Nubia and north into Syria-Palestine. Just as Egypt had virtually colonized Nubia during the Middle Kingdom, the Theban kings now realized the economic benefits of once again controlling Nubia. As early as Ahmose I's reign, Egyptian troops marched south to reassert Egyptian influence, and Amenhotep I concentrated on securing Ahmose's gains. Various titles—"King's Son of Cush," "Commandant of (Fort) Buhen," and "Overseer of Southern Lands"—indicate a significant bureaucracy governing Nubia.[144]

Before Thutmose III was able to secure the throne and establish Egypt's empire, he had to watch from the sidelines as coregent while his aunt, Hatshepsut, wife of Thutmose II and daughter of Thutmose I, ruled for twenty-one years.[145] For two decades Egypt enjoyed prosperity and peace under this dowager queen. She built extensively at Karnak in the Theban area, including temples and two towering 97-foot obelisks made of single pieces of granite. The one that still stands is inscribed with all the titles of kingship and with her speech to the patron of Thebes, Amon, for whom she built.[146] Her impressive funerary temple at Deir el-Bahri in western Thebes records many of her achievements, including a celebrated expedition to the mysterious land of Punt to obtain gold and incense.[147]

Only a matter of weeks after Hatshepsut's demise, Thutmose III launched his first campaign into western Asia because of a rebellious coalition rallied at Megiddo by the king of Kadesh.[148] Between his twenty-second and forty-

142. Hoffmeier, "Reconsidering Egypt's Part," 190.

143. For a documentation of these sorties, see ibid., 182–88; Donald B. Redford, "A Gate Inscription from Karnak and Egyptian Involvement in Western Asia during the Early 18th Dynasty," *Journal of the American Oriental Society* 99 (1979): 270–87; idem, "Contact between Egypt and Jordan," 115–19; idem, *Egypt, Canaan and Israel*, 138–40.

144. Gardiner, *Egypt of the Pharaohs*, 169–70.

145. William C. Hayes, "Egypt: Internal Affairs from Tuthmosis I to the Death of Amenophis III," in *CAH* 2/1:316–17.

146. Lichtheim, *Ancient Egyptian Literature*, 2:25–29.

147. See Édouard Naville, *The Temple of Deir el-Bahri*, vols. 3–4 (London: Quaritch, 1898–1908).

148. W. J. Murnane, "Rhetorical History? The Beginning of Thutmose III's First Campaign to Western Asia," *Journal of the American Research Center in Egypt* 26 (1989): 183–89.

second regnal years, Thutmose III sent expeditions into the Levant nearly every year to collect taxes or to establish order. Thutmose III's annals were inscribed on the walls of his Karnak temple at Thebes.[149]

Under the succeeding kings, Amenhotep II, Thutmose IV, and Amenhotep III, Egypt's interests in Syria-Palestine and Nubia were maintained, and commercial contact with the Aegean was established. The resulting booty, tribute, and trade brought incredible wealth and prosperity to Egypt. Beginning with Thutmose I, the kings of the New Kingdom were buried in lavishly decorated tombs in the Valley of the Kings in western Thebes, while massive funerary temples and estates were built at the edge of the flood plain. Little remains of the mortuary establishments of the early Eighteenth Dynasty pharaohs in this area. Of Amenhotep III's temple, only the famous Colossi of Memnon (actually statues of Amenhotep III) stand at what was the entrance to his temple, while a few blocks are found at the rear of the temple along with a large stele that chronicled his many building accomplishments.[150] During Amenhotep III's thirty-eight-year reign, he built a new palace at Malqata (western Thebes), an adjacent lake (or harbor) that measured 6,200 feet by 1,200 feet,[151] and temples at Karnak, Luxor, and Nubia. Amenhotep III's political marriages saw Mitanni and Babylonian princesses come to Egypt. While the practice of diplomatic marriage precedes this period, during Dynasties 18 and 19 it was especially used to solidify diplomatic ties throughout the realm.[152]

Born during this heyday of the empire period, Amenhotep IV succeeded his father around 1353. Shortly after his accession he changed his name to Akhenaten and elevated Aten, the visible image of the sun, to a place of supremacy and closed the temples of other deities. During his first five years he built an extensive temple complex for Aten at Karnak called *pr-itn* ("the domain of the Aten"). After his death, these temples were unceremoniously dismantled and many of the blocks reused in other building projects.[153] The

149. Kurt Sethe, *Urkunden der 18. Dynastie* (Berlin: Akademie Verlag, 1961), 647–734. Portions of the annals are translated in *ANET* 234–38 and Lichtheim, *Ancient Egyptian Literature*, 2:29–35.

150. Lichtheim, *Ancient Egyptian Literature*, 2:43–48.

151. Gardiner, *Egypt of the Pharaohs*, 206–7.

152. Alan R. Schulman, "Diplomatic Marriage in the Egyptian New Kingdom," *Journal of Near Eastern Studies* 38 (1979): 177–93.

153. For the excavations of the Akhenaten Temple Project, see Donald B. Redford, *Akhenaten the Heretic King* (Princeton: Princeton University Press, 1984), chaps. 5–8; R. W. Smith, Donald B. Redford, et al., *Akhenaten Temple Project*, vol. 1 (Warminster: Aris & Phillips, 1976); and Donald B. Redford (ed.), *Akhenaten Temple Project*, vol. 2, Aegypti Texta Propositaque 1 (Toronto: University of Toronto Press, 1988).

Karnak temples were found in 1975–76 in the area where a number of colossal statues of Akhenaten had been discovered in 1922.[154]

For about a decade Akhenaten relocated his capital to what is now modern el-Amarna, a site north of Thebes in Middle Egypt. According to the boundary steles that surrounded this capital (inscribed in his sixth year), he dedicated this area to Aten and declared his intention to stay there the rest of his life.[155]

Irrespective of whether Akhenaten was a monotheist, his expression of Aten worship had some unique elements (as the famous "Hymn to Aten" attests), but it drew largely on Old Kingdom solar theology.[156] Akhenaten's concern with religious matters and building projects may have prevented his maintaining firm control in Palestine, since his "preoccupation in his intellectual revolution permitted . . . disintegration."[157] To be sure, the disintegration began as early as Amenhotep II; nevertheless, Akhenaten is blamed for letting the empire slip away. The Amarna letters from Egyptian vassal-kings in Palestine and Syria and from rulers in Anatolia and Mesopotamia indicate internecine strife in the Levant.[158] Since we do not have the Egyptian responses to these requests for help, it is generally assumed that Akhenaten did nothing.[159] However, Alan R. Schulman maintains that Akhenaten initiated military activity beyond Egypt's borders,[160] a view reinforced by the discovery of reliefs at Karnak showing battle scenes with Hittites.[161] Akhenaten apparently was not negligent in maintaining the empire, but sent his general, Horemhab, on military missions.

154. Redford, *Akhenaten the Heretic King*, 89.

155. Lichtheim, *Ancient Egyptian Literature*, 2:48–51.

156. James K. Hoffmeier, "Hymns to Aten: Their Antecedents and Implications," in *Tell el-Amarna, 1887–1987*, ed. Barry Beitzel and Gordon D. Young (Winona Lake, Ind.: Eisenbrauns, forthcoming). This volume will contain many essays on the Amarna period in Egypt and Palestine, including several papers dealing with the famous Amarna letters.

157. Wilson, *Culture of Ancient Egypt*, 230.

158. Some of the letters are translated in *ANET*; a complete authoritative translation of the letters is William L. Moran's *Les Lettres d'el-Amarna: Correspondance Diplomatique du Pharaon* (Paris: Cerf, 1987), now available in English: *The Amarna Letters* (Baltimore: Johns Hopkins University Press, 1992).

159. Robert North, "Akhenaten Secularized?" *Biblica* 58 (1977): 249–52; Cyril Aldred, *Akhenaten Pharaoh of Egypt: A New Study* (London: Thames & Hudson, 1968), 65–68.

160. Alan R. Schulman, "Some Observations on the Military Background to the Amarna Period," *Journal of the American Research Center in Egypt* 3 (1964): 51–69; idem, "The Nubian War of Akhenaten," in *L'Égyptologie en 1979: Axes Prioritaires de Recherches* (Paris: CNRS, 1982), 1:307–11.

161. Alan R. Schulman, "Hittites, Helmets and Amarna: Akhenaten's First Hittite War," in *Akhenaten Temple Project*, vol. 2, ed. Donald B. Redford, Aegypti Texta Propositaque 1 (Toronto: University of Toronto Press, 1988), 53–79. Schulman firmly believes that the reliefs belong to Akhenaten, although he refers to scholars who maintain that they belong to Tutankhamun.

Because Akhenaten was branded a heretic, much information about him and his immediate successors (Smenkhkare, Tutankhamun, and Ay) has been lost. King lists (e.g., the Abydos list) skip over these four kings. In the same way that Akhenaten and his iconoclastic followers hacked out the name of Amon and other gods from monuments, so Horemhab eradicated the memory of the Amarna kings. Tutankhamun apparently sought to restore relations with the Amon priests in Thebes and reopen the temples.[162] If it were not for the discovery of the tomb of Tutankhamun with its splendid contents, very little would be known about this king.

Although not related to the royal family, Horemhab (Akhenaten's general) took the throne and is usually listed as the last king of Dynasty 18. He apparently lacked a male heir, and so the torch passed to an elderly military colleague, Ramesses, whose origin was in the delta. Although Ramesses reigned only sixteen months, he was the founder of Dynasty 19, which ran from 1295 to 1187.[163] The practice of burying kings in the Valley of the Kings (traced to Thutmose I) continued with Ramesses I down to the end of Dynasty 20 in 1069.[164]

Seti I was an energetic king who placed Egypt on a track like his empire-minded predecessors Thutmose III and Amenhotep II. His building at Karnak included work on the famed Hypostyle Hall, which was begun under Horemhab and continued briefly under Ramesses I.[165] One of its walls records numerous scenes of Seti's military campaigns into Syria-Palestine.[166] Seti built a summer palace at Avaris in the shadow of the old Hyksos capital.[167] He also built a magnificent cenotaph at Abydos, which contains the famous Abydos King List.

Ramesses II (the Great) succeeded Seti and went on to become one of Egypt's most celebrated monarchs and one of its most prolific builders. Characterized by their grand size, his temples can be found from the delta to Nubia, including the famous Abu Simbel temples that had to be relocated during

---

162. Tutankhamun's stele documenting this restoration was usurped by Horemhab; see *ANET* 251–52.

163. Kenneth A. Kitchen, *Pharaoh Triumphant: The Life and Times of Ramesses II* (Warminster: Aris & Phillips, 1982), 18–20.

164. On the Valley of the Kings, see C. N. Reeves, *The Valley of the Kings: The Decline of the Royal Necropolis* (London/New York: Kegan Paul, 1990); idem (ed.), *After Tutankhamun: Research and Excavation in the Valley of the Kings* (London/New York: Kegan Paul, 1992).

165. Gardiner, *Egypt of the Pharaohs*, 245, 255.

166. For a historical interpretation of these reliefs, see W. J. Murnane, *The Road to Kadesh: A Historical Interpretation of the Battle Reliefs of King Sety I at Karnak*, 2d ed., Studies in Ancient Oriental Civilization 42 (Chicago: Oriental Institute, 1990).

167. Raymond O. Faulkner, "Egypt: From the Inception of the Nineteenth Dynasty to the Death of Ramesses III," in *CAH* 2/2:222.

Seti I (Dynasty 19) bowing before the god Thoth, 1294–1279 B.C. (height: 30.3″; width: 42.4″)
Courtesy of the Cincinnati Art Museum, John J. Emery Fund

the Nubian salvage campaign in the 1960s.[168] While Thebes and Memphis remained capitals, Ramesses built a new capital just northeast of Seti's summer palace and named it Pi-Ramesses ("the house [or domain] of Ramesses").[169] This name is likely behind the toponym *Rameses* in Exodus 1:11.[170] By locating his capital in the northeast delta, Ramesses was able to keep a close watch on affairs in western Asia, which would become an epicenter of military activity.

In Ramesses' fourth year he campaigned in Palestine, followed the next year by the famous Battle of Kadesh against the armies of Ḥattushili III, the

---

168. For a popular treatment of this project, see Georg Gerster, "Abu Simbel's Ancient Temples Reborn," *National Geographic* 135.5 (May 1969): 724–44.

169. Kitchen, *Pharaoh Triumphant*, 119–23.

170. Edward F. Wente, "Rameses," in *ABD* 5:617–18; Manfred Bietak, *Avaris and Piramesse* (Oxford: British Academy, 1979); E. P. Uphill, "Pithom and Raamses: Their Location and Significance," *Journal of Near Eastern Studies* 27 (1968): 291–316; idem, "Pithom and Raamses: Their Location and Significance," *Journal of Near Eastern Studies* 27 (1969): 15–39; idem, *The Temples of Per Ramesses* (Warminster: Aris & Phillips, 1984).

Hittite king—an event well documented in Egyptian sources.[171] The near military disaster for Ramesses and his forces was turned into a victory by propagandistic rhetoric and monumental battle scenes at the Luxor temple, the Ramesseum (his mortuary temple in western Thebes), and Abu Simbel. Relations remained cool between the two superpowers for over a decade, but gradually warmed up. The rising power of Assyria prompted Hattushili to take a conciliatory approach with Egypt, which led to a treaty with Ramesses and eventually a diplomatic marriage between the Hittite and Egyptian courts.[172]

Ramesses outlived his first twelve sons (he ruled into his sixty-seventh year) and was succeeded by Merenptah, the thirteenth, who was in his fifties when crowned.[173] Despite his age, he apparently led the campaign into Canaan recorded on the famous Israel Stele—the earliest nonbiblical attestation of Israel.[174] Frank Yurco suggests that a sequence of Karnak reliefs is a pictorial version of the renowned stele.[175] One of the vignettes, Yurco believes, portrays the Israelites in Canaanite attire and coiffure.

After Merenptah's death, Dynasty 19 limped along with several kings whose combined reigns lasted only thirty years and then concluded with Queen Tewosret. The Ramesside family, it appears, died off, bringing the dynasty to an end and resulting in the emergence of Dynasty 20. According to the Great Harris Papyrus, Setnakht, the founder of Dynasty 20, claims that he took control of Egypt after a period of social upheaval in which "Isru the Asiatic was with them as chief."[176] Isru may have been Bay, a Syrian who bore the title *Chancellor of the Entire Land*,[177] but it is unclear whether he ruled before or after Tewosret.

171. Alan H. Gardiner, *The Kadesh Inscriptions of Ramses II* (Oxford: Oxford University Press, 1960); Lichtheim, *Ancient Egyptian Literature*, 2:57–72.

172. Kitchen, *Pharaoh Triumphant*, 74–81. For Hittite and Egyptian versions of the treaty, see Ernst F. Weidner, *Politische Dokumente aus Kleinasien*, Boghazköi Studien 8–9 (Leipzig: Hinrichs, 1923), 112–23; and Kenneth A. Kitchen, *Ramesside Inscriptions* (Oxford: Blackwell, 1970), 2/5:225–32; with translations in *ANET* 199–203. The Hittite princess arrived in Egypt in 1245, but Ramesses did not reciprocate; see Kitchen, *Pharaoh Triumphant*, 83–88. This one-sided policy of welcoming foreign princesses to Egypt but not sending the pharaoh's daughters abroad continued until the time of Solomon (1 Kings 3:1); see Schulman, "Diplomatic Marriage."

173. Faulkner, "Egypt," 232.

174. William M. F. Petrie, *Six Temples at Thebes* (London: Quaritch, 1897), pls. xiii–xiv; for a translation, see Lichtheim, *Ancient Egyptian Literature*, 2:74–78.

175. Frank Yurco, "Merenptah's Canaanite Campaign," *Journal of the American Research Center in Egypt* 23 (1986): 189–215; idem, "3,200-Year-Old Picture of Israelites Found in Egypt," *Biblical Archaeology Review* 16.5 (1990): 20–38.

176. Faulkner, "Egypt," 240.

177. Ibid., 240–41.

Ramesses III is the only Twentieth Dynasty monarch to distinguish himself by his building projects and international affairs. His mortuary temple at Medinet Habu in western Thebes is the best surviving of New Kingdom funerary estates. The inscriptions and scenes provide a detailed report of much of his reign, including extensive reliefs of the Sea Peoples invasion, which included the biblical Philistines.[178] While Egypt was able to defend itself against this invasion, it never really recovered. The debate on whether the Egyptians relocated the Philistines to the coastal area of Canaan or whether they settled there on their own accord has recently been rekindled.[179] While an Egyptian presence in Palestine is attested as late as the time of Ramesses VI (1143–1136), its influence was clearly beginning to wane.[180]

Troubled by strikes and inflation at home toward the end of Ramesses III's reign,[181] Dynasty 20 quickly declined. Before the death of Ramesses XI in 1069, Herihor, the priest of Amon and "commander of the army," was the *de facto* ruler in Thebes.[182] Meanwhile in the north, Smendes established a rival dynasty (Manetho's Twenty-first) in Tanis, a newly founded city.[183] With this political bifurcation, Egypt entered the so-called Third Intermediate period. Except for a few futile attempts during the next centuries by Neco II and Apries, Egypt would never again be a dominant force in the Near East. The Late Egyptian "Tale of Wenamon" well reflects this situation.[184] Wenamon, a Theban official, confers with Smendes in Tanis before embarking for Phoenicia to buy timber. Upon his arrival in Byblos, he is rudely treated by the prince. After being snubbed for twenty-nine days, Wenamon is finally granted an audience, thanks to the divine intervention of Amon via an ecstatic utterance by a young man. The treatment of this royal envoy shows that Egypt was no longer held in high esteem in the Levant. The once-proud empire could be aptly called "that splintered reed of a staff" by the Assyrian emperor Sennacherib in 701 (2 Kings 18:21).

---

178. *Medinet Habu*, 4 vols., Oriental Institute Publications 8, 9, 23, 51 (Chicago: Oriental Institute, 1930–40).

179. Bryant G. Wood, "The Philistines Enter Canaan—Were They Egyptian Lackeys or Invading Conquerors," *Biblical Archaeology Review* 17.6 (1991): 44–52; and Itamar Singer, "How Did the Philistines Enter Canaan? A Rejoinder," *Biblical Archaeology Review* 18.6 (1992): 44–46. See also the entry "Philistines" in this volume.

180. Mazar, *Archaeology of the Land of the Bible*, 296–300.

181. Trigger et al., *Ancient Egypt*, 226–29; William F. Edgerton, "The Strikes in Ramses III's Twenty-ninth Year," *Journal of Near Eastern Studies* 10 (1933): 135–45; J. Janssen, "Background Information on the Strikes of Year 29 of Ramesses III," *Oriens Antiquus* 18 (1979): 301–8.

182. Gardiner, *Egypt of the Pharaohs*, 302–3.

183. Kenneth A. Kitchen, *The Third Intermediate Period (1100–650 B.C.)*, 2d ed. (Warminster: Aris & Phillips, 1982), 6–9.

184. Lichtheim, *Ancient Egyptian Literature*, 2:224–30; ANET 25–29.

Third Intermediate Period and Beyond (1100 to the Christian Era)

Egypt was politically divided for much of the Third Intermediate period, except for part of Dynasty 22, all of Dynasty 26, and brief intervals between foreign conquests. Undoubtedly because of Egypt's weakness during this time, Israel's monarchy was able to flourish and, for a short time, become a major power in the Levant.

Under the energetic Shoshenq I (biblical Shishak), Egypt was reunited, even as far south as Thebes, by his fifth year.[185] He was of Libyan origin[186] and hailed from the delta city of Bubastis, but Tanis remained his capital. In his penultimate year, Shoshenq invaded Palestine, received tribute from Rehoboam in Jerusalem (1 Kings 14:25), and attacked the northern kingdom of Israel.[187]

Dynasties 23 and 24 were of little significance and, in fact, overlapped toward the end of the eighth century. Dynasty 25 was made up of Cushite kings from Nubia. For reasons that remain unclear, Piankhy (or Piye) sailed north from Napata (just above the fourth cataract), conquered Egypt, and claimed to be the legitimate pharaoh. His campaign is well documented in the annalistic style of the New Kingdom.[188] After uniting Egypt, Piankhy returned to Napata. Perhaps as a result of seeing the Egyptian pyramids, Piankhy abandoned the mastaba and used a small pyramid as his burial structure, a practice continued by his successors.[189]

Dynasties 25 and 26 were characterized by an artistic and literary renaissance.[190] Pyramid and Coffin texts from the Old and Middle Kingdoms were utilized on coffins and in tombs of this period. In the Memphite Theology on the famous black stone now in the British Museum, Shabako (Piankhy's successor) states, "This writing was copied out anew . . . for his majesty found it to be a work of the ancestors which was worm-eaten, so that it could not be understood from beginning to end."[191] This renewed interest in the literature of the past was not limited to Egypt, but is also found in Assyria (as the

185. Kitchen, *Third Intermediate Period*, 287–88.

186. The origin of the Libyans in Egypt can be traced to the late New Kingdom; see Kenneth A. Kitchen, "The Arrival of the Libyans in Late New Kingdom Egypt," in *Libya and Egypt: c. 1300–750 B.C.*, ed. A. Leahy (London: School of Oriental and African Studies, Center of Near and Middle Eastern Studies, 1990).

187. Evidence for this campaign comes from a toponym list inscribed at Karnak and a Megiddo stele fragment bearing this monarch's name; see *ANET* 263; and Mazar, *Archaeology of the Land of the Bible*, 398.

188. N. C. Grimal, *La Stèle Triomphale de Pi(ʿankh)y au Musée du Caire* (Cairo: IFAO, 1981); for English translation, see Lichtheim, *Ancient Egyptian Literature*, 3:66–84.

189. Edwards, *Pyramids of Egypt*, 250.

190. Aldred, *Egyptians*, 176.

191. Lichtheim, *Ancient Egyptian Literature*, 1:52.

discovery of Ashurbanipal's library attests)[192] and Israel, where Hezekiah was actively editing earlier Solomonic wisdom texts and adding them to the corpus of Proverbs (cf. Prov. 25:1).

A series of invasions by the Assyrians during the reigns of Esarhaddon and Ashurbanipal rocked Egypt,[193] resulting in the demise of Dynasty 25. In anticipation of these events, the Cushites tried to stymie the Assyrians in Palestine, hence Taharqa's intervention when Sennacherib attacked Hekeziah in Jerusalem in 701.[194] Despite Taharqa's valiant efforts, the Assyrians prevailed, and Thebes was sacked (cf. Nah. 3:8).[195] Subsequently, an Egyptian prince from Sais in the western delta was appointed king.[196] This Neco (I) is credited with founding Dynasty 26, although it was his successor, Psammetichus I, who reunited and rebuilt Egypt after the Assyrian invasion.[197] With the crum-

Head of a king (late Dynasty 25), ca. 690–656 B.C. (height: 8.1″; width: 3.0″; diameter: 4.5″)

Courtesy of the Cincinnati Art Museum, John J. Emery Memorial Fund, A. J. Howe Endowment, Henry Meis Endowment, Phyllis H. Thayer Purchase Fund, Israel and Caroline Wilson Fund, On To The Second Century Art Purchase Fund, and Museum Purchase: Various Deaccession Funds

192. Simo Parpola, "Assyrian Library Records," *Journal of Near Eastern Studies* 42 (1983): 1–29.

193. A. Kirk Grayson, "Assyria's Foreign Policy in Relation to Egypt in the Eighth and Seventh Centuries B.C.," *Journal of the Society for the Study of Egyptian Antiquities* 11 (1981): 85–88; Anthony J. Spalinger, "Essarhaddon and Egypt: An Analysis of the First Invasion of Egypt," *Orientalia* 43 (1974): 295–326, and idem, "Ashurbanipal and Egypt: A Source Study," *Journal of the American Oriental Society* 94 (1974): 316–28.

194. Kitchen, *Third Intermediate Period*, 383–86; idem, "Egypt, the Levant and Assyria in 701 B.C.," in *Fontes atque Pontes: Eine Festgabe für Hellmut Brunner*, ed. Manfred Görg, Ägypten und Altes Testament 5 (Wiesbaden: Harrassowitz, 1983), 243–53; Alan R. Millard, "Sennacherib's Attack on Hezekiah," *Tyndale Bulletin* 36 (1985): 61–77; and James K. Hoffmeier, "Egypt as an Arm of Flesh: A Prophetic Response," in *Israel's Apostasy and Restoration: Essays in Honor of Roland K. Harrison*, ed. Avraham Gileadi (Grand Rapids: Baker, 1988), 88–90.

195. Georges Roux, *Ancient Iraq*, 3d ed. (Baltimore: Penguin, 1992), 331.

196. Gardiner, *Egypt of the Pharaohs*, 352.

197. Anthony J. Spalinger, "The Concept of the Monarchy during the Saite Epoch—an Essay of Synthesis," *Orientalia* 47 (1978): 12–36.

bling of Assyria and the rise of Babylon, Neco II saw his chance to reassert Egyptian influence in Syria-Palestine, and he marched to the Euphrates to stake his claim. En route, he was opposed by King Josiah of Judah, who was killed at Megiddo (2 Kings 23:29–30). From 609 to 605, Egyptian troops occupied Carchemish and manipulated events in Judah. But with the coronation of Nebuchadnezzar, the new Babylonian king moved quickly to oust the Egyptian garrison,[198] thus opening the way to control Palestine and eventually invade Egypt in 568.

Under Cambyses, Egypt was invaded and made a Persian satrapy from 525 to 404. During the Persian era (Manetho's Dynasty 27), temples continued to be built and decorated in the Egyptian artistic tradition, and the name of Darius appears as a dedicatory inscription on the sarcophagus of the Apis bull at Sakkara.[199] Inscriptions record that Cambyses ordered the removal of squatters in the temple precinct of Neith in Sais, indicating Persian support for Egyptian traditions.[200]

Dynasties 28–30 represent the last periods of Egyptian independence, because in Dynasty 31 Egypt fell back under Persian control until Alexander's conquest in 332. The Hellenization of Egypt continued under Ptolemy I and his successors,[201] and the Ptolemaic period saw the blending of Egyptian and Greek cultures. Egyptian temples, such as those of Horus at Edfu and Isis at Philae, continued to display traditional Egyptian architecture and were covered with hieroglyphic inscriptions, some of them harking back to the Old and Middle Kingdoms.[202]

Despite the arrival of Greek culture with the Ptolemaic kings and the subsequent domination by Rome, Egyptian religion and culture were not dismantled. Ironically, what finally pulled Egypt out of its ancient polytheism was not an invading army, but Christianity. By the early fourth century, Christianity was the dominant force in Egypt.[203] Egyptian worship centers became churches, and the name of Ramesses the Great was plastered over and replaced by Christian symbols. Centuries earlier, Isaiah of Jerusalem

198. Translated by Donald J. Wiseman in *Documents from Old Testament Times*, ed. D. Winton Thomas (London: Nelson, 1958), 78–79.

199. Gardiner, *Egypt of the Pharaohs*, 364.

200. For recent translation and discussion of this text, see, James K. Hoffmeier, *"Sacred" in the Vocabulary of Ancient Egypt*, Orbis Biblicus et Orientalis 59 (Göttingen: Vandenhoeck & Ruprecht/Freiburg: Universitätsverlag, 1985), 216–17.

201. For a survey of this period down to the Arab invasion in A.D. 642, see A. K. Bowman, *Egypt after the Pharaohs, 332 BC–AD 642* (Berkeley: University of California Press, 1986).

202. L. V. Žabkar, "Adaptation of Ancient Egyptian Texts to the Temple Ritual at Philae," *Journal of Egyptian Archaeology* 66 (1980): 127–36; see also, Bowman, *Egypt after the Pharaohs*, 165–202.

203. Harold I. Bell, *Cults and Creeds in Graeco-Roman Egypt* (Liverpool: Liverpool University Press, 1953, repr. Chicago: Ares, 1975), 78–105.

said, "The LORD will make himself known to the Egyptians, and in that day they will acknowledge the LORD" (19:21 NIV). In a sense, the birth of Christianity heralded the death of Egypt as it had been known. Today in Egypt, six to eight million Christians think of themselves as Egyptians, not Arabs. In the liturgy of the Egyptian Orthodox Church, Coptic—the last vestige of the ancient Egyptian language—can still be heard.

Religion

As in all ancient societies, religion was a dominating factor in Pharaonic Egypt. Even in the twilight of Egyptian history, Herodotus observed, "They are beyond measure religious, more than any other nation. . . . Their religious observances are, one might say, innumerable" (2:37).

Even before Menes united Egypt, the Egyptian pharaohs were viewed as divine and were associated with Horus.[204] The foundation for this belief was rooted in the myth of Osiris, Horus, and Seth, which is known from the Old Kingdom Pyramid Texts, the later Coffin Texts, and the Memphite Theology.[205] Because of this mythic foundation, the pharaoh was always the focal point of Egyptian religion, the ultimate high priest who built temples and oversaw their maintenance.

Egyptian religion can be divided into three areas: state, popular, and funerary. The foundation of state religion was laid in the previous paragraph, and a number of excellent studies on state religion and the gods are available.[206] Major deities like Atum-Re of Heliopolis, Ptah of Memphis, and Amon of Thebes dominate much of Egyptian history, but scores of other divinities were worshiped at local sanctuaries.

Popular religion, perhaps owing to the less glamorous nature of the evidence compared with that of state religion, has not been thoroughly studied. Ashraf Sadek corrects this imbalance by introducing the sources for the study of the religious practices of the common folk.[207] While in their basic assump-

204. Frankfort, *Kingship and the Gods*, 15–50.
205. For translations, see Faulkner, *Egyptian Pyramid Texts*; idem, *The Egyptian Coffin Texts*, vols. 1–3 (Warminster: Aris & Phillips, 1973–77); and Lichtheim, *Ancient Egyptian Literature*, 1:51–57.
206. S. Morenz, *Egyptian Religion* (Ithaca: Cornell University Press, 1973); Erik Hornung, *Conceptions of God in Ancient Egyptian: The One and the Many* (Ithaca: Cornell University Press, 1982); A. Rosalie David, *The Ancient Egyptians: Religious Beliefs and Practices* (New York/London: Routledge & Kegan Paul, 1982); and Byron Shafer (ed.), *Religion in Ancient Egypt: Gods, Myths and Personal Practice* (Ithaca: Cornell University Press, 1991).
207. Ashraf I. Sadek, *Popular Religion in Egypt during the New Kingdom*, Hildesheimer Ägyptologische Beiträge 27 (Hildesheim: Gerstenberg, 1987). See my favorable review in *Journal of Egyptian Archaeology* 78 (1992): 338–39.

tions the two branches are identical, the differences come in practice. The large New Kingdom temples at Karnak and Luxor, for instance, were not normally accessible to the common people. Only on special festive occasions were they able to enter the massive walls, but they could not enter the holy place, which was reserved for the priesthood.[208] Perhaps because of this exclusion from or limited access to state temples, small cult centers were established close to towns and villages in the Old and Middle Kingdoms.[209] It is only in the New Kingdom that sufficient evidence survives to enable a fuller description of these religious practices. Lay priests operated small chapels at Deir el-Medineh, where hundreds of small offering steles and votive objects have been found.[210] The votive objects show that the same deities worshiped in the state religion were also revered by common people. However, the latter had patron deities that were not worshiped elsewhere, such as the divinized Amenhotep I.[211]

Yielding perhaps the largest body of sources for the study of religion, burial customs are well attested in Egypt from predynastic through Roman times.[212] In addition to the corpora of funerary texts mentioned already,[213] the Book of the Dead (a later development of the Pyramid and Coffin texts recorded on papyrus) was popular from the New Kingdom on.[214]

From the various mortuary sources, it is evident that a mythic foundation stands behind funerary practices. The god Osiris, who presides over the netherworld and before whom everyone stands for judgment, appears to have been a historical figure of predynastic times who was killed by his violent brother Seth.[215] Isis, the sister-wife of Osiris, wept and searched for him. Through sexual union with Osiris, Isis gave birth to Horus, who succeeded his father. Anubis gathered the fallen Osiris and assisted in his mummification and burial. While in the Old Kingdom only royalty was associated with Osiris in the next life, the funerary cult was democratized during the First Intermediate period (as seen in the Coffin Texts), and others were able to share in the same privilege.[216]

208. Hoffmeier, *"Sacred" in the Vocabulary of Ancient Egypt*, 208–20.

209. Sadek, *Popular Religion*, 5–10.

210. Ibid., 79–83.

211. Ibid., 131–40.

212. For a comprehensive study of Egyptian burial practices, see A. J. Spencer, *Death in Ancient Egypt* (Middlesex: Penguin, 1982).

213. See n. 205.

214. Raymond O. Faulkner, *The Ancient Egyptian Book of the Dead*, ed. Carol Andrews (Austin: University of Texas Press, 1990).

215. J. G. Griffiths, *The Conflict of Horus and Seth* (Liverpool: University of Liverpool Press, 1960), 2–22; idem, *The Origins of Osiris and His Cult* (Leiden: Brill, 1980).

216. Wilson, *Culture of Ancient Egypt*, 116.

Because people had to stand before Osiris's tribunal for judgment, it was necessary to live according to *maat*, the Egyptian concept of justice and righteousness.[217] Admission to heaven was contingent on an individual's being pronounced "*maa ḫrw.*" Spell 125 (the so-called negative confession) of the Book of the Dead contains a list of sins and taboos that the deceased claims not to have done so as to merit divine favor. These provide good insights into Egyptian morals and ethics. It could be that the moral dimension of Egyptian wisdom literature served as a practical guide to help individuals live according to the principles of *maat* and thus be vindicated in the judgment.

Tombs and their accompanying chapels or temples aimed to preserve the body of the deceased and provide a place for the Ka (the spirit or alter ego) to come and go. Through the so-called false door of the chapel, the Ka could return to eat and drink the foodstuffs placed on altars.[218] It was, naturally, the obligation of the family to provide the offerings on behalf of the departed. In the New Kingdom, a type of ancestor worship developed, as the *3ḫ iḳr in Rc* steles show.[219]

Because of the plethora of information regarding mortuary religion, one might think that the Egyptians were preoccupied with death, and thus lived morbid lives. However, from Dynasty 5 onward, tomb scenes make it clear that this is not so. On the contrary, in paintings and reliefs we see people engaged in various types of recreation—hunting and fishing being favorites. Egyptian nobility and middle classes frequented parties with music, dancing, drinking, and banqueting, as paintings of the New Kingdom illustrate.[220]

Herodotus was right: the Egyptians were a most religious people. Religion affected every area of life: piety, ethics, politics, and death. If we eliminate all the archeological remains connected to religion (i.e., temples, funerary structures, cultic statues, steles, etc.), little would remain.

Egypt and Israel

During the Second Millennium B.C.

Abraham had a brief visit to Egypt sometime in the early second millennium (Gen. 12:10–20). Since the name of the Egyptian monarch is not given, only the title *Pharaoh*, there is no way to determine the identity of the king. If

217. Morenz, *Egyptian Religion*, 113–30.
218. Spencer, *Death in Ancient Egypt*, 58.
219. R. J. Demaree, *The 3ḫ iḳr in Rc-Stelae: On Ancestor Worship in Ancient Egypt* (Leiden: Nederlands Historisch-Archaeologisch Instituut in het Nabije Oosten, 1983).
220. Examples of this type of scene are found in the tomb of Nefer at Sakkara and on the relief of Hetep Horakhti at Leiden.

Abraham is placed broadly within the first third of the second millennium,[221] Dynasties 12–13 would be a likely period for his descent to Egypt.

The next contact between the Hebrews and Egypt is found in the Joseph story of Genesis 39–50. Once again, the biblical text is vague about historical matters, making the dating of the accounts difficult. However, Egyptian coloring to the story is well established, which lends credibility to the historicity of the Joseph cycle.[222] Redford argues that the Egyptian personal names in the story, Potiphar and Asenath, point to the first millennium.[223] However, equally compelling arguments have been offered for the antiquity of the Genesis record.[224] Joseph's rise to power from a domestic to a high-ranking official is not without parallel in Egypt. Bay, a non-Egyptian, was elevated to "Chancellor of the Entire Land" during Dynasty 20. Gardiner writes, "There is good reason for thinking that Bay was a Syrian by birth, possibly one of those court officials who in this age frequently rose to power by the royal favor."[225] The Hyksos period, when foreigners controlled the delta and northern Egypt, is a likely time for Joseph to have come to prominence and for Jacob's family to have settled in Goshen in the delta.

In the years intervening between Joseph's death and the birth of Moses, the Hebrew population grew to the point that the Egyptian pharaoh saw their presence as threatening. Exodus 1:8 reports that "a new king, who did not know about Joseph, came to power in Egypt." Clearly, time had passed since the death of Joseph (Exod. 1:6), and the *new king* probably refers to a new dynasty, not just a different king than the one mentioned in Genesis.[226] The

---

221. This dating is challenged by John Van Seters, *Abraham in History and Tradition* (New Haven: Yale University Press, 1975); and Thomas L. Thompson, *The Historicity of the Patriarchal Narratives: The Quest for the Historical Abraham*, Beiheft zur Zeitschrift für die Alttestamentliche Wissenschaft 133 (Berlin: de Gruyter, 1974). For criticism of these works, which question the historicity of the Genesis patriarchs, see Alan R. Millard and Donald J. Wiseman (eds.), *Essays on the Patriarchal Narratives* (Winona Lake, Ind.: Eisenbrauns, 1983); Alan R. Millard, "Abraham," in *ABD* 1:35–41; and James K. Hoffmeier, "The Wives' Tales of Genesis 12, 20 and 36 and the Covenants at Beersheba," *Tyndale Bulletin* 43 (1992): 81–99.

222. J. M. A. Janssen, "Egyptological Remarks on the Story of Joseph in Genesis," *Jaarbericht . . . ex Oriente Lux* 14 (1955–56): 63–72; Jozef Vergote, *Joseph en Égypte*, Orientalia et Biblica Lovaniensia 3 (Louvain: Peeters, 1959); idem, "'Joseph en Egypte': 25 Ans Après," in *Pharaonic Egypt: The Bible and Christianity*, ed. Sarah Israelit-Groll (Jerusalem: Magnes, 1985), 289–306; Kenneth A. Kitchen, "Joseph," in *The Illustrated Bible Dictionary*, ed. James D. Douglas et al. (Leicester: Inter-Varsity/Wheaton, Ill.: Tyndale, 1980), 812–15; and idem, "Joseph," in *ISBE* 2:1126–30.

223. Donald B. Redford, *A Study of the Biblical Story of Joseph (Genesis 37–50)*, Vetus Testamentum Supplement 20 (Leiden: Brill, 1970).

224. See Kitchen's two articles on Joseph in n. 222 and his review of Redford's book (cited in n. 223) in *Oriens Antiquus* 12 (1973): 233–42.

225. Gardiner, *Egypt of the Pharaohs*, 277.

226. Nahum M. Sarna, *Exploring Exodus* (New York: Schocken, 1986), 15.

expulsion of the Hyksos and the establishment of the New Kingdom with Dynasty 18 seems to be a logical time for the change in attitude toward the Israelites. One can imagine Ahmose's exasperation upon finding a sizable Semitic population in the very region where the hated Hyksos had lived. This new king feared that the Hebrews would join his enemies if war broke out (Exod. 1:10). Could Egypt's enemies have been the Hyksos?

The absence of direct archeological or historical evidence for the Israelite sojourn and exodus from Egypt leads some scholars to question the historicity of the exodus narratives.[227] The result is to regard Israel as just another Canaanite tribe that emerged from obscurity to become a nation.[228] However, the exodus tradition is too deeply entrenched in the Old Testament to be dismissed as an innovation of the late period of Israelite history.[229] Similarly, the historicity of Moses is undeniable, although his name is not attested in any contemporary literature and even though his precise historical setting cannot be proven. Siegfried Herrmann affirms this conclusion: "Thus we are left ultimately with only the mighty figure of Moses, which cannot be put aside as invention or interpolation, but which is constitutive for the whole account."[230]

In recent decades, two main positions have emerged on the dating of the exodus from Egypt.[231] The so-called early date is computed from 1 Kings 6:1: 967 (Solomon's fourth year) + 480 years (from the exodus to Solomon) = 1447.[232] A second view, the late date, regards the figure 480 as the result of multiplying 12 x 40 years (the symbolic length of a generation). Since a generation is actually closer to 25 years, 967 + 300 (12 x 25) = 1267, which would fall in the reign of Ramesses II.[233] That the Israelites were forced to

227. Donald B. Redford, "An Egyptological Perspective on the Exodus Narrative," in *Egypt, Israel, Sinai: Archaeological and Historical Relationships in the Biblical Period*, ed. Anson F. Rainey (Tel Aviv: Tel Aviv University Press, 1987), 138–61; idem, *Egypt, Canaan, and Israel in Ancient Times*, 257–80.

228. Gösta W. Ahlström, *Who Were the Israelites?* (Winona Lake, Ind.: Eisenbrauns, 1986); Robert B. Coote, *Early Israel: A New Horizon* (Minneapolis: Fortress, 1990).

229. See Kenneth A. Kitchen, "Exodus, The," in *ABD* 2:700–708; and Nahum M. Sarna, "Exodus, Book of," in *ABD* 2:689–700. In addition, the lengthy sojourn of the Israelites is reflected in Egyptian influence on Hebrew history and culture, and some of the Hebrew names of this period were likely Egyptian: Moses, Merari, Phinehas, and Miriam.

230. Siegfried Herrmann, *Israel in Egypt* (Philadelphia: Fortress, 1973), 41–42.

231. For an evaluation of both positions' merits and weaknesses, see William Stiebing, *Out of the Desert?* (Buffalo, N.Y.: Prometheus, 1989).

232. Charles Aling, *Egypt and Bible History from Earliest Times to 1000 B.C.* (Grand Rapids: Baker, 1981), 77–96.

233. Kenneth A. Kitchen, *The Bible in Its World: The Bible and Archaeology Today* (Downers Grove, Ill.: InterVarsity, 1977), 75–79; idem, *Pharaoh Triumphant*, 70–71; and Roland K. Harrison, *Introduction to the Old Testament* (Grand Rapids: Eerdmans, 1969), 315–25.

help build a city called Rameses (Exod. 1:11) is regarded as supporting this conclusion.

Despite the inability of historians and biblical scholars to agree on the dating of the exodus event, there can be little doubt that the exodus narratives reflect New Kingdom conditions, such as forced labor for building projects and brick making by quota.[234] In Exodus the language of the conflict between pharaoh and God has a decisively Egyptian flavor.[235] This struggle is brought to a climax through the plagues, which demonstrate that Yahweh, the God of Israel, is responsible for maintaining cosmic order.[236] In Egyptian thought, the king was responsible for the proper functioning of the Nile, agricultural fertility, and even the sun's shining. All of these are shown to be controlled by Moses' God, not pharaoh.

The geography of the exodus route from Rameses to the Sea of Reeds (Exod. 14:1–2; Num. 33:5–8) appears to be an authentic itinerary that makes good, geographical sense in the eastern delta and Sinai area.[237] The biblical data combined with the supporting (albeit secondary) evidence from Egypt supports the conclusion of John Bright: "There can really be little doubt that ancestors of Israel had been slaves in Egypt and had escaped in some marvelous way."[238]

While it remains unclear when the Israelites entered and departed Egypt, it is certain that by 1208 they had reached Canaan. In this year, the fifth year of Merenptah, the famous Israel Stele was inscribed to celebrate the pharaoh's triumph in Palestine, including an encounter with some Israelites. For the balance of the second millennium, there is little evidence of contact between Israel and Egypt. That picture changes considerably during the next millennium.

234. Kenneth A. Kitchen, "From the Brickfields of Egypt," *Tyndale Bulletin* 27 (1976): 137–47.

235. James K. Hoffmeier, "The Arm of God Versus the Arm of Pharaoh in the Exodus Narratives," *Biblica* 67 (1986): 378–87; Manfred Görg, " 'Der Starke Arm Pharos' Beobachtungen zum Belegspektrum einer Metapher in Palästina und Ägypten," in *Hommages à François Daumas* (Montpellier: Université de Montpellier, 1986), 323–30.

236. James K. Hoffmeier, "Egypt, Plagues in," in *ABD* 2:374–78.

237. "Sea of Reeds" is the Hebrew reading of the body of water through which the Israelites passed in Exod. 14; the Septuagint has "Red Sea." The Reed Sea is probably one of the lakes along Egypt's border with Sinai (Timsah, el-Ballah, or Bitter); see James B. Pritchard (ed.), *The Harper Atlas of the Bible* (San Francisco: Harper & Row, 1987), 57; James K. Hoffmeier, "Moses," in *ISBE* 3:420–21; and idem, "Toponymns of the Exodus" (paper read at 1987 symposium "Who Was the Pharaoh of the Exodus?" in Memphis, Tenn.; audio tape available from the Near Eastern Archaeological Society). Redford's argument ("Egyptological Perspective") for a Saite-Persian background for the geographical terms is simply not compelling.

238. John Bright, *A History of Israel*, 3d ed. (Philadelphia: Fortress, 1981), 120.

During the First Millennium B.C.

Solomon married an Egyptian princess (1 Kings 3:1)—likely the daughter of Siamun of Tanis (Dynasty 21)[239]—to formalize a treaty between the two nations. And he may well have been familiar with the Egyptian treatises of Any and Amenemope. Ongoing contact between Egypt and Israel and Judah existed from the days of Solomon down to the destruction of Jerusalem in 586.

In later history, Egypt was both friend and foe of Israel and Judah. Shishak (Shoshenq I) invaded Palestine, as witnessed by his relief at Karnak temple, taking the gold of the temple and inflicting considerable pain on his former friend Jeroboam I (1 Kings 14:25–26). Solomon's vast gold reserves may have ended up as part of Shishak's funerary cache or of the enormous temple donations made by his son Osorkon I.[240] Hoshea of Samaria called on Egypt for help on the eve of Israel's destruction by the Assyrians (2 Kings 17:4). But help was not forthcoming owing to the weakness of a politically divided Egypt. Neco II (610–595; Dynasty 26) slew the godly king Josiah in battle (2 Kings 23:29), a disaster from which Judah never recovered.

In the years that followed, Babylon became the superpower, and many Jews fled to Egypt, hoping to find safe haven there. Included in one of the last flights to Egypt was Jeremiah the prophet, whose writings contain some intriguing insights on Egypt (Jer. 46).[241] From the Jewish community who lived in Egypt ultimately came the Septuagint, the translation of the Hebrew Scriptures in Alexandria in the third century and later.

Recommended Reading

Aldred, Cyril. *The Egyptians.* Rev. ed. London: Thames & Hudson, 1984.

Baines, John, and Jaromír Málek. *Atlas of Ancient Egypt.* New York: Facts on File, 1980.

David, A. Rosalie. *The Ancient Egyptians: Religious Beliefs and Practices.* New York/London: Routledge & Kegan Paul, 1982.

Davies, W. V. *Egyptian Hieroglyphs.* Reading the Past 6. Berkeley: University of California Press/London: British Museum, 1987.

Faulkner, Raymond O. *The Ancient Egyptian Pyramid Texts.* Oxford: Clarendon, 1969.

---

239. Kitchen, *Third Intermediate Period,* 280; Hoffmeier, "Egypt as an Arm of Flesh," 81.

240. Kenneth A. Kitchen, "Egypt and Israel during the First Millennium B.C.," in *Congress Volume: Jerusalem 1986,* ed. John A. Emerton, Vetus Testamentum Supplement 40 (Leiden: Brill, 1988), 117–18; idem, "Where Did Solomon's Gold Go?" *Biblical Archaeology Review* 15.3 (May/June 1989): 30.

241. James K. Hoffmeier, "A New Insight on Pharaoh Apries From Herodotus, Diodorus, and Jeremiah 46:17," *Journal of the Society for the Study of Egyptian Antiquities* 11 (1981): 167.

————. *The Ancient Egyptian Book of the Dead.* Edited by Carol Andrews. Austin: University of Texas Press, 1990.

————. *The Egyptian Coffin Texts.* 3 vols. Warminster: Aris & Phillips, 1973–77.

Gardiner, Alan H. *Egypt of the Pharaohs.* Oxford: Oxford University Press, 1961.

Hallo, William W., and William K. Simpson. *The Ancient Near East: A History.* New York: Harcourt Brace Jovanovich, 1971.

Hobson, Christine. *The World of the Pharaohs.* New York: Thames & Hudson, 1987.

Kitchen, Kenneth A. "Egypt and Israel during the First Millennium B.C." Pp. 107–23 in *Congress Volume: Jerusalem 1986.* Edited by John A. Emerton. Vetus Testamentum Supplement 40. Leiden: Brill, 1988

————. *Pharaoh Triumphant: The Life and Times of Ramesses II.* Warminster: Aris & Phillips, 1982.

————. *The Third Intermediate Period (1100–650 B.C.).* 2d ed. Warminster: Aris & Phillips, 1982.

Lichtheim, Miriam. *Ancient Egyptian Literature.* 3 vols. Berkeley: University of California Press, 1973–80.

Moran, William L. *The Amarna Letters.* Baltimore: Johns Hopkins University Press, 1992.

Morenz, S. *Egyptian Religion.* Ithaca: Cornell University Press, 1973.

Rainey, Anson F. (ed.). *Egypt, Israel, Sinai: Archaeological and Historical Relationships in the Biblical Period.* Jerusalem: Tel Aviv University Press, 1987.

Redford, Donald B. *Akhenaten: The Heretic King.* Princeton: Princeton University Press, 1984.

Sadek, Ashraf I. *Popular Religion in Egypt during the New Kingdom.* Hildesheimer Ägyptologische Beiträge 27. Hildesheim: Gerstenberg, 1987.

Shafer, Byron (ed.). *Religion in Ancient Egypt: Gods, Myths and Personal Practice.* Ithaca: Cornell University Press, 1991.

Simpson, William K. (ed.). *The Literature of Ancient Egypt: An Anthology of Stories, Instructions, and Poetry.* Revised edition. New Haven: Yale University Press, 1973.

Smith, W. S. *The Art and Architecture of Ancient Egypt.* Rev. edition by William K. Simpson. New York: Penguin, 1981.

Spencer, A. J. *Death in Ancient Egypt.* Middlesex: Penguin, 1982.

Trigger, Bruce G., et al. *Ancient Egypt: A Social History.* Cambridge: Cambridge University Press, 1983.

Wilson, John. *The Culture of Ancient Egypt.* Chicago: University of Chicago Press, 1951.

Part 3

Transjordan

Ammonites

Randall W. Younker

The king of the Ammonites answered Jephthah's messengers,
"When Israel came up out of Egypt, they took away my land
from the Arnon to the Jabbok, all the way to the Jordan."
—*Judges 11:13*

The Ammonites, known from both biblical and extrabiblical
sources, were an ancient people who inhabited the central Transjordanian
plateau from about the middle of the second millennium until the middle of
the first millennium. Their country was known as Ammon, and their capital
was called Rabbah-ammon or Amman. They are best known for their numerous encounters with the biblical Israelites. In spite of their appearance in the
biblical record, few scholars have seriously studied the Ammonites,[1] largely
because they are seldom mentioned in extrabiblical texts and, until recently,
little archeological research had been done within the boundaries of their ancient territory. Nearly a century of exploration and the recent increase in archeological survey and excavation have greatly expanded our knowledge of
the Ammonites.

Exploration and Excavations

Transjordan was included on the itineraries of many of the nineteenth century's adventurous Western explorers. Several of the better known
travelers who visited the city of Amman or its environs are Ulrich Seetzen
(1806), Johann Burckhardt (1812), James Buckingham (1816), Henry B.
Tristram (1863–64), and Charles Warren (1867). The first systematic exploration of Amman and its hinterland was by Claude R. Conder in 1881, fol-

---

1. To date, the only major study in English on the Ammonites is George M. Landes, *A His-
tory of the Ammonites* (Ph.D. diss., Johns Hopkins University, 1956). See also Ulrich Hübner,
*Die Ammoniter: Untersuchungen zur Geschichte, Kultur und Religion eines transjordanischen
Volkes im I. Jahrtausend v. Chr.* (Wiesbaden: Harrassowitz, 1992).

lowed by a more extensive survey by Howard C. Butler in 1907. Perhaps the most important exploration of Ammonite territory was conducted by Nelson Glueck in the 1930s.[2] His survey discovered numerous small villages, farmsteads, and agricultural and defensive "watchtowers," many of them dating to the Iron Age, especially Iron Age II (ninth–sixth centuries), when Ammonite civilization was at its peak.

Excavations within Ammonite territory proceeded slowly during the first half of this century; the most important were those of the ancient Ammonite capital initiated by G. Guidi in 1927 and continued under R. Bartoccini from 1929 to 1933. However, rapid development of the modern city of Amman and its environs during the last thirty-five years has led to numerous archeological discoveries in the heartland of the ancient Ammonites. For example, in 1955 a temple from the Late Bronze Age was discovered during expansion of the airport northeast of the city. The expansion also led to salvage excavations of several tombs and towers, most dating to Iron Age II.[3] During this same time German scholars conducted several important surveys, especially to the west and south of Amman. The objective of most of their explorations was to test Glueck's original assertion that Ammonite borders during the early Iron Age were defined by a strong line of defensive towers.

In addition to surveys and salvage projects, there have been full-scale excavations, some of which are still ongoing, at Umm ad-Dananir, Tell Safut, Tell Siran, Tell Sahab, Tell el-ʿUmeiri, Tell Jawa (South), and Amman.[4] Ma-

---

2. See Nelson Glueck, "Explorations in the Land of Ammon," *Bulletin of the American Schools of Oriental Research* 68 (1937): 13–21; idem, *Explorations in Eastern Palestine*, part 3, Annual of the American Schools of Oriental Research 18–19 (New Haven: American Schools of Oriental Research, 1939), 151–251.

3. For the tombs around Amman see William F. Albright, "An Anthropoid Clay Coffin from Sahab in Transjordan," *American Journal of Archaeology* 36 (1932): 295–306; G. Lankester Harding, "Two Iron Age Tombs from ʿAmman," *Quarterly of the Department of Antiquities of Palestine* 11 (1944): 67–74; idem, "Two Iron-Age Tombs in Amman," *Annual of the Department of Antiquities of Jordan* 1 (1951): 37–40; idem, "The Tomb of Adoni Nur in Amman," *Palestine Exploration Fund Annual* 6 (1953): 48–65; Rafik W. Dajani, "An Iron Age Tomb from Amman," *Annual of the Department of Antiquities of Jordan* 11 (1966): 41–47; idem, "Jebel Nuzha Tomb at Amman," *Annual of the Department of Antiquities of Jordan* 11 (1966): 48–52; idem, "Late Bronze–Iron Age Tomb Excavated at Sahab, 1968," *Annual of the Department of Antiquities of Jordan* 15 (1970): 29–34; Rudolph H. Dornemann, *The Archaeology of the Transjordan in the Bronze and Iron Ages* (Milwaukee: Milwaukee Public Museum, 1983), 47 n. 3; Adnan Hadidi, "An Ammonite Tomb at Amman," *Levant* 19 (1987): 101–20.

4. For Umm ad-Dananir, see Patrick E. McGovern, *The Late Bronze Age and Early Iron Ages of Central Transjordan: The Beqʿah Valley Project, 1977–1981* (Philadelphia: University Museum, 1986). For Tell Safut, see Donald H. Wimmer, "The Excavations at Tell Safut," in *Studies in the History and Archaeology of Jordan*, ed. Adnan Hadidi (Amman: Department of Antiquities of Jordan, 1987), 3:279–82; idem, "Tell Safut Excavations, 1982–85: A Preliminary Report," *Annual of the Department of Antiquities of Jordan* 31 (1987): 159–74. For Tell Sahab,

jor excavations have also been conducted at Tell el-Mazar and Tell Hesban (not necessarily to be identified with biblical Heshbon), which were probably originally outside the borders of ancient Ammon, but later incorporated into the kingdom at the height of its power during the eighth–sixth centuries.[5]

Name

According to Genesis 19:38, the ancestor of the Ammonites was Ben-ʿammi, the son of an incestuous relationship between Lot and his younger daughter. Some scholars assume that the name, which means "son of my people" or "son of my paternal father," was a popular etymology developed in support of a tradition of a kindred relationship between Ammon and Israel. However, George M. Landes shows from Ugaritic texts that Ben-ʿammi was both a genuine clan and a personal name.[6] Daniel I. Block further shows that *bny ʿmwn* (the Hebrew expression for the Ammonite people) cannot be interpreted in the same way as *bny yśrʾl* ("sons of Israel"), even though they appear to be analogous. Rather, the prefixed element *bn* or *bny* was an integral part of the full name, similar to the well-known Semitic name *Benjamin*. Thus, the proper designation for the land of the Ammonites was not Ammon, but Bene-ʿammon.[7] Similarly, the full and proper form of the name for the eponymous ancestor of the Ammonites is Ben-ʿammi. Thus, while it

---

see Rafik W. Dajani, "A Late Bronze–Iron Age Tomb Excavated at Sahab, 1968," *Annual of the Department of Antiquities of Jordan* 15 (1970): 29–34; Moawiyah M. Ibrahim, "Second Season of Excavations at Sahab, 1973," *Annual of the Department of Antiquities of Jordan* 19 (1974): 55–61, 187–98; idem, "Third Season of Excavations at Sahab, 1975," *Annual of the Department of Antiquities of Jordan* 20 (1975): 69–82, 169–78. For Tell el-ʿUmeiri and Tell Jawa (South), see Randall W. Younker et al., "The Joint Madaba Plains Project: A Preliminary Report of the 1989 Season, Including the Regional Survey and Excavations at el-Dreijat, Tell Jawa, and Tell el-ʿUmeiri (June 19 to August 8, 1989)," *Andrews University Seminary Studies* 28 (1990): 5–52. For the Tell el-ʿUmeiri survey, see Robert G. Boling, "Site Survey," in *Madaba Plains Project*, vol. 1: *The 1984 Season at Tell el-ʿUmeiri and Vicinity and Subsequent Studies*, ed. Lawrence T. Geraty et al. (Berrien Springs, Mich.: Andrews University Press, 1989), 98–188. For the Amman airport temple, see John B. Hennessy, "Excavation of a Late Bronze Age Temple at Amman," *Palestine Exploration Quarterly* 98 (1966): 155–62. For probes at the Amman Citadel, see Dornemann, *Archaeology of the Transjordan*, 22.

5. For the Hesban survey, see Robert D. Ibach Jr., *Archaeological Survey of the Hesban Region: Catalogue of Sites and Characterization of Periods*, Heshbon Excavations Final Reports 5 (Berrien Springs, Mich.: Andrews University Press, 1987). For Tell el-Mazar, see Khair N. Yassine, *The Archaeology of Jordan: Essays and Reports* (Amman: Department of Archaeology, University of Jordan, 1988), 73–155.

6. Landes, *History of the Ammonites*, 4–6.

7. Daniel I. Block, "*Bny ʿmwn*: The Sons of Ammon," *Andrews University Seminary Studies* 22 (1984): 197–212.

is highly unlikely that the existence of Lot's son could be historically established apart from the biblical record, the idea that the Ammonites had an ancestor with such a name is not at all impossible.

Geographical Boundaries

The most prominent geophysical feature that biblical writers used to define Ammonite territory was the Jabbok River (Deut. 3:16; Josh. 12:2).[8] Its sources are near modern Amman. From this point the Jabbok's upper courses flow in a northeasterly direction to the modern town of Zerqa. From there the stream curves around to the west where the lower courses rapidly descend into the Great Rift Valley, a drop from 2,700 feet above sea level to 1,000 feet below. It joins the Jordan River just north of Adam, 23 miles north of the Dead Sea. Its total length is about 62 miles.

A question concerning which part of the river served as the Ammonite border derives from the circular route the Jabbok follows. Based on the general understanding that the river commences from the base of Citadel Hill in modern Amman, scholars assume that only this downstream portion of the Jabbok served as the border in the biblical text—either the upper north-south stretch running out from modern Amman or the east-west stretch farther downstream. Landes, following the view of Glueck and others, maintains that the biblical text describes only the upper stretch of the Jabbok located northeast of Ammon, flowing in a south-north direction. If so, the Ammonites were located on the east side of this stretch.[9] Bustenay Oded interprets the same archeological evidence to show that the biblical text refers to the east-west stretch of the Jabbok.[10]

It is possible that the biblical texts do not exclusively refer to either the east-west or the south-north stretch of the Jabbok. Although there is a major spring in the wadi at the foot of Amman, the wadi itself does not begin there. Rather, it can be traced back through a number of confluences to what is today known as Wadi Hannutiya, near Umm es-Summaq, at least six miles northwest of Amman.[11] The upper reaches of this wadi (geophysically a sin-

8. Now known as Wadi Zerqa or Nahr ez-Zerqa ("the blue river").

9. Landes, *History of the Ammonites*, 70. If the south-north stretch of the Jabbok formed the Ammonite western border, as Glueck (*Explorations in Eastern Palestine*, 246) assumes, the Ammonites would have been crowded into an unrealistic, narrow corridor between this part of the Jabbok and the desert. Landes also points out that the archeological evidence clearly indicates the Ammonites settled west of this stretch of the Jabbok well before the tenth century.

10. Bustenay Oded, "Ammon, Ammonites," in *Encyclopaedia Judaica* (Jerusalem: Keter, 1971), 2:854.

11. A similar observation is made by Zechariah Kallai, *Historical Geography of the Bible* (Jerusalem: Magnes, 1986), 298 n. 35.

gle feature) assume various names as it winds along—names of recent origin, having been assigned by farmsteads or villages standing adjacent to the various stretches. However, there is no evidence that this toponymic classification existed in antiquity. Indeed, it is likely that the ancient Ammonites used a single name for both the principal wadi and its tributaries.[12]

Recognizing that the ancient Jabbok included the upper reaches of the wadi and its numerous tributaries and that it can be traced west and northwest of Amman means that the Jabbok essentially formed a complete circle around the ancient kingdom of Ammon. Its territory included a considerable amount of land to the south, west, and northwest of the old capital city, probably the "land along the course of the Jabbok" referred to in Deuteronomy 2:37.[13] The hill country of the Ammonites mentioned in this same verse could refer to the hills adjacent to the Jabbok's tributaries and also the range of undulations south of Amman that form a natural geographical division between ancient Ammon and the Madaba Plains, traditional Moabite (and later Amorite and Israelite) territory. It is within these southern hills that several distinctive Ammonite sites have been excavated, including Tell el-ʿUmeiri, Tell Jawa (South), and Tell Sahab—all of which appear to have been continuously occupied from at least Late Bronze Age times (ca. 1400) down to the end of the Iron Age and perhaps into the Persian period.

Origin and Early History

The biblical tradition views the Ammonites as an indigenous people who descended directly from Lot. According to Deuteronomy 2:20–21 the Ammonites eventually grew strong enough to displace an ancient people known as the Rephaim (called the Zamzummim by the Ammonites) from the headwaters of the Jabbok. There the Ammonites established their capital, Rabbah-ammon (2 Sam. 12:27). Thus, the biblical record indicates that the

12. Andrew Dearman notes a similar situation for the ancient Arnon River (modern Wadi Mujib): *Arnon* was applied not only to the main artery but to the tributaries as well. If ancient geographers considered the many tributaries and branches of the Arnon River as part of a single water system, there is no reason to deny a similar understanding of the Jabbok River. See Dearman, "The Levitical Cities of Reuben and Moabite Toponymy," *Bulletin of the American Schools of Oriental Research* 276 (1989): 58.

13. Oded provides a description of the Ammonite borders similar to my own, with conclusions likewise based on biblical, archeological, and topographical factors; see Oded, "Ammon, Ammonites," 854. Elsewhere, Oded suggests that the ridge separating the tributaries of the upper Jabbok from those of Wadi Shueʿib, Wadi es-Sir, Wadi Kafrein, and Wadi Hesban formed a partition between the land of the Ammonites and the settlements of the Israelites; see Bustenay Oded, "Neighbors on the East," in *The Age of the Monarchies: Political History*, ed. Abraham Malamat, World History of the Jewish People (Jerusalem: Massada, 1979), 259.

Ammonites occupied the central Transjordanian plateau for some time before the Israelites arrived on the scene (Gen. 19:38; Num. 21:24; Deut. 2:19).

From a purely scientific perspective, it is presently impossible to either prove or disprove the Bible's view of Ammonite origins. Critical scholarship tends to view the biblical account of Ammonite origins as an Israelite attempt to disparage their long-time enemies, and it generally prefers to look for an exogenous origin of the Ammonites.[14] This approach received impetus after Glueck reported that there appeared to be an occupational gap in Transjordan prior to 1300.

If Glueck is right that no Ammonites were in Transjordan prior to 1300, scholars have naturally asked where the Ammonites came from and what caused them to settle in Transjordan at this particular time. Most suggest that the Ammonites (along with other ancient Palestinian peoples) originated in the north as part of an Amorite or Aramean migration.[15] George E. Mendenhall suggests that many of the peoples of Palestine and Transjordan (including the Ammonites) moved south from Anatolia and northern Syria during a widespread socioeconomic collapse that engulfed much of the Levant during the latter part of the Late Bronze Age. While it is assumed that many of these immigrants moved into and took over the collapsing lowland Canaanite cities (which were affected by the same socioeconomic crisis that struck the north), others are believed to have moved into the lightly populated highlands of Palestine and Transjordan. These highland settlers from the north were joined by local inhabitants fleeing the collapsing Canaanite cities. Through the embracing of new ideologies, new people groups were formed that would become known as the Israelites, Ammonites, etc.

The views of Norman K. Gottwald somewhat follow the proposals of Mendenhall, but focus more on the indigenous population of Palestine. According to Gottwald, the bulk of the new Israelite and Transjordanian populations were derived from Canaan itself. Although people from the north and elsewhere certainly could have been involved, Gottwald views the migration as an essentially local one in which lower-class Canaanites fled the socioeconomic inequalities of the urban centers, usually located in the lowlands, into

---

14. For a recent example of how these origin narratives are treated, see J. Maxwell Miller, "Moab and the Moabites," in *Studies in the Mesha Inscription and Moab*, ed. J. Andrew Dearman (Atlanta: Scholars Press, 1989), 18–19.

15. See Landes, *History of the Ammonites*, 31–35; Glueck, *Explorations in Eastern Palestine*, 160; J. F. Fenlon, "Ammonites," in *The Catholic Encyclopedia* (New York: Appleton, 1907), 1:431; Martin Noth, *The History of Israel*, 2d ed. (New York: Harper & Row, 1960), 157. Representative are the views of George E. Mendenhall: *The Tenth Generation: The Origins of Biblical Tradition* (Baltimore: Johns Hopkins University Press, 1973), 167–68; "Ancient Israel's Hyphenated History," in *Palestine in Transition: The Emergence of Ancient Israel*, ed. David N. Freedman and David F. Graf (Sheffield: Almond, 1983), 94–100.

the uninhabited highlands of Canaan and Transjordan where they established new ethnic identities.[16]

Patrick E. McGovern, researching the central Transjordanian plateau, localizes the nature of the migration and social transformation even more than Gottwald. The recognition that central Transjordan had its own Late Bronze settlements prompts McGovern to suggest that there was a local movement from the city to the countryside in the Late Bronze and early Iron periods and back again into an urban mode (often in new locations) in Iron Age IC, at which time the Ammonite and Israelite kingdoms were formed.[17] A site like Umm ad-Dananir thus shrank in size during Iron Age IA as people moved into the hinterland; it was apparently abandoned after 1050 (Iron Age IC), just before true Ammonite and Israelite kingdoms were established in the region.

While this view that the Ammonites, Israelites, and other ancient Palestinian peoples arose from the fleeing populations of collapsing Canaanite city-states has, with variations, been adopted by an increasing number of scholars, there is some dissension. For example, Israeli archeologist Israel Finkelstein vigorously denies a direct connection between the highland Israelites and the Late Bronze Age urban Canaanites.[18] Specifically, Finkelstein argues that certain aspects of the material culture—such as pillared buildings, elliptical site plans, lack of fortifications, and a limited pottery repertoire exhibiting regionalism—are all unique to the Iron Age I highlanders and indicate that they could not have come directly from the Late Bronze Age urban Canaanites. (There are those who argue that the Iron Age material culture is a direct development from the Late Bronze Age, but Finkelstein argues the similarities are only the result of two peoples living in close physical proximity.)

If the Iron Age peoples did not migrate into the Canaan and Transjordanian highlands from the Canaanite cities, where did they come from? Finkelstein argues that they did not come from anywhere; rather, they were already in the highlands during the Late Bronze Age, living as seminomadic pastoralists and, thus, left little for the archeological record. They become visible in the archeological record of the Iron Age simply because the collapse of the Late Bronze Canaanite cities forced (or encouraged) the highland pastoral-

---

16. Norman K. Gottwald, *The Tribes of Yahweh: A Sociology of the Religion of Liberated Israel, 1250–1050 b.c.e.* (Maryknoll, N.Y.: Orbis, 1979), 429, 433. For a similar approach dealing specifically with the settlement in Transjordan, see Robert G. Boling, *The Early Biblical Community in Transjordan* (Sheffield: Almond, 1988), 21–22, 35.

17. McGovern, *Beqʿah Valley Project*, 341.

18. Israel Finkelstein, *The Archaeology of the Israelite Settlement* (Jerusalem: Israel Exploration Society, 1988), 307, 312, 314, 338.

ists to settle down and adopt a more sedentary lifestyle with an emphasis on agriculture.[19]

Late Bronze Age

While Finkelstein has difficulty in finding evidence for the presence of seminomadic pastoralists (early Israelites) in the highlands of western Palestine, there may be such evidence for the central Transjordan plateau (early Ammonites?). Very few societies that specialize in pastoralism are completely self-sufficient.[20] Since they require certain foods and materials that only sedentary folks can provide, pastoralists generally have a symbiotic relationship with sedentary folks.[21] While this type of relationship can still retain a degree of tension between the cooperating parties, especially if they come from different sociopolitical or kinship backgrounds, in many cases a single tribe will provide both sedentary and nomadic elements.[22] This appears to be the situation in Late Bronze Age central Transjordan.

There is now increasing evidence of sedentary occupation in central Transjordan during the Late Bronze Age, contrary to Glueck's original gap hypothesis. Examples of occupation include Umm ad-Dananir, Tell Sahab, Tell Safut, the Amman airport temple, soundings from the Amman Citadel, Tell el-ʿUmeiri, possibly Tell Jawa (South), and a number of tombs at Amman and Umm ad-Dananir. Regional surveys of Hesban and the Madaba Plains also reveal some additional Late Bronze Age sites in the hinterland.

This new evidence for Late Bronze Age settlements in central Transjordan leads some scholars to suggest that a thriving urban civilization was

19. Finkelstein's evidence for a pastoral background for the Iron Age Israelites includes those same unique elements of Israel's material culture that distinguish it from the Canaanite cities—pillared buildings, grain silos, elliptical settlement plans. All of these characteristics, according to Finkelstein, reflect the pastoral backgrounds of the early Israelites.

20. One of the pioneering studies in this area is J. Tracy Luke's dissertation: *Pastoralism and Politics in the Mari Period: A Reexamination of the Character and Political Significance of the Major West Semitic Tribal Groups on the Middle Euphrates, ca. 1828–1758 B.C.* (Ph.D. diss., University of Michigan, 1965).

21. This realization led Michael B. Rowton to describe the interactions of ancient Near Eastern society as occurring within two major "dimorphs"—between urban and rural populations, in general, and between the sedentary farmer and nomadic pastoralist (who can belong to the same tribe). For a brief summary of Rowton's views and his complete bibliography see Kathryn A. Kamp and Norman Yoffee, "Ethnicity in Ancient Western Asia during the Early Second Millennium B.C.: Archaeological Assessments and Ethnoarchaeological Prospectives," *Bulletin of the American Schools of Oriental Research* 237 (1980): 85–104.

22. See Michael B. Rowton, "Enclosed Nomadism," *Journal of the Economic and Social History of the Orient* 17 (1974): 7 n. 3; Kay Prag, "Ancient and Modern Pastoral Migration in the Levant," *Levant* 17 (1985): 81–88.

there at this time, identical or at least comparable to that of the Canaanite city-states to the west.[23] However, a cursory view of western Palestine's Late Bronze Age sites shows considerable variation in their size and function. Megiddo, a major center, exhibits a city plan that reflects a complex, kinship-based social organization; especially significant is the separation of the palace from the main temple, indicating competing centers of authority within the social organization. Aphek, a smaller settlement, appears to be a residency for Egyptian governors, pointing to another facet in Canaan's complex social structure. Mevorakh and Lachish, isolated temple sites, reflect a variety of religious practices and beliefs. Small settlements were probably simple agricultural villages. This rather sophisticated and complex view of Canaanite society is also depicted in Egyptian sources like the Amarna letters.

The picture in Transjordan during this same time, however, appears to be different. Besides the possibility that Transjordan appears to have developed its own unique pottery tradition,[24] the variety and complexity seen in western

---

23. See McGovern, *Beqᶜah Valley Project*, 340. McGovern's argument that the settlement at Umm ad-Dananir was urban is based, in part, on the presence of certain cultivants (bread and immer wheat) and the bones of large draft animals, such as cattle. He also assumes a population density of 400–500 persons per hectare, which would create a fairly substantial population for the site. However, these data do not necessarily reflect an urban society. Cattle bones in the Umm ad-Dananir collection are only 0.82% of the total number of bones, which is considerably lower than the percentage from urban phases at Heshbon, where the percent of cattle bones from the Iron Age was 16%, the Hellenistic/Roman period nearly 12%, and the Mamluk 12%. As for botanical remains, there was no positive data for grape or tree crop production; the cultivants McGovern reports can be found among nomads as well as sedentary folks; see Frank Hole, "Pastoral Nomadism in Western Iran," in *Explorations in Ethnoarchaeology*, ed. Richard A. Gould (Albuquerque: University of New Mexico Press, 1978), 158. Finally, the population estimates McGovern uses appear to be twice as high as they should be, according to recent ethnographic and anthropological data compiled by Steve Falconer; see *Heartland of Villages: Reconsidering Early Urbanism in the Southern Levant* (Ph.D. diss., University of Arizona, 1987), 58–70.

24. H. J. Franken and W. J. A. Power, "Glueck's *Explorations in Eastern Palestine* in the Light of Recent Evidence," *Vetus Testamentum* 21 (1971): 119–23; Dornemann, *Archaeology of the Transjordan*, 23. Franken and Power note that analysis of Deir ᶜAlla pottery shows that "tribes from the east had their own pottery repertoire, which can be distinguished from the Late Bronze Age Canaanite repertoire" and "that much, which hitherto has been thought to be a simple development from Canaanite traditions, is in fact the continuation of Transjordanian traditions of the thirteenth century B.C. and not of Palestinian traditions" (121). Although Franken and Power allow that the Deir ᶜAlla pottery "is in some respects analogous to that of the transitional Late Bronze–Iron Age of Palestine," it is "not entirely so" (122). While Deir ᶜAlla is not on the central Transjordan plateau proper, its location to the west, between western Palestine and the Transjordanian plateau, makes it likely that the plateau's pottery followed its own lines of development. This conclusion is supported by some unique forms that appear in the Late Bronze Age repertoire of Umm ad-Dananir. For example, McGovern notes that "the LB II bowl types in the Baqᶜah had already diverged somewhat from the western Palestinian repertoire" (*Beqᶜah Valley Project*, 69). That Transjordan developed its own unique pottery tradition may

Palestine's settlements is missing in central Transjordan. None of the Late Bronze Age sites in central Transjordan display the complex city planning (and the accompanying social organization) seen at Megiddo and Hazor. Indeed, important Late Bronze Age settlements are limited to Ammon (although little is known about its Late Bronze Age settlement), Tell Safut, Tell Sahab, and possibly Tell el-ʿUmeiri and Tell Jawa (South).[25] So far, no monumental architecture has been recovered: no palaces or governors' residencies, and the only possible temple that has been recovered (the enigmatic Amman airport structure) appears to be a Hittite intrusion.[26] With the possible exceptions of Amman and Tell el-ʿUmeiri, none of these sites are comparable to the larger sites in western Palestine,[27] and all were probably self-sufficient in terms of subsistence.[28]

Yet, while Transjordan's Late Bronze Age settlements were self-sufficient in terms of subsistence, this does not mean they practiced intensive agriculture (a strategy usually associated with urban societies). Indeed, diachronic studies of central Transjordan's subsistence systems suggest that the Late Bronze Age was at a low ebb in terms of agriculture. Indicators for intensive agriculture such as higher numbers of cattle bones, seeds of tree crops, hinterland farmsteads, etc., are low for the Late Bronze Age when compared to

---

have sociopolitical implications; see Gloria London, "A Comparison of Two Contemporaneous Lifestyles of the Late Second Millennium B.C.," *Bulletin of the American Schools of Oriental Research* 273 (1989): 37–55.

25. As Boling notes, the Hesban survey turned up only six Late Bronze Age sites. Of these, two were dismissed as insignificant (the sites are small and the few Late Bronze Age sherds questionable). Of the other four, only Tell el-ʿUmeiri and Umm es-Sahab fall within traditional Ammonite territory, and only el-ʿUmeiri is classified as a major site. The el-ʿUmeiri Survey shows similar results: of fifty-five sites, only three were recorded as possible Late Bronze Age sites in the hinterland; see Boling, *Early Biblical Community,* 32–34. While Umm ad-Dananir is located on the central Transjordanian plateau, there is some question as to the ethnicity of the occupants. McGovern does not address this question, but Kallai suggests that Umm ad-Dananir was an Israelite site, just over the border from Ammon; see *Historical Geography,* 298 n. 36. While this suggestion is in harmony with my placement of the western boundary of Ammon, excavations there have so far turned up nothing uniquely Israelite. At any rate, Umm ad-Dananir is better classified as an important agricultural village, rather than a city, in my opinion.

26. See Larry G. Herr, "The Amman Airport Structure and the Geopolitics of Ancient Transjordan," *Biblical Archaeologist* 46 (1983): 223–29.

27. Wimmer records the area of Tell Safut as 17,728 square meters; "Excavations at Tell Safut," 279. Ibrahim describes Late Bronze Age Tell Sahab as covering over 20 dunums in area; "Sahab and Its Foreign Relations," in *Studies in the History and Archaeology of Jordan,* ed. Adnan Hadidi (Amman: Department of Antiquities of Jordan, 1987), 3:77.

28. This latter point is especially significant if one accepts Falconer's argument that the only settlements to be classified as true cities are those that are not self-sufficient. Thus, none of Transjordan's (or even western Palestine's) Late Bronze Age settlements can be properly defined as cities; see Falconer, *Heartland of Villages,* 315.

earlier and later periods in Transjordan.[29] While a similar period of abatement is seen in western Palestine, the indicators for intensive agriculture are still significantly higher there than for Transjordan.[30] Thus, it appears that the Late Bronze people of Transjordan were clearly more oriented toward sheep and goat pastoralism than their contemporaries in western Palestine.

In short, peoples east of the Jordan undoubtedly had contacts and relations with western Palestine during the Late Bronze Age. However, they not only developed a distinctive pottery tradition, they also maintained a less complex social system (reflected in smaller, homogenous settlements) and pursued their own self-sufficient subsistence strategy, which during the Late Bronze Age had oscillated toward a greater emphasis on pastoralism. Thus, rather than reflecting the Canaanite urban system to the west, the Late Bronze Age Transjordanian settlements appear to represent the sedentary component of a tribal society that was predominately pastoral in nature.[31]

This new understanding of indigenous oscillating settlement and subsistence patterns is beginning to influence the way some biblical scholars view the origins of the peoples of Transjordan. John Bartlett notes that "positive

29. Such oscillations have been documented for this region from the present back to Roman times and probably go back to the Early Bronze Age; see Øystein S. LaBianca, *Sedentarization and Nomadization: Food System Cycles at Hesban and Vicinity in Transjordan*, Heshbon Excavations Final Reports 1 (Berrien Springs, Mich.: Andrews University Press, 1990).

30. For example, at Ekron, Bronze Age cattle bones are fewer than those of the Iron Age, but still notably more frequent than those from the Late Bronze Age at Umm ad-Dananir; see Brian Hesse, "Animal Use at Tel Miqne–Ekron in the Bronze Age and Iron Age," *Bulletin of the American Schools of Oriental Research* 264 (1986): 17–27. Further evidence for intensive agricultural practices in western Palestine during the Late Bronze Age is seen in the Amarna letters, which report the collection of olive and grape crops for the Egyptian authorities in Canaan. See S. Ahituv, "Economic Factors in the Egyptian Conquest of Canaan," *Israel Exploration Journal* 28 (1978): 93–105.

31. Lack of literary and material remains makes it difficult to reconstruct the nature of the earliest Ammonite sociopolitical structure. However, Landes (*History of the Ammonites*, 178–79) argues that the persistent use of the element *Ammon* with the prefix *ben* in the Hebrew Bible indicates that the people of Ammon continued to be recognized as descendants of their tribal ancestor down to the seventh century (as opposed to the Moabites and Edomites whose names are not prefixed with *ben* or *beni*). The Ammonites thus never completely lost their identification with some form of tribal organization. In this connection it is interesting to note that, when Glueck came to realize that the so-called Edomite and Moabite border forts he discovered did not date to the time of the conquest, he conceded that these peoples may not have been organized into a state with a sedentary population. However, he still maintained that these people could have been present as semi-Bedouin and that they could have had "such strong possession of their areas as to be able to oppose the Israelites with sufficient strength to turn them aside and force them to make the long detour to the east of the lands they controlled"; see *Explorations in Eastern Palestine*, 153–54. Although "semi-Bedouin" may not be appropriate anthropological terminology, it seems probable that a similar situation existed with regard to the Ammonites during the latter part of the Late Bronze Age.

evidence for the origins of the Ammonites, Moabites and Edomites is not easy to find" and that "the recovery of the population had less to do with the invasion of peoples from Syria or North Arabian desert" than with natural "economic and environmental" oscillations. Bartlett concludes by saying that in the absence of any clear evidence Transjordan was "resettled by the invasion of foreign groups with new and distinctive ways of life" and that "the indigenous, if limited, population expanded with improving economic conditions."[32]

This idea of an indigenous origin of the Iron Age Ammonites is also supported by an increasing recognition of occupational continuity at central Transjordanian sites. At Tell Safut, for example, Donald H. Wimmer notes the continuity of occupation from Late Bronze Age II to Iron Age I. Specifically, he notes that "occupation of Tell Safut apparently continued with no clear destruction layers to interrupt its continued existence into the Late Iron Age in which there is ample testimony to a flourishing Ammonite population. This may suggest that the Ammonites entered the region long before current opinion likes to place them there."[33]

While it may be impossible to determine exactly when the people who came to be known as Ammonites achieved their national self-identity, there is no reason not to assume that the Iron Age Ammonites were derived directly from the Late Bronze Age population of central Transjordan.

Early Expansion and Conflict with Israel (Twelfth and Eleventh Centuries)

The earliest record of hostilities between the Ammonites and Israel is recorded in Judges 3:12–14, where the Ammonites are said to have joined with the Moabites and Amalekites against Israel. The coalition was apparently successful, for Israel was subject to King Eglon of Moab for eighteen years. The oppression was finally lifted when Ehud, the son of Gera the Benjamite, assassinated Eglon and led Israel in a successful campaign against Moab, leading to the latter's subjection for eighty years. Although the Ammonites are mentioned as participants in Moab's initial aggression, there is no indication what Ammon received for its assistance. It may not have been much, for there is no evidence that Ammon came to Moab's aid when the latter was later attacked by Israel.

32. John R. Bartlett, *Edom and the Edomites*, Journal for the Study of the Old Testament Supplement 77 (Sheffield: JSOT Press, 1989), 64–65.
33. See Wimmer, "Tell Safut Excavations," 165.

Whatever the case, it appears that the Ammonite sociopolitical system continued to develop to a point so that power was eventually concentrated in the office of king. Judges 11 mentions an unidentified Ammonite king whom Jephthah confronts. The first Ammonite king recorded by name is Nahash, noted for his conquest of Israelite territories bordering Ammon, especially his invasion across the Jabbok and the siege of Jabesh-Gilead (1 Sam. 11:1–11). His abhorrent command to put out the right eye of every Israelite incited the Israelites to rally around their own king, Saul, who led them to victory.[34]

Although there is no direct archeological evidence for these events, during this period (Iron Age IA–B) there is a distinct increase in the number of sites within Ammonite territory.[35] In addition to the Iron Age IA–B pottery recovered from excavations at Madaba, Tell Sahab, Hesban, Khirbet Hajjar, the Amman Citadel, Baqʿa Valley, and Tell el-ʿUmeiri, numerous sites from this period have turned up in hinterland surveys. It is also clear that a discernible transformation appears during this period as agricultural settlements sprouted throughout the countryside and the subsistence mode shifted from an emphasis on pastoralism to intensive agriculture.[36]

It used to be thought that the "megalithic towers" that archeological surveys had turned up around Amman were evidence of this early period of Ammonite expansion, but further analysis indicates that most of them probably date to the Iron Age II period (eighth–sixth centuries).

Contact with the Monarchy of Israel (Tenth and Ninth Centuries)

In spite of Saul's success against the Ammonites, Nahash retained his throne and eventually obtained a small amount of revenge by providing sanc-

---

34. In 1952 Roland de Vaux discovered in Dead Sea Cave 4 a manuscript of 1 Sam. 11 that indicates Nahash had already subjected Gad and Reuben prior to his demanding the surrender of Jabesh-Gilead. In essence, Nahash was demanding the surrender of rebels. Frank M. Cross suggests that this manuscript (now known as 4QSamᵃ) represents an early original account that was later dropped out of the Masoretic Text; see "The Ammonite Oppression of the Tribes of Gad and Reuben: Missing Verses from 1 Samuel 11 Found in 4QSamuelᵃ," in *History, Historiography, and Interpretation: Studies in Biblical and Cuneiform Literatures*, ed. Hayim Tadmor and Moshe Weinfeld (Jerusalem: Magnes, 1983), 153. Alexander Rofé, on the other hand, believes the additional material was the product of late scribal activity that expanded and revised the biblical manuscripts; see "The Acts of Nahash according to 4QSamᵃ," *Israel Exploration Journal* 32 (1982): 129–33. See also Terry L. Eves, "One Ammonite Invasion or Two? 1 Sam 10:27–11:2 in the Light of 4QSamᵃ," *Westminster Theological Journal* 44 (1982): 308–26.

35. Dornemann, *Archaeology of the Transjordan*, 163.

36. Øystein S. LaBianca, "Intensification of the Food System in Central Transjordan during the Ammonite Period," *Andrews University Seminary Studies* 27 (1989): 169–78.

tuary to Saul's antagonist, David. In time David himself became king of Israel, and when Nahash died David sent an envoy to Hanun, the son and successor of his former benefactor, to express sympathy (2 Sam. 10:1–2). Hanun's advisors, however, accused David's delegates of being spies and persuaded Hanun to humiliate and return them to David. This outrageous act incited David to immediately initiate a war against the Ammonites. In desperation, the Ammonites hired Aramean mercenaries to assist in their defense, but to no avail. Under the leadership of commanders Joab and Abishai (2 Sam. 10; 1 Chron. 19) the Israelites defeated the Ammonite-led coalition in the field and eventually captured their capital city, Rabbah, as well (2 Sam. 11:1; 12:26–31; 1 Chron. 20:1–3).[37] Whether Hanun was killed for his impudence is uncertain, but it seems clear that he did not continue in power, for after pillaging the city David seized the royal crown and placed it upon his own head. The crowns sculpted on male busts found in Amman and nearby regions may be typical depictions of the Ammonite royal diadem. Although Hanun's fate is unknown, it is of interest that, when David was forced to flee from his own son Absalom many years later, he headed toward Ammon, where he was ministered to by Shobi, the son of Nahash—probably a brother of Hanun (2 Sam. 17:27).

It is generally assumed that the Ammonites remained under the suzerainty of Israel during Solomon's reign. Ammonites were among the many foreign women whom Solomon loved (1 Kings 11:1) and married, and under whose influence the king was persuaded to build a sanctuary to their god Milcom or Molech (1 Kings 11:7).[38] One of these women, Naamah, was the mother of Rehoboam, who inherited the throne of Israel (1 Kings 14:21, 31; 2 Chron. 12:13) and whose intransigence led to the division of the monarchy.

Archeological evidence for this period (Iron Age IC, 1000–918), while still sparse, is increasing. Some remains have been recovered at Tell Sahab, Khirbet Hajjar, and the tomb at Madaba. New material from this period was found during the 1987 and 1989 seasons at Tell el-ʿUmeiri. The most dramatic find, on the western slope of the tell, was an Iron Age I casemate fortification system, including a rampart and a dry moat.[39] A destruction layer 6.6

---

37. For more on David's conflicts with the Ammonites, see John I. Lawlor, "Theology and Art in the Narrative of the Ammonite War (2 Samuel 10–12)," *Grace Theological Journal* 3 (1982): 193–205.

38. On Milcom, see Émile Puech, "Milkom, le Dieu Ammonite, en Amos i 15," *Vetus Testamentum* 27 (1977): 117–25.

39. See Lawrence T. Geraty et al., "Madaba Plains Project: A Preliminary Report of the 1987 Season at Tell el-ʿUmeiri and Vicinity," in *Preliminary Reports of ASOR-Sponsored Excavations, 1983–87,* ed. Walter E. Rast, Bulletin of the American Schools of Oriental Research Supplement 26 (Baltimore: Johns Hopkins University Press for the American Schools of Oriental Research, 1990), 59–88.

inches thick, composed of burned mud bricks, stones, and wooden roofing beams, was found inside the casemate. Several smashed collared-rim storage jars, typical of Iron Age I, were also found underneath the debris. Ash layers separated Iron Age I and Iron Age II occupation in other sections of the tell as well, suggesting the destruction of the whole site. Larry G. Herr, co-director of the Madaba Plains Project, suggests that this destruction could have been caused by King David's campaign against the Ammonites. Although the storage jars probably date to the earlier part of Iron Age I, it is not uncommon for such jars to be used for long periods of time.[40] Unfortunately, no unequivocal clues as to the identity of the destroyers of the city have yet been found, so the association with David's campaign remains only a suggestion.

Several Ammonite artifact types, which reached their zenith in Iron Age II (ninth to sixth centuries), find their predecessors in the tenth century, although they are not very abundant. These include the earlier figurine forms of a woman holding a tambourine, terra-cotta shrines, and anthropoid coffins.[41] Most metal objects are made of bronze and include knives, straight toggle pins, arrowheads, spearheads, bracelets, anklets, earrings, finger-rings, razors, and armor scales.[42]

Zenith of the Ammonite Kingdom (Ninth through Sixth Centuries)

During the early period of the divided monarchy, the Ammonites continued to be subjugated to the kingdom of Judah, as evidenced by the payment of tribute to kings Uzziah and Jotham (2 Chron. 26:8; 27:5). Later, when the Assyrian juggernaut rolled through the region, the Ammonites joined other Syro-Palestinian kingdoms in a coalition of resistance. The Ammonite army, led by King Ba'sa, son of Ruhubi, joined the alliance arrayed against Shalmaneser III at Qarqar in 853. After this event, it appears that the Israelites became involved in a conflict with the Arameans. The Ammonites, who may have enjoyed a degree of independence since the division of the Israelite monarchy, used this opportunity to join the Moabites and Meunites and invade Judah—possibly at the instigation of the Arameans (2 Chron. 20). Although Judah's king, Jehoshaphat, rallied his army to meet this threat, the Transjordan coalition fell apart before the soldiers of Judah arrived.

40. See London, "Comparison of Two Contemporaneous Lifestyles," 46.
41. Anthropoid coffins around the Amman area include those found at Tell Sahab Tomb A (ten–ninth century) and two types from the Royal Palace Tomb in Amman (dated respectively from the ten–ninth century and ten–seventh century); see Yassine, *Archaeology of Jordan*, 37.
42. Dornemann, *Archaeology of the Transjordan*, 149.

Archeological and extrabiblical sources are quite abundant for this period of Ammonite history (Iron Age II), especially during the eighth through the sixth centuries. This may be due to the Ammonites' liberation from the western kingdoms of Israel and Judah, caused in large part by the intervention of the Mesopotamian empires. This led to a period of tremendous economic growth. Indeed, Assyrian records suggest that by the time of Ashurbanipal (668–627), the Ammonites had become the wealthiest of all the Palestinian kingdoms—and had the dubious honor of paying the highest tribute to the Assyrian coffers (assuming that this higher tribute is a measure of wealth and not disloyalty).[43]

At any rate, the material culture of the Ammonites clearly reached its florescence during this period, as evidenced from the findings of numerous tomb deposits. Figurines are fairly abundant in these deposits (although some have been found in tell excavations). Most common is the "woman holding the tambourine" (continued from Iron Age I), which can be found as either a plaque (handmade or molded) or a pillar figurine. The majority of male figurines seem to belong to the "horse and rider" type, which Landes believes may suggest the existence of an Ammonite cavalry.[44] Other Ammonite figurines of the Iron Age include depictions of horses, camels, fish, and the Egyptian household god Bes.

A particularly interesting Ammonite figurine fragment was found during the 1989 season of the Madaba Plains Project at Tell Jawa (South), a border city that Albrecht Alt identifies as the Moabite city of Mephaath (Jer. 48:21–24), although the excavators question this identification.[45] The fragment depicts the head of a male wearing a headdress similar to the Egyptian *atef* crown and identical to those depicted on the well-known limestone busts displayed in the Amman Museum. Siegfried H. Horn suggests that these headdresses represent the crown worn exclusively by the Ammonite kings.[46] Although Horn suggests that this style of crown may date back to the time of

---

43. See *ANET* 301; Dornemann, *Archaeology of the Transjordan*, 180.

44. George M. Landes, "The Material Civilization of the Ammonites," *Biblical Archaeologist* 24 (1961): 66–86. While uncertain of their exact function, Dornemann (*Archaeology of the Transjordan*, 140) believes these figurines (which are almost always found in tombs) possibly had something to do with the mortuary cult, although the figurines represent human and not divine beings. Perhaps they were intended to represent individuals who belonged to socially honored or elite groups.

45. Albrecht Alt, "Das Institut im Jahr 1932," *Palästinajahrbuch des Deutschen evangelischen Instituts für Altertumswissenschaft des Heiligen Landes zu Jerusalem* 29 (1933): 26; Randall W. Younker and P. Michelle Daviau, "Is Mefaᶜat to Be Found at Tell Jawa (South)?" *Israel Exploration Journal* 43 (1993): 23–28.

46. Siegfried H. Horn, "The Crown of the King of the Ammonites," *Andrews University Seminary Studies* 11 (1973): 170–80 and pls. xvii–xx.

David, most of the archeological representations date from the eighth to the sixth centuries.[47]

In addition to the limestone busts, several other sculptures have been found in ancient Ammon. Indeed, more sculpture has been found in this region than anywhere else in Palestine. Male statues are for the most part free standing and seem to depict noble or royal personages.[48] One of the statues has an inscription that Fawzi Zayadine translates as "of Yarah-ʿazar, son of Zakir(?), son of Shanib."[49] Zayadine equates Shanib with a certain Shanipu, an Ammonite king mentioned in the second campaign account of Tiglath-pileser III. Zayadine further suggests that both Yarah-ʿazar and Zakir were Ammonite kings, thus extending the list of known kings of Ammon by two. Female sculptures are restricted to double-faced heads that may have served an architectural function. Based on the reverential attitude that many of the statues display, Rudolph H. Dornemann believes some if not most of them were created for display within a sacred precinct, perhaps a temple or a shrine. Al-

Male figure wearing an Atef crown, 8th–6th century B.C. (height: 3.1″)

Courtesy of Randall W. Younker

47. If so, this artifact would suggest that Tell Jawa (South) was within the Ammonite (rather than Moabite) sphere of influence at this time and would render the identification of earlier scholars unlikely. An Ammonite occupation of this site is also supported by the pottery, which is typical of Ammonite sites such as nearby Tell el-ʿUmeiri. It should also be noted that an expansion of Ammonite borders is suggested by archeological data from Tell Hesban (see also Jer. 48:21–24), Tell Mazar, and Tell Safut; see W. Vyhmeister, "The History of Heshbon from Literary Sources," in *Historical Foundations: Studies of Literary References to Hesban and Vicinity*, ed. Lawrence T. Geraty and Leona G. Running, Heshbon Excavations Final Reports 3 (Berrien Springs, Mich.: Andrews University Press, 1989), 9–10; Yassine, *Archaeology of Jordan*, 87–88; Wimmer, "Tell Safut Excavations," 165. See also the references in n. 45 above. The southern extension of Ammonite territory to Heshbon would make it even more likely that Tell Jawa (South) was within Ammonite territory.

48. For description and bibliography of these statues, see Dornemann, *Archaeology of the Transjordan*, 153–63.

49. Fawzi Zayadine, "Note sur l'Inscription de la Statue d'Amman J. 1656," *Syria* 51 (1974): 129–36.

though Egyptian and Syrian influences can be seen in the work, they all appear to be the work of indigenous artisans who created a distinctive local flavor.

In 1966 an Iron Age tomb was found on the grounds of the Raghdan Royal Palace, which contained five anthropomorphic (or anthropoid) coffins, similar to the well-known Philistine coffins from western Palestine. Jordanian archeologist Khair N. Yassine suggests that these coffins were used to bury Ammonite chiefs. Some scholars believe that both the Philistine and Transjordanian coffins reflect an Egyptian influence since similar coffins were used for the burial of royal and noble Egyptian mummies, although the Palestinian versions are more crude and grotesque.[50]

Metal objects from the Iron Age II also continue Iron Age I traditions, although there are some distinct stylistic changes and some new forms do appear.[51] The Iron Age II corpus continued from earlier traditions includes bracelets, earrings, finger-rings, knife blades, and bronze vessels (a wine service). New forms include bronze mirrors, fibulas, new types of arrow points, long kohl sticks, and new types of finger-rings and earrings.

While these small finds are interesting, probably the most exciting artifacts an archeologist recovers are objects with writing—usually either ostraca or seal impressions. The lack of any extensive ancient Ammonite literary works naturally impedes a complete understanding of that ancient language, but enough has been found to assign Ammonite to the Canaanite family of languages, closely related to Hebrew.[52] Indeed, discoveries during the last thirty years have greatly increased the corpus of Ammonite inscriptions to over 130 stamps and seal impressions, nearly a score of ostraca, and several important inscriptions.

One of the most important inscriptional finds is the bronze bottle exca-

---

50. Yassine, *Archaeology of Jordan*, 33–46.
51. Dornemann, *Archaeology of the Transjordan*, 150.
52. On the Ammonite script see Larry G. Herr, "The Formal Scripts of Iron Age Transjordan," *Bulletin of the American Schools of Oriental Research* 238 (1980): 21–34. On the Ammonite language see Kent P. Jackson, *The Ammonite Language of the Iron Age*, Harvard Semitic Monographs 27 (Chico, Calif.: Scholars Press, 1983); cf. the review by Walter E. Aufrecht, *Bulletin of the American Schools of Oriental Research* 266 (1987): 85–95. See also Kent P. Jackson, "Ammonite Personal Names in the Context of the West Semitic Onomasticon," in *The Word of the Lord Shall Go Forth: Essays in Honor of David Noel Freedman*, ed. Carol L. Meyers and Michael P. O'Connor (Winona Lake, Ind.: Eisenbrauns, 1983), 507–21; B. Becking, "Kann das Ostrakon ND 6231 von Nimrud für ammonitisch gehalten werden?" *Zeitschrift des Deutschen Palästina-Vereins* 104 (1988): 59–67; Paul E. Dion, "Notes d'Épigraphie Ammonite," *Revue Biblique* 82 (1975): 24–33; Michael P. O'Connor, "The Ammonite Onomasticon: Semantic Problems," *Andrews University Seminary Studies* 25 (1987): 51–64. For a comprehensive bibliography of studies of Ammonite inscriptions up to 1989 see Walter E. Aufrecht, *A Corpus of Ammonite Inscriptions* (Lewiston, N.Y.: Mellen, 1989).

vated at Tell Siran bearing a complete Ammonite inscription.[53] The inscription mentions two individuals named Amminadab, who each ruled as an Ammonite king. Their reigns were separated by a certain Hissal-El. The name *Amminadab* is also inscribed on two seals discovered in tombs near Amman—an individual generally equated with the Ammonite king of the same name known from a 687 inscription of the Assyrian king Ashurbanipal. Since the Siran bottle lists two Ammonite kings with this same name, it is difficult to know which, if either, is to be equated with Ashurbanipal's inscription and the seals. The bottle's inscription is variously interpreted as a building inscription, a love song, and a drinking song. It talks of a vineyard, gardens, a channel or temple(?), and cisterns. Grains placed in the bottle include two species of wheat and one of barley.[54] Whatever the exact function of the bottle, it reflects the agricultural intensity and success that is corroborated by other archeological data.

The ninth-century Amman Citadel Inscription was found by Rafik W. Dajani in 1961. The text consists of thirty-three words carved on a limestone block, approximately 10.25 inches by 7.5 inches. Because the inscription is incomplete, it has been interpreted in a variety of ways.[55] Several scholars understand it as a building inscription, perhaps of a temple or citadel. Others see it as an oracle from the Ammonite god Milcom, ordering the construction of defensive towers around the perimeter of Rabbah-ammon. In spite of its uncertain meaning, it provides important clues about the linguistic and paleographic characteristics of the Ammonite language.

---

53. See Henry O. Thompson and Fawzi Zayadine, "The Tell Siran Inscription," *Bulletin of the American Schools of Oriental Research* 212 (1973): 5–11; Frank M. Cross, "Notes on the Ammonite Inscription from Tell Sīrān," *Bulletin of the American Schools of Oriental Research* 212 (1973): 12–15; Charles R. Krahmalkov, "An Ammonite Lyric Poem," *Bulletin of the American Schools of Oriental Research* 223 (1976): 55–57; Oswald Loretz, "Die ammonitische Inschrift von Tell Siran," *Ugarit-Forschungen* 9 (1977): 169–71; William H. Shea, "Siran Inscription: Amminadab's Drinking Song," *Palestine Exploration Quarterly* 110 (1978): 107–12; John A. Emerton, "The Meaning of the Ammonite Inscription from Tell Siran," in *Von Kanaan bis Kerala: Festschrift für . . . J. P. M. van der Ploeg,* ed. W. C. Delsman et al., Alter Orient und Altes Testament 211 (Kevelaer: Butzon & Bercker/Neukirchener-Vluyn: Neukirchener Verlag, 1982), 367–78; Gösta W. Ahlström, "The Tell Siran Bottle Inscription," *Palestine Exploration Quarterly* 116 (1984): 12–15.

54. Hans Halbaek, "Grain from the Tell Siran Bronze Bottle," *Annual of the Department of Antiquities of Jordan* 19 (1974): 167–68.

55. See Siegfried H. Horn, "The Ammân Citadel Inscription," *Bulletin of the American Schools of Oriental Research* 193 (1969): 2–13; Frank M. Cross, "Epigraphic Notes on the Ammān Citadel Inscription," *Bulletin of the American Schools of Oriental Research* 193 (1969): 13–19; V. Sasson, "The 'Amman Citadel Inscription as an Oracle Promising Divine Protection," *Palestine Exploration Quarterly* 111 (1979): 117–25; William H. Shea, "The Amman Citadel Inscription Again," *Palestine Exploration Quarterly* 113 (1981): 105–10.

Interestingly, seals and seal impressions provide one of our few insights into Ammonite religion. According to 1 Kings 11:5 the national god of the Ammonites was Milcom. This name appears on a seal from the Neo-Babylonian period and on another from the Persian period. It also appears as a theophoric element in names on several other Ammonite seals, for example, Milkom-ʾur, the servant of the Ammonite king Baalis inscribed on a seal impression found at Tell el-ʿUmeiri.[56]

Little else is currently known about Ammonite religion. It is often assumed that the biblical references to burning children to Molech has something to do with the Ammonite cult, although this is far from certain.[57] Like many peoples in the area, the Ammonites practiced circumcision (Jer. 9:25–26 [MT 9:24–25]), but details on its significance for the Ammonites are lacking.

Besides the numerous small objects and inscriptions from the ninth to sixth centuries just described, there have been a number of large architectural finds. The most impressive of these are the numerous megalithic structures throughout the Ammonite countryside. Glueck (and a number of scholars following him) identifies most of these structures as towers, assumed to have been part of an elaborate defensive system constructed by the early Ammonites during the thirteenth and twelfth centuries to prevent encroachment upon their territory by neighboring kingdoms.[58] However, excavations of several of these towers reveal that they were built no earlier than Iron Age II, perhaps sometime between the eighth and sixth centuries.[59]

End of the Ammonite Kingdom

The latter part of the Iron Age II (seventh–sixth centuries) continued

---

56. See Larry G. Herr, "The Servant of Baalis," *Biblical Archaeologist* 48 (1985): 169–72.

57. On the vexed problem of Molech, see Alberto R. W. Green, *The Role of Human Sacrifice in the Ancient Near East*, American Schools of Oriental Research Dissertation Series 1 (Missoula, Mont.: Scholars Press for American Schools of Oriental Research, 1975), 179–87.

58. Glueck, *Explorations in Eastern Palestine*, 163; Landes, *History of the Ammonites*, 74.

59. There is, of course, the possibility that the pottery found in some of these structures represents only the latest occupation of a particular phase and that construction could be pushed back to a slightly earlier period, although Iron Age I (twelfth century) sherds have only been reported from one excavated site, so far; see Henry O. Thompson, "The Ammonite Remains at Khirbet al-Hajjar," *Bulletin of the American Schools of Oriental Research* 227 (1979): 29. Shea makes an interesting suggestion that the Amman Citadel Inscription was intended to be an oracle of the god Milcom to an Ammonite king in which the latter is instructed to build round towers to defend the approaches of Ammon. Since the inscription has been dated to about the middle of the ninth century or the first half of the eighth century, it would roughly correspond to the earliest construction date for these "towers." See William H. Shea, "Milkom as the Architect of Rabbath-Ammon's Natural Defenses in the Amman Citadel Inscription," *Palestine Exploration Quarterly* 111 (1979): 18–25.

to witness increased economic and political power for the Ammonites.[60] This success is reflected in Jeremiah 49, where the prophet rebukes the Ammonites for taking advantage of Judah's misfortunes by moving into the territory of Gad: "Why do you boast of your valleys, boast of your valleys so fruitful? O unfaithful daughter, you trust in your riches and say, 'Who will attack me?' " (v. 4 NIV). The Hesban and Madaba Plains surveys have recorded a number of contemporary structures throughout the Ammonite hinterland that appear to be part of well-planned agricultural complexes. This interpretation is confirmed by the presence of enclosure walls, cisterns, winepresses, cupholes, terraces, smaller field towers, and other associated food-production features found in the vicinity of these structures.[61] Obviously, Ammonite agricultural success provided a firm economic base that in turn led to the political confidence, which provoked the prophet's rebuke.

It was this same economic and political confidence that undoubtedly led to the events described in Jeremiah 27 and 40, where the prophet accuses an unnamed Ammonite king of leading a rebellion against Babylon. Jeremiah later identifies Baalis as the one responsible for the assassination of the Babylonian-appointed governor, Gedaliah. A seal impression with an Ammonite inscription, discovered in 1984 at Tell el-ʿUmeiri, reads, "Belonging to Milkom-ʾur, servant of Baʿal-yashaʿ." The owner's name contains the theophoric element *Milcom*, the primary Ammonite deity; the king's name, *bʿlyshʿ*, may be identified with Baalis of Jeremiah 40:14.[62] The identification of the person on this seal with the Ammonite king is also supported by the date of the script (ca. 600) and by the iconography, which includes the four-winged scarab, formerly used as a royal motif of the western kingdoms of Israel and Judah. Ammonite adaptation of this symbol is another indication that political power and prestige had gravitated to the Ammonite ruler by the seventh and sixth centuries.[63]

60. Evidence for an increase in Ammonite political strength is also supported by the expansion of its borders at this time: Ammonite remains have been reported at Hesban in the south, Mazar in the Jordan Valley, and the Baqʿa Valley in the north. See the references in n. 4 above.

61. Reexamination of the location of some of Glueck's original "towers" as well as recent studies of related structures in the vicinity of Hesban and Tell el-ʿUmeiri show that many of these buildings were not strategically located; see Dornemann, *Archaeology of the Transjordan*, 123; Lawrence T. Geraty et al., "Madaba Plains Project: A Preliminary Report of the 1984 Season at Tell el-ʿUmeiri and Vicinity," in *Preliminary Reports of ASOR-Sponsored Excavations, 1980–84*, ed. Walter E. Rast, Bulletin of the American Schools of Oriental Research Supplement 24 (Winona Lake, Ind.: Eisenbrauns for the American Schools of Oriental Research, 1986), 123.

62. Herr, "Servant of Baalis."

63. Randall W. Younker, "Israel, Judah, and Ammon and the Motifs on the Baalis Seal from Tell el-ʿUmeiri," *Biblical Archaeologist* 48 (1985): 173–80.

Seal of Milkom-ʾur, servant of Baʿal-yashaʿ (cf. Baalis in Jer. 40:14), 6th century B.C. (diameter: 0.8″)

Courtesy of Randall W. Younker

It would seem unusual for the Babylonians to ignore the blatant murder of their own appointed leader of Judah (Gedaliah), and, indeed, Josephus claims that Nebuchadnezzar conducted a punitive campaign against the Ammonites in his twenty-third year (582–581).[64] There is some indication that Josephus's account of Nebuchadnezzar's punitive campaign against the Ammonites is historical. Occupation at several Ammonite sites such as Tell Safut, Tell el-Mazar, Tell Jawa (South), and Tell Hesban may have been terminated or interrupted at this time.[65]

While it may be that the Ammonite kingdom ceased to function as an independent or semi-independent polity about this time, the Ammonite people appear to have continued to occupy their land well into Hellenistic times and beyond. This is supported by later literary references to Ammonites and the recent archeological findings of the Madaba Plains Project, which show continuous occupation in Ammonite territory down into the Persian and perhaps early Hellenistic periods.[66]

64. Josephus also provides a full account of the assassination of Gedaliah; see *Antiquities* 10:9:3–4 §163–73.

65. Yassine suggests that stratum 3 at Tell el-Mazar, which he believes was in Ammonite hands at this time, was possibly destroyed by this campaign of Nebuchadnezzar. Another site possibly destroyed at this time is Tell Safut, although the excavator, Donald H. Wimmer, does not attempt to tie the destruction to any known historical event. Some scholars suggest that Heshbon, which also was apparently in Ammonite hands at this time (Jer. 49:3) was also sacked during this campaign.

66. See James A. Sauer, "Transjordan in the Bronze and Iron Ages: A Critique of Glueck's Synthesis," *Bulletin of the American Schools of Oriental Research* 263 (1986): 18; Lawrence T.

Key biblical references for Ammonite activity during this period are Nehemiah 2:10, 19; 4:3 [MT 3:35]; 4:7 [MT 4:1]; 6:1, 12, 14; 13:4–8. These texts describe the actions of a certain Tobiah, an Ammonite official (Hebrew *ᶜebed*) who resisted Nehemiah's restoration program in Jerusalem.[67] The activities of the Tobiad family, which was apparently part Jewish, continued in Transjordan well into Hellenistic and later times, as indicated by Josephus (*Antiquities* 12:4:2 §160).[68]

Evidence for the Tobiads in Transjordan has been found in the Wadi es-Sir at Iraq el-Amir, west of Amman. The name *Tobiah* is actually carved on the entrances of two caves on the north side of the wadi in old Hebrew characters. Epigraphers date the inscriptions between the second and fourth centuries.[69] A large second-century building, known locally as Qasr el-Abd ("the castle of the slave"), is believed to be either the fort or the palace of the Tobiads.[70]

Conclusion

The Ammonite people resided on the central Transjordanian plain from at least the Late Bronze Age until the end of the Iron Age, and perhaps beyond. For much of their early existence the Ammonites were integrated with the political/economic system of the Cisjordanian kingdoms of Israel and Judah, as reflected in the transformation of their socioeconomic structure from a pastoral mode to one of intensive agriculture. While their initial interaction with and domination by Israel and Judah may have contributed in their socioeconomic development, it was not until they were freed of the dominance of the west that they were really able to develop. They reached the zenith of their power in the seventh and sixth centuries. Sometime during the sixth century their power seems to have waned, although their occupation of the land continued into the Persian and Hellenistic periods.

Geraty et al., "The Madaba Plains Project: A Preliminary Report of the 1987 Season at Tell el-ᶜUmeiri and Vicinity," *Andrews University Seminary Studies* 26 (1988): 226; Younker et al., "Joint Madaba Plains Project," 13, 22.

67. For more on Tobiah the Ammonite, see Edwin M. Yamauchi, "Ezra–Nehemiah," in *The Expositor's Bible Commentary*, ed. Frank E. Gaebelein (Grand Rapids: Zondervan, 1988), 4:687–88.

68. For fuller discussions on the Tobiads see Benjamin Mazar, "The Tobiads," *Israel Exploration Journal* 7 (1957): 140–41; Dov Gera, "On the Credibility of the History of the Tobiads," in *Greece and Rome in Eretz Israel*, ed. Aryeh Kasher, Uriel Rappaport, and Gideon Fuks (Jerusalem: Israel Exploration Society, 1990), 21–38.

69. See Frank M. Cross, "The Development of the Jewish Scripts," in *The Bible and the Ancient Near East: Essays in Honor of William Foxwell Albright*, ed. G. Ernest Wright (Winona Lake, Ind.: Eisenbrauns, 1979), 191 n. 13.

70. See Gera, "History of the Tobiads," 26.

Recommended Reading

Aufrecht, Walter E. *A Corpus of Ammonite Inscriptions.* Lewiston, N.Y.: Mellen, 1989.

Block, Daniel I. *"Bny ʿmwn:* The Sons of Ammon." *Andrews University Seminary Studies* 22 (1984): 197–212.

Dornemann, Rudolph. *The Archaeology of the Transjordan in the Bronze and Iron Ages.* Milwaukee: Milwaukee Public Museum, 1983.

Glueck, Nelson. *Explorations in Eastern Palestine,* part 3. Annual of the American Schools of Oriental Research 18–19. New Haven: American Schools of Oriental Research, 1939.

——. "Explorations in the Land of Ammon." *Bulletin of the American Schools of Oriental Research* 68 (1937): 13–21.

Herr, Larry G. "Whatever Happened to the Ammonites?" *Biblical Archaeology Review* 19.6 (Nov.–Dec. 1993): 26–35, 68.

Jackson, Kent P. *The Ammonite Language of the Iron Age.* Harvard Semitic Monographs 27. Chico, Calif.: Scholars Press, 1983.

Landes, George M. *A History of the Ammonites.* Ph.D. diss., Johns Hopkins University, 1956.

McGovern, Patrick E. *The Late Bronze Age and Early Iron Ages of Central Transjordan: The Baqʿah Valley Project, 1977–1981.* Philadelphia: University Museum, 1986.

Yassine, Khair N. *The Archaeology of Jordan: Essays and Reports.* Amman: Department of Archaeology, University of Jordan, 1988.

Moabites

Gerald L. Mattingly

Now Mesha king of Moab raised sheep, and he had to supply the king of Israel with a hundred thousand lambs and with the wool of a hundred thousand rams. But after Ahab died, the king of Moab rebelled against the king of Israel.

—2 Kings 3:4–5

In 1924, the great Orientalist William F. Albright made the following observation:

> For many years students of Palestine have been painfully aware of a serious lacuna in their knowledge of the land and its antiquities. Much explored as the Holy Land has been, there are sections which virtually remain *terra incognita*, which have not even been geographically surveyed, and still less archaeologically. Even Western Palestine is inadequately studied, and Eastern Palestine still contains districts which are an archaeological blank.[1]

The last seven decades have witnessed a rapid expansion in our knowledge of Syro-Palestinian archeology. In recent years, the accumulation of primary evidence and the construction of theories based on that data have brought remarkable progress to our understanding of ancient Jordan, along with other Middle Eastern countries.[2] Nelson Glueck's surface survey of the Transjordan, launched in 1933 and published in his monumental *Explorations in Eastern Palestine*, provided a point of departure for many subsequent inves-

1. William F. Albright, "The Archaeological Results of an Expedition to Moab and the Dead Sea," *Bulletin of the American Schools of Oriental Research* 14 (1924): 2.
2. The investigation of Jordan's history and culture is moving at a rapid pace. For a sample of the different avenues of inquiry being pursued at present, see *Studies in the History and Archaeology of Jordan*, ed. Adnan Hadidi et al., vols. 1–4 (Amman: Department of Antiquities, 1982–92). Each issue of the *Annual of the Department of Antiquities of Jordan* contains much valuable research.

tigations of the region's history and culture.[3] This is especially true for those interested in the rise, development, and collapse of the kingdoms of Ammon, Moab, and Edom—names well known to students of the Old Testament.

Despite advances in our understanding of Jordan's past, there are still unanswered questions concerning the nature and density of human occupation in specific regions and periods, and it may sometimes appear that little progress has been made—at least on the level of historical-cultural synthesis—since Glueck's pioneering efforts in the 1930s. Although the Moabite plateau of central Jordan is no longer *terra incognita*, it has not been subjected to the historical and archeological inquiry it deserves. Until recently, very few research projects have been conducted in this territory, which has been fully accessible to archeologists for many years. Following an overview of Moabite history and culture, I will identify some important steps made in the archeological investigation of ancient Moab, an effort in which I have been involved for a number of years.

Geography and Chronology

Before examining the details of Moab's history and culture,[4] it is necessary to define the terms *Moab* and *Moabite*, since these words narrow the geographical limits and chronological focus of this survey. *Moab* refers to a people and their territory, just as, for example, the name *Israel* was used to designate a land and its population within a specific period of history. In geographical terms, Moab was that part of the Transjordanian plateau located immediately east of the Dead Sea Valley. While the southern border of Moabite territory was fixed by the biblical Brook Zered (modern Wadi el-Ḥesa), with Edom to the south, Moab's northern boundary changed from time to

3. Any reference to Nelson Glueck must be prefaced with praise for his remarkable accomplishments, though his work is now subject to revision. Glueck's primary findings were published in the Annual of the American Schools of Oriental Research (nos. 14, 15, 18–19, and 25–28) between 1934 and 1951, under the title *Explorations in Eastern Palestine*, parts 1–4. Part 1 focuses on the Moabite territory south of Wadi el-Mujib, but Glueck deals with "Greater Moab" in parts 2 and 3 as well. Glueck's major secondary work is *The Other Side of the Jordan*, rev. ed. (Cambridge, Mass.: American Schools of Oriental Research, 1970).

4. Until recent years, the standard source on all things Moabite was A. H. Van Zyl, *The Moabites* (Leiden: Brill, 1960), but this volume is outdated—though not without continuing value for its reconstruction of Moabite history and culture. Nowadays the major studies on Moab's history are J. Andrew Dearman (ed.), *Studies in the Mesha Inscription and Moab* (Atlanta: Scholars Press, 1989); Stefan Timm, *Moab zwischen den Mächten: Studien zu historischen Denkmälern und Texten* (Wiesbaden: Harrassowitz, 1989); and J. Maxwell Miller (ed.), *Archaeological Survey of the Kerak Plateau* (Atlanta: Scholars Press/American Schools of Oriental Research, 1991). Also important is John R. Bartlett, "The Moabites and Edomites," in *Peoples of Old Testament Times*, ed. Donald J. Wiseman (Oxford: Clarendon, 1973), 229–58.

time. During periods of national strength, the Moabites controlled land that stretched from the Zered (Num. 21:12; Deut. 2:13–14) to the vicinity of ancient Heshbon, a territory whose maximum north-south extent was only about sixty miles and beyond whose northern frontier lay the kingdom of Ammon. When Moabite power waned, as in the heyday of the Amorite king Sihon and during periods of Israelite control in Transjordan, their domain was reduced to the undisputed heartland of Moab—the region between the Zered and the biblical River Arnon (modern Wadi el-Mujib). This northern boundary fluctuated because of political and military conditions, as attested in the Bible and the Mesha Inscription (also known as the Moabite Stone).[5]

The territory north of Wadi el-Mujib is called northern Moab, and it corresponds to what the biblical writers called the *mîšôr* ("the tableland") or the "tableland of Madaba," after its major town. Attached to this northern section is the area known in the Bible as the "Plains of Moab." Southern Moab, located south of the Mujib, was Moabite territory par excellence, but it was not as well known to the Old Testament authors.

While the Arabah, which is part of a major geological fault that cuts across the Levant into east Africa, provided an effective boundary between Judah and Moab (thereby restricting Moabite-Israelite contact), the eastern desert was both a blessing and a curse to the Moabites, since it provided protection from some enemies but convenient access to the plateau for various Arab peoples over the centuries. Although environmental factors did not make Moab as inhospitable as is often portrayed, it is true that most of this region's sedentary population was restricted to a narrow strip of cultivable land that was sandwiched between the Dead Sea escarpment and the fringe of the Syrian Desert, a zone that extended only about fifteen miles east of the plateau's rim.[6]

The national or ethnic designation *Moabite* refers to the people who inhabited this tiny kingdom from near the end of the Late Bronze Age until the end of the Iron Age (i.e., from ca. 1300 to 600). Iron Age Moabite culture was, no doubt, influenced by the pre-Moabite population of this region,

---

5. See especially J. Andrew Dearman, "Historical Reconstruction and the Meshaᶜ Inscription," in *Studies in the Mesha Inscription and Moab*, ed. J. Andrew Dearman (Atlanta: Scholars Press, 1989), 155–210.

6. For more detailed descriptions of the Moabite region, see Gerald L. Mattingly, "The Natural Environment of Central Moab," *Annual of the Department of Antiquities of Jordan* 27 (1983): 597–605; Frank L. Koucky, "The Regional Environment," in *The Roman Frontier in Central Jordan*, ed. S. Thomas Parker (Oxford: British Archaeological Reports, 1987), 11–40; Jack R. Harlan, "The Early Bronze Age Environment of the Southern Ghor and the Moab Plateau," in *Studies in the History and Archaeology of Jordan*, ed. Adnan Hadidi (Amman: Department of Antiquities, 1985), 2:125–29. A massive treatment of the total environmental context for this region is Øystein S. LaBianca and Larry Lacelle (eds.), *Environmental Foundations*, Heshbon Excavations Final Reports 2 (Berrien Springs, Mich.: Andrews University Press, 1986).

which can be called "Canaanite" for lack of a better term.[7] Like their Judean, Ammonite, and Edomite neighbors, the Moabites lost their autonomy during the Babylonian invasion of the early sixth century. The Moabite kingdom never reappeared, and with the arrival of new peoples (with their material cultures, languages, and religions), Moabite identity was gradually lost, though, in certain respects, Moabite culture proved to be remarkably durable. Although it was a tiny state, the Bible reflects the significance of this people in the Hebrew purview, since the words *Moab* and *Moabite* appear nearly two hundred times in the Old Testament.

Land and Economy

The terrain of Moab may be described as gently rolling tableland, but numerous streams—winter torrents (i.e., wadis) dry throughout most of the year—drain the plateau and have cut deep ravines across its surface; these wadis run in all directions, but the major systems empty into the Dead Sea canyon on the west. The plateau's western side has a higher elevation than the lower desert fringe on the east; this western half of the plateau receives more rainfall and is therefore better suited to agriculture. As is still the case today, the land of Moab has always been famous for its pasturage; 2 Kings 3:4 reports that "King Mesha of Moab was a sheep breeder, who used to deliver to the king of Israel [Ahab] one hundred thousand lambs, and the wool of one hundred thousand rams" (NRSV). Not to be overlooked are Moab's Mediterranean soils and climate, which allow for the growing of wheat and barley, along with a variety of other crops, including fruit trees and vineyards. Average precipitation is around fourteen inches per year, and the tableland's residents have always depended on a small number of springs, a few perennial streams, and cisterns cut into the plateau's limestone bedrock. Another factor in the Moabite economy was the ancient dynamic between "the desert and the sown." This symbiotic relationship between townsfolk, villagers, and nomadic groups was critical to the ebb and flow of the region's history and culture.[8]

Moab is also famous for its connection to the biblical narrative involving Moses, the Hebrews, and the so-called King's Highway, the *derek hammelek* (lit., "the royal way"). Mentioned in Numbers 20:17 and 21:22 (cf. Deut.

---

7. On Moab in the Early Bronze Age, see Gerald L. Mattingly, "Settlement Patterns and Sociocultural Reconstruction," in *Benchmarks in Time and Culture: An Introduction to Palestinian Archaeology*, ed. Joel F. Drinkard Jr., Gerald L. Mattingly, and J. Maxwell Miller (Atlanta: Scholars Press, 1988), 389–415.

8. Miller, *Archaeological Survey of the Kerak Plateau*, 5–6.

2:27), this road is considered the major international highway traversing the Transjordanian plateau from end to end. It is not necessary to imagine that the modern highway that mainly follows the Roman road (the *Via Nova Traiana*) corresponds to the biblical King's Highway. The plateau was certainly traversed by trade routes in antiquity (including several royal roads), but there was not a significant line of settlements along a single road in Moab's remote past, as Glueck postulates. Water and farmland were more critical in the distribution of ancient settlements, at least until the Romans constructed a rather straight route across the tableland, shortly after A.D. 106.[9]

Origin and Early History

The origin of this Semitic people is described in a straightforward way in Genesis 19:37: the Moabites descended from Moab, the son of Lot and his older daughter.[10] According to Deuteronomy 2:10–11, the Emim or Emites ("terrible ones" or "frightful ones") were the giant, pre-Moabite occupants of this region defeated by Chedorlaomer and his military coalition long before the Israelites encountered them (Gen. 14:5).[11] Archeological investigations indicate that the Moabite plateau, including the Dead Sea Valley at the foot of the escarpment, contained a significant population and a substantial culture in the third millennium, the Early Bronze Age.[12]

Though Glueck's view concerning an occupational gap in Moab during much of the second millennium is now in need of revision, it does appear that there was a decline in population (or a shift away from a sedentary lifestyle) during the Middle Bronze Age and the first part of the Late Bronze Age (i.e., from ca. 1900 to 1300). Any explanation given for this phenomenon must also take into account the appearance of a Moabite kingdom, sometime around 1300. This population decline or a change in the nature of settlement—either of which could have produced the apparent scarcity in the amount of archeological data that come from this period—has been used to

9. James R. Kautz III, "King's Highway," in *ISBE* 3:39. Cf. Bustenay Oded, "Observations on Methods of Assyrian Rule in Transjordania after the Palestinian Campaign of Tiglath-pileser III," *Journal of Near Eastern Studies* 29 (1970): 177–86.

10. On Moabite origins in general, see the essays by Dearman, Miller, and Mattingly in *Early Edom and Moab: The Beginning of the Iron Age in Southern Jordan*, ed. Piotr Bienkowski (Sheffield: Collis, 1992). These papers were read at the colloquium "The Beginning of the Iron Age in Southern Jordan," Liverpool, May 1991.

11. See Albrecht Alt, "Emiter und Moabiter," *Palästina-Jahrbuch* 36 (1940): 29–43.

12. See the important publications of the Expedition to the Dead Sea Plain, Jordan, whose principal investigators are Walter E. Rast and R. Thomas Schaub. The first volume is *Bâb edh-Dhraʿ: Excavations in the Cemetery Directed by Paul Lapp (1965–67)* (Winona Lake, Ind.: Eisenbrauns, 1989).

support a late date for the exodus and conquest. The archeological evidence from southern and central Transjordan is important in this debate, since the Hebrew Bible (Num. 20–21; Judg. 11) indicates that the Hebrews, while migrating to the land of Canaan, met significant opposition from Edomite, Moabite, and Amorite kings who controlled territory on the east side of the Jordan. The current consensus points to the need for modifying Glueck's gap hypothesis—a modification that leaves open the possibility of a more substantial population in Transjordan during the Late Bronze Age (ca. 1550–1200) than previously suggested. This means that the nature or extent of the population in Edom, Moab, and Ammon is a neutral factor in the debate over the date of the Hebrew exodus and conquest.[13]

Though Glueck's pioneering studies in Moab have been supplemented by recent surveys and excavations, considerable controversy continues because of the inconclusive nature of various kinds of evidence: (1) the historical trustworthiness and intention of the biblical narratives, (2) the implications of references to Moab in Egyptian texts, and (3) the dating assigned to archeological data recovered at a number of sites in this region. The third point prompts two major observations. On the one hand, it is clear that many Moabite sites—sites not mentioned in the biblical accounts of the Hebrew migration—were occupied during the Late Bronze Age.[14] On the other hand, most of the archeological sites associated with the Hebrew migration through and settlement of Transjordan have yielded little or no evidence of Late Bronze occupation.

13. On this topic in general, see John J. Bimson, *Redating the Exodus and Conquest*, Journal for the Study of the Old Testament Supplement 5 (Sheffield: Almond, 1978), esp. 61–68; Manfred Weippert, "The Israelite 'Conquest' and the Evidence from Transjordan," in *Symposia Celebrating the Seventy-fifth Anniversary of the Founding of the American Schools of Oriental Research (1900–1975)*, ed. Frank M. Cross (Cambridge, Mass.: American Schools of Oriental Research, 1979), 15–34; Rudolph H. Dornemann, *The Archaeology of the Transjordan in the Bronze and Iron Ages* (Milwaukee: Milwaukee Public Museum, 1983), esp. 20–24; Gerald L. Mattingly, "The Exodus-Conquest and the Archaeology of Transjordan: New Light on an Old Problem," *Grace Theological Journal* 4 (1983): 245–62; James A. Sauer, "Transjordan in the Bronze and Iron Ages: A Critique of Glueck's Synthesis," *Bulletin of the American Schools of Oriental Research* 263 (1986): 4–9. See also Patrick E. McGovern, *The Late Bronze Age and Early Iron Ages of Central Transjordan: The Baqʿah Valley Project, 1977–1981* (Philadelphia: University Museum, 1986); J. Maxwell Miller "The Israelite Journey through (around) Moab and Moabite Toponymy," *Journal of Biblical Literature* 108 (1989): 577–95.

14. The most important survey reports for this region are Robert D. Ibach Jr., *Archaeological Survey of the Hesban Region*, Heshbon Excavations Final Reports 5 (Berrien Springs, Mich.: Andrews University Press, 1987); Miller, *Archaeological Survey of the Kerak Plateau*. See also Zeidan A. Kafafi, *Late Bronze Age Pottery in Jordan (East Bank) 1575–1200 B.C.* (M.A. thesis, University of Jordan, 1977).

Illustrative of this latter point are the excavations at ʿAraʿir (biblical Aroer), Dhiban (Dibon), and Tell Ḥesbân (Heshbon, the capital of the Amorite king Sihon). Late Bronze Age remains from ʿAraʿir and Dhiban are meager, but Heshbon is problematic since the data recovered in its extensive excavations show that it was not occupied before 1200. Discussing various explanations for the lack of Late Bronze evidence at Heshbon, Lawrence T. Geraty concludes that Late Bronze Age Heshbon was located at Tell Jalul (east of Madaba) and that the name migrated when "the Reubenites built the *new* Heshbon at Tell Ḥesbân."[15] David Merling proposes that Heshbon was a regional name and that Sihon's "city" in Heshbon was an encampment that would not be expected to leave much that can be recovered through archeological investigation.[16] These suggestions are intriguing, but their speculative nature precludes acceptance as definitive solutions to the Ḥesbân problem. Such proposals also enhance the significance attached to the ongoing research of the Madaba Plains Project, which includes new excavations at Tell Jalul.

Unfortunately, our understanding concerning the establishment of the tiny kingdom of Moab is quite limited, but bits of information are provided by archeology and textual sources. Although the archeological and epigraphic data that connect Egypt with Transjordan, especially the central and southern regions, are relatively few, there is enough evidence to demonstrate that the pharaohs of the New Kingdom were interested in and on occasion directly involved in the affairs of the peoples east of the Jordan Rift Valley.[17] If the Shasu Bedouin mentioned in an account of Thutmose II's campaign were natives of Transjordan, this reference would be especially important because of the text's early date. Especially intriguing is the possibility that a toponym list of Thutmose III points to this pharaoh's activity in Transjordan in the fif-

15. Lawrence T. Geraty, "Heshbon: The First Casualty in the Israelite Quest for the Kingdom of God," in *The Quest for the Kingdom of God: Studies in Honor of George E. Mendenhall*, ed. Herbert B. Huffmon, Frank A. Spina, and Alberto R. W. Green (Winona Lake, Ind.: Eisenbrauns, 1983), 239–48.

16. David Merling, "Heshbon: A Lost City of the Bible," *Archaeology in the Biblical World* 1.2 (Fall 1991): 10–17. See also Siegfried H. Horn, *Heshbon in the Bible and Archaeology* (Berrien Springs, Mich.: Horn Archaeological Museum, 1982); and Larry G. Herr, "The Search for Biblical Heshbon," *Biblical Archaeology Review* 19.6 (1993): 36–37.

17. See especially Kenneth A. Kitchen, "The Egyptian Evidence on Ancient Jordan," in *Early Edom and Moab: The Beginning of the Iron Age in Southern Jordan*, ed. Piotr Bienkowski (Sheffield: Collis, 1992), 21–34; cf. idem, "Some New Light on the Asiatic Wars of Ramesses II," *Journal of Egyptian Archaeology* 50 (1964): 47–70; S. Aḥituv, "Did Ramesses II Conquer Dibon?" *Israel Exploration Journal* 22 (1972): 141–42; Donald B. Redford, "Contacts between Egypt and Jordan in the New Kingdom: Some Comments on Sources," in *Studies in the History and Archaeology of Jordan*, ed. Adnan Hadidi (Amman: Department of Antiquities, 1982), 1:115–20; Udo Worschech, *Die Beziehungen Moabs zu Israel und Ägypten in der Eisenzeit* (Wiesbaden: Harrassowitz, 1990); Miller, *Archaeological Survey of the Kerak Plateau*, 6–9.

teenth century. If Donald B. Redford is correct, several sites in this military itinerary are located on a route that stretches from Gilead to Moab: Dibon, a watercourse that may be Wadi el-Mujib, and Yarut (a Moabite site south of Wadi el-Mujib).[18]

The name *Moab* is mentioned at least twice in ancient Egyptian sources, with both instances dating to the reign of Ramesses II. A topographical list at Luxor mentions the region, and a description of Ramesses II's campaign in Transjordan around 1270 also refers to the "land of Moab." Though S. Ahituv agrees that Moab is mentioned in this latter text, along with an unidentified Moabite site (i.e., Botirat), he does not follow the suggestions of Kitchen and Redford that Moabite Dibon appears in this same document.

The only Late Bronze Age Egyptian artifact recovered in southern Transjordan is a fragmentary scarab of Amenhotep III, reportedly found near Petra. The Egyptian monuments from Tell esh-Shihab (a Seti I stele) and Sheikh Saʿid (a Ramesses II stele) are the only true Egyptian steles found in Transjordan. James M. Weinstein is probably correct in referring to the Baluʿ Stele as a "pseudo-Egyptian monument," a designation that is almost universally accepted.[19] This Egyptianized relief, discovered just south of Wadi el-Mujib, portrays three figures, two gods, and a mortal usually identified as a Moabite king. Most important is the central figure's dress—the typical garb of Shasu Bedouin.[20] Though far from certain, it is possible that the Baluʿ Stele portrays a belief in divine support of the Shasu, who had become, by the time this monument was carved around 1200, a significant component of Moab's population.[21]

These Egyptian references to Transjordan, and to Moab in particular, do not provide the kind of information that allows us to reconstruct early Moabite history with any exactitude, but it is important to reiterate that the name *Moab* appears in two of Ramesses II's inscriptions at Karnak. These earliest nonbiblical references to Moab thereby confirm that this designation was known by the thirteenth century, which, according to some historical reconstructions, was about the same time the Hebrews migrated through this territory.

18. Redford, "Contacts between Egypt and Jordan," 119.

19. James M. Weinstein, "The Egyptian Empire in Palestine: A Reassessment," *Bulletin of the American Schools of Oriental Research* 241 (1981): 1–28.

20. On the Shasu in general, see Raphael Giveon, *Les Bédouins Shosou des Documents Égyptiens* (Leiden: Brill, 1971); William A. Ward, "The Shasu 'Bedouin': Notes on a Recent Publication," *Journal of the Economic and Social History of the Orient* 15 (1972): 35–60.

21. The most important study on the Baluʿ Stele is William A. Ward and M. F. Martin, "The Baluʿa Stele: A New Transcription with Palaeographical and Historical Notes," *Annual of the Department of Antiquities of Jordan* 8–9 (1964): 5–29. See also E. Drioton, "A Propos de Stele du Balouʿa," *Revue Biblique* 42 (1933): 353–65.

North Syrian influence on early Moab is reflected in the Shihan Warrior Stele (ninth–eighth century), which was found near Jebel Shihan in southern Moab. Some scholars equate this javelin-wielding warrior with the Moabite god Kemosh, who is often identified as a god of war.[22] Connection between Syria and early Moab is also inferred from references to a god named Kamish in the recently discovered Ebla Tablets.[23] This Kamish, one of the principal deities of the Eblaites in the latter half of the third millennium, is almost certainly an archaic form of the name *Kemosh*, who was without question the chief god of Moab. Though far from conclusive, the available data at least hint that Moabite origins can be sought in an amalgamation that involved the indigenous Canaanite population and elements of or influences from such disparate peoples as the Shasu Bedouin, Syrians, and Midianites.

According to Numbers 21:13, 26, the Moabites did not control the region north of the River Arnon at the time of the Hebrew migration, since the Amorite king Sihon had assumed power in this area and ruled from Heshbon. Numbers 21:21–32 reports that the Hebrews soundly defeated Sihon when he

Shihan warrior stele, 9th–8th century B.C. (height: 3′ 5″)

Courtesy of the Louvre Museum

22. On the Shihan Warrior, see E. Warmenbol, "La Stèle de Ruǧm el-ʿAbd (Louvre AO 5055): Une Image de Divinité Moabite du IXème–VIIIème Siècle av. N.E.," *Levant* 15 (1983): 63–75.

23. On Kamish in the pantheon of ancient Ebla, see Gerald L. Mattingly, "Moabite Religion and the Meshaʿ Inscription," in *Studies in the Mesha Inscription and Moab*, ed. J. Andrew Dearman (Atlanta: Scholars Press, 1989), 216–17.

refused them permission to pass through Moabite territory. The famous episode involving the professional diviner Balaam occurred when Balak of Moab feared the presence of the powerful Israelites in his realm (Num. 22–24; Josh. 24:9).[24] Ultimately, the Hebrew tribes of Reuben and Gad occupied Sihon's territory, with the Arnon serving as the new boundary between Israel and Moab proper (Num. 32).[25] The Moabite plateau on the northern side of the Arnon was, thereafter, a source of contention between the Israelites and Moabites.[26]

Later History

In the period of the judges, the Moabite king Eglon oppressed the Hebrews, an indication that Moabite power had increased once more, but he was assassinated by Ehud (Judg. 3:12–30). Northern Moab came under the control of Israel once again by the time of Jephthah (Judg. 11:26), but the Book of Ruth seems to point to a time when Israel and Moab lived in peace. The latter story also reflects one kind of reaction to famine in antiquity: migration to another land (in this case Moab) where climatic conditions were more favorable and food more abundant.

24. It is important to note that the Balaam narrative has assumed a high profile in scholarship nowadays because of the recovery of a fascinating inscription from Tell Deir ʿAlla in the Jordan Valley, a nonbiblical text from ca. 700 that names Balaam and identifies him as a seer. Though this text was recovered in the Jordan Valley, just west of the Gilead Mountains, it has enormous implications for the historicity of the Balaam episode and its relation to Moabite religion. On the Balaam narrative in general, see the up-to-date treatment in Philip J. Budd, *Numbers*, Word Biblical Commentary 5 (Waco: Word, 1984), 248–73; H. Rouillard, *La Pericope de Balaam (Nombres 22–24)* (Paris: Gabalda, 1987); Michael S. Moore, "Another Look at Balaam," *Revue Biblique* 97 (1990): 359–78. The Tell Deir ʿAlla inscription itself has generated a large number of studies, including Jo Ann Hackett, *The Balaam Text from Deir ʿAlla* (Chico, Calif.: Scholars Press, 1984); idem, "Religious Traditions in Israelite Transjordan," in *Ancient Israelite Religion: Essays in Honor of Frank Moore Cross*, ed. Patrick D. Miller Jr., Paul D. Hanson, and S. Dean McBride (Philadelphia: Fortress, 1987), 125–36; André Lemaire, "Fragments from the Book of Balaam Found at Deir Alla: Text Foretells Cosmic Disaster," *Biblical Archaeology Review* 11.5 (1985): 27–39; Helmer Ringgren, "Balaam and the Deir ʿAlla Inscription," in *Essays on the Bible and the Ancient World*, ed. Alexander Rofé and Yair Zakovitch (Jerusalem: Rubenstein, 1985), 3:93–98; V. Sasson, "The Book of Oracular Visions of Balaam from Deir ʿAlla," *Ugarit-Forschungen* 17 (1985): 283–309; Al Wolters, "The Balaamites of Deir ʿAlla as Aramean Deportees," *Hebrew Union College Annual* 59 (1988): 101–13.

25. Cf. J. Andrew Dearman, "The Levitical Cities of Reuben and Moabite Toponymy," *Bulletin of the American Schools of Oriental Research* 276 (1989): 55–66.

26. Among other sources that deal with this problematic history, see John R. Bartlett, "Sihon and Og, Kings of the Amorites," *Vetus Testamentum* 20 (1970): 257–77; idem, "The Conquest of Sihon's Kingdom: A Literary Reexamination," *Journal of Biblical Literature* 97 (1978): 347–51; John Van Seters, "The Conquest of Sihon's Kingdom: A Literary Examination," *Journal of Biblical Literature* 91 (1972): 182–97; idem, "Once Again—The Conquest of Sihon's Kingdom," *Journal of Biblical Literature* 99 (1980): 117–19.

The age of Saul and David, the late eleventh through mid-tenth centuries, witnessed the return of a bitter hostility between Israel and Moab. According to 1 Samuel 14:47 and 2 Samuel 8:2, it would seem that Israel was usually more powerful, a situation that continued into Solomon's reign. Most interesting is the biblical reference to the presence of Moabite women in Solomon's harem (1 Kings 11:1), which caused him to build a high place for the Moabite god Kemosh at Jerusalem (1 Kings 11:7, 33).

The Moabites exerted their independence at the beginning of Israel's divided monarchy, but King Omri subjected these traditional foes to Israelite control once again in the ninth century. One of the most important discoveries in the history of Syro-Palestinian archeology, the thirty-four-line Mesha Inscription (or Moabite Stone), which dates to approximately 830, provides important illumination on this relationship (cf. 2 Kings 3). The Mesha Inscription, which was found at Dhiban (biblical Dibon), commemorates Mesha's achievements and Moab's autonomy from Omride oppression after the death of Omri. Though the Old Testament provides much incidental and useful information concerning the Moabites, this memorial stele remains the single most important primary source on Moab.[27]

Without question, King Mesha is the best known figure from Moabite history, though our knowledge of this monarch is tantalizingly scanty. He is also one of the best known non-Israelite kings, since so much attention is given to Mesha in 2 Kings 3. It is likely that both Mesha and his father, whose name was probably Kemosh-yat(ti), were from Dibon. According to the Mesha Inscription (lines 3, 21–25), King Mesha expended considerable energy in restoring Dibon, once his rebellion against Israel was complete. It is most appropriate that the Mesha Inscription, a testimony to Mesha's military and building activities, emphasizes the mighty deeds of Kemosh, Moab's chief deity (lines 4–5, 7, and 9).[28]

27. The Mesha Inscription has been studied and interpreted repeatedly since its discovery in 1868. Dearman's *Studies in the Mesha Inscription and Moab* provides much of the bibliography on this inscription. On the discovery of the text, see Siegfried H. Horn, "The Discovery of the Moabite Stone," in *The Word of the Lord Shall Go Forth: Essays in Honor of David Noel Freedman*, ed. Carol L. Meyers and Michael P. O'Connor (Winona Lake, Ind.: Eisenbrauns, 1983), 497–505; M. Patrick Graham, "The Discovery and Reconstruction of the Meshaᶜ Inscription," in *Studies in the Mesha Inscription and Moab*, ed. J. Andrew Dearman (Atlanta: Scholars Press, 1989), 41–92. See also Klaus A. D. Smelik, "The Literary Structure of King Mesha's Inscription," *Journal for the Study of the Old Testament* 46 (1990): 21–30; idem, *Studies in Ancient Israelite and Moabite Historiography* (Leiden: Brill, 1992). It is important to note that the Mesha Inscription is supplemented by fragmentary inscriptions from the same general area; cf. Miller, *Archaeological Survey of the Kerak Plateau*, 9–10.

28. Along with Dearman's detailed study of the Omride-Mesha conflict ("Historical Reconstruction and the Mesha Inscription"), see Karl-Heinz Bernhardt, "The Political Situation in the East of Jordan during the Time of King Mesha," in *Studies in the History and Archaeology of*

After Mesha's day, Moab's conflicts with the surrounding nations (Israel, Judah, Edom, and Assyria) were brought to an end with the Babylonian invasion, when Nebuchadnezzar destroyed the Moabite kingdom in 582, according to Josephus, *Antiquities* 10:9:7 §§180–82. Moab's conflict with and vassal relationship to Assyria, which began in the eighth century, is well documented in Assyrian texts, which name four additional Moabite kings: Shalamanu, Kamoshnadab, Musuri, and Kamoshᶜasa. No precise chronology of their reigns is available.[29]

The age-old conflict between Moab, Israel, and Judah is highlighted by numerous prophetic indictments leveled against the Moabites (Isa. 15–16; Jer. 9:25–26 [MT 9:24–25]; 48; Amos 2:1–3; Zeph. 2:8–11). In Isaiah 15:1, the prophet introduced his oracle by referring to the destruction of two prominent Moabite towns, Ar (perhaps modern Rabbah or Baluᶜ) and Kir (Kir-hareseth/Kir-heres = modern Kerak), after which Isaiah listed other settlements in Moab that stood under Yahweh's judgment.[30]

Following the Babylonian conquest, the kingdom of Moab never reappeared. The former Moabite territory eventually came under Persian control, but very little is known about this period.[31] A variety of Arab peoples moved into southern Transjordan, a process that had been underway since before the Babylonian invasion, but the Nabatean Arabs emerged by the fourth century as the dominant inhabitants of this region.[32] Since the Jewish community sought to observe the law of Deuteronomy 23:3–6 [MT 23:4–7], people of Moabite ancestry were still identified as such in postexilic times (Ezra 9:1; Neh. 13:1, 23).

Religion

The principal sources of information concerning Moabite religion

Jordan, ed. Adnan Hadidi (Amman: Department of Antiquities, 1982), 1:163–67; André Lemaire, "Les Territoires d'Ammon, Moab et Edom dans le Deuxième Moitié du Iˣᵉ S. avant Notre Ère," in *Studies in the History and Archaeology of Jordan*, ed. Muna Zaghloul et al. (Amman: Department of Antiquities, 1992), 4:209–14.

29. See Miller, *Archaeological Survey of the Kerak Plateau*, 10–11.

30. Bartlett, "Moabites and Edomites," 241–43. On the identification of these sites, see Miller, "Israelite Journey," 577–95; Brian C. Jones, "In Search of Kir Hareseth: A Case Study in Site Identification," *Journal for the Study of the Old Testament* 52 (1991): 3–24.

31. On the relation between Transjordan and the Mesopotamian empires, see Manfred Weippert, "The Relations of the States East of the Jordan with the Mesopotamian Powers during the First Millennium B.C.," in *Studies in the History and Archaeology of Jordan*, ed. Adnan Hadidi (Amman: Department of Antiquities, 1987), 3:97–105.

32. On the rise of the Nabateans in Moab, see Gerald L. Mattingly, "Settlement on Jordan's Kerak Plateau from Iron Age IIC through the Early Roman Period," *ARAM Periodical* 2.1–2 (1990): 309–35.

are the Mesha Inscription and the Hebrew Bible, but significant insights are provided from other textual references and a wide range of archeological evidence.[33] While our knowledge of Moabite religion is limited, it is clear that there were many similarities with the religious practices of Canaan and Israel, among others. By the time the Moabite kingdom emerged, however, there were distinctive features in the beliefs and rituals of Moab. Most important was the worship of the national or ethnic god Kemosh, though it is now known that this deity was part of a much older Semitic pantheon. Numbers 21:29 and Jeremiah 48:46 refer to the Moabites as the "people of Kemosh," and the frequent references to this god in Moabite personal names and in the Mesha Inscription point to Kemosh's role in personal and national life, especially to his intervention in behalf of Moab in it's conflict with Israel. Whatever developmental process the worship of Kemosh may have taken, it appears that this deity had emerged by the time of the Iron Age kingdom of Moab as the chief god, in much the same way that Yahweh, Milcom, and Qaus were recognized in Israel, Ammon, and Edom, respectively.

Moabite stone, 9th century B.C. (height: 3′ 9″)
Courtesy of Scholars Press;
drawing by Joel F. Drinkard Jr.

33. For a much more detailed examination of Moabite religion, see Mattingly, "Moabite Religion and the Mesha Inscription," 211–38; idem., "Moabite Religion," in *The Encyclopedia of Religion*, ed. Mircea Eliade (New York: Macmillan, 1987), 10:1–3.

Numbers 22–24 indicates that the Moabites sought divine guidance and that diviners and oracles were highly respected. Moabite religion included a priesthood (Jer. 48:7) and a sacrificial system (Num. 22:40–23:30; 25:1–5; 2 Kings 3:27; Jer. 48:35). What has been identified as a Moabite sanctuary has been uncovered at Dhiban; both the Mesha Inscription and the Hebrew Bible (1 Kings 11:7–8; 2 Kings 23:13) indicate that such structures existed.

History of Research

During the nineteenth century, Transjordan was visited by a number of European explorers, adventurers, scholars, and scientists, many of whom had an interest in the Bible and its setting. Northern Moab was included on the itinerary of most of these early travelers; southern Moab was not visited as frequently, though it was not ignored entirely. The region south of Wadi el-Mujib was not investigated often, since it was more isolated, less secure, and had fewer major tells and biblical sites than Palestine or the Moabite territory north of the Mujib. Nevertheless, the list of those intrepid souls who visited and wrote about their travels in Moab includes some of the most distinguished scholars of their day. Ulrich Seetzen (1806) and Johann Burckhardt (1812) were the first modern travelers to enter the Bedouin realm of southern Moab and write accounts of their journeys. Other travelers to this region were Charles L. Irby and James Mangles (1818), Henry B. Tristram (1872), and Charles Doughty (1875). In terms of contributions to history and archeology, the most important scholars to penetrate southern Moab were Felicien de Saulcy (who discovered the Shihan Stele at Rujm el-ᶜAbd in 1851), F. A. Klein (who discovered the Mesha Inscription in 1868), Rudolf E. Brünnow and Alfred von Domaszewski (who explored ancient roads and fortifications in Transjordan in the 1890s), Alois Musil (who investigated the geography and ruins of southern Transjordan between 1896 and 1902), and George Adam Smith, the famous biblical scholar (who studied the Roman road between Kerak and Madaba in 1904).

Early twentieth-century investigators of this region include William F. Albright (who visited Jebel Shihan, Faquᶜ, Adir, Rabbah, Khanzirah, Kerak, and Bâb edh-Dhraᶜ in 1924; and made soundings at Adir in 1933), Reginald Head (who discovered the Baluᶜ Stele at Khirbet el-Baluᶜ in 1930), and J. W. Crowfoot (who made soundings at Baluᶜ in 1933). Nelson Glueck launched his important survey of Transjordan, beginning in southern Moab in 1933.

In more recent times, excavations have been conducted at the following sites in and around Moab:

ʿAraʿir	Khirbet Iskander
Bâb edh-Dhraʿ	Lehun
Dhiban	Lejjun (and vicinity)
Khirbet el-ʿAl	Madaba (and vicinity)
Khirbet el-Baluʿ	Numeira
Khirbet Mdeinet el-Muʿrrajeh	Shuqairah
Khirbet et-Tannur	Tell Ḥesbân
Khirbet Faris	Tell Jalul[34]

A new and exciting discovery from the ongoing excavation at Umm er-Resas, near Dhiban, is a seventh-century A.D. mosaic that identifies modern Umm er-Resas as Mephaath, one of the Levitical cities named in Joshua 21:36–37, 1 Chronicles 6:79 [MT 6:64], and Jeremiah 48:21.[35]

Small-scale archeological surveys have been undertaken in parts of Moab in recent years, but a major effort to locate and study all of surface ruins and remains in southern Moab was undertaken for the first time during the summers of 1978, 1979, 1982, and 1983. The purpose of this project, the "Archaeological Survey of Central and Southern Moab," was to recover the occupational history of a region of the Hashemite Kingdom of Jordan that was, in the mid-1970s, relatively unexamined from an archeological perspective. Sponsored by Emory University, this survey was conducted under the auspices of Jordan's Department of Antiquities and affiliated with the American Center of Oriental Research (the Amman branch of the American Schools of Oriental Research). J. Maxwell Miller and Jack M. Pinkerton directed the project, and staff members came from a number of colleges, universities, and seminaries in North America and Europe.[36]

The survey investigated the tableland (500 square miles) between Wadi el-Mujib and Wadi el-Ḥesa, a region also known as the Kerak Plateau, and studied 443 archeological sites during the four seasons of fieldwork. (Glueck examined only 110 sites in this same territory.) The Emory survey provided thorough coverage of a full spectrum of site types (large vs. small, single vs.

---

34. Bibliographic references for these sites are found in Denyse Homès-Fredericq and John B. Hennessy (eds.), *Archaeology of Jordan I: Bibliography* (Leuven: Peeters, 1986); and idem, *Archaeology of Jordan II.1–2: Field Reports; Surveys and Sites* (Leuven: Peeters, 1989).

35. For discussion and bibliography, see Dearman, "Historical Reconstruction and the Mesha Inscription," 183–84. Cf. Randall W. Younker and P. Michelle Daviau, "Is Mefaʿat to Be Found at Tell Jawa (South)?" *Israel Exploration Journal* 43 (1993): 23–28.

36. Of Miller's studies that deal with the history of exploration in Moab, the most recent and best documented is *Archaeological Survey of the Kerak Plateau*, 14–17. See also the important essay by Hannes Olivier, "Nineteenth-Century Travelogues and the Land of Moab," in *Pillars of Smoke and Fire: The Holy Land in History and Thought*, ed. Moshe Sharon (Johannesburg: Southern, 1988), 80–95.

multiple period), ranging in date from prehistoric to Ottoman times. In an attempt to avoid the dangers of ecological determinism, team members studied the Kerak Plateau in full awareness that a variety of determinants are "reflected" in settlement patterns. Beyond the publication of the survey's primary data, project participants hope to produce synthetic reports on each occupational period.

The final report of the Emory survey was recently published under the title *Archaeological Survey of the Kerak Plateau.*[37] The product of years of painstaking effort, representing the most thorough study of southern Moab's archeological resources, it includes history of research on the Kerak Plateau, full description of every site investigated, study of the region's toponymy (ancient and modern), comparative typology and chronology for the ceramics of the Kerak Plateau, maps, photographs, pottery plates, and full bibliography. In order to promote future studies of this data, all artifacts retrieved during the Moab survey are fully cataloged and housed in Emory University's Museum of Art and Archaeology in Atlanta.

In addition to primary research, the recent flurry of secondary studies on various aspects of Moab's history and culture includes an up-to-date reassessment of the Mesha Inscription and its contribution to our understanding of Iron Age Moab. Edited by Andrew Dearman, *Studies in the Mesha Inscription and Moab* contains essays by eight authors.[38] Interested scholars are encouraged to obtain the *Central Jordan Network*, a quarterly newsletter that enables those studying the histories and cultures of Ammon, Moab, and Edom to keep abreast of what others are investigating and writing.[39]

A major project continues to investigate the region of northern Moab and Ammon, the Madaba Plains Project, which is in many ways a continuation of Andrews University's long-term archeological inquiry at Tell Ḥesbân and its environs.[40]

While many areas of inquiry concerning ancient Moab remain virtually untouched (e.g., the linking of ancient place-names with modern archeological sites, a better understanding of the ceramic traditions of ancient Moabite potters [and the subsequent refinement of Moab's settlement history], the nature of interregional trade), a wealth of recently recovered data and many new avenues of research promise to provide additional insights into this

37. J. Maxwell Miller (ed.), *Archaeological Survey of the Kerak Plateau* (Atlanta: Scholars Press/American Schools of Oriental Research, 1991).

38. J. Andrew Dearman (ed.), *Studies in the Mesha Inscription and Moab* (Atlanta: Scholars Press, 1989).

39. Edited by Gerald L. Mattingly, 7900 Johnson Drive, Knoxville, Tennessee 37998.

40. See especially Larry G. Herr, "Whatever Happened to the Ammonites?" *Biblical Archaeology Review* 19.6 (1993): 26–35, 68.33

land's past. Students interested in the peoples of the Old Testament world will not be disappointed, since the Bible will be illuminated by much of this study. In other words, there can be no doubt that inquiries into Moabite history and culture have a bright future, since there is much that is new on old Moab.

Recommended Reading

Bartlett, John R. "The Moabites and Edomites." Pp. 229–58 in *Peoples of Old Testament Times*. Edited by Donald J. Wiseman. Oxford: Clarendon, 1973.

Bienkowski, Piotr (ed.). *Early Edom and Moab: The Beginning of the Iron Age in Southern Jordan*. Sheffield: Collis, 1992.

———. *Treasures from an Ancient Land: The Art of Jordan*. Wolfeboro Falls, N.H.: Sutton, 1991.

Dearman, J. Andrew (ed.). *Studies in the Mesha Inscription and Moab*. Atlanta: Scholars Press, 1989. Contains full bibliography on numerous aspects of ancient Moab's history and culture.

Dornemann, Rudolph H. *The Archaeology of the Transjordan in the Bronze and Iron Ages*. Milwaukee: Milwaukee Public Museum, 1983.

Glueck, Nelson. *The Other Side of the Jordan*. Revised edition. Cambridge, Mass.: American Schools of Oriental Research, 1970.

Kautz, James R. "Tracking the Ancient Moabites." *Biblical Archaeologist* 44 (1981): 27–35.

Mattingly, Gerald L. "The Exodus-Conquest and the Archaeology of Transjordan: New Light on an Old Problem." *Grace Theological Journal* 4 (1983): 245–62.

Miller, J. Maxwell (ed.). *Archaeological Survey of the Kerak Plateau*. Atlanta: Scholars Press, 1991. Contains full bibliography, including references to Miller's extensive publications on ancient Moab.

Sauer, James A. "Transjordan in the Bronze and Iron Ages: A Critique of Glueck's Synthesis." *Bulletin of the American Schools of Oriental Research* 263 (1986): 1–26.

Timm, Stefan. *Moab zwishen den Mächten: Studien zu historischen Denkmälern und Texten*. Wiesbaden: Harrassowitz, 1989.

Van Zyl, A. H. *The Moabites*. Leiden: Brill, 1960.

Edomites

Kenneth G. Hoglund

Remember, O LORD, what the Edomites did
  on the day Jerusalem fell.
"Tear it down," they cried,
  "tear it down to its foundations!"
                          —Psalm 137:7

Of the many different cultures that inhabited Syria-Palestine in the first millennium, perhaps none were as closely related to Israel as the Edomites. In Genesis, Esau's nickname was "Edom" (25:30), and following his reconciliation with his brother Jacob he lived in the region of Edom (36:1–8). When Israel encountered Edom during the wilderness wandering, its king was addressed as "brother" (Num. 20:14). Despite this close relationship, following the Babylonian destruction of Jerusalem in 587, Israel came to look upon the Edomites with great bitterness (e.g., Ps. 137:7; Obadiah). This shift in attitude can only be appreciated by knowing something of the history and culture of Israel's "brothers" to the east.

In reconstructing the world of the Edomites, we are dependent on what the surrounding cultures tell us about them, since there are no surviving Edomite records of their own history. Of these sources, Egyptian records are the earliest (from the fifteenth century on), occasionally noting encounters with groups from Edom and Seir called *Shasu*.[1] The Egyptian term *Shasu* designates a nomadic group, although these references are largely from military contexts and merely note that Egyptian forces engaged these groups in bat-

---

1. See John R. Bartlett, *Edom and the Edomites*, Journal for the Study of the Old Testament Supplement 77 (Sheffield: Sheffield Academic Press, 1989), 77–80, for a helpful survey of this data. The earliest mention of Edom is apparently in a campaign list of Thutmose III (1479–1425); see W. Helck, *Die Beziehungen Ägyptens zu Vorderasien im 3. und 2. Jahrtausand vor Chr.*, 2d ed. (Wiesbaden: Harrassowitz, 1971), 243.

tle.[2] As a consequence, the Egyptian kings of Dynasties 18–20 (ca. 1550–1085) only mention battles with the "nomads of Edom" and provide no further insight on the size or social complexity of these groups.

That the Egyptian records mention "nomads of Edom" and "nomads of Seir" as two distinct groups raises a complication in any effort to understand these ancient sources. The Old Testament occasionally reflects the same distinction between Edom and Seir (e.g., Isa. 21:11 mentions only Seir), although more frequently it treats the two terms as one region (e.g., Num. 24:18; Judg. 5:4). This may suggest that Edom and Seir were two adjacent locations that by the time of Israel's monarchy had become indistinguishable.[3] From the cities and place-names associated with Edom in the Old Testament, it is apparent that the biblical writers understood Edom to refer to the region from Wadi el-Ḥesa in modern Jordan south along the high plateau east of Wadi Arabah to the shores of the Gulf of Aqabah.[4]

Geography and Economy

The environmental character of this region is forbidding, the rocky crags of the plateau soaring some four thousand feet above the floor of Wadi Arabah, the deep rift depression running from the southern end of the Dead Sea to the Gulf of Aqabah. Wadi Arabah, undoubtedly a major trade passageway from the Gulf of Aqabah northward into Judah, would have shaped the perception found in passages such as Jeremiah 49:16 that the Edomites "nested with the eagles." Once on top of this plateau, there are relatively few obstacles to movement north and south, which resulted in this region's being traversed by several important trade routes, including the fabled King's Highway (Num. 20:17).[5] The rapid rise of the plateau from the floor of Wadi Arabah has a negative impact on rainfall, sufficient rain for agriculture falling only along the western slopes of the region. On the top of the plateau itself, rainfall is scarce, capable of supporting only seasonal grasslands and encouraging pastoral nomadism.

2. See the comments of William A. Ward, "The Shasu 'Bedouin': Notes on a Recent Publication," *Journal of the Economic and Social History of the Orient* 15 (1972): 50–56. For the *Shasu* in general, see Raphael Giveon, *Les Bédouins Shosu des Documents Égyptiens* (Leiden: Brill, 1971).

3. "Seir perhaps denoted the wilder, scrubby land south of Judah and Mount Halak and between Kadesh and the Gulf of Aqabah. This region was never claimed by Judah as its own, and its borders were never very clearly defined"; Bartlett, *Edom and the Edomites*, 44.

4. For a detailed examination of the specific sites, see ibid., 44–54.

5. Yohanan Aharoni, *The Land of the Bible: A Historical Geography*, rev. ed., trans. and ed. Anson F. Rainey (Philadelphia: Westminster, 1979), 54–57.

Recent research indicates that copper production was another basic piece in the economic mosaic of the region. Extensive copper mining and smelting operations were carried out in the Wadi Feinan region in the central portion of the plateau since the Early Bronze Age. Ceramic evidence points to Edomite utilization of these copper resources around the same time as settlements were being founded in the Edomite heartland, approximately the eighth century.[6]

Although there have been several significant archeological excavations in the region during the last two decades, there is still insufficient knowledge from these investigations to say much beyond the records of the surrounding cultures. Recent surveys of site remains suggest that the Egyptian picture of a region inhabited by nomadic groups in the second millennium is largely correct, as the first general pattern of settlements emerged in the transitional period from Late Bronze Age to Iron Age I (1300–1000).[7] While some infer from this that the biblical notice of Edomite kings prior to the development of the Israelite monarchy in the tenth century (Gen. 36:31) is really the product of a much later period, there are no convincing reasons to draw this conclusion.[8] Nomadic groups could have considered their leaders kings, the term itself being used to denote a broad range of leadership positions in the ancient Near East.[9]

History

Early Contact with Israel

While Israel's earliest contact with the Edomites may have been with nomadic groups, the situation seems to have been dramatically different by the

6. Ernst A. Knauf and C. J. Lenzen, "Edomite Copper Industry," in *Studies in the History and Archaeology of Jordan*, ed. Adnan Hadidi (Amman: Department of Antiquities, 1987), 3:83–88.

7. This is mainly true for the northern portion of the region; see Burton MacDonald, "The Wâdi el-Ḥasâ Survey 1979 and Previous Archaeological Work in Southern Jordan," *Bulletin of the American Schools of Oriental Research* 245 (1982): 35–52; Bartlett, *Edom and the Edomites*, 70–73. For the southern regions, settlement occurs much later in the eighth and seventh centuries; Stephen Hart, "Preliminary Thoughts on Settlement in Southern Edom," *Levant* 18 (1986): 51–58. For more detailed discussion on this transitional period, see the various essays in Piotr Bienkowski (ed.), *Early Edom and Moab: The Beginning of the Iron Age in Southern Jordan* (Sheffield: Collis, 1992).

8. See Bartlett, *Edom and the Edomites*, 83–90.

9. In the Old Testament itself, there is a consciousness of a "chiefdom" in Edom at an early stage (Gen. 36:40–43; Exod. 15:15). That these "chiefs" are cataloged in the same lists as "kings" may suggest that the two terms are used interchangeably with respect to the leadership of Edom.

time of David's reign over Israel.[10] The Bible records that David defeated the Edomites and brought them under direct Israelite control through the establishment of garrisons throughout the country (2 Sam. 8:13–14). This initiated a period of Israelite control over the Edomites for nearly 150 years until Edom was able to assert its independence from Judah. While some question has been raised regarding the extent to which David would have moved to the east of Wadi Arabah, there is clear evidence that Edomite settlements were increasing at this time.[11] The movement of settled populations to an area where they could threaten the Judean hill country would have provided the stimulus for David to seek greater control over this region.[12]

According to the implication of 1–2 Kings, the Judean kings (ruling from Jerusalem) controlled Edom from the time of David until the Edomites successfully revolted during the reign of Jehoram of Judah (ca. 854–841).[13] There are, however, no direct explanations of how this control was exercised or what benefits Judah gained from dominating Edom. Nor, for that matter, do the Egyptian records provide any notice of Edom at this time, suggesting that the region had no independent status. The act of throwing off Judean control may have been stimulated by the successful revolt of Moab against the northern kingdom of Israel (2 Kings 3:4–27), Moab being the immediate northern neighbor of Edom.[14]

Contact with Assyria and Babylon

Once freed of Judean control, the Edomite state enjoyed a brief moment of

10. The biblical notice of Saul's battling the Edomites (1 Sam. 14:47–48) is part of a larger summary of military victories by the first king of Israel. While in previous accounts Saul is shown battling the armies of the other enemies, in this summary there are no such accounts of a war with Edom. This has led a number of scholars to suggest that 1 Sam. 14:47–52 has been modified to conform to the pattern of David's military success recorded in 2 Sam. 8. This would suggest that Saul may not have engaged the Edomites in battle. For a helpful discussion of this problem, see Ralph W. Klein, *1 Samuel*, Word Biblical Commentary 10 (Waco: Word, 1983), 141.

11. Questioning the extent of David's movements east of the Wadi Arabah are J. Maxwell Miller and John H. Hayes, *A History of Ancient Israel and Judah* (Philadelphia: Westminster, 1986), 182.

12. See the comments of Bartlett, *Edom and the Edomites*, 106–7. See also Alan R. Schulman, "The Curious Case of Hadad the Edomite," in *Egyptological Studies in Honor of Richard A. Parker*, ed. Leonard H. Lesko (Hanover, N.H.: University Press of New England for Brown University Press, 1986), 122–35.

13. 1 Kings 11:14–22 contains the odd account of Hadad the Edomite who fled to the Egyptian court, where he was sheltered until returning to Edom to be an "adversary" to King Solomon. He is said to have "done mischief" to Solomon (1 Kings 11:25), though there is no specification as to what this entailed. A thorough discussion of this narrative may be found in Bartlett, *Edom and the Edomites*, 107–11.

14. On Moab's revolt from Israel, see Miller and Hayes, *History of Ancient Israel and Judah*, 282–83.

self-determination before the westward movement of the Assyrians brought a new tyranny into the region. There are no direct literary references to this independent state until the western Assyrian campaigns, though the archeological evidence points toward a flourishing society. This is particularly true at Bozrah (modern Buseirah), one of Edom's most important urban centers (Amos 1:12). Excavations conducted at Buseirah demonstrate that this city was founded in the eighth century and enjoyed considerable prosperity until its destruction in the sixth century.[15] Similarly, at the important urban center of Tawilan, excavations indicate that the primary phase of architectural development was in the eighth and seventh centuries.[16]

The first Assyrian king to claim to have forced Edom into vassalage was Adad-nirari III (810–783), though it is possible that Edom voluntarily entered into a vassal relationship with Assyria as protection from its more powerful neighbors.[17] Judean interest in reestablishing a port facility at Elath at the southern end of Wadi Arabah (2 Kings 14:22) early in the reign of Uzziah of Judah (792–740) increased the pressure on Edom.

It was not until the vigorous westward expansion of Assyria under Tiglath-pileser III (744–727) that the Edomite kingdom faced its greatest peril. Apparently Edom had thrown its support behind a coalition led by Rezin, the king of Damascus (2 Kings 16:6). In 733 Rezin revolted and the Assyrians attacked Damascus, killed Rezin, and demanded tribute from all states formerly associated with Rezin. Edom, among a number of other countries, is listed in the Assyrian annals as having capitulated to the Assyrian demand.[18] Edomite support for an abortive revolt by the king of Ashdod in 713 also brought new demands for tribute from the Assyrian rulers.[19]

The seventh century marks the emergence of Edom as a prosperous kingdom, though still under the domination of the Assyrian Empire for the first

---

15. Crystal M. Bennett, "Excavations at Buseirah (Biblical Bozrah)," in *Midian, Moab and Edom: The History and Archaeology of Late Bronze and Iron Age Jordan and North-West Arabia*, ed. John F. A. Sawyer and David J. A. Clines, Journal for the Study of the Old Testament Supplement 24 (Sheffield: JSOT Press, 1983), 9–17.

16. Crystal M. Bennett, "Excavations at Tawilan in Southern Jordan, 1982," *Levant* 16 (1984): 1–19.

17. On this point, see Bartlett, *Edom and the Edomites*, 124–25. See also Manfred Weippert, "The Relations of the States East of the Jordan with the Mesopotamian Powers during the First Millennium B.C.," in *Studies in the History and Archaeology of Jordan*, ed. Adnan Hadidi (Amman: Department of Antiquities, 1987), 3:97–105. On the subject of Neo-Assyrian activity in Edom, see Alan R. Millard, "Assyrian Involvement in Edom," *Early Edom and Moab: The Beginning of the Iron Age in Southern Jordan*, ed. Piotr Bienkowski (Sheffield: Collis, 1992), 35–39.

18. See Miller and Hayes, *History of Ancient Israel and Judah*, 323–32, for a detailed discussion of this period in the history of the region.

19. See Bartlett, *Edom and the Edomites*, 130–31, for a discussion of this campaign and Edom's role in it.

portion of the century. The decline of Judah following Hezekiah's disastrous revolt of 701 gave Edom the opportunity to begin expanding into portions of the eastern Negev that had formerly been held by Judah. An inscription from the Judean fortress at Arad mentions an "evil" done by Edom in the eastern Negev, possibly the forcible seizure of Judean lands.[20] Other Negev sites have also yielded Edomite texts from the same period, though these texts fail to provide direct evidence for why Edomite groups had moved westward into Judah.[21]

The westward expansion of Edomites continued, following the entry of the Babylonian Empire in the west with the campaigns of Nebuchadnezzar II in 605. Judah, apparently in a weakened state, was unable to resist the appropriation of territory by its eastern neighbors. Ostraca from an Arad stratum dated toward the end of the Judean monarchy mention an anticipated Edomite attack.[22]

Perhaps the most remarkable evidence for Edomite movements into Judah is the Negev site of Ḥorvat Qitmit, excavated in 1984–86. Here, archeologists revealed a religious center complete with a circular altar and a building consisting of three chambers open to the south (i.e., facing Edom). Each room contained a podium about three feet high, which at some point apparently supported an idol or other sacred object. There was clear evidence of sacrifi-

---

20. For the inscription, see Yohanan Aharoni, *Arad Inscriptions* (Jerusalem: Israel Exploration Society, 1981), 70–74. The excavators placed the ostraca in stratum 8, dated at the end of the eighth century, but noted some confusion as to the stratigraphic character of the locus. In their dating, the "evil" relates to Edom's quick capitulation to Assyria when Sennacherib marched westward. Since the excavations were published without reporting the stratigraphy, it is necessary to rely on more subjective indications to date this inscription. The paleography is more consistent with an early seventh-century date, and one would suspect that two local fortress commanders would be more likely to discuss regional issues in such correspondence than comment on international affairs. Thus, this important text would fit more comfortably into the first quarter of the seventh century, or Arad stratum 7, exactly where the excavators first assigned it.

21. For example, see the Edomite ostracon from Ḥorvat ʿUza dated to the late seventh century; Itzhaq Beit-Arieh and Bruce C. Cresson, "An Edomite Ostracon from Ḥorvat ʿUza," *Tel Aviv* 12 (1985): 96–101. Further archeological evidence for Edomite intrusion into Judean territory may be found in the Edomite pottery that bears seal impressions reading "Belonging to Qous-ʿanal, servant of the king" found at Tell el-Kheleifeh, now dated to the late seventh century; Gary D. Pratico, "Nelson Glueck's 1938–1940 Excavations at Tell el-Kheleifeh: A Reappraisal," *Bulletin of the American Schools of Oriental Research* 259 (1985): 1–32. Robert D. Haak offers the intriguing suggestion that during the reign of Josiah the Judean court actually sought to cooperate with Edom to strengthen trade patterns that had proven profitable under Assyrian domination. In Haak's view, this condition would explain why the prophet Zephaniah—who prophesied against both Ammon and Moab—gave no oracles against Edom. I thank Professor Haak for sharing his unpublished work on this issue with me.

22. The text may be found in inscription 24 from stratum 6; Aharoni, *Arad Inscriptions*, 46–49. Inscription 3 from the same stratum contains an incidental reference to Edom; Aharoni, *Arad Inscriptions*, 17–18.

cial animals having been burnt at the altar and in the chambers. The site was also rich with figural ceramic objects, some probably used in worship, others possibly reflecting votive offerings or symbolic worshipers. The more common ceramic vessels of the site are characteristic of pottery found in the Edomite heartland at sites such as Buseirah.[23]

Later Contact with Israel

Edom's continual movement into the southern Judean region generated tension between Edom and its "brother." Further strains came about as Judah plotted a final revolt against the Neo-Babylonian Empire. While there are some indications that Edom was part of the plot at first, by the time of the revolt of 587 (see Jer. 27:1–15), Edom stood by and watched as Judah was annihilated. While it is clear from the accounts that Edom did not play an active role in the destruction of Jerusalem, the biblical writers accused Edom of gloating over Judah's demise (Obad. 11–14).[24] Edom was apparently untouched by the western Babylonian campaign, and refugees from the destruction

Goddess with horned headdress from Qitmit, 7th–6th century B.C. (height: 5.1″)

Courtesy of Itzhaq Beit-Arieh and the University of Tel Aviv, Department of Archaeology and Near Eastern Studies

23. There have only been fragmentary reports on the excavations at Ḥorvat Qitmit in English. The most comprehensive presentation is Itzhaq Beit-Arieh, "An Edomite Sanctuary at Ḥorvat Qitmit in the Judean Negev: A Preliminary Report," *Eretz-Israel* 20 (1989): 135–46 [Hebrew]. A short English summary may be found in Itzhaq Beit-Arieh, "Ḥ. Qitmit," *Israel Exploration Journal* 35 (1985): 201–2; and a popularization in "New Light on the Edomites," *Biblical Archaeology Review* 14.2 (1988): 28–41.

24. On Edom's noninvolvement with the siege against Jerusalem, see Bartlett, *Edom and the Edomites*, 154–55.

of Judah fled to Edom for safety until the fighting had ceased (Jer. 40:11–12).

With the demise of the Judean kingdom, Edomite groups apparently moved into and occupied the southern portions of Judah (Ezek. 35:10–12). Spared the judgment of destruction, Edom's seeking to benefit from Judah's misfortune appeared morally reprehensible to the biblical writers. This treachery on the part of Edom drew broad condemnation from Israel's prophets, and oracles against Edom became a standard part of the prophetic denunciation of Israel's enemies (Jer. 9:25–26 [MT 9:24–25]; 25:17–26; 49:7–22; Ezek. 25:12–14; 32:29; 35; Joel 3:19 [MT 4:19]).[25] The prophet Obadiah reverses Edomite occupation of Judean lands: "People from the Negev will occupy the mountains of Esau" (19 NIV). Even the psalmist joined in the call for God to recall the Edomite pleasure at Judah's destruction (Ps. 137:7).

Edom's destruction was not far behind Jerusalem's. From scattered evidence, both literary and archeological, it is possible to conclude that the Babylonian king Nabonidus attacked and destroyed Edom during a campaign against the west in the mid-sixth century.[26] Edom's desolation after this point is reflected in the opening verses of Malachi; "'Was not Esau Jacob's brother?' the LORD says, 'Yet I have loved Jacob, but Esau I have hated, and I have turned his mountains into a wasteland and left his inheritance to the desert

Kneeling figure (or dancer) from the high place at Qitmit, 6th century B.C. (height: 6.9″)

Courtesy of Itzhaq Beit-Arieh and the University of Tel Aviv, Department of Archaeology and Near Eastern Studies

25. For a full exposition of this prophetic attitude, see Bruce C. Cresson, "The Condemnation of Edom in Postexilic Judaism," in *The Use of the Old Testament in the New and Other Essays: Studies in Honor of William Franklin Stinespring*, ed. James A. Efird (Durham: Duke University Press, 1972), 125–48.

26. See the summary of the evidence in Bartlett, *Edom and the Edomites*, 157–61.

jackals'" (1:2–3 NIV). The evidence of archeological surveys in the region points to the destruction and abandonment of urban areas during this period and a probable return to the pastoral nomadism that characterized Edom prior to its organization into a kingdom.[27] Following the Persian conquest of Babylon in 539 and the establishment of the new Persian Empire in the Near East, some archeological evidence suggests that several urban sites east of Wadi Arabah, such as Buseirah and Tawilan, were utilized as administrative centers. However, the overall picture from archeological surveys is the continued desolation of much of the Edomite homeland.

While central Edom may have been desolate, there is evidence that the Edomite settlements that resulted from the movement of peoples west of Wadi Arabah continued to thrive under the Persians. The exact extent of these settlements is somewhat debated. Some scholars, following indications in several late sources, place the Edomites as far north as Beth-zur, just fifteen miles south of Jerusalem.[28] Assuming this to be the case, several scholars argue that the presence of Edomites so close to Judah's traditional capital led the Persians to rebuild Jerusalem's fortifications under the administration of Nehemiah.[29] A fundamental problem with this view is the lack of evidence in contemporaneous sources; the biblical accounts of Ezra and Nehemiah, for example, never mention the Edomites. A more probable boundary would be just south of Hebron, where changes in rainfall and elevation create a distinct environmental zone similar to that of the Edomite heartland.

Contact with Persia

Wherever their northern boundary was located, there is little doubt that the Edomite settlements in former Judean territories flourished in the Persian pe-

---

27. As indicated by the data presented in Stephen Hart, "Excavations at Ghrareh, 1986: Preliminary Report," *Levant* 20 (1988): 89–99; and idem, "Five Soundings in Southern Jordan," *Levant* 19 (1989): 33–47.

28. Charles C. Torrey, "The Edomites in Southern Judah," *Journal of Biblical Literature* 17 (1898): 16–20; and Jacob M. Myers, "Edom and Judah in the Sixth–Fifth Centuries B.C.," in *Near Eastern Studies in Honor of William Foxwell Albright*, ed. Hans Goedicke (Baltimore: Johns Hopkins University Press, 1971), 377–92. The argument is made on the basis of several references to Idumeans around the Dead Sea area by Diodorus of Sicily, a writer of the first century (recounting a campaign of one of Alexander's successors in 312), and an account in 1 Esdr. 4:50 that claims the Persian monarch Darius I (521–486) ordered the Edomites to surrender several Judean villages to the returning exiles. As for the first point, even if Diodorus is accurate in his account, the placement of Edomites in the region of the Dead Sea would not imply that they also settled in the more agriculturally important region to the west. As for the narrative in 1 Esdras, it is part of a composite narrative of Persian favor toward the Postexilic community and reflects more the circumstances of the second century than the Persian period itself.

29. Most notably Morton Smith, *Palestinian Parties and Politics That Shaped the Old Testament* (New York: Columbia University Press, 1971), 127–28.

riod (539–332). Archeological remains from Tell el-Kheleifeh, including several epigraphic finds, suggest an occupation in the fifth century.[30] Aramaic ostraca from Arad in the Persian period list several Edomite names, presumably of people in the immediate area. Individuals bearing Edomite names also appear among the Beer-sheba ostraca from the same period.[31] The conclusion from this evidence is that the Edomite settlements were healthy under Persian supervision.

Possibly sometime during the later Persian period, these Edomite settlements were consolidated into an imperial province with a probable capital at Lachish.[32] By the Hellenistic period (332–165) this region became known as Idumea, and when the Hasmonean Dynasty came to power in Jerusalem, the Idumeans were eventually forced to adopt normative Jewish customs.[33] The validity of Idumean "Jewishness" was always regarded with suspicion by the Jerusalem establishment, and this led to some of the disdain with which Herod the Great (47–4), an Idumean, was regarded.[34] Interestingly, in Mark 3:8 people from Idumea are listed among the earliest listeners to Jesus' preaching.

Nabateans

In the region to the east of Wadi Arabah, a new people were settling the former Edomite centers: the Nabateans, who skillfully adapted to the arid conditions of the region and established a prosperous trading empire centered at Petra, a city whose ruins still draw admiration from visitors. Many of the former Edomite cities were reinhabited by the Nabateans, leading some to propose a formal relationship between the Edomites and the Nabateans.[35] However, not all of the Edomite centers were reestablished, and linguistic and religious differences existed between these two groups, suggesting that the relationship between the Edomites and later Nabateans was more complex

30. Nelson Glueck, "Tell el-Kheleifeh Inscriptions," in *Near Eastern Studies in Honor of William Foxwell Albright*, ed. Hans Goedicke (Baltimore: Johns Hopkins University Press, 1971), 225–42; and Pratico, "Nelson Glueck's 1938–40 Excavations at Tell el-Kheleifeh," 22.

31. See Ephraim Stern, *Material Culture of the Land of the Bible in the Persian Period, 538–332 B.C.* (Warminster: Aris & Phillips, 1982), 44–45.

32. André Lemaire, "Populations et Territoires de la Palestine à l'Époque Perse," *Transeuphratène* 3 (1990): 40–54.

33. 1 Macc. 4:61 records that Beth-zur was fortified against an independent Idumea, and Josephus records that under John Hyrcanus I (ca. 125) Idumea was forcibly annexed to the Jewish state (*Antiquities* 13:9:1 §§257–58). For further discussion of the troubled relationship between the Jewish and Idumean communities, see Arayeh Kasher, *Jews, Idumaeans, and Ancient Arabs*, Texte und Studien zum Antiken Judentum 18 (Tübingen: Mohr, 1988).

34. See further, Harold W. Hoehner, "Herod," in *ISBE* 2:689–94.

35. John R. Bartlett, "From Edomites to Nabataeans: A Study in Continuity," *Palestine Exploration Quarterly* 111 (1979): 53–66.

than a simple reconsolidation of economic and political power. Perhaps in time, new discoveries will provide additional data on this relationship.

Language

The Edomites spoke a language scholars call "Edomite." Though only relatively few, short inscriptions have been found thus far, Edomite appears to have been in the larger family of Northwest Semitic languages and in structure resembles Hebrew and Phoenician. In its written form, Edomite betrays some unusual letter forms, providing scholars with the surest means of classifying an inscription as Edomite.[36] How widespread literacy was among the Edomites is uncertain.

Religion

The religion of the Edomites provides a further puzzle for scholars. In the Assyrian records, several Edomite kings are noted, most bearing names built around the divine name *Qos* (or *Qaus*). For example, a Qausmalaka ("Qaus has become king") is noted from the time of Tiglath-pileser III, and a Qosmalak ("Qos is king") is one of the names from the Beer-sheba ostraca.[37] Josephus, writing many centuries after the fall of Edom as a political power, wrote that an Idumean family worshiped Koze, the god of the Idumeans.[38]

There has been considerable discussion among scholars as to the identity of this god and the possible meaning of the name, the general consensus being that Qos is related to the Arabic word *qaus* ("bow"). In many of the polytheistic cultures surrounding ancient Israel, storm gods were depicted holding bows with which they launched lightning bolts, their "arrows." Consequently, the Edomite deity Qos may have been conceived of as a storm god, similar perhaps to the god Hadad of the Arameans.[39] However, as John Bart-

36. For a full corpus of Edomite inscriptions and helpful overall discussion, see Bartlett, *Edom and the Edomites*, 209–28. On the Edomite script, see Larry G. Herr, "The Formal Scripts of Iron Age Transjordan," *Bulletin of the American Schools of Oriental Research* 238 (1981): 21–34.

37. For a listing of attested names using the divine name Qos, see Bartlett, *Edom and the Edomites*, 204–7. For the Egyptian evidence, see Bustenay Oded, "Egyptian References to the Edomite Deity Qaus," *Andrews University Seminary Studies* 9 (1971): 47–50.

38. *Antiquities* 15:7:9 §253.

39. Bartlett, *Edom and the Edomites*, 201–2, has a concise discussion of these complex linguistic issues. On Qos and Hadad possibly being identical, note the biblical references to several Edomites bearing names formed from Hadad: a king of Edom (Gen. 36:35; 1 Chron. 1:46); Hadad (or Hadar) (Gen. 36:39; 1 Chron. 1:50); and Hadad from the Edomite royal line (1 Kings 11:14–22).

lett notes, many of the names using compounds of Qos reflect a kinder figure than is usually found in conceptions of storm gods.[40]

While the evidence from names might suggest that Qos was the primary deity worshiped by the Edomites, the shrine at Horvat Qitmit, with its three identically sized rooms and podiums, suggests that a grouping of deities may have been worshiped (the identity of these gods is unknown). Complicating the picture is Qitmit's being the only clear example of an Edomite place of worship. There are no certain examples of Edomite sanctuaries east of Wadi Arabah.

The biblical picture of Edom's religion is also puzzling. Unlike the perspectives on the other peoples to its east, the biblical writers neither attack Edom's gods by name nor include Edom in lists of countries practicing "abominations."[41] Moreover, there are references to theophanies by Israel's God in areas traditionally associated with the Edomites. For example, in quoting an ancient hymn, the prophet Habakkuk claims that "God came from Teman, the Holy One from Mount Paran" (3:3 NIV). Teman was always regarded as part of Edom by the biblical writers.[42] In the Song of Deborah, the victory hymn claims, "O LORD, when you went out from Seir, when you marched from the land of Edom, the earth shook, the heavens poured, the clouds poured down water" (Judg. 5:4 NIV). Seir and the "land of Edom" clearly imply some connection to traditional Edomite regions.

Scholars are divided on how to account for this benign approach to Edomite religion, especially in consideration of the scorn heaped on the Edomites following the destruction of Judah by the Babylonians. Some believe these theophanies have their origins in a time when encounters among groups of *Shasu* led to the adoption by some portions of these peoples of the God of Israel as their exclusive deity. These peoples later became the tribes of Israel and saw their God as having come from the east.[43] Others argue that the God of Israel was among the deities worshiped in Edom and that this recognition of religious commonality made Israel speak of the Edomites as their "brothers" despite their treachery toward Israel.[44] For example, during the time of David the Bible speaks of Doeg the Edomite worshiping Israel's God at the Israelite sanctuary at Nob (1 Sam. 21:7 [MT 21:8]).

---

40. Bartlett, *Edom and the Edomites*, 204.

41. See ibid., 194–96, for summary.

42. On Teman, see Gen. 36:11, 15, 34; Jer. 49:20. On Mount Paran, see Num. 10:12; 12:16. Though not explicitly identified as Edomite, the region of Paran was conceived of as being to the far south of Judah.

43. Lars E. Axelsson, *The Lord Rose up from Seir: Studies in the History and Traditions of the Negev and Southern Judah*, Coniectanea Biblica, Old Testament 25 (Lund: Almqvist & Wiksell, 1987).

44. Bartlett, *Edom and the Edomites*, 198–99.

Whatever the reasons for Israel's nonconfrontation with Edomite religion, the Old Testament treats the Edomites with a respect accorded no other neighboring people. The Book of Deuteronomy holds out the possibility of Edomites—unlike the Ammonites and Moabites—becoming part of the "assembly of the LORD" (23:8 NIV [MT 23:9]). The biblical writers revered Edomite wisdom traditions (Jer. 49:7), and Job, who was said to dwell in the land of Uz, may have been conceived as having some Edomite connection (Lam. 4:21).[45]

The long political and economic encounter between Edom and Israel, beginning in the reign of David and extending past the domination of the region by the Babylonian kings, engendered both bitterness and respect. Both emotions find their expression in the Old Testament as Israel struggled to understand how God's actions in their own national history were intertwined with alliances and betrayals by their "brothers" to the east.

Recommended Reading

Bartlett, John R. *Edom and the Edomites.* Journal for the Study of the Old Testament Supplement 77. Sheffield: Sheffield Academic Press, 1989.

Bienkowski, Piotr (ed.). *Early Edom and Moab: The Beginning of the Iron Age in Southern Jordan.* Sheffield: Collis, 1992.

Cresson, Bruce C. "The Condemnation of Edom in Postexilic Judaism." Pp. 125–48 in *The Use of the Old Testament in the New and Other Essays: Studies in Honor of William Franklin Stinespring.* Edited by James A. Efird. Durham: Duke University Press, 1972.

Hart, Stephen. *The Archaeology of the Land of Edom.* Ph.D. diss., Macquarie University, 1989.

MacDonald, Burton. "Edom, Edomites." Vol. 2 / pp. 18–21 in *The International Standard Bible Encyclopedia.* Edited by Geoffrey W. Bromiley et al. Grand Rapids: Eerdmans, 1982.

Myers, Jacob M. "Edom and Judah in the Sixth–Fifth Centuries B.C." Pp. 377–92 in *Near Eastern Studies in Honor of William Foxwell Albright.* Edited by Hans Goedicke. Baltimore: Johns Hopkins University Press, 1971.

---

45. "We do not know who wrote the book of Job or when he lived. Nor do we know where"; Francis I. Andersen, *Job*, Tyndale Old Testament Commentaries (Downers Grove, Ill.: InterVarsity, 1976), 61. See further Andersen's able comments on p. 77.

Subject Index

Place-names containing foreign geographical terms—such as el- (including ed-, en-, er-, es-, eṣ-, esh-, et-, and ez-), Ḥorvat, Jebel, Khirbet, Tel, Tell, Tepe, Til, and Wadi—are inverted and alphabetized under the main name (e.g., Amarna, el-; Dan, Tell). English geographical terms are handled similarly (e.g., Van, Lake; Hermon, Mount). Alternate spellings or names of ancient place-names and personal names are placed in parentheses: Agga (Akkad); Byblos (Gebal).

349

Author Index

Scripture Index